ANATOMY OF
A COVER-UP

ANATOMY OF A COVER-UP

THE TRUTH ABOUT
THE RCMP AND THE
NOVA SCOTIA MASSACRES

PAUL PALANGO

RANDOM HOUSE CANADA

PUBLISHED IN 2025 BY RANDOM HOUSE CANADA

Random House Canada, a division of Penguin Random House Canada Limited
320 Front Street West, Suite 1400
Toronto, Ontario, M5V 3B6, Canada
penguinrandomhouse.ca

Random House Canada and colophon are registered trademarks of Penguin Random House LLC

The authorized representative in the EU for product safety and compliance is
Penguin Random House Ireland, Morrison Chambers, 32 Nassau Street,
Dublin D02 YH68, Ireland. https://eu-contact.penguin.ie

LIBRARY AND ARCHIVES CANADA CATALOGUING IN PUBLICATION
Title: Anatomy of a cover-up : the truth about the RCMP and
the Nova Scotia massacres / Paul Palango.
Names: Palango, Paul, 1950-
Description: Includes bibliographical references and index.
Identifiers: Canadiana (print) 20240417496 | Canadiana (ebook) 2024041859X |
ISBN 9781039010123 (softcover) | ISBN 9781039010130 (EPUB)
Subjects: LCSH: Mass shootings—Nova Scotia—Portapique. | LCSH: Mass murder—Nova
Scotia—Portapique. | LCSH: Mass murder investigation—Nova Scotia—Portapique. | LCSH:
Royal Canadian Mounted Police—Corrupt practices. | LCSH: Police corruption—Canada |
LCSH: Political corruption—Canada. | LCSH: Mass Casualty Commission. | LCSH:
Governmental investigations—Canada.
Classification: LCC HV6536.6.C32 N67 2025 | DDC 364.152/340971612—dc23

Cover design: Matthew Flute
Text design and maps: Matthew Flute
Typesetting: Erin Cooper
Image credits: (police car) mathieukor, (sky) kevinjeon00 | Getty Images;
(clouds) Michael | Adobe Stock

Printed in Canada

2 4 6 8 9 7 5 3 1

Penguin
Random House
RANDOM HOUSE CANADA

DEDICATED TO

TRUE BLUE, a heroic whistleblower who single-handedly
punctured the official narrative

The more than 3,200 current and former members of the
Royal Canadian Mounted Police who have blown the
whistle on *some* of the force's long-standing unethical and
illegal behaviour and practices

IN MEMORY OF

LEON JOUDREY, who never wavered about his version
of events, and **RICK HOWE**, a radio talk-show host
who made a difference

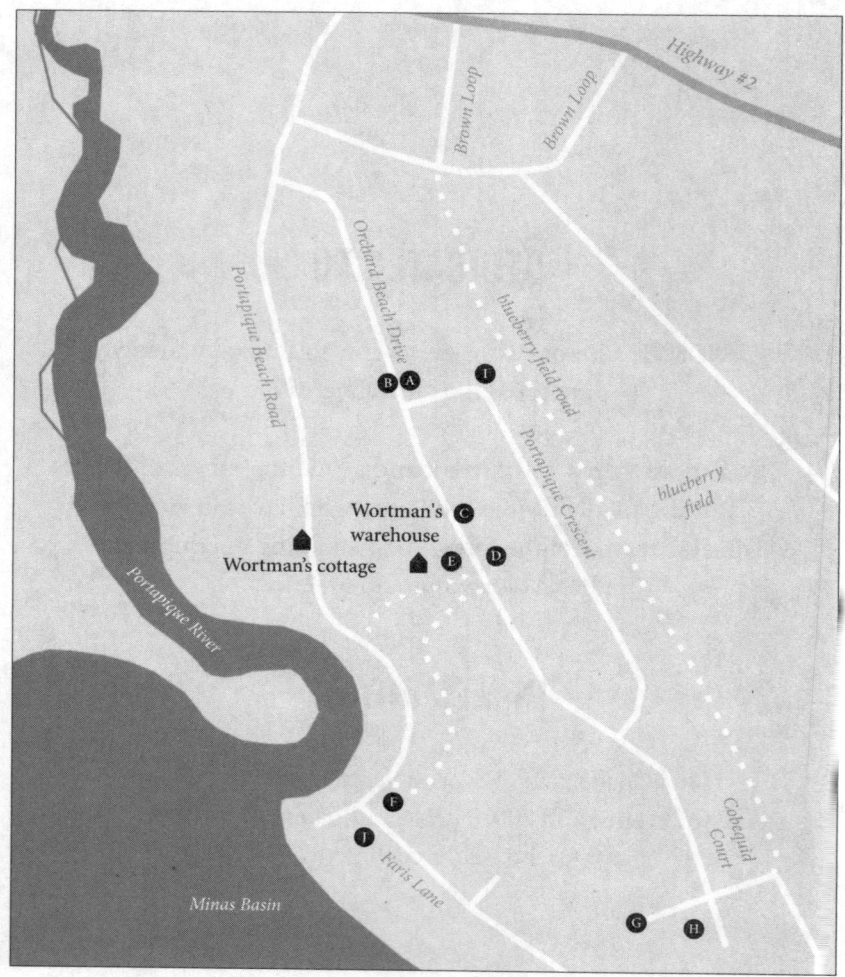

APRIL 18, PORTAPIQUE BEACH

Ⓐ Dawn and Frank Gulenchyn

Ⓑ Andrew MacDonald (injured)

Ⓒ Greg and Jamie Blair

Ⓓ Lisa McCully

Ⓔ Corrie Ellison

Ⓕ Elizabeth Joanne Thomas
and John Zahl

Ⓖ Joy and Peter Bond

Ⓗ Aaron Tuck, Emily Tuck,
and Jolene Oliver

Ⓘ Joudrey residence

Ⓙ Griffon residence

One-Lane Roads ▪▪▪

Footpath ▶▶▶

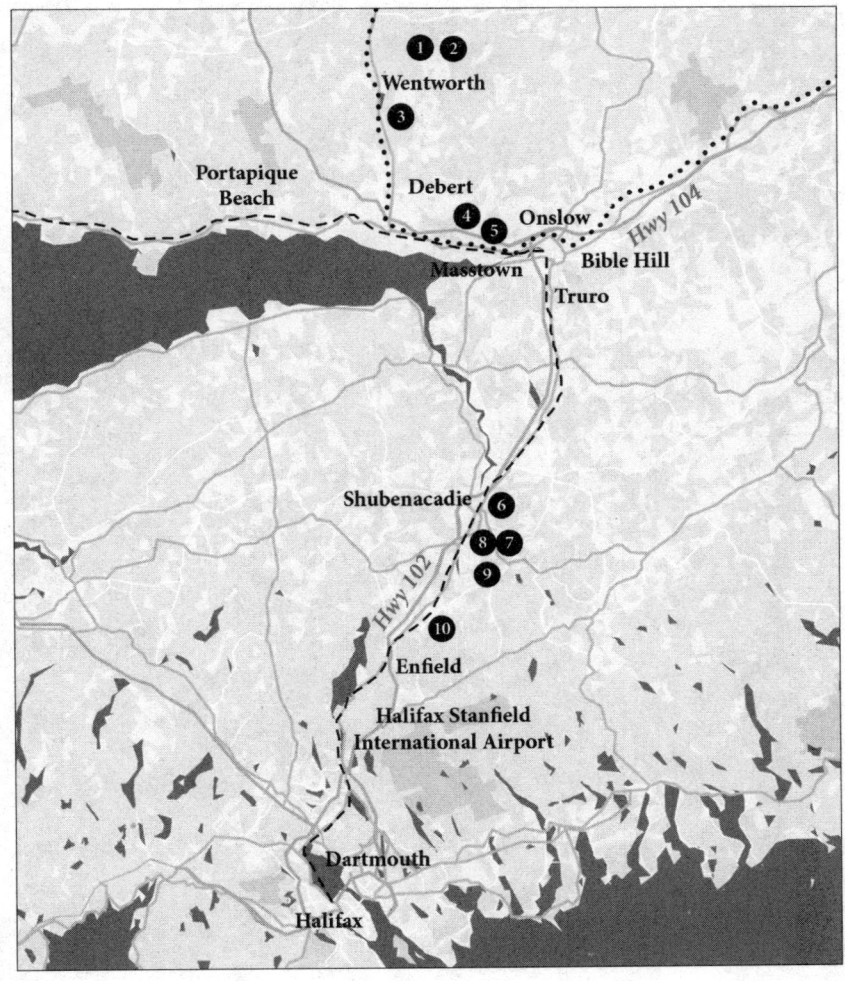

APRIL 19, NOVA SCOTIA

1. Alanna Jenkins
   and Sean McLeod
2. Tom Bagley
3. Lillian Campbell Hyslop
4. Kristin Beaton
5. Heather O'Brien
6. Chad Morrison (injured)

7. Heidi Stevenson
8. Joey Webber
9. Gina Goulet
10. Irving Big Stop

Highway 2 •••
Highway 4 ---

CONTENTS

PREFACE

There are twenty-five truths about the Nova Scotia massacres.

Twenty-two of those truths have names and indisputable fact on their side. They are the people who were shot dead by Nova Scotia denturist Gabriel Wortman. On Saturday night, April 18, 2020, thirteen of them died in Portapique, some while the Royal Canadian Mounted Police were on scene trying to figure out what to do. We still don't know the order in which they died or the precise details of many of the murders. We just know their names: Greg Blair, Jamie Blair, Lisa McCully, Corrie Ellison, Frank Gulenchyn, Dawn Madsen Gulenchyn, John Zahl, Elizabeth Joanne (Jo) Thomas, Peter Bond, Joy Bond, Aaron Tuck, Jolene Oliver and Emily Tuck.

The next morning, as the Mounties were still trying to make sense of the situation, in distinctly different circumstances, nine more people were murdered: Sean McLeod, Alanna Jenkins, Tom Bagley, Lillian Campbell Hyslop, Heather O'Brien, Kristen Beaton, Heidi Stevenson, Joey Webber and Gina Goulet.

The twenty-third truth is that while only three people, including Wortman's common-law wife, Lisa Banfield, suffered non-life-threatening injuries, hundreds if not thousands were emotionally or psychologically damaged by what happened.

The twenty-fourth truth is that although a handful of Mounties did indeed put their lives on the line in exceptionally trying circumstances, a few who offered to do so were not allowed to. Other Mounties, meanwhile, were anything but brave. In a profession where the preservation of life is the first priority, the Mounties saved no one who was in danger by the time they got there. It was anything but a great moment in policing. Not one Mountie's actions would make a heroes' highlight reel.

The twenty-fifth truth is that the RCMP and its enablers in government and the justice system have not been entirely honest about what happened before, during and after the massacres. From its first comments, the RCMP attributed the actions of gunman Gabriel Wortman to the fallout from a long-standing domestic-violence environment exacerbated by paranoia over the COVID pandemic and the lockdown in Nova Scotia. This official narrative was immediately picked up by Prime Minister Justin Trudeau and the federal and provincial governments. During the summer of 2020, the governments reluctantly called a joint federal-provincial public inquiry, the Mass Casualty Commission (MCC), headed by three commissioners: former Nova Scotia chief justice J. Michael MacDonald, former Fredericton police chief Leanne J. Fitch and Toronto lawyer Dr. Kim Stanton. The families of the victims, and the public in general, hoped that the commission would get to the truth of the matter, whatever it might be.

What's the Big Secret?

That's the last line of my previous book, *22 Murders*, which documented the two massacres and critiqued the police response. In that book, I also presented evidence that suggested that Wortman or someone close to him might have been an informant for or working undercover with the RCMP, perhaps involved in their efforts to quell the outlaw biker gangs in the Maritimes—a line of inquiry that might cast Wortman's killing spree in a new light. Had something gone sideways with an operation?

22 Murders was published in early 2022, prior to the MCC's hearings. The full title was *22 Murders: Investigating the Massacres, Cover-Up and Obstacles to Justice in Nova Scotia*. Some thought it was reckless and bold that I would dare describe what was going on in Nova Scotia in that fashion, without the MCC having held a single hearing. My sources were shy, but solid. I had confidence in what I was reporting.

Among the first obstacles in the pursuit of the truth was the government mandate that the MCC be "trauma-informed." There were also demands from various quarters that any inquiry be viewed through "a feminist lens." To me, the overriding problem seemed easily quantified: the RCMP's broken culture and poor performance, and the public's insistence on not holding the force accountable for its myriad failures.

When the commission held a "virtual progress update" on September 9, 2021, *Frank* magazine editor Andrew Douglas insisted that I participate. There was nothing new in what the commissioners had to say, but what commission chair Michael MacDonald did say foreshadowed what would eventually unfold. I described it this way in a subsequent *Frank* piece, part of which read:

> MacDonald, speaking in a flat, almost lifeless tone of voice, said the commission had a two-year mandate and was going to conduct its own investigation to create "an evidence-based record" and "foundational documents." He tossed around words like "consultative" and "collaborative."
>
> "We continue to subpoena documents and interview witnesses to ensure that we are able to get to the bottom of what happened and why," the former judge said. "We are committed to doing our work transparently and respectfully. We are also approaching our work in a trauma-informed manner. We will do our utmost to make sure that we will not cause more harm to those who have already suffered. . . . We must balance two competing but important considerations. Honouring the public's right to understand what happened while protecting the privacy and dignity of those who have already suffered so much."

Almost from the moment Gabriel Wortman was shot at the Irving Big Stop in Enfield, government officials and the RCMP have been promoting the notion that they were all determined to protect the survivors of the dead from further trauma. That's become their collective mantra. They seem to have forgotten that the real victims are the 22 dead and that our society demands answers in their name. That's how the justice system is supposed to work, as difficult as that might be for some of the families to accept.

"I would like to stress that our commission is not a court. Our approach is very different from a civil trial or a criminal prosecution, which are adversarial. We cannot and will not make findings of civil or criminal liability or assign punishment," he said.

The commission was an inquisition whose intended purpose was to find the truth, he said. Somebody else could always come along after the fact, pick up the commission's evidence and run with it, but who? The RCMP won't be interested, of that we can be sure.

"However, difficult precedents and uncomfortable truths will be explored," MacDonald continued, "to get to the bottom of what happened and why."

After it handed down its voluminous final report in March 2023, MacDonald and his co-commissioners proclaimed that they had thoroughly examined the issue. Most media observers praised their efforts, although there were dissenters, including family members who were baffled by what had transpired.

Throughout it all, I sat back and monitored what was going on. Based on my considerable experience, I sensed what the commission was actually going to do. With that in mind, I didn't attend a single hearing, but I and my band of citizen investigators followed every move made by the government, the commission and the RCMP, by either perusing their documents or watching the televised proceedings. My intention was this: when it was all over, I would dissect it and show the public how, unbelievable as it might seem to some, the three parties had worked together to pull off a cover-up in plain sight. This is my report.

I

TURNING THE TIDE

On March 30, 2023, my wife, Sharon, and I made our way from our home on the South Shore of Nova Scotia to the Truro Trade and Convention Centre inside the Best Western Truro-Glengarry Hotel, where the Mass Casualty Commission would be issuing its final report, nearly three years after the massacres.

The commission had come out of a public outcry for answers about what had happened those fateful days of April 18 and 19, 2020, and particularly the RCMP's fumbled response. On the morning of July 22, 2020, the families of the twenty-two victims and their friends and supporters marched on the Bible Hill RCMP detachment. Darcy Dobson, the daughter of Gabriel Wortman's nineteenth victim, nurse Heather O'Brien, was one of the organizers of the event. She told Nicole Munro of the Halifax *Chronicle Herald*, "There were so many things that were done wrong, even afterwards, so we want to know why, and we want to make sure this never happens to another family again. We want a full public inquiry with full transparency."

The political point men in this exercise were Mark Furey and Bill Blair, two former police officers. Furey was a retired RCMP staff sergeant who was now the Nova Scotia justice minister and attorney general. Blair, a former Toronto police chief, was the federal public safety minister. Their response was to set up a joint federal-provincial review of what had happened. Essentially, a select panel would go over the RCMP's paperwork behind closed doors—there would be no public hearings or cross-examination of witnesses by lawyers. In that way, the politicians said, families and those affected in the wider public would suffer no further harm—they would be shielded from reliving the trauma. The overarching focus of politicians at all levels was the narrative that the massacres were the result of domestic violence and that any examination of what happened should be viewed through "a feminist lens."

If the federal and provincial governments thought they had addressed the public's request for transparency, they were instantly disabused of that notion. Many people complained publicly that the plan for a review was unseemly in the circumstances and could in no way be called a thorough investigation. Patterson Law, the Truro firm representing many of the families, issued a statement that read, in part:

> The "Independent Review" announced by Ministers Furey and Blair is wholly insufficient to meet the objectives of providing full and transparent answers to the families and the public, identifying deficiencies in responses, and providing meaningful lessons to be learned to avoid similar future tragedies. . . .
>
> Most disappointingly, Ministers Furey and Blair have hidden behind their contrived notion of a "trauma-free" process to exclude the full participation of the families under the guise of protecting them from further trauma. This is not how the families wish to be treated. I know that Minister Furey has spoken with the families, so he must know that they want to participate, not to be protected by an incomplete process.
>
> The families want a full and transparent public inquiry. Why will Minister Furey not give them this? Why will he not give the citizens of Nova Scotia this? "We are all in this together" has been the slogan throughout 2020—the families simply want us all, the public, to be in this together now to figure out a better tomorrow for families and the Province.

Tim Bousquet, publisher, editor, and reporter of the *Halifax Examiner*, summed up the public sentiment well in a commentary published on July 23, 2020, headlined "Not Having a Public Inquiry into the Mass Murders Is a Disservice to Victim's Families, the Public, and Common Sense." In the piece, he quoted from his interview with Dalhousie University law professor Archibald Kaiser:

I thought that their defense of the methodology they've chosen was utterly without any legal or logical foundation. It's as if they're living in some kind of alternate reality, particularly on the points of independence and transparency that they allege would infuse the independent review. I don't understand how they maintained their positions, frankly, with a straight face. . . . The minister is entirely incorrect in saying that this process is transparent. It is not.

Bousquet wrote:

I've never seen a public policy announcement rejected by the public with such unanimity. I heard from hundreds of people yesterday about the review panel, and I'm not aware that even one person supported that approach. I wasn't even trolled on this, and I'm trolled on everything. So far as I can see, no one at all supports this; it is roundly and universally condemned. . . . Twenty-two people were murdered. People were frightened and the murder spree will remain one of the most traumatic events in Nova Scotians' collective memory for a very long time. As more than one person expressed it yesterday: If *this* doesn't deserve a public inquiry, what does? I don't know what led to the decision not to have a public inquiry. I do know, however, that that decision is feeding public mistrust: *What are they hiding?*

Five days later, Furey and Blair caved to public pressure and announced there would be a joint federal-provincial *public inquiry*, which would, according to Blair, "have the power to summon witnesses and require them to give evidence orally or in writing . . . and . . .

produce such documents and things as the commissioners deem requisite to the full investigation."

The public inquiry, which would come to be known as the Mass Casualty Commission (MCC), was heralded as a victory for the victims' families. They were promised answers, but they would have to wait for the commission and its investigators to do a thorough review.

The original plan for the MCC was that it would hold its first public hearings in October 2021, more than a year after it had been empanelled. (This date would eventually be postponed to February 2022.) During that period, the commission intimated that it was scouring the earth for information about the massacres. Investigators were flying everywhere. Anyone and everyone was being interviewed. Mountains of files were being built. The commission set out to "front-end load" the process by gathering and predigesting all the available facts into foundational documents, "an efficient and effective . . . common information base about what happened." The process would be totally transparent, it said. The intent was to "share the key facts and events leading up to, during and after the mass casualty." In addition, there would be "supplementary reports . . . to support the overall understanding of the facts of what happened, how and why. Each report contains the results of further investigation into specific questions or events."

Meanwhile, the public was still waiting.

In total, the commission took twenty-six months, just over two years, and spent an estimated $50 million or more on their investigation and ancillary matters. From June to December 2021, they held fourteen open houses—meet-and-greets with community groups and tribal band councils in the key towns involved in the massacres, whether it was where people had died, Wortman had driven through, or RCMP responders had detachments. Beginning in Colchester, home to Portapique, these open houses seemed intended to win the confidence of the public by showing how open and approachable the commissioners and their staff were.

In the early days of the meet-and-greets, Charlene Bagley, whose father, Tom, was Wortman's sixteenth murder victim, all but shouted out her contempt for the commission. On August 14, 2021, she published a letter on her Facebook page that read, in part:

Losing a parent is difficult enough, but to lose your father so tragically and to not have answers as to what happened is beyond comprehension some days. My healing process has been prolonged due to the lack of information and transparency since day one. I was raised to respect our RCMP and government and to be proud to say I am from Nova Scotia. This is becoming harder for me to do. I was also raised to not give up, even though things get hard, and to speak up when I need to when something is not right.

When we as families had to fight for this Inquiry was when I first began to realize not everyone wanted the truth to come out. As time passed this became blatantly obvious. . . . I can now say in confidence that we have been let down and may never find out the truth about my beloved father. Considering your claim to be using the trauma-informed approach, I will end with this: We are losing more faith by the day . . .

To some, including me, it looked as if the commission was plowing ahead with its original mandate—a review—and disguising it as a public inquiry. Behind closed doors, it was determining what was going to be addressed and what was going to be excluded from the record. I—along with Andrew Douglas, editor at *Frank* magazine, and other citizen investigators—was hearing concerning reports from my sources, including one called True Blue, whom I introduced readers to in *22 Murders*, about non-disclosure agreements being signed, key witnesses not yet being interviewed by commission investigators, and the RCMP refusing to co-operate.

We published the results of our ongoing parallel investigation in *Frank* in August 2021. Here is an excerpt:

THE PORTAPIQUE PAPERS

The RCMP is stalling the release of as many as 50,000 documents or pieces of evidence pertaining to the Nova Scotia massacres that are being sought by the Mass Casualty Commission, according to various sources close to the Commission.

Although public hearings are slated to begin in October, it appears that the RCMP, backed by federal government lawyers, is deliberately balking at being anywhere close to transparent about the role its members played before, during and after the massacres in which 22 people were killed on April 18 and 19, 2020.

"There is frustration inside the Commission over the obvious stonewalling by the RCMP," said one source familiar with the internal operations of the MCC, which is technically a creature of both the federal and provincial governments.

"The province is finding that it can't get answers to anything," another source said. "The feds are controlling everything."

These new sources confirm and expand upon what another source, dubbed True Blue, has previously told Frank Magazine about what the RCMP is and has been doing.

All the sources have sought anonymity out of fear of retaliation by the RCMP and/or the federal and provincial governments.

In June, True Blue described to Frank Magazine how there are approximately 60 lawyers and investigators operating on behalf of the RCMP and the federal government. At that time, he said that the Commission's investigators have had difficulty obtaining key evidence which the RCMP is refusing to disclose.

Up to that point, for example, True Blue said the Commission had virtually no information about killer Gabriel Wortman's common-law wife, Lisa Banfield, other than her driver's license and vehicle registration.

"Banfield was apparently the last person to be with him before he began his rampage," one source put it. "She is the most important witness and the RCMP won't tell the Commission anything about her."

It is not known if the Commission has received more information about Banfield since that point.

The 50,000 documents being sought by the Commission fall into a wide range of categories, including old case files and RCMP procedures, but among the most sensitive would be the encrypted conversations between Mounties on April 18th and 19th as well as any information about whether Wortman or someone in his circle of friends and acquaintances was a RCMP informant or agent, as sources have suggested may have been the case.

It seemed to us that the RCMP and the federal and provincial governments wanted the public to believe everything was moving along as expected as the inquiry approached, but every indication suggested that commission investigators were becoming disgruntled about the way things were unfolding.

"The mood there is foul," said a source close to the commission.

Finally, the formal hearings began in February 2022, five months after originally scheduled. They ran until September 23, 2022, a total of seventy-six hearings. Afterwards, the commission adjourned for six more months to prepare its final report and recommendations, which were now, at long last, being released.

◆

The title of the report was *Turning the Tide Together*, which was a head-scratcher for anyone who knows about the nature of tides. Nova Scotia enjoys the highest tides in the world in the Bay of Fundy. Twice daily, the mountains of sea water roll in and out, gently tilting the entire province as they come and go. No human can cause them to change their course—which, ironically, might also describe how the RCMP has survived over the years.

The unveiling of the report would be the commission's last public meeting, but the first I planned to attend in person.

Citizen investigator Ryan Potter was instantly given accreditation as a journalist. Potter, who was in his forties, worked at an assisted-living home and was a mixed martial arts referee on weekends. He began commenting on the massacres on his own before joining forces with me after the publication of *22 Murders*. He found it somewhat amusing that he was accredited but I wasn't, since the commission stalled on approving me, claiming that I wasn't a working journalist.

Perhaps they didn't like *22 Murders* or appreciate the dozens of stories Andrew Douglas and I had broken in *Frank* magazine. Maybe something I said had offended them, like occasionally referring to the three commissioners, Justice J. Michael MacDonald, former Fredericton police chief Leanne Fitch and Dr. Kim Stanton, as "The Three Stone-Faced Puppets" on the *Nighttime* podcast with Jordan Bonaparte. It had been nothing personal, just professional irreverence. No matter how much they protested their honest intent, everything they had said and done made it seem as if someone else was pulling their strings, as this book will show. After the commission was called, the mainstream and even the alternative media had treated them with deference. I felt that I had a duty to get under their skin with my stories and my commentary, to keep them on their toes and hold them accountable.

Three days before the release of the final report, the commission's Hannah Langille notified me that I would be issued credentials, claiming that my application had been lost in the pile. What really happened was that Halifax *Chronicle Herald* reporter Andrew Rankin got wind of what was going on, called them and asked why I was being blocked.

Inside the convention centre's main hall that morning, friends and families of the victims mingled with the media and the Mounties scattered around the room, waiting for the proceedings to begin. After three years of working on this single story, I continued to be an outsider. Most of the family members refused to acknowledge me. In their view, at least according to what they said on social media—and sometimes to me directly—I was little more than an opportunistic hack who was only in it for the money. The few who thought otherwise were warm and cordial to both Sharon and me.

We took our seats in the second-last row of the first section. My podcast buddy, lawyer Adam Rodgers, and Ryan Potter sat behind us. Just off to our left, Prime Minister Justin Trudeau strode into the room and sat in the first row of the second section, flanked by two of his cabinet members, Sean Fraser and Marco Mendicino. Behind Trudeau was Nova Scotia premier Tim Houston.

After holding everyone at bay for six quiet months, the commission had created a sense of urgency about the final report. Advance copies were not released to approved people until a few hours before the meeting. Some got it only a few minutes before commission chairman MacDonald began speaking.

At one point during the presentation, Potter turned around in his seat to hide a yawn and caught Trudeau's eye. "He was staring down at the floor, and then he looked up and looked me in the eye," Potter recalled. "I nodded hi to him. He acknowledged me and then put his head back down and stared at the floor. I don't think he wanted to be there."

The MCC's final report contained seven chewy volumes, along with an executive summary, published in digital form on its website. In all, there were 3,153 pages, broken up into seven sections (page lengths in brackets): *Executive Summary* (298); *Context and Purpose* (74); *What Happened* (358); *Violence* (496); *Community* (707); *Policing* (703); *Implementation* (70); and, finally, *Process* (277), with an additional 218 pages of appendices. The combined volumes contained almost twice as many pages as the aggregate of my first four books on the RCMP. At approximately 300 words per page, there were about one million words in the report, plus charts and graphs. In addition, there were likely a couple of million more words in supporting documents.

All this documentation was what I had been hoping for ever since the public inquiry was announced. Why? Because the RCMP had not been forthcoming in the aftermath of the massacres, which made getting answers about what had happened incredibly difficult. Despite what my sources had said about the RCMP's lack of co-operation with the commission, the process of creating the report would have forced the RCMP to put down things on paper, whether good or bad. It was going to take some time and work to sift through it all, but I was ready.

The commission didn't make it easy. The report was published digitally as a PDF. Nothing was searchable within the documents. Nothing could be copied, not the website or any of its component elements. Every document had to be read. Once something worth noting was located and identified, it had to be retyped, word by word. With immediate deadlines, journalists would have to rely on the executive summary, with its predigested information served up to them on a platter.

The titles of each of the 130 recommendations showed that the commission, at least on the surface, had stayed true to its mandate. Here are some from the first 49: "Framework for Tracking Mass Casualty Incidents"; "A Public Health Approach to Preventing Mass Casualties"; "External Evaluation of RCMP Behavioural Sciences Branch"; "Conflict of Interest in Forensic Psychological Assessment"; "Intimate Partner Violence and Police and Prosecutorial Discretion to Lay Criminal Charges"; "Countering Victim Blaming and Hyper-Responsibilization [*sic*] of Women Survivors"; "Women-Centric Risk Assessments"; "Creating Safe Spaces to Report Violence"; "Replacement of Mandatory Arrest and Charging Policies and Protocols for Intimate Partner Violence Offences"; and, in that same vein, logically, "Promoting and Supporting Healthy Masculinities."

It wasn't until its fiftieth recommendation that the commission segued from social issues to the RCMP. About fifty of the recommendations were aimed at the RCMP. The most telling recommendation, from my perspective, was number 46: "Implementing the 2007 Recommendations of the Brown Task Force." That task force had described the RCMP as having "a management structure and corporate governance that isn't working . . . fundamental change is required to create a modern, accountable and healthy police force." Sixteen years passed, and the RCMP and its government enablers had stalled, deflected and ignored the devastating report, with dire consequences. What would be different this time?

The surprise was that many of the commission's recommendations seemed to be tougher and more critical of the RCMP than anyone might have imagined. For example, the commission acknowledged that the Mounties had failed to detect Wortman, contain him in the original site or impede his way the next day while he killed nine more people. The Mounties were so confused about what to do that the force failed to engage the Alert Ready system to warn the public about the danger.

After scuffling about with a series of what seemed like housekeeping recommendations, the commission fired its big gun in its ninety-ninth recommendation: the RCMP should no longer be involved in contract policing.

Where did that rocket come from?

Contract policing is a uniquely Canadian hybridized policing structure. The RCMP is a federal police force, like the FBI in the United States, but it rents itself out to the provinces, aside from Ontario and Quebec, to provide provincial and largely rural policing across the country in marked RCMP cars. The federal government subsidizes all this, creating the illusion of a national police force that, for the most part, patrols the boonies of eastern and western Canada. The majority of the RCMP's personnel are devoted to contract policing. Ontario and Quebec have their own provincial and municipal police forces. In those provinces, the RCMP is an all-but-invisible federal police service.

The recommendation by the commission to stop contract policing made me wonder if I had fallen asleep for longer than I thought during the public hearings. Nothing like that had ever been discussed. As I would come to realize later, the recommendation came not from the MCC hearings, but from *Broken Dreams, Broken Lives*, the 2020 report on the RCMP from former Supreme Court justice J.E. Michel Bastarache. As with other reports over the years, the RCMP and federal and provincial governments ignored Bastarache, a tactic the government had used for decades with similar recommendations. People soon forgot, and the RCMP continued on its way. Was the commission hoping for the same outcome?

To add to the confusion, in recommendation number 101—two after the one about ending contract policing—the commission advised that the RCMP should be given *more* money for contract policing. Recommendation number 102 stated that the RCMP should *revitalize* rural policing: "The RCMP should establish an attractive career stream for members who wish to develop specialization in rural or remote policing." Then, two recommendations after that, the commission recommended that the RCMP training facility, Depot, be shut down and that all police candidates have a three-year degree-based education.

It looked like a dog's breakfast, but there was a glittery headline available for every dogged journalist that day, no matter how specific their news appetite might be.

As the presentation came to a close, I ducked out of the hall to do a live radio report for *The Todd Veinotte Show* in Halifax. Trudeau's security team, a couple of men and a woman with earbuds, were conspicuously leaning against the wall, pretending to be just hanging out. I found a quiet spot at the end of the hallway and began my report. The next thing I knew, the prime minister was walking toward me, flanked by other members of his security detail. I got the sense from his expression that he knew who I was and didn't think much of what he was seeing. I took it as a compliment. What I didn't realize was that he was heading to a room off to my left, where a rolling press conference was being held.

I don't do press conferences, but after finishing my report, I peeked in while Trudeau was still speaking.

"It was important for me to be here today to support the families, to show that all Canadians continue to stand with the family members, the community, the people of Nova Scotia and elsewhere, who have been so deeply affected over the three years almost since this horrific, horrific day," Trudeau said. "Obviously, I thank the commissioners for their comprehensive work, looking at all aspects of what happened and how we need to move forward."

The funny thing was, I didn't see Trudeau talking to a single person, other than briefly being cornered by family member Scott McLeod, before he was whisked away. His mere presence, I guess, was meant to convey comfort.

Meanwhile, the RCMP's Acting Commissioner Mike Duheme and Assistant Commissioner Dennis Daley took to the podium and said that they hadn't had time to read the commission's recommendations and therefore couldn't comment. That seemed unlikely, but convenient. I soon returned to the original hall, where people were now standing around chatting and television reporters were conducting on-camera interviews, dutifully repeating the various story angles that the commission had outlined in their executive summary.

It appealed to all the right emotions, but I remained skeptical. I had spent almost three years following this story, and what was being said didn't jibe with my own investigation and observations. I returned home and dove into the deepest reaches of the commission's report, territory where few modern reporters dared venture without a few hits of extra-strength NoDoz.

2

THE ILLUSION OF TRANSPARENCY

Previous Canadian public inquiries had taught me that critical bits and pieces of the true story were likely buried somewhere in the final stages of the official report, just about the last place a reporter would search with a deadline in their face. Take, for example, the O'Connor Commission into the treatment of Maher Arar.

The story began with news reports in 2002 that Arar, a telecommunications engineer with dual Syrian and Canadian citizenships, had been detained as a suspected terrorist while passing through New York's John F. Kennedy International Airport. Arar was travelling alone back to Canada, where he had lived since 1987, after a family vacation in Tunisia. After 13 days in custody, he was shipped to Syria, where he was allegedly tortured and kept captive for 374 days.

His case raised issues about illegal extraordinary renditions by the US government and the degree of co-operation by Canadian authorities, particularly the RCMP. A Mountie unit had first encountered Arar walking in the rain outside Mango's Café with fellow Syrian Abdullah Almalki, who had also immigrated to Canada in 1987. Almalki, an electrical engineer, was under surveillance for ties to suspected terrorists.

On February 5, 2004, Prime Minister Paul Martin set up the Commission of Inquiry into the Actions of Canadian Officials in Relation to Maher Arar. The commission was led by Dennis O'Connor, associate chief justice of Ontario, who conducted hearings and testimony over nineteen months. On the surface, it looked like a credible and thorough inquiry, though much of the proceedings were behind closed doors. In the end, O'Connor exonerated Arar of any wrongdoing, finding that he was a likely a victim of inaccurate and unfair information provided to US authorities by the RCMP. On January 26, 2007, Prime Minister Stephen Harper issued a formal apology to Arar on behalf of the Canadian government and awarded him $10.5 million, plus an additional $1 million for legal costs. Everyone in Canada was happy, even me, until I started doing research for a planned chapter on the Arar case for my book *Dispersing the Fog*.

I began with an attempt to interview Maher Arar myself, but he declined to answer any of my questions. As I investigated, I noticed that no matter how much I read about Arar, there was no clear biographical information, other than that he grew up in Aleppo and Damascus and came to Canada in 1987. His public profile was little more than a stickman drawing. The commission made him out to be a dull, dweeby telecommunications engineer, but there were no real specifics about that, either. There was not enough information available to describe the real Arar. It was like trying to nail Jell-O to a wall.

There were so many obvious gaps in Arar's backstory that I originally suspected he really was a terrorist who had slipped through the cracks. There were numerous "leaks" from within security circles suggesting just that. But as I analyzed the evidence, I made a 180-degree turn in my suspicions: maybe he was working *with* the government. But which one?

The natural suspect was the US government. After the 9/11 attacks, President George Bush proclaimed a Declaration of National Emergency by Reason of Certain Terrorist Attacks, which gave him extraordinary powers to deal with the terrorist crisis. Vice President Dick Cheney also made this momentous statement: "This is a different kind of war. You're not going to see our victories. Our victories are going to occur in the dark alleys as our intelligence forces and law enforcement forces go after this threat."

If Arar *was* a government agent—a brave soldier, as it were—his credentials as a suspected terrorist were instantly embellished by the news story about his being held for thirteen days in New York. At the Syrian prison he was sent to, he was likely not met with much suspicion by others incarcerated there. He would have been the perfect mole.

After being released from prison and returned to Canada in 2003, Arar declined to undergo a physical examination by a doctor. It was claimed that he was shy and that the process would be too traumatizing for him. His medical assessment was based upon a verbal interview. He did not have to testify at the O'Connor Commission inquiry. He did not talk to the media, other than the *Globe and Mail*.

For its part, the RCMP was given short shrift by the commission. Even for a long-time RCMP critic like me, the hearings, led by Toronto lawyer Paul Cavalluzzo, were extremely hard on the Mounties. Cavalluzzo took almost any opportunity he could to lambaste the force, which was essentially not allowed to defend itself. The RCMP set up Project A-O Canada to investigate what had happened and found some previous links between Almalki and Arar, including signatures on a lease signed in 1997, that had all got lost in the shuffle. The Mounties even drew up a large chart showing the intertwined relationships the force had found, but the commission ignored 90 percent of it, focusing instead on how Arar didn't really know Abdullah Almalki. Arar said that he didn't know Almalki very well and had met with him only to find an obstetrician for his wife, which seemed to be a dubious alibi. His wife, Tunisian-born Monia Mazigh, was already in the second trimester of her second pregnancy. She was a bright, relatively independent woman who had earned a doctorate in finance from McGill University.

Two other men were also reportedly wrongfully imprisoned and tortured in Syria. Along with Almalki, they were not allowed to sit in on the hearings, much of which were conducted in camera—a courtroom closed to the public. Why? If the four men were all victims of the same set of circumstances, why weren't they treated equally by the commission? Why couldn't they hear what was going on? What made them different from Arar? None of it made sense to me.

As I leafed through the first volumes of the O'Connor Commission report, I found a thread that, when I tugged on it, revealed some of the story that was being hidden. In its "biographical" information on Arar, the commission referred to a mysterious Montreal company he had worked for, called CIM21000 Inc. When I tried to locate the company's address, I couldn't find it in Montreal or anywhere else in the world. It didn't seem to exist. The commission seemed to throw up its hands, too, and moved on.

When the O'Connor Commission published its first volumes of findings in 2006, the media covered it feverishly. Then, in 2007, the commission released its "second addendum" to the report, containing previously redacted information. On page 506 was this: "August 2004: In August, Project A-O Canada produced several pages of documents, both personal and commercial, indicating contact between the following individuals and companies: Abdullah Almalki, Youssef Almalki, Safa Almalki, Nazih Almalki, Maher Arar, Mourad Mazigh, and CIM2000. The documentation ranged in date from 1996 to 2002, often related to computer equipment."

I deduced that the initial reference to CIM21000 Inc. was a deliberate typo introduced to deter unwanted investigators. It's an old police technique that includes altering the proper spelling of names on a file listing. The company's real name was CIM 2000 Inc. According to corporate records in Quebec, the sole director was a person named Parto Navidi.

Many months later, I tracked down Navidi in Ottawa, where she ran a hair salon in the city's west end. As it turned out, Navidi had been married to Arar's brother-in-law, Mourad Mazigh. Arar and his wife, Monia, had lived with Navidi and Mourad in a single house at 13309 Chelsea in the northwestern Montreal suburb of Pierrefonds. Their landlord for seven years was a shady fellow named Pietro Rigolli, who used at least five aliases, his favourite being Ian Falcon.

Rigolli was arrested in 1999 in a joint action involving US and Canadian authorities. He had been charged with illegally selling airplane parts to Iran, extradited to the United States, convicted in an all-but-secret trial in Connecticut and imprisoned in the federal penitentiary at Otisville, New York. One would have thought that Arar would have popped up on the radar at that time, but apparently not.

In 1999, Arar and Mazigh moved to the Boston suburb of Natick, where he took up a position with the MathWorks, a privately owned company that specializes in mathematical computing software. It looked innocuous enough, but upon closer inspection I learned something rather intriguing: the MathWorks had worked on every major aeronautical and outer space development over the previous four decades for either the US Department of Defense or the CIA.

The obvious question became: If Arar and his family had been living in illegal arms dealer Pietro Rigolli's house for seven years, how, after Rigolli's arrest, did Arar get hired so easily in the United States by a company with such close ties to US military and intelligence agencies? When I asked that question among my sources, I was told that a long-held suspicion in the world of spies was that the MathWorks is a CIA front company.

None of this was addressed by the O'Connor Commission, and there was nothing more I could say about it. I couldn't find a CIA or FBI pay stub for Arar, and no one would answer my questions on the record.

The RCMP documents released in the second addendum clearly showed not only that Almalki and his brothers were doing business with CIM 2000 Inc., but also that Arar didn't work for the company; he owned it, along with his brother-in-law. The Mounties knew this, but it was never brought up by the commission. The story should have been a bombshell, but the media had moved on.

A major obstacle for the media in telling the whole story was that, by that time, Arar had been lauded by, among others, *Time* magazine as Canada's newsmaker of the year in 2004, and one of the most influential people in the world. I strongly suspected that Arar was not a victim hero but a different kind of hero: a gutsy government agent.

Shirley Heafey, who spent eight years heading the RCMP Public Complaints Commission, which included the time during which the O'Connor Commission sat, believed that Arar was victimized by shoddy RCMP police work. However, even she conceded that she wasn't aware of the Pietro Rigolli investigation, the implications of Arar's hiring by the MathWorks afterwards or Arar's ownership of CIM 2000 Inc. and his long-time hidden relationship with Almalki. What she did know, however, was how Ottawa conducted investigations.

She described a situation under Prime Minister Brian Mulroney that occurred amid a sensitive investigation she had been conducting. She said she was approached by former MP Ron Atkey, who at the time was chairman of the Security Intelligence Review Committee, which oversaw the activities of the Canadian Security Intelligence Service (CSIS). "Ron Atkey wanted me to not dig so deeply in my investigation," Heafey said. "I didn't understand what he was trying to do. I was stunned. That was not my style. My father taught me to do the best job possible."

Misdirection and confusion are highlights of any controversy involving security and intelligence services. Silence is enforced by the Security of Information Act.

The O'Connor Commission was not the last word on the matter. Although Almalki and the two other detainees were excluded from the hearings, afterwards the government dealt with them separately. Like Arar, without so much as a critical question being asked of them, they were each eventually given an apology and a combined $31.5 million settlement. Why?

In 2023, a person close to the Arar investigation told me they had learned a little more about the case over time. "Arar was a CIA operator," the highly placed source said. "One of the other guys was CSIS."

There was no way anyone would corroborate that. It would mean arrest and jail time for the source. If Arar was an agent, perhaps that is why the US refused to apologize to him. The US intransigence subtly continued to paint Arar as a possible terrorist, giving him street cred among those being targeted.

The questions remain: Why did O'Connor let that critical, previously undisclosed information about Arar's involvement with CIM 2000 Inc., slip into the second addendum? Were Mounties or others threatening to go public with the information after they were berated for incompetence before the commission? Was it designed to give him plausible deniability should the true story come out later? Not everything was actually hidden. You just had to persevere and find it.

Which brings me back to the Mass Casualty Commission.

◆

From the moment it was empanelled in 2020 to the last words Commissioner Michael MacDonald spoke on March 30, 2023, the commission insisted that it was committed to being open and forthcoming. I was determined to test that claim. Like a spelunker entering a cave, I opened the 3,153-page PDF and waded into the final volume: *Process*. On page 32 of that volume, the commission described its vision and values:

> Our vision was to provide clarity around the causes, context, and circumstances that led to the April 2020 mass casualty in Nova Scotia. To create a thorough, evidence-based record, we knew that difficult questions would need to be asked and uncomfortable facts would need to be considered. We sought to perform our duties with compassion and with an unwavering commitment to a full, transparent and independent inquiry. . . . We strove to make the Commission's process inclusive, accessible, transparent and conducted with humanity.

The commission said it was guided by its "pledge" to put into practice the principles of "human-centred" Indigenous restorative justice.

> That pledge did not compromise procedural fairness, nor did it mean avoiding disagreements or not sharing emotional or difficult information. Rather, it meant taking active steps to avoid harm wherever possible. . . . Fostering a restorative approach was an indispensable yet largely misunderstood method, underappreciated by critics as a legitimate part of our mandate.

They took their cue from Prime Minister Trudeau, who was the country's biggest promoter of restorative justice, in which all parties to a crime gather in a room and make amends. Even Trudeau seemed to have missed a key principle about the Indigenous justice regime: that it can't be used in murder cases, especially in this case. Since the killer was dead, who was going to apologize for him? Or was restorative justice pointed at the Mounties? Were they expected to apologize? That would be a rare moment in Canada.

It smacked of virtue signalling, a concept conceived in 2015 by British conservative James Bartholomew, writing in *The Spectator* magazine. "One of the crucial aspects of virtue signalling is that it does not require doing anything virtuous. It does not involve delivering lunches to elderly neighbours or staying together with a spouse for the sake of the children. It takes no effort or sacrifice at all."

US linguist John McWhorter, a liberal Black professor, has written extensively about the hollowness of virtue signalling, calling it a new religion. "The way we talk about white privilege is eerily consonant with the way one talks about original sin," McWhorter said in an interview with NPR Radio in November 2021. "You have it from the beginning, it's a stain that you'll never get rid of . . . White privilege becomes the original sin that you're supposed to live in a kind of atonement for."

On the surface, at least, it seemed as if the commission was infected with that religion. It went to great lengths to *say* that it was committed to doing the right thing at all times, trumpeting the importance of language: "One of our guiding principles was to be respectful and to recognize that 'every word matters.' The commission prepared an internal lexicon on key terms that we considered through a trauma-informed lens and aligned with our mandate and our integrated team approach."

For example, the commission was diligent that Gabriel Wortman not be named, to avoid his being glorified for his infamy, as the prime minister stated in his first comments about the massacres and his government's subsequent actions. Wortman would be reduced to "the perpetrator," "the gunman," "the shooter" or "a lone wolf." The massacres would be called the more inclusive "mass casualty," which would encompass all those who felt injured, not just those who had been murdered.

Although all those murdered that weekend were white men and women, and they were killed by a white man, the commission applauded itself for its gentle approach to "Differentially Affected Groups":

Given the many past reports which indicated that actions related to aspects of our mandate, such as policing and gender-based violence, can have disproportionate effects on Black, Indigenous, Two-Spirit, lesbian, gay, bisexual, trans, queer and intersex people (2SLGBTQI+), and other historically disadvantaged groups, we made efforts to include those perspectives in our process.

The commission also vowed to never use the word "victim." "Our decision was consistent with restorative principles. . . . We used the phrase 'those most affected' as an inclusive term to refer to the affected individuals, families, first responders, service providers and communities." Under that definition, just about everyone, including the commission, was allowed to claim victimhood under another name.

This approach affected the very nature of the hearings, which the commission had promised on page 32 would provide clarity and ask difficult questions, but page 162 told a different story:

> This inquiry incorporated a restorative approach to all its processes.
> A process that would seek to lay blame or create a public spectacle
> of someone is unlikely to produce that person's best evidence. In our
> inclusive approach, first responders were among those most affected,
> and they are also the people who we want to answer the call when
> the next critical incident happens. An inquisitorial approach accepts
> that there are many ways to seek reliable information, and cross-
> examination of witnesses is often not the most effective means of
> getting people to be forthcoming with their evidence. . . . It was not
> necessary to call witnesses to appear in a public forum if we could
> obtain their evidence in some other reliable manner.

This seemed like a massive conflict between the vision and how it would be carried out. How would the commission provide clarity into what happened if they didn't ask difficult questions and test the veracity of witnesses' statements? In some cases, the witness didn't have to appear at a hearing. One of those "reliable manners" was accepting the notes of interviews with key witnesses that were conducted by the RCMP. This certainly expedited the process but left no room for follow-up and ignored the possibility that police interrogators can shape stories with the questions they ask and the notes they take, overstating or discrediting a witness's reliability. If this was the approach, how could the public possibly get the answers they had been demanding? How would the RCMP be truly held to account for its failure to protect the citizens of Nova Scotia?

The future of the RCMP was under threat and yet the commission seemed to assume that the red serge uniform automatically made the Mounties honourable. There was no acknowledgement whatsoever that the RCMP might be motivated by self-interest. None of the commission's members seemed to have heard the old joke that the most dangerous place is between a cop and their pension.

My doubts weren't unfounded. As I reported in *Frank* magazine and in *22 Murders*, sources had told me that the force was hiding, altering and destroying evidence in the Wortman case. In December 2020, an internal RCMP document ordering a moratorium on the destruction of information about Gabriel Wortman, issued October 15, 2020, had fallen into our hands. Here's an excerpt of what I wrote at the time:

> The trigger for the moratorium on destruction of evidence appears to be a Canada Labour Code investigation undertaken by Employment and Social Development Canada into the matter.
>
> The four-page document is dated October 15, 2020. It appears to come from an internal RCMP web page and is headlined: "MD-218— Moratorium on the destruction of information involving Gabriel Wortman pertaining to the investigation of the mass shooting in Nova Scotia on 2020-04-18 and 2020-04-19." The URL for the web page is: http://infoweb.rcmp-grc.gc.ca/manuals-manuels/national /moratorium-moratoire/md-218-.
>
> The last bit of information is missing from the photocopy.
>
> The document first was sent anonymously to *Little Grey Cells*, a YouTube channel, which operates out of Alberta. The show's host, Seamus Gorman (real name Paul Ragona), has been discussing it for the past few days in his broadcasts as part of a group called The Discord. It is comprised of 380 citizen investigators who have banded together since the massacre to dig up information.
>
> The timing and wording of the memorandum strongly suggests that the RCMP has been destroying documents and data in the case. Since May, multiple anonymous sources close to the investigation

have suggested the RCMP was destroying or altering paper and electronic evidence. This has previously been reported in the *Halifax Examiner* and on the Halifax talk show hosted by Rick Howe. The RCMP has not commented on the allegations to date.

The order commands the RCMP to collect, protect and retain every kind of evidence in the case, including paper documents, electronic data, 911 calls and radio communications.

To date the RCMP has resisted releasing any information or answering any questions about what it did and didn't do before, during and after the shootings on April 18 and 19.

In the new documents the RCMP is ordered to collect and retain "all records, documents, and information pertaining to communications and dealings with Gabriel Wortman, and all occurrences linked or related to Gabriel Wortman, including intelligence reports, citizen reports, calls for service and occurrence reports."

The RCMP has been told to collect and retain "all occurrence reports, briefing notes, SITreps, taskings and regular members' notes of the incidents, including notes or regular members who responded from 'H' Division," which is Nova Scotia. . . .

In recent months a current RCMP member has been quoted on numerous occasions in the *Halifax Examiner* and elsewhere as saying that the RCMP was attempting to "pasteurize" the evidence in the case. The member said there are ways the force can alter electronic files and data, "or even make it disappear."

Another current member said in an interview that the biggest problem from a public interest point of view is that the RCMP data management system, known by its acronym PROS, can be manipulated by senior officers.

"There has never been an audit conducted on the integrity of data in the PROS system," the ranking officer said. "The force has had six months to play with the evidence. Now, these investigators aren't going to take 'the dog ate my homework' for an answer. They will demand answers to their questions."

A third former RCMP officer who is familiar with the current inner workings of the force said this in an interview: "This is the nightmare for the force that I've been expecting. They have been doing everything they can to hide information. They have likely been trying to scrub the database to get rid of anything incriminating." . . .

A former executive-level officer in the RCMP says the revelation of this memo is devastating to the organization.

"It shows how corrupt the force is, and how it has to be disbanded," the former officer tells *Frank*.

"They use the word 'moratorium'? That means not preserving evidence is a regular thing. That means they're gonna continue to do it all the time."

Meantime, a former member of the judiciary says they are "really surprised" that a moratorium is required.

"Especially in this case where they would have known there was going to be at least a SIRT inquiry, evidence should have been retained."

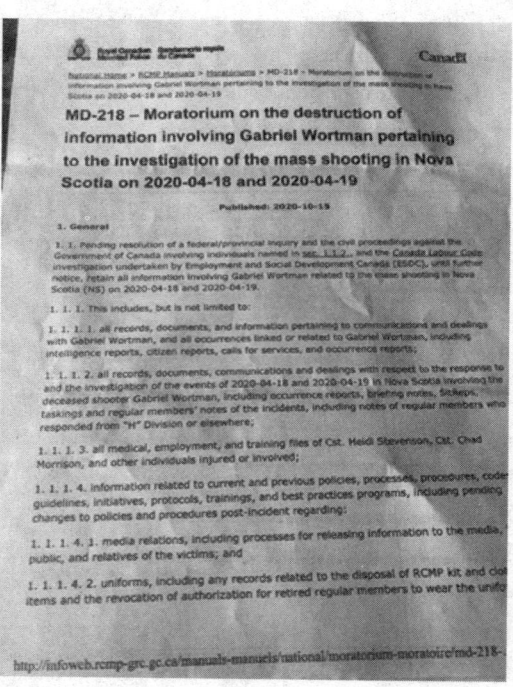

This wasn't anything new. Some observers, myself included, have long suspected some police forces of hiding or destroying documents in cases where the force could be proven to have done something wrong. In Nova Scotia, the RCMP uncovered the fact that the now defunct Sydney Police Department had ignored exculpatory evidence that would have exonerated Donald Marshall of a murder in 1972. In 1999, Glenn Assoun of Halifax was convicted in a similar murder case in which the RCMP was involved in hiding or overlooking evidence. Each case was settled with massive settlements provided by the taxpayer, while the offending police officers were given a slap on the wrist, if that.

In *22 Murders*, I laid out how the RCMP, specifically, had the ability and, according to insiders, a track record of manipulating data and evidence within its computerized records system to make it nearly impossible for nosey lawyers and other investigators to find information the force preferred to keep hidden.

Days after the story about the moratorium was published, RCMP spokesperson Corporal Lisa Croteau sent a lengthy email to *Frank* editor Andrew Douglas claiming that the documents were authentic and that the RCMP had done nothing wrong—just normal housekeeping. Croteau said documents are destroyed if they have "no business value." She concluded by saying this, regarding the RCMP's investigation of the massacres, which was dubbed Operation H-Strong:

> From the outset of the H-Strong investigation, the RCMP committed to keeping victim's [*sic*] families informed as well as providing the public and media with the facts related to H-Strong, while maintaining the integrity of the investigation.
>
> The RCMP's commitment to transparency and accountability includes publicly reporting on our activities to help achieve those objectives and we have done so since April 19, 2020.
>
> The RCMP recognizes the need to provide the factual account of what transpired this past April. With the public inquiry now ongoing, the most appropriate and unbiased opportunity to do so is with our full participation in the inquiry.

The inquiry is underway and RCMP is fully cooperating. The RCMP will respectfully refrain from further commenting on these matters outside of the inquiry.

The RCMP's defence didn't make sense—though take special note of its commitment to transparency. Like any successful magic trick, the illusion of transparency is built upon a well-constructed foundation of distraction. My sources told me that the RCMP records everything, including what it destroys, but I couldn't find a reference to the moratorium in the million words of the commission's final report.

However, I did find something else. Just as with the O'Connor Commission, it was buried deep in the report, sandwiched between the commission's description of how it had prepared legislative briefs and policy documents and where it expressed its gratitude "for the guidance of Mi'kmaw Elder Marlene Companion, who helped us proceed in a good way by smudging and offering prayers." It was a reference to missing documents. It was like finding fingerprints of the invisible hand.

On page 124 of Volume 7—effectively page 2,829 of the final report—the commission wrote:

In any public inquiry, there are three fundamental and related tasks. The first, document production, is our obligation to obtain all the relevant documents from all the people or institutions that are in possession of them. The second, document management, is to organize and categorize these documents, combing through them line by line and identifying privacy and other issues that need to be protected from public disclosure. Commission staff often consulted on specific issues with the families and those most affected. The third, disclosure, is to release all documents not identified as protected, first to the Participants and then to the public. We faced considerable challenges with each of these tasks.

The commission went on to describe how it had issued more than 100 subpoenas and had gathered not 50,000 documents, as previously reported, but more than 80,000 documents. Yet it still failed to get everything it was looking for. "The Commission experienced some delays in the document production process . . . the most significant delay was due to the pace and manner of disclosure by the RCMP and the Attorney General of Canada."

Almost two years after the massacres, contrary to what the RCMP was telling the public, the force was dragging its feet when it came to co-operating with the commission. This was precisely what we had been reporting in *Frank* magazine all along. Our journalism had been dismissed because our sources were not foolish enough to put their names on the record, even if the documents themselves were verified. Now, after everything was over and the commission was finished, it was admitting that everything inside was anything but kumbaya.

The commission investigators detected obvious gaps in the RCMP disclosures and other apparent examples of game playing.

The late disclosure of various RCMP members' and officers' notes also hampered our ability to gain a complete understanding of the RCMP's critical incident response. In our decision of March 9, 2022, . . . we confirmed that the Commission would be calling a number of senior RCMP witnesses to testify during upcoming public hearings. Therefore, the RCMP and Attorney General of Canada were aware by no later than March 9, 2022, that they should be producing documents relevant to at least three senior RCMP members. In our previous subpoenas, dated March 25, 2021, and June 15, 2021, we required the production of all documents requisite to our mandate, including police notes and reports as well as relevant emails and other correspondence. In some cases, though, we did not receive relevant documents, including notes, until after a member's scheduled interview and even, in some instances, until after the witness had testified, despite our request that documents be provided in advance. . . . The manner in which materials were produced created an enormous task of review and analysis for the Commission and Participants. Many of the RCMP documents had meaningless titles and little contextual information and required detailed review by the document management and analysis team.

The poorly organized state of the materials received from the Attorney General of Canada on behalf of the RCMP was a source of frustration for both Commission staff and the Participants and caused significant delays . . . and costly additional work as staff analyzed what the commission had received.

The commission had tight deadlines and no flexibility, so full and quick disclosure was a must if they were to keep to their schedule. When the commission fought the Attorney General of Canada for quicker disclosure, Ottawa negotiated a variation: it would release documents sooner but could claw them back if it was later determined that privileged documents had been "inadvertently disclosed." The commission thought that was a good compromise until they saw what the Attorney General's lawyers had in mind.

The arrangement unfortunately met with two unintended challenges. First, there was no time limit on when the Attorney General could demand a claw back. On at least one occasion, the Attorney General required us to claw back a document after it had been posted on our website. It had to be taken down immediately, redacted to remove the privileged aspects and then reposted. This led to a media backlash, alleging that we were not being transparent as a commission. Secondly, the Attorney General had on occasion sought to claw back information in a particular document, only to have us later discover that this same information was contained in other documents that had also been disclosed and relied upon by the Attorney General (for example, as a response to a request for written evidence). This arrangement caused enormous challenges for our Commission counsel and document management teams.

The RCMP's hollow promise to fully co-operate with the commission was being backed surreptitiously by the federal Attorney General's office. While this kind of behaviour was the Canada I had come to know, the commission and its legal counsel acted as if they had never seen it before. The mischief by the Attorney General's office played out in many ways.

The Attorney General of Canada on behalf of the RCMP also relied on what is known as "litigation privilege" to justify withholding certain documents. This privilege protects parties immersed in the adversarial system from disclosing documents prepared primarily to protect their interests in litigation that is either anticipated, contemplated, or ongoing. It is very much aligned to the adversarial process. Here the Attorney General of Canada on behalf of the RCMP maintained that litigation privilege applied to documents prepared in contemplation of this inquiry. In other words, it withheld certain documents that it asserts were created for the dominant purpose of representing its interests before the inquiry. This begs a fundamental question: does litigation privilege attach to non-adversarial public inquiries such as ours?

Even though the hearings were not criminal proceedings and the commission wasn't taking an adversarial approach (remember, restorative justice), the RCMP was withholding documents under the auspices of privacy and self-protection. The lawyers for the Attorney General refused to budge on that one, which meant the commission didn't get all the documents it required.

In the end, the commission steamed ahead, reiterating what MacDonald had stated on the opening day of their work more than a year earlier: "We did not want the work to drag on for years, because that might only prolong the grieving process for many people."

But the above passages tell a different story from what had been reported since the inquiry was called in 2020. They are clear proof that both the federal Attorney General and the RCMP were not comporting themselves transparently. Why? If the official narrative was indeed the truth, what need was there for the police and the government to resort to so many shenanigans?

The even bigger mystery was why the commission wasn't more curious about what was in those missing documents. Furthermore, if the commission was truly being transparent, it would have let the public know all about this *before* it published its report and recommendations. Unlike a journalist or curious citizen, the commission didn't have to file a Freedom of Information request and rely upon the good graces of government to get what it needed. It appeared to have more than enough power to pierce the veil of secrecy and get its hands on what it wanted or needed. What was the information that it couldn't get from the police and the Attorney General of Canada? What was being massaged? What was being hidden? What had been destroyed? What was being covered up?

It made me wonder why the commissioners had bothered to reveal the problems they faced in such detail. Were they rattled by our investigation, which seemed able to reach inside the walls of the RCMP, the government and the commission and extract valuable information?

Was their well-concealed admission about the lack of co-operation by the RCMP a strategic move, should something come out later? If so, I could imagine their response going something like: "Oh, that. We covered it in our final report. No big deal. Nothing to see there."

Or did the commissioners feel personally bruised by their experience and worried that their legacies had been tarnished? Was it all just a backwards way of promoting their own integrity? "We did our best in the face of withering obstruction!"

Or were the commissioners and some of their staff active participants in a cover-up?

On April 3, four days after the report was released, I tried to get more than a dozen journalists from around the country interested in what was contained in Volume 7. "The lede was buried," I wrote in emails extending a professional courtesy, as it were. I cheekily suggested what the story was, without pointing them to the exact spot. I was eager to see if any one of them would expend an ounce of energy to pursue the lead I had handed them. All it would have taken was a phone call and I would have told them.

"Interesting," a veteran CBC investigative reporter responded by return email, the only journalist to do so. Neither he nor anyone else seemed to think it was a story, and the commission closed up shop and disappeared into the wind. There was no one available to answer any questions.

The bottom line for me was that since the commission didn't get everything it was looking for from the RCMP and the Attorney General, it was fair to infer that there was a shaky foundation for its recommendations. The commission had failed. Justice hadn't been done. The official narrative was not the truth. There was still a story to be told.

3

PATTI STARR AND THE GELDING OF PUBLIC INQUIRIES

After the Nova Scotia massacres, policing experts told me there was plenty of evidence that there should have been an independent criminal investigation into certain aspects of what the RCMP had done and not done. For example, the Mounties had refused to call for help from other police agencies or accept it, even though it was offered; instead, they waited on help from the New Brunswick RCMP, a move that may have prolonged the time before Wortman's capture and put more lives at risk. The Mounties had also not put out a public alert to warn people that a gunman was roaming the province, instead relying on Twitter updates.

The RCMP was quick to announce that it was investigating itself, but how could it do so impartially? "Protect the Buffalo" appears to be the force's unofficial code, a reference to the giant mounted buffalo head in the commissioner's Ottawa office.

An ex-Mountie whom I'll call Carl Filbert makes a compelling case, supported by other Mounties, that like many before and after him, he had been targeted and railroaded out of the force for not playing the game the way the RCMP wanted him to play it.

Filbert was serving in Halifax at the time when RCMP staff sergeant Craig Robert Burnett was charged with stealing 10 kilograms of cocaine, breach of trust and laundering the proceeds of crime, among other offences. The drugs were taken from a police exhibit locker. Burnett protested his innocence. His family and friends took to social media to raise money for his defence, crying foul all the way to and during Burnett's trial in 2019. They said he was being framed by his criminal associates, but the court didn't buy that argument. He was convicted of all seven charges against him and imprisoned for ten years. It looked like a simple case of a financially strapped man going through a divorce who let his greed rule his better judgment.

Not everyone saw it that way, however. Burnett was the commanding officer of the National Port Enforcement Team, which is a big job in Halifax, being that the city is one of the largest seaports on the east coast of North America. He was heavily in debt from gambling, and during that period the outlaw biker gang the Hells Angels was controlling the port. The bikers had key people inside working the port for them. While Burnett was on the job, the RCMP experienced several blown operations.

"That Burnett was working at the port wasn't a coincidence," said Filbert. "I had the port under surveillance and had an informant working inside the union. Yet the closer I got, the more heat was on me from above to leave them alone. We knew there was a mole or two inside our operation. Every time we went to do a raid, everything would disappear just before we got there."

Burnett was charged after he cut out one of his criminal accomplices, who was miffed and got his revenge by going to a clean Mountie and filing a complaint about "a dirty cop." The case was handed over to the Serious Incident Response Team (SIRT). Burnett was the only police officer charged and convicted.

"He couldn't have done it alone," Filbert said. "There were others inside who were helping him, but they weren't touched. The RCMP would be too embarrassed to get to the bottom of it all . . . you gotta protect the Buffalo first."

New recruits to the RCMP swear an oath to the force, not the country. It's such a subtle distinction that many Mounties don't even recall doing it, but it doesn't take long for the majority to fall into line.

Josh O'Brien was a late bloomer who joined the RCMP after first working for twenty years for large companies in the private sector. He spent twenty-five years as a constable in Alberta before retiring from the force in 2022. He is now a real estate agent. In an interview with me, O'Brien compared the differing approaches of journalism, which police often malign, and policing itself and its culture erected upon a foundation of blue lies: "In my twenty-five-year career, I've never seen police patrolmen come together to openly denounce their fellow officers who are producing thousands of false reports a day . . . Journalists and their institutions do not hesitate to uncover impostors, isolate them and denounce their colleagues without any social pressure. It is they themselves who have uncovered the lack of integrity.

"By comparison, within the police culture, while their false reports send thousands of innocent people to prison, often for decades, their unions defend their members mercilessly. Not only do the unions defend their corrupt cops, but they also sue prosecutors who refuse to accept the testimony of thousands of police officers who regularly lie to the courts.

"No journalistic association protects their rapist-killer journalists— yet in police culture, this is the norm. The police continue to walk around with badges on their shoulders that often read 'integrity, honour, transparency, justice' without behaving accordingly . . . They systematically choose the blue wall of silence—and make citizens pay for it in the billions of dollars."

O'Brien, like many experienced police officers before him, says the police culture is sick: "Bad cops should fear good cops—not the other way around."

There are viable laws on the books that could be used to hold police accountable, but there appears to be no one capable of conducting an impartial investigation. If an outside force were called in to investigate the RCMP in Nova Scotia, who could be trusted to conduct it? The Ontario Provincial Police? The Sûreté du Québec (Quebec's provincial police)? The Toronto Police? The Calgary Police, the third-largest municipal force in the country? They are the only forces with enough experienced personnel to take on such an investigation, but all of them are compromised in one way or another. They each have signed agreements with each other that include non-disparagement clauses—they can't say anything bad about each other. It should come as no surprise, therefore, that each force has historically shown itself reluctant to find any wrongdoing by other departments. In the great tradition of Canadian governance, they may wear different uniforms, but they are all on the same team, working as one.

The answer seemed to be civilian oversight. In 2010, Nova Scotia's provincial government legislated creation of the Serious Incident Response Team (SIRT), an independent investigative agency "tasked with the investigations of serious incidents involving police in Nova Scotia." It might have looked great on paper; in reality, it turned out to be anything but. Those appointed to operate SIRT had ties to the justice system. The investigators were police seconded from the forces that were supposedly being overseen, or were former, recently retired police officers. And the director of SIRT at the time of the massacres was Felix Cacchione, a former Nova Scotia Supreme Court judge who, as I reported in 22 Murders, had been appointed to hear the case of Aimé Simard and Dany Kane, two Hells Angels hit men who had been arrested for the 1997 murder of former Hells Angel Robert MacFarlane. However, the two men were set free after Cacchione stayed the proceedings, ostensibly because of contradictory RCMP evidence. At the time, Kane was working as an RCMP confidential informant.

It all begged a question: Could SIRT be trusted to be disinterested?

In the end, SIRT would investigate two incidents of the massacres, not the entire shooting spree and the role played by the RCMP, which most experts in policing believed it should have done. Instead, as we know, public outcry from the families led to a public inquiry, which was celebrated as a major win. People were desperate for a serious and thorough public airing, but what neither the lawyers for the families nor the media seemed to appreciate was that the inquiry process had been rendered ineffective by politics.

Allow me to take you on a journey back to the 1980s and introduce you to Patti Starr.

◆

In 1979 and 1980, there were two federal elections, nine months apart. In the first, Progressive Conservative Joe Clark was elected prime minister, but he soon bumbled his way out of office, paving the way for the return of Pierre Elliott Trudeau.

During those campaigns, I met David Peterson, whose older brother, James, ran in both elections in the north Toronto federal riding of Willowdale. While I was covering a boring campaign event one night, David and I retired to my admittedly pimpish-looking powder-blue 1974 Plymouth Satellite Sebring (with white interior!) to smoke a cigarette or two and kick back and get to know each other. We had quite a few laughs. Some might have thought that would lead to a *Casablanca*-type beautiful friendship: he'd help me with my future reportage and I would, in return, protect him from nasty headlines. That's how some journalists work. Not me.

Our lives changed dramatically over the next few years. David Peterson was elected leader of the Ontario Liberal Party and in 1985 became the premier of Ontario, ending a forty-two-year reign by the Progressive Conservatives. I became a senior editor at the *Globe and Mail* and was placed in charge of investigative reporting. The first thing I did was disband the "investigative" unit and make every reporter an investigator—assigned to dig as deeply as they could into their designated areas of coverage.

In 1988, I oversaw a number of high-profile investigations, the most spectacular of which involved reporters Linda McQuaig, Jock Ferguson and Dawn King and columnist Michael Valpy. It began with an investigation into the largely unknown land developers of Tridel Corporation Inc., who had become incredibly wealthy and politically influential. This morphed into a twenty-two-day series focusing on the activities of

Toronto fundraiser Patricia (Patti) Starr, who was washing money from Tridel through the National Council of Jewish Women, which she ran, and funnelling it into Ontario Liberal Party coffers. We managed to unravel much of the scheme, including juicy nuggets like one about how one of Premier Peterson's closest advisers, lawyer Gordon Ashworth, had received a new refrigerator and free house painting from a development company.

The revelations proved devastating for Premier Peterson, who wasn't at all happy with me. The last time I saw him, when he was visiting the newsroom, he scowled at me and muttered a few words of contempt under his breath.

Shortly thereafter, on a single day, nine Ontario cabinet ministers were removed from their portfolios, including five who had received money from land developers via Starr's charity. Although Peterson had one of the largest majorities ever enjoyed by an Ontario government—95 of 125 seats in the Legislature—public opinion polls deemed him and his party to be untrustworthy. The usually swaggering Peterson had lost his mojo.

On June 23, 1989, he called a public inquiry, to be headed by Mr. Justice Lloyd Houlden. "I think the inquiry will be a positive thing," said Starr, who had not been charged with any crimes at that point.

Once the inquiry began, her tune changed. She had two top-drawer lawyers in Austin Cooper and Peter West. Tridel Corporation Inc. was represented by Earl A. Cherniak, QC, and partners. Together, the lawyers challenged the very existence of the inquiry, arguing, among other things, that the province did not have proper jurisdiction and that the Houlden Inquiry could potentially affect the rights of an individual to due process, which was guaranteed by the Charter of Rights and Freedoms as embodied in the Canadian Constitution.

Both the Ontario Divisional Court and the Ontario Court of Appeal dismissed the case, which was appealed to the Supreme Court of Canada. The Supreme Court overturned the Ontario decisions in a 6–1 ruling, led by Chief Justice Brian Dickson and supported by justices Charles Gonthier, John Sopinka, Gérard La Forest, Peter Cory and Antonio Lamer. The majority took the position that the province was exceeding its jurisdiction and that the Houlden Inquiry was effectively conducting a police investigation or preliminary inquiry. "The inquiry process cannot be used to circumvent federally prescribed criminal procedure," the judges wrote. "It is coercive and quite incompatible with our notion of justice in the investigation of a particular crime and the determination of actual or probable criminal or civil responsibility. The pith and substance of a provincial commission must be firmly anchored to a provincial head of power and cannot be used, either purposely or through its effect, as a means to investigate and determine the criminal responsibility of specific individuals for specific offenses."

Claire L'Heureux-Dubé, a frequent dissenter on the Supreme Court, believed that Charter rights were not absolute and that there was no hierarchy of rights. Her philosophy was that all rights must be balanced against each other. She thought the Ontario government had a right to proceed with the inquiry, writing: "The profound concern about alleged improprieties against government officials and employees extended far beyond the appellants and provided the necessary framework of the commission's mandate. . . . The terms of reference do not invade the federal criminal law power. . . . Indeed, any resemblance is immaterial. . . . The terms of reference serve only to define the scope of an investigation which is expressly prohibited from making criminal findings. An otherwise constitutional provincial inquiry cannot be barred absolutely by the possibility of a subsequent prosecution."

After the inquiry was quashed by the Supreme Court ruling, Patti Starr was hit with seventy-six charges, including thirty violations of election spending laws. Other Liberals who were party to the scheme were also charged. In June 1991, Starr pled guilty to eight charges of election fraud expense and two charges of breach of trust. She was sentenced to two six-month terms in jail, which were served concurrently.

In her first book, *Tempting Fate: A Cautionary Tale of Power and Politics*, Starr claimed that David Peterson made her a scapegoat to avoid scrutiny of other government activities. Starr invited me to attend the launch party for her second book, *Deadly Justice*, which I did. I purchased a copy, which she inscribed with: "Dear Paul, without your investigations, I wouldn't be a writer. xxxx Patti Starr."

If anything, Starr's gesture showed that not everyone who was the target of my journalism thought ill of me. Peterson, meanwhile, never recovered and his government was effectively demolished by the New Democratic Party in the provincial election held September 6, 1990. The Liberals lost fifty-nine seats. In true Canadian fashion, however, Peterson afterwards continued to thrive with significant corporate appointments and as an éminence grise of the Liberal Party.

The Patti Starr affair, as it came to be known, might seem obscure now, but the legal decisions made in her case had an enormous impact on how the Nova Scotia massacres were handled by governments. The Starr decision established that no inquiry could delve into possible criminal behaviour. The Supreme Court had placed its faith in the police to do their job and hold the powerful to account. What this meant was that, should the police or the courts fail to mount a successful investigation, suspects were safe from prosecution, even if a public inquiry were to be called. And the hands of Parliament would be tied. It also meant that if it wasn't in the interest of the police to succeed in their investigation, there would be no oversight to hold them or those truly responsible to account, leaving the police vulnerable to influence by high-profile actors and politicians. Corruption was protected by the Constitution.

In Nova Scotia, the killer was dead. The police were investigating, but it was obvious to anyone who paid attention that the RCMP hadn't done what the police should have done: respond quickly in force, protect citizens in danger, identify and contain the suspect and, failing that, alert the community about a dangerous man on the loose. The first priority of police is the preservation of life. The RCMP saved no one that weekend. If, in their investigation, they discovered evidence that reflected poorly on them, would they be forthcoming? I suspected not. They had a Buffalo to protect.

4

WELCOME TO THE "SPINQUIRY"

February 22, 2022, was a cloudy and cool Tuesday morning in Halifax when the Mass Casualty Commission's formal public hearings finally began. The first hearing was held at the new Halifax Convention Centre, which sits halfway up the hill that runs from the harbour to the Citadel in the old downtown. The commission had optimistically booked another venue nearby for the public to watch the televised proceedings, but the locations were anything but a lure for the public. Parking rates in the area are forbidding. Interest in the story had waned over the 674 days since Gabriel Wortman had been shot dead at the Irving Big Stop in Enfield. Combined with the ongoing COVID lockdown, the massacres had become an "oh, that" story for those who recalled it.

That first day there were about forty-five mask-wearing people in attendance, safely spread out from one another, making the cavernous room look even larger than it was. Three of the people who did dare attend were Scott McLeod, Darrell Currie and Greg Muise. McLeod's brother, corrections officer Sean McLeod, had been one of Gabriel Wortman's twenty-two victims. Currie, the deputy fire chief at the Onslow Belmont fire hall, and Muise, the fire chief, were nearly shot by Mounties who were frantically chasing Wortman and who had fired wildly into their fire hall. Others would come and go, but the presence of these three would be a constant throughout the hearings.

Also in attendance were the three people who had been named as commissioners: J. Michael MacDonald, the former chief justice of Nova Scotia, who would serve as chairman of the commission; Leanne Fitch, a former Fredericton police chief; and Dr. Kim Stanton, a specialist in women's issues, equality and Aboriginal rights, who took the place of Anne McLellan, a former cabinet minister who had stepped down when the review turned into a public inquiry.

As I described in *22 Murders*, each commissioner had a personal history that "called into question their so-called independence." MacDonald was the uncle of Andrew MacDonald, one of the victims whom Wortman wounded but did not murder. Andrew and his father owned Maritime Auto Parts, which sponsored the police hockey team in the local beer league.

MacDonald's title, former chief justice of Nova Scotia, conveyed the image of a man who was a paragon of virtue and impartiality, perfect for the difficult task at hand. But there were others who saw it differently. Any chief justice is appointed by the federal government of the day; in MacDonald's case, it was former prime minister Paul Martin who had recommended him. Like many of his colleagues, MacDonald had first been a lawyer working inside the federal Liberal Party, as the registered official agent for then federal cabinet minister David Dingwall, the king of patronage in the Maritimes at the time. It was the kind of volunteer work that gets a lawyer like him worthwhile rewards later.

While MacDonald had had a long and seemingly illustrious career on the Nova Scotia bench, there was one case over which the controversy has never diminished. MacDonald was the judge in the 1998 trial of former Nova Scotia premier Gerald Regan. The RCMP had charged Regan with nineteen criminal counts involving sexual misconduct with young girls and women. As I wrote in *22 Murders*, "It looked like a slam-dunk case, but once again a miracle happened in a Nova Scotia court. Justice J. Michael MacDonald stayed the nine most serious charges against Regan, and Regan eventually beat the others (the stayed charges were reinstated years later after a ruling by the province's Court of

Appeal, but were never prosecuted before Regan's death in 2019)." This all happened well before being trauma-informed was adopted as a judicial approach, because "traumatized" would accurately describe the state of mind of the young victims of Regan and their families after what took place in MacDonald's courtroom in 1998.

What most people also missed or simply glossed over in MacDonald's qualifications for the commission was a single word—"former." He was just an ordinary citizen who was merely acting like a judge. It was an important distinction because MacDonald ultimately had no judicial power or authority to compel the RCMP to co-operate with the commission or answer questions about delicate matters that it didn't want to answer.

Joining MacDonald was former Fredericton police chief Leanne Fitch. The first openly gay woman to be named a police chief in Canada, she was hailed as an expert on domestic violence and women's issues, which seemed to make her a perfect fit for the commission. However, many people, including myself, questioned her ability to be impartial to the RCMP's involvement in the case. Not only did Fitch come from a family of police officers, her father was a Mountie. Her wife was also a Fredericton cop. As Fredericton police chief, Fitch had worked closely with the Mounties in New Brunswick as part of the Combined Forces Special Enforcement Unit there. As I reported in *22 Murders*, "Gabriel Wortman was conducting criminal activities in New Brunswick and central Nova Scotia for almost thirty years, smuggling cigarettes, alcohol and guns over the border. Anything he was noticed doing would have been caught on Fitch's radar." It was very likely that she had known about Wortman.

I also noted that Fitch was on the RCMP Management Advisory Board: "in February 2020, she was photographed for the RCMP standing beside a gleaming Assistant Commissioner Lee Bergerman. The occasion was to celebrate Fitch's appointment to the RCMP Management Advisory Board, where she would have worked shoulder to shoulder with Bergerman. Fitch, therefore, was conducting an investigation into a colleague, something Blair and Furey forgot to mention in their joint announcement of the review. Weeks later, Fitch resigned from her RCMP management advisory role."

Even her fellow police officers were aghast at her appointment. "Having her there is a joke," one well-placed New Brunswick police officer told me, echoing the sentiments of many others.

"I got along fine with Leanne," another New Brunswick police officer said, "but there were plenty of problems with her. But there was no one to complain to about any of it, especially if you wanted to continue with your career and get your pension."

Rounding out the commission was Dr. Kim Stanton, a specialist in social issues who had published a book, *Reconciling Truths: Reimagining Public Inquiries in Canada*, about how public inquiries should be employed as a medium to address "deep societal challenges" rather than as an investigative tool. After Patti Starr, it was the only thing a public inquiry could do.

My initial reaction to Stanton was that she was just another university-approved social engineer who was going to make the world a better place, even if it meant pounding a massive square peg into a narrow round hole. Then it struck me that Stanton was not just a garden-variety social engineer; she was an historian as well. Inadvertently or otherwise, she was describing not only the raison d'être of these political creations but how the creatures had actually functioned, even before the Patti Starr decision. What she was describing was the postmodernist concept of a public inquiry—reason, logic, facts and the truth were tossed out the window, if need be. When confronted with a controversial issue, the outcome of any such inquiry would be predetermined by government and its bureaucracy and then, if required, reinforced with new legislation, regulations or subsidies.

Stanton was also a legal director of the Women's Legal Education and Action Fund (LEAF), from which she resigned when she took the appointment to become commissioner. LEAF would appear before her at the hearings, but no one questioned that potential conflict of interest.

All this biographical background somehow escaped the media that were covering the creation of the MCC. In fact, the three commissioners were treated as all but angels descending from heaven. As I first reported in *22 Murders*, *Maclean's* magazine's Nick Taylor-Vaisey included them in an aspirational year-end list of the "50 Canadians Who Are Breaking

Ground, Leading the Debate and Shaping How We Think and Live."
Taylor-Vaisey wrote, in part:

> The results of their inquiry could be monumental for a national
> police force struggling with its underfunded rural policing model,
> a change-resistant culture and ongoing charges of systemic racism.
> Michael MacDonald, Leanne J. Fitch and Kim Stanton will face
> intense pressure to tell uncomfortable truths for the families, and for
> a police force in need of reform.

Once the three commissioners were in place, a large team was assembled around them. The commission set up two offices, one in Halifax and the other in Truro, to be near the people most closely involved in the massacres. Sixty full-time staff were hired, including fourteen lawyers who would serve as commission counsels, managers, policy advisers and communications specialists.

The ten investigators and an intelligence specialist were mostly retired Toronto police officers. Many of them had served under federal public safety minister Bill Blair, a former Toronto police chief and current political boss of the MCC. The investigations director was Toronto deputy police chief Barbara McLean. The MCC's lead investigator was former Toronto officer Scott Spicer, who was now employed by the Privy Council Office, which oversees the bureaucracy and policy implementation of the federal government. One couldn't help but wonder why he was there. The entire episode in Nova Scotia appeared to be a provincial matter. The RCMP was hired as a contract police force to enforce provincial laws. Everything had happened inside Nova Scotia, but Ottawa had taken total control of the investigation afterwards and the provincial government appeared to be sitting on its hands. That seemed odd to me. It suggested that there was more going on than first met the eye.

◆

On the morning of February 22, MacDonald began his opening speech. He tried to project the air of a wise and learned sixty-eight-year-old jurist; just another day at work, but it wasn't. He was no longer in the flak-free world of the bench. He was an ordinary joe with privileges and a hefty retainer in the $2,000 to $2,500 per day range, and he was taking incoming fire from all sides, even from lawyers and politicians who were being openly critical of him.

"Some people are concerned about the commission's independence, believing we may be susceptible to covering up for either the RCMP or government," MacDonald said in his thirty-five-minute address. "Let me assure you, nothing could be further from the truth . . . I was a chief justice in this province for over twenty years. Protecting the judiciary from outside interference was fundamental to that role. I would never tolerate any attempt by any institution or individual to tamper with our independence. I am absolutely committed to the independence of this commission, its findings and recommendations—as is the entire commission team."

Family members of the murder victims were each given $100,000 to hire a lawyer to represent them at the commission. They and others like firefighters Muise and Currie were subsidized by the commission to attend. They were put up in hotels and had their meals paid for. Other groups who applied for standing were also funded. Even Lisa Banfield, Wortman's common-law wife, apparently received financial support, which I reported about in *Frank*. The monies came with a string attached: non-disclosure agreements, which served to seal almost everyone's lips, making accurate and timely reporting about what was going on significantly more difficult.

A week before the commission hearings were to open, Patterson Law, the legal firm representing twenty-three participants, including the families of fourteen of the murder victims, put out a hard-hitting public statement expressing its concerns about the commission. Even though they were being funded by the commission, Patterson Law lawyers Robert Pineo, Sandra McCulloch and Michael Scott and their team felt that they were being kept in the dark about the process. I've included their unedited comments below.

Our concerns about the completeness of the Commission's fact-finding process are aggravated by the lack of information with which we have been provided in regards to what the public proceedings will entail, including:

- Who will be called as a witness during the public proceedings, how they will be asked or required to give evidence, and upon what subject matter(s) they will be directed to speak;
- Whether we, on behalf of our clients, will be permitted opportunity to examine any such witnesses, whether on the subject matter we judge appropriate, or at all;
- What the revised Foundational Documents will look like (only three of which have been made available to us in the past two weeks);
- When we will have access to the outstanding source materials which inform/are expected to inform the revised Foundational Documents;
- Whether and what opportunities we, on behalf of our clients, will be afforded to test evidence presented to the Commissioners, whether presented in the form of revised Foundational Documents, source materials, witnesses or otherwise;
- Whether and what opportunities we, on behalf of our clients, will be afforded to raise objections to evidence which is *not* presented to the Commissioners during the public proceedings, including objections we have to Commission Counsels' decisions *not* to call particular individuals as witnesses to give any evidence during public proceedings;
- What further disclosure we should anticipate to receive in advance of or during the public proceedings, and when (such that we cannot know whether we have had access to all of the evidence which will inform the revised Foundational Documents, whether in advance or any opportunities for us to make submissions or otherwise);
- What opportunities we will have to make submissions about various matters during the public proceedings, and during those opportunities, what matters we will be permitted to make submissions about;

- In what manner we and our clients will be permitted to appear; in person or otherwise, at the public proceedings, the particulars of which have yet to be provided to us.

They painted a vivid picture of the commission's modus operandi. Everything was being controlled from the inside. Even the parties who were supposedly part of the process were complaining, publicly and privately, about being blocked from fully participating. It was the closed-door review that the government had originally planned, but with the name of a public inquiry.

Patterson Law client Nick Beaton, whose pregnant wife, Kristen, was Wortman's eighteenth murder victim, added: "This has been the review we fought against. We wanted the tools that a public inquiry would give us, that a review would not. . . . All this has done is cost taxpayers millions of dollars, only to give us a review anyway."

The recent missive from Patterson Law lawyers had been amplified that very morning by Nova Scotia premier Tim Houston. "The reason Nova Scotians pulled together and pushed for an inquiry as opposed to a review was to ensure that it was honest, comprehensive, detailed and most importantly, designed to answer questions," said Houston, who otherwise had not said much of anything substantial about the matter. "Yet, it is still not even known if key witnesses have been subpoenaed to testify, if there will be an opportunity to cross-examine them or if it will be a comprehensive list of witnesses. This uncertainty is causing further, unnecessary trauma.

"For these reasons, the commission should meet with the families and their counsel to listen to their concerns and provide them with a plan that gives them confidence in the process," Houston said, accurately summarizing the discontent that was apparent to anyone paying attention.

MacDonald bristled at what he thought was Houston's "political interference" and felt compelled to respond to both the lawyers and the Nova Scotia premier. "Cross-examination is one way to do that and, rest assured, where appropriate, including questioning by counsel for the participants, it will happen—and the commission will be robust in its response if witnesses try to be misleading."

Finally, MacDonald defended the planned brisk schedule for the hear-ings, arguing that the inquiry "could drift and drag on for years if we called all the witnesses involved. This process cannot drag on for five years."

While it was slow getting started, the MCC's public hearings would not drag on. The hearings would run from February 22 to September 23, 2022—seven months. While that might sound like ample time for it to do its work, the commission seemed to abide by the maxim that less is more. During that period, it would hold seventy-six public hearings, but even that was deceptive. About half of those seventy-six hearings would be devoted to round-table discussions, witness panels, participant sub-missions and virtual hearings—the antithesis of drama.

In its pursuit of being "trauma-informed," the commission opted to take the stress out of the experience of testifying. In fact, testifying was not how the commission described what was about to take place. These were public interviews. The commission was going to show the world that it had a sensitive touch. It supposedly had the power to subpoena people to attend its hearings, but some people, including police officers, just ignored the subpoenas, and there is no indication that any were ever pursued by the commission.

Lawyer Josh Bryson, who represented the Bond family, was in pri-vate practice but moonlighted as a federal prosecutor. He immediately recognized the practical problem of taking the trauma-informed approach. "As a federal prosecutor, I have put seven-year-old children on the witness stand to be cross-examined by the defence," Bryson told me. "As soon as you announce everything is going to be trauma-informed, everyone would suddenly be too stressed to testify."

That's precisely what happened.

Although the public face of the RCMP was that it welcomed an inquiry, the Mounties were reluctant participants, pretending to co-operate. The public perception of police officers is that they all have a duty to testify and tell the truth—the fundamental requirements of their job—but the Mounties appeared to be running for cover.

Before the first Mountie was even called as a witness, an issue was raised about whether the Mounties would be required to swear an oath. If the story of the massacres was what the force said it was, a domestic violence case gone wrong, nothing would need to be hidden from the public. But the Mounties were clearly jittery about something and were attempting to hide behind mental-health concerns about not just one or two Mounties, but *all* who were involved.

Union president Sergeant Brian Sauvé made that case in an affidavit submitted to the commission, arguing that the RCMP members had already told their stories to other RCMP members and to commission investigators. It was all in their individual notes and statements. Nothing more was needed from them, the union argued.

The union's lawyer Nasha Nijhawan argued that all RCMP members who responded that weekend should be shielded from hard questions because of their everlasting traumatization. She even offered to provide an expert witness, a clinical psychologist from the RCMP's home turf in Regina, to make the case. The commission declined.

One of the lawyers who addressed the issue was Stephen Topshee, who represented the families of four of the murder victims. He spoke specifically about Acting Corporal Stuart Beselt, the first Mountie to arrive on the scene that Saturday night, but his argument could have been applied to every Mountie. "There are a lot of facts to be known from his evidence," Topshee said. ". . . There's a lot of evidence. Questions that will never be answered . . . It's not to put him on the stand to cross-examine him, per se, in my view. It's to get to the truth and get to the facts. It's not a blame-seeking situation here. It's an inquisitorial fact-seeking situation . . . and it's necessary to have him on the stand in that regard."

Federal government lawyers were also running interference that benefited the Mounties. The Attorney General of Canada's lawyers applied for and were granted a Rule 43 accommodation for certain witnesses, most of them Mounties, without disclosing the underlying reasons why each needed special treatment. These protected witnesses were allowed to tell their version of events without being challenged by questions that were not first approved by federal government lawyers from the commission. Some witnesses who claimed that the hearings would be too traumatizing for them were allowed to do it via the Internet. When they did muster up the strength and courage to come to the hearings, there was nothing conventional about the circumstances. Some witnesses were allowed to "testify" in groups, with family members or human support animals, all protected by the commission from probing questions.

Portapique resident Jerry Murphy recalled watching it all on television. "I remember when the Department of Justice lawyers came in that morning, the camera panned to Judge MacDonald . . . I think that was the moment he realized that it wasn't *his* commission. It was going to be run by the Department of Justice in Ottawa. It turned it all into nothing but a shit show."

On the *Nighttime* podcast, we held an audience participation contest to come up with an appropriate nickname for the commission. The winner was Spinquiry.

◆

If Mounties weren't testifying in person, their accounts could be read in the foundational documents, in which the disjointed threads of the story were spread across more pages than many people could read or absorb.

The commission had taken more than a year to create the foundational documents and was still doing so after the hearings had begun. People were interviewed and everything was supposedly recorded and transcribed. The documents would become the commission's bible. Lawyers for the families could ask questions only about information contained within the documents. Anything else was deemed an invitation to spreading conspiracy theories. The storylines built into the documents would be followed religiously, even though the transcriptions themselves were criticized for being sloppy, inaccurate and, sometimes, misleading, a point addressed by RCMP constable Greg Wiley, who appeared before the commission via closed video link: "The transcript was being handed around for people to read," Wiley told the MCC. "And if they are not getting clear information—and I think I speak English quite well—if they weren't getting clear information from the get-go from my transcript, then that's a very weak foundation to build your questions upon, and this whole—your inquiry is almost like an investigation, and our statements are the key building blocks of evidence for you . . . I think people who were looking at this, all of the lawyers who have been looking at this, have a hard time. I had a hard time looking at my own statement."

The RCMP union fought behind the scenes to limit the scope of questioning of its members about their training and work histories. It was well known in policing circles that some of the Mounties in Nova Scotia had sketchy work histories and had been moved from detachment to detachment, à la the Catholic Church and wayward priests. One key senior Mountie, reliable sources said, was involved with his wife in the local swingers' community, which may well have extended into Wortman's ambit. Though not a criminal act, it raised questions about their decision-making processes. Lawyers from the federal Department of Justice, who were effectively running the commission, seemed more than eager to accommodate and assuage the Mounties. The end result was that none of the above was deemed to be fair game for the commission.

The individual Mounties would be allowed to say what they wanted to say, and Commissioner MacDonald would rely upon his self-proclaimed superior senses to detect lies. Most of what the Mounties said was likely true, but at the same time it was impossible to know for certain, because nothing was challenged. In this fantasy world, it was as if the commissioners had never heard that police will all too often shade the truth or lie, even under oath, if it comes down to protecting their livelihoods, their jobs or those of their preferred colleagues.

A good example of how the process worked was the way Corporal Natasha Jamieson was handled. She was one of the first at the scene in Portapique on the evening of April 18, 2020. In the aftermath of the massacres, multiple police sources told me that an RCMP corporal had blocked other members from entering the neighbourhood, saying: "If you go down there, this will be your last shift in the RCMP." As I reported in both the *Halifax Examiner* and *22 Murders*, multiple sources told me that a corporal had hidden in the bushes and left their gun there. Who was that corporal? What happened? I believed that knowing the answers to those questions appeared to be in the public interest.

Since she was there and held the rank of corporal, Jamieson seemed like a key Mountie to interview, but the commission took its time getting to her. Remember that the MCC was supposed to begin its hearings in October 2021, but announced in September 2021 that the opening would be delayed for another four months. The commission finally got around talking to Jamieson on December 10, 2021, when she gave a "voluntary statement."

Jamieson's interview was conducted at RCMP headquarters, at 80 Garland Avenue in Dartmouth. She was accompanied by Corporal Chantelle Egan, the force's wellness coordinator. Heidi Collicutt, a lawyer from the Attorney General of Canada's office, represented her. The interviewers were two former Toronto police detectives, Wayne Fowler and Will Crews.

Jamieson said she joined the RCMP in 1997 after signing up for an Aboriginal cadet development program. On the force, she had worked in general duty, as a school liaison officer for four years, as an acting supervisor at Indian Brook First Nation for four years and as the force's human trafficking awareness coordinator for another four years. She worked in federal crime units until 2017, when she received a promotion to corporal and was posted to the Millbrook First Nation, where she was working the night the massacres began.

According to her statement, Jamieson did not arrive in Portapique until about an hour after the first 911 call, which suggested that she was not the corporal who hid in the woods that night. She conceded that she had not taken the training needed to carry a carbine and was therefore excluded from participating in the dangerous search for Wortman in Portapique. After the massacres, Jamieson was one of about seventy Mounties who took the summer of 2020 off work on paid stress leave.

There were a couple of moments during Jamieson's interview with Fowler and Crews that gave plenty of fodder for a cross-examination that would never occur. On page 20 of the transcript, for example, Jamieson stopped herself while relating an incident: "Oh, my goodness, the most . . . important part I totally forgot. . . . Sorry, I'm going backwards here, and I really had hoped my prep session was going to result in me not being all over the place."

Like most Mounties' versions of events, Jamieson's statement was accepted at face value, reduced to a transcript and labelled a foundational paper. She did not appear before the commission.

Among the many others who were not called as witnesses was Detective Sergeant William (Bill) Raaymakers, the lead investigator during the first week after the massacres. He oversaw operations, examination, interviews and searches. Portapique-area resident Nathan Staples said Raaymakers visited him shortly after the massacres and seemed disturbed by what the force had done. Staples said Raaymakers personally apologized for the Mounties' behaviour that night. The commission posted some of Raaymakers's notes, but he was not interviewed. My efforts to reach him for comment were unsuccessful. He retired from the force less than two weeks after the massacres.

Another lead investigator was Corporal Gerard (Gerry) Rose-Berthiaume. He was interviewed by the MCC and a transcript was posted on its website, but the corporal was never called to testify in public.

Someone who *was* called on two different occasions as an expert witness, however, was retired constable Brian Carter, president of the Nova Scotia branch of the RCMP Veterans' Association. A rabid defender of the RCMP, Carter bled red serge. He was called on early in the commission's hearings to discuss police paraphernalia—the pride he had in the uniform—and later as an expert on the organization of policing in Nova Scotia.

If there was a common thread to be found in how the commission treated Mounties, it was that RCMP members had been coddled and coached and had rehearsed their "testimony." To reiterate, the commission showed no interest in pursuing the strong possibility, based on the RCMP's own verified documents, that it had destroyed or manipulated information in the case. Why? What was destroyed?

The MCC was presenting itself as conducting a robust search for the truth, but in spite of Commissioner MacDonald's declarations to the contrary, the truth it was seeking seemed predetermined, as if everything had been storyboarded beforehand. Meanwhile, the whole truth, whatever it might be, continued to be hidden in the glaring omissions, obfuscation and outright fabrications. As you shall learn, the commission accepted the versions of events as described by the RCMP and seconded by SIRT director Felix Cacchione when video and eyewitness testimony described a narrative that was much less favourable to the RCMP.

All this transcribing created a mountain of paper. Recall that the commission was seeking 80,000 documents, a total it didn't come close to achieving. Each document was numbered. The first was COMM0000001 and the last was COMM0065782. That was daunting enough, but the commission made it even more difficult. Documents would appear on its website with no apparent rhyme or reason, as if there were a ghost in the machine. Sometimes foundational documents were released on the day a witness would be appearing, and other times not. Documents would be posted on the website, then disappear, and then reappear days or weeks later in a slightly altered form. It was up to the reader to figure out what had changed in them.

Citizen investigator Ryan Potter, who closely monitored the commission's activities, experienced this capriciousness several times, usually after he copied curious sections from a document and posted them on the Internet. One 407-page document from the Halifax Police Department suddenly disappeared after Potter began pointing out what was contained in it. It was later replaced by a five-page summary. "They were watching what I was doing," Potter said. "I was always under the assumption that one or two parties were monitoring the [*Nighttime*] podcast, YouTube chat and some social media. A few times, I suspected things were pulled or redacted because we were talking about it."

Even after the hearings formally ended, a tsunami of 2,000 documents was made public one day, long after the media had lost the scent. Soon afterwards, the commission shut down, so that there was no one left to answer questions about what was in those documents.

The fact that the commission had 65,782 numbered documents suggested that it had done a thorough job and had left no stone unturned, but the total number was misleading. Only 6,000 documents were released in PDF form, and there were giant gaps in suspicious places. For example, in a section where RCMP staff sergeant Greg Vardy's handwritten notes were published, the document run goes like this: 6032, 6033, 6034, and then jumps to 6053 and notes taken by Constable Mike Woolcock. Among other roles, Vardy was Lisa Banfield's main interviewer and had interviewed her under caution as he touched on the source of Wortman's munitions. The gap in the numbers made me wonder if anything had been left out.

Typical of the omissions was the range numbered from 10000 to 11000. In the "Foundational Documents" ledger for that range, there were not 1,000 documents but only 88. Another two in that range were located in the "Research Documents" ledger. Those two involved Lisa Banfield and her brother-in-law Brian Brewster. Where were the other 910? Even this understates the extent of the gaps. The last document in the above range was 10990, and the next one was 11086. What was in those unseen 81 documents?

It was a pattern repeated across the board.

The commission had located almost 2,000 of Wortman's emails but released only a handful. It released none of the emails it described as being degrading of Banfield. It didn't reveal what it knew about Wortman's Internet searches. It didn't release information contained on many phones, including those used by Mounties on the job that weekend. The Mounties like to use WhatsApp as an alternative communication platform because it leaves no traces. The commission didn't appear interested in who might have been using the app.

If all that wasn't enough to make one skeptical about the process, a closer examination of some of the documents would help illustrate a deeper issue regarding the commission's credibility. For that, we need to move to the second day of the public hearings, to the panel discussion on the structure of policing in Nova Scotia.

5

THE INVISIBLE HAND IN POLICING

Not every police chief in Nova Scotia was a bad guy in a uniform. Against the odds, some tried to do the right thing. One of those was Edgar MacLeod. He graduated from the Atlantic Police Academy in 1973 and was offered a job by the Shelburne Police Department on Nova Scotia's South Shore, which his father, desperate to see his son get a job, made him take.

Shelburne was created largely by United Empire Loyalists who had fled the United States after the British lost the American War of Independence. Many of the new settlers were Black. In 1783, Shelburne was the fourth-largest municipality in North America, with 17,000 residents, but by the 1820s the population had shrunk to just 300. By the time MacLeod arrived for work in Shelburne, the population was at a 1970s high of about 2,300. The main industries were fishing and shipbuilding.

When MacLeod received his first paycheque in Shelburne, he noticed something extremely odd about it. The cheque had been issued by Bob Douglas Security Agency, Dartmouth, Nova Scotia. When MacLeod investigated, he found the strangest of arrangements: Shelburne's was one of a number of small Nova Scotia police services that fell under the umbrella of the private Dartmouth company.

Five months after joining the Shelburne police force, the twenty-one-year-old MacLeod was made deputy police chief. A year and a half later, MacLeod was made chief when his predecessor left for a better job—manager of the local liquor store.

According to MacLeod, his demise on the force came after a key Shelburne citizen was arrested for creating a disturbance and drunk and disorderly conduct. The arrested man was a financial supporter of the mayor (now long since dead), who called MacLeod into his office. "There was some discussion," MacLeod recalled. "And the mayor said, 'I expect you to look after these charges. It's a bit of an embarrassment and he's a big supporter and a friend.'

"I was in shock that he would even approach a chief of police with that kind of a notion. 'I don't even know if you know who you are talking to, Your Worship,'" MacLeod said, conscious of paying respect to the office. "'I'm going to pretend this conversation didn't happen . . . The charges stand and it's going to court.' And the mayor said: 'I don't know if you know who I am. I am the chief magistrate. I expect you to look after this.'"

MacLeod asked the mayor: "What will happen if I don't look after this?"

He said the mayor replied that he would go to his council and have a resolution passed to dismiss MacLeod by a motion of council.

"I'm never going to resign," MacLeod said, and he stormed out of the office. "He told me the town didn't want to bring the Mounties in, but they were in a dilemma because I wasn't going to co-operate."

About three months later, a resolution was passed. MacLeod was gone. The Shelburne police force was eliminated. The plan was that the RCMP would be contracted on a short-term basis to provide municipal policing until a new local force could be assembled.

The RCMP jumped at the opportunity. It promised the world to Shelburne: better policing that would be cheaper, thanks to federal subsidies. The town wouldn't have to worry about the messiness of overseeing the RCMP. It would all be handled by the federal government.

Before long, other small Nova Scotia municipal forces were disbanded and the RCMP moved in. In 1975 the Nova Scotia Police Act came into force, putting the Bob Douglas Security Agency out of the policing business. As the Mounties grew their contract operations, municipalities noticed that their promised gratis services began to disappear. There were financial charges for everything, and virtually no way for municipalities to control the Mounties or hold the force accountable.

MacLeod went on to have a stellar career in law enforcement. He spent twelve years in the Sydney, Nova Scotia, police force before becoming the chief of police in nearby New Waterford. Until 1995, the greater Sydney area employed seven different police agencies, with the RCMP assigned to the rural areas. MacLeod was one of the leaders in the fight to amalgamate the services into one, a move that the RCMP strenuously objected to, but unsuccessfully. The Mounties were kicked out of the community and replaced by the Cape Breton Regional Police under MacLeod, who served for twelve years in the post. Further aggravating the Mounties was the defection of two Cape Breton First Nations reserves, Membertou and Eskasoni. Each was disgruntled by the spotty service provided by the RCMP under federal contracts. They liked what MacLeod's force had to offer and, in a move unprecedented in Canada, switched their business to the municipal force.

In September 2017, MacLeod was named the executive director of his old alma mater, the Atlantic Police Academy in Summerside, Prince Edward Island. Over the years he has received many accolades and has become known as an articulate and well-respected analyst and thinker in Canadian policing circles.

Now retired and living in PEI, MacLeod says the failings of the RCMP at the federal level have had an unacknowledged but profound effect on Canadian society. "Governments at all levels are failing to make the connection between the lack of federal enforcement and the unprecedented conditions facing our local communities," MacLeod said. "We've never had more homeless people or people with psychiatric problems. There have never been more illegal drugs on our streets. Why? It can all be traced back to the impact of international crime, including organized commercial crime, drug trafficking and money laundering. The federal government is largely responsible. The RCMP is tasked with the responsibility of federal law enforcement, but federal policing enforcement has not kept pace. Instead, we see more and more of our federal policing dollars being invested into a fundamentally flawed structure where the RCMP is stretched well beyond its primary mandate."

The RCMP has long been a coddled problem child for governments. Over the past several decades, repeated headlines have informed the public about convincing and disturbing tales of incompetence (the National Security and Intelligence Committee of Parliamentarians warned in November 2023 that "the committee does not believe that federal policing is effective, efficient, flexible or accountable"), deceit ("Despite Denials, RCMP Used Facial Recognition Program"—*The Tyee*, March 10, 2020), and far too many tragedies to enumerate but including shootings of RCMP officers in Mayerthorpe in 2005, Spiritwood in 2006, and Moncton in 2014, and the killing of Polish tourist Robert Dziekański at Vancouver International Airport in October 2007. Behind the scenes, one independent study after another has found the force to be in tatters, suffering from a cult-like toxic and broken culture ("Scathing Report Calls Out RCMP's Toxic Culture"—National Association of Federal Employees, February 25, 2021), a lack of accountability ("The Dark Side of the RCMP"—*The Walrus*, October 20, 2021), and an unsustainable structure ("RCMP Facing 'Systemic Sustainability Challenges' Due to Provincial Policing Role"—*CTV News*, May 24, 2020). Fixing the RCMP is about as unpalatable a subject as there might be for Canadian politicians. They just keep throwing money at the problem, now more than $5 billion a year.

"Give us some of that money and we'll show you how policing should work," one Canadian municipal police chief, who was reluctant to speak on the record out of a very real fear of retribution from the RCMP, told me.

But no matter what the RCMP does wrong, it continues to have access to the public purse. The RCMP's Kevlar is that it has long been an informal yet indelible symbol of the country. It is a guardian institution but operates and comports itself like a business. It's the Canadian way. Canada has never been about lofty ideals, and its symbols are not aspirational, like those of some countries. There are no suns or stars or majestic eagles or lions. Canada has always been about business. One of its national symbols is a semi-aquatic rodent, the beaver, whose pelts were the basis of the country's original industry and wealth. One of the first and most important duties of the RCMP in 1874 was to protect trappers collecting those pelts in the late stages of that industry.

Some prime ministers have spoken about the RCMP's problems. At the turn of the twentieth century, when they were still known as the Northwest Mounted Police, Prime Minister Louis St. Laurent wanted to get rid of them, but soon relented. Instead, the Mounties were deemed to be "Royal," a moniker they kept when they transitioned into the Royal Canadian Mounted Police a few years later.

In the years leading up to his campaign for office in early 2006, Stephen Harper championed reforming and reimagining the RCMP. Once he was elected prime minister, that all got put on the back burner and was forgotten.

In the lexicon of modern business, with about 30,000 employees, the RCMP is deemed to be too big to fail and too important an institution for the country. That's the myth-making government and RCMP marketing departments at work.

While it appears to be a giant national police force, in reality, the RCMP is less than the sum of its parts. Its unorthodox hybridized structure has reduced it largely to a publicly funded, politically controlled rent-a-cop system, providing policing to provinces, territories and municipalities across the country on a contract basis. Those buying RCMP services think they are getting a deal—the best police force in the country at a discounted rate, because of subsidies from the federal government.

When the RCMP markets its policing services to provinces and communities, one of the things it promotes is that Mounties are well rounded. Their individual careers are built on multiple assignments in different locales. Many have travelled the world on international peacekeeping missions or training police in third-world countries. When a Mountie arrives in a Canadian community, they have highly buffed credentials. While they are often outsiders, the theoretical advantage is that not being part of the society they are policing makes them incorruptible. The Mounties promise to dish out the law fairly and without favour. Sounds great on paper.

In fact, the personnel pool that the RCMP draws from is much smaller than it might seem: about 20,000 serving Mounties. Over the past three decades of writing about the RCMP, dozens of Mounties have told me that the open secret for getting ahead is not based so much on merit as it is on family history inside the force, hidden connections and favouritism. Under this regime, upwardly mobile Mounties tend to have curated careers in which they are all but sheltered from harm, controversy and obstacles as they quickly climb the rungs of the organization. The single most important ingredient in their rise through the ranks is a willingness every few years to pack up their family, load their worldly possessions into a moving van and head out on an adventure. It's the RCMP way, reliving the vagabond glory of the Great March West over and over again, without acknowledging that the world has changed a little since 1874.

It's not exactly a recipe for excellence, because many of the best Mounties are unwilling to sacrifice a normal life for themselves and their families to chase the pot of gold promised to them at the end of their career rainbows. Once a Mountie arrives in a new location, they tend not to know anyone but other Mounties. Their knowledge of a community and its criminal players tends to be superficial and anything but second nature to them. They are strangers in a strange land.

Modern Canadian governments have little appetite for big projects, a reluctance noted by Canadian constitutional lawyer Deborah Coyne in a July 2021 ebook: *Canada's Faux Democracy: What Are We Going to Do about It?* Coyne's daughter is Prime Minister Justin Trudeau's half-sister. Coyne says governments refuse to undertake "long-term initiatives to address major challenges we face as Canadians. Such challenges are too often considered high risk politically. And, because they may take more than a four-year term to resolve, deliver no neatly packaged success stories to present at election time. Majority governments—common under our antiquated first-past-the-post electoral system—allow faux democrats to govern using a short-term electoral calculus, in which winning the next election trumps the broader collective interests of Canadians."

Echoing Coyne's thoughts, Edgar MacLeod said: "Governments are not thinking far enough ahead down the road. Everything is very short-term. They don't want to get involved in any meaningful change because that is too difficult. It's all about the next election."

Governments instead promote "the partnership model," as MacLeod puts it, the fairy tale that all police forces are working together like a consortium of businesses. "That structure promotes a lack of accountability and fails to serve the public interest. The partnership policing model has become the classic problem where everyone is responsible for everything, but nobody is accountable for anything. The ambiguous federal, provincial, and local governments' policing responsibilities will unfortunately lead to further erosion of peace and security."

MacLeod has also been highly critical of the lack of uniform standards and governance for police across the country, another subject politicians have refused to address. The reason for that is obvious. If there were a single standard for police training and accountability, the logical choice would *not* be the Mountie way of doing things, a move that the RCMP would resist to its death.

Needless to say, MacLeod's criticism has made him unpopular with the Mounties.

◆

When the Mass Casualty Commission was looking for someone credible to analyze and discuss the state of policing in Nova Scotia, someone like Edgar MacLeod would seem to have been a knowledgeable, fair and appropriate candidate. The RCMP model of policing is an inherent problem. The force specializes in underpolicing communities, understaffing and slow response times, while proclaiming that these policies make it efficient and a cheaper alternative to municipal and provincial police forces. In a province of almost a million residents at the time of the massacres, about half of Nova Scotians lived in communities served by municipal police forces. The other half were spread out in tiny communities across the province that were being served by fifty-three RCMP detachments. In some of those communities, however, the RCMP presence was merely a building and few, if any, officers. It was a crazy, entrenched patchwork that the RCMP fought to maintain in spite of the enormous costs of the infrastructure alone.

But the commission soft-pedalled these issues, choosing Barry MacKnight as their expert. On paper, he looked like another Edgar

MacLeod, but his 1,500-page report in the foundational documents seemed to sugar-coat the entire situation. The first thing that struck me as odd about the report was the anodyne biographical information about MacKnight. Why were there no specifics? It didn't take long to find an answer.

MacKnight had begun his policing career as a Mountie. He then moved over to the Fredericton Police Force, where he rose to become chief of police. In 2012, he suddenly left that job at the relatively young age of forty-nine to, as it's often put in similar circumstances, "pursue other opportunities." He was now running his own consulting service in Hanwell, New Brunswick, specializing in workplace and professional misconduct investigations. His successor in Fredericton was an officer he had groomed for the job, Leanne Fitch, now one of the commissioners. One police source in New Brunswick described MacKnight as "strategically careful to never offend anyone." Another spoke of his tenure as "unspectacular," while a third said, "By the time he left, the force was in a mess. Fitch didn't do anything to fix it."

MacKnight's report was loaded with numbers and graphs and read like a virtual press release, as if the structure of policing in Nova Scotia were a well-oiled machine that just needed a little tinkering to run better. A casual reader would not find any mention of the force's above-noted shortcomings. At the very bottom of his report, for example, MacKnight produced the training records for what appeared to be about a dozen RCMP members at Bible Hill. Their names and any identifying characteristics were redacted. Each showed pages and pages of training achievements, as if this mattered in the real world. Former Mountie Janet Merlo showed how phony the training is in her 2021 book *No One to Tell: Breaking My Silence on Life in the RCMP*. Merlo described how a single Mountie at a detachment would log into a computer terminal and do the tests for perhaps forty other members at once. Many other Mounties have confirmed what she wrote.

In his hagiographic assessment of the RCMP, MacKnight failed to acknowledge, among other things, that the Mounties are extremely secretive and see information-sharing with other police forces as a one-way street.

Although his report was completed in November 2021, like most of the foundational documents, it was kept under wraps until it was released by the commission just prior to MacKnight's session.

Five days after the report was made public, on February 28, 2022, Jeffrey D. Waugh of the Nova Scotia Department of Justice's Legal Services Division weighed in with a complaint about it. Waugh said that his department had been given the opportunity to review MacKnight's draft but "due to an oversight" failed to do so. One of the issues Waugh focused on was public safety access points (PSAPs), suggesting the statements MacKnight had made about them were wrong. But then Waugh added this about the commission and MacKnight's views:

> It was confirmed in an email from the Commission Council on February 25, 2022, the presentation is akin to oral submissions of council and not evidence. The Department is concerned that this submission [by MacKnight] could create a misperception.
>
> The Department is concerned that the statement identifies this as a problem or possible communication shortfall. In our view, this comment requires additional context to help explain the significance of that fact to the public.
>
> If the comment is taken at face value, there is a possible suggestion that all police should be automatically able to hear all other police on a common system. As if all police were essentially on a "party line."
>
> From our perspective, and very likely that of all police agencies, such an arrangement could create operational chaos. Police agencies do not want to hear all the communications traffic of other police agencies. That would create confusion. . . . Some agencies, like the RCMP, have strict rules about what talk groups or channels they will or will not share with other police agencies.

Waugh seemed to be telling the commission, belated as his statement was, that despite its marketing to the contrary, the RCMP has never been a true team player when it comes to co-operating with other police forces. He also perfectly explained the problem with much of the purportedly sacred foundational documents: they were just words and not evidence.

Coming as it did on the second day of the hearings, MacKnight's report signalled that the commission was not going to be digging all that deeply into the root of the problem—the historical rotten foundations of policing in Nova Scotia—and it didn't. It also seemed apparent that the commission wasn't all that interested in how the RCMP came to be so poorly organized in Nova Scotia. Bad decisions had to have been made, but who made them? The RCMP has long been adept at hiding behind the red serge to protect individual officers from facing accountability.

Not everyone saw it that way.

Nova Scotia–born and then Ottawa-based freelance journalist Dean Beeby was once Halifax bureau chief for the Canadian Press and had worked for the CBC on Parliament Hill. He had fond memories of the times in his childhood when his family vacationed in the area just west of Portapique. Beeby used the commission's record as the foundation for his 2023 book *Mass Murder, Police Mayhem: The Mass Casualty Commission— The Facts, the Findings, and What Must Be Done*. The slim 208-page book was "intended to give readers access to the key content of this important public record" and tell them "exactly what happened." True to his mainstream journalism training, Beeby accepted the official narrative as the default truth while skipping past the inconveniences that could not be readily explained. There was little if any on-the-ground reporting. I heard from countless readers that Beeby's breathtakingly uncritical approach was surprising considering that the story cried out for his talents: Beeby billed himself as an expert on Freedom of Information searches. I could find no evidence in his book that he had put in a single such request in his research

It all made me wonder whether I and others who thought like me were just imagining that something was fundamentally wrong with the commission. It looked as if the dreaded invisible hand was fiddling with the evidence, but where was the proof?

We are now headed back to Portapique, to revisit what the RCMP did before, during and after the massacres in light of what the commission said—and the new evidence that my citizen investigators and I have uncovered.

6

WITNESSES WHO
OFFICIALLY SAW NOTHING

A key to unlocking the whole truth begins with those who were deemed by the authorities to have seen or heard nothing of real importance. They are the people whose testimonies were reduced to paper and distilled into dry, voiceless accounts within the mounds of commission documents. Their stories will propel this one forward, beginning with that fateful Saturday night, when it was not only what these witnesses saw, but also what they *didn't* see, that sometimes mattered most.

Twenty-one months before the massacres, Gerald and Floria Murphy had bought the modest house at 121 Portapique Beach Road for $126,000. Originally from Curling, a residential neighbourhood in Corner Brook, Newfoundland, the couple had spent their working years in bustling Kitchener, Ontario, and thought the quiet neighbourhood of Portapique was an attractive place to retire. It was remote and peaceful; the population was perhaps 100 people in the winter, swelling to a high of 250 at the height of the summer.

The house sat on 1.2 acres of land and had a view of the mouth of the Portapique River. Across and up the road was the old Portaupique

Cemetery (which used the old spelling for the community), on the other side of which was Wortman's log cabin. At the rear of the Murphys' house and a few lots to the south was Wortman's warehouse, at 136 Orchard Beach Drive.

Gerald, who went by Jerry, was an affable fellow who got along with everyone in a "how ya doin'?" neighbourly fashion. When Sharon and I, who had never met them, showed up unannounced at their door late one Sunday afternoon in 2022, the Murphys were happy to see us. Jerry had been reading my stories and had heard me on the radio, and had put out the word with those who knew me that he'd like to meet me. They poured us drinks and set places for us at the table for dinner. It reminded me of the old saw about the hospitality of Newfoundlanders, with a sign on their front lawn that read: "Beware!!! Trespassers will be fed and boarded."

Jerry described his dealings with Wortman as limited but informative. Once, when Wortman was hauling something large around the neighbourhood, as was his habit, he had clipped the Murphys' mailbox and knocked it down. Some say it was an accident, others that Wortman wanted to introduce himself to his new neighbours.

Wortman immediately knocked on the door and apologized for the accident, insisting that he would fix it. "I'm going to go home and grab a drill," he said. "I'm Gabriel."

Jerry said, "No, don't be bothered . . . It's not necessary to do that at all."

"Oh yeah," Wortman replied. "I've gotta do this because I never met a Newfoundlander I didn't like."

In the end, Jerry found that the post was rotten to its core and took on the job himself.

Wortman's decommissioned police car collection—and his replica police car—were anything but secrets. Jerry described how on Thanksgiving weekend in 2019 (October 12–14 for Canadians), Floria, who goes by Florie, and their daughter, who was visiting from Ontario, went for a walk down the road past Wortman's cottage. An RCMP cruiser was sitting outside with no licence plate. "I thought that was funny. I thought he must have some friends who are friends with the police," Jerry said, although his daughter was somewhat suspicious. She mused to her mother, "How can a guy on a police salary afford that great big chalet?"

Florie liked taking long walks in the neighbourhood and enjoying the magnificent views of the Bay of Fundy and the distant Cobequid Mountains. Another person who liked to walk the neighbourhood when they were there was Wortman's partner, Lisa Banfield, who was usually on her phone the entire time. She wasn't much for chitchatting with the neighbours, Florie said. "She was a bit reclusive that way."

Florie remembers cutting through the woods one day and coming across Wortman and Banfield. Wortman said hello, then abruptly told Florie that he and Banfield were "heading to the warehouse to have sex." It wasn't the first time the uninhibited Wortman had said something like that to a neighbour.

"I thought it was kind of rude of him to say that to a stranger," Florie said. "I didn't need to know that."

One incident involving Wortman has stuck in Jerry's mind. He told me about it that first night over dinner. "One time he drove one of his old white police cars off the road into the ditch. Two RCMP cars came, and a tow truck. I remember the Mounties helping him carry some boxes up from the car and putting them in their car. I thought it was strange."

Jerry couldn't remember the date or, as it turned out, the make of the vehicle, but he was right about the incident. *Frank* magazine editor Andrew Douglas put in a request to the RCMP for details about the accident. He soon received a reply from RCMP corporal Chris Marshall:

On April 24, 2019, at approximately 9:40 p.m., Colchester County District RCMP responded to a report of a single vehicle collision on Portapique Beach Rd. in Portapique. The complainant, a 51-year-old man (at the time), advised that he had swerved to avoid a collision with a deer and went over an embankment. The man was uninjured. A tow truck was called to the scene and the vehicle, a 2015 Mercedes-Benz C30, was removed from the ditch.

We do not have any information that relates to a negative interaction during this incident.

Thank you,

Chris

The Mercedes, actually a model C300, was Lisa Banfield's. It had sustained an estimated $13,600 damage in the collision. Wortman handled the insurance claim. He took a cash payout for the damage because he thought he could fix the car for about $3,000.

"Thanks, hon," Banfield emailed him on May 7, 2019. "You mean the world to me and I'm so lucky to have you as My Person and best friend. I love you. ♡" The email was disclosed by the Mass Casualty Commission, but the media generally ignored it, likely because it portrayed Banfield and Wortman's relationship in a more positive light than did the official narrative.

In his request to the RCMP about the incident, Douglas never suggested any "negative interaction." In fact, Jerry had thought the opposite was the case. He suspected that Wortman may have been drinking and speeding, neither being out of character for him. From what Jerry could discern, it seemed like Wortman and the RCMP had an unusually friendly relationship.

On the night the massacres began, Jerry and Florie were at home when they first heard the shots. "I was in on the bed," Jerry described, "probably with the iPad or reading a book or something, and I hear *pop, pop, pop. Pop, pop, pop. Pop, pop, pop.*" He left the bedroom and asked Florie, "Did you hear that?"

"Yes, it sounds like gunshots," she said.

The Murphys didn't investigate because, according to Jerry, "there was nothing happening that would indicate there was anything going on. Everything was as black as a witch's tit."

There was no way Jerry could know that the *pop, pop, pops* were the sound of his neighbours being murdered on Orchard Beach Drive, the road behind his house to the east. As he said, it was dark and quiet between the *pop pops*—just another night in rural Nova Scotia.

Then Florie went to the fridge and noticed flames on the other side of the tree line. She also noticed the time on the microwave clock: 11:14 p.m. "Jerry," she said, "somebody got a bonfire. There's a bonfire over on the other road behind us."

Jerry took a look and recognized that it was much bigger than that: "That's not a bonfire. That's something on fire."

He changed back into his workpants and sneakers and went out onto his balcony. "We could hear a bang, like a propane tank or something going off. And then, after that, we heard *pop, pop, pop, pop, pop, pop, pop, pop, pop*. So I said, 'My God, there's something going on.'"

Jerry walked to the back of his property, where his neighbour, carpenter Bjorn Merzbach, met him on the other side of the fence. Merzbach had his dog, Ford, with him. Merzbach had heard shots, too, and said the Gulenchyn house across from his property had gone up in flames.

"You could hear the crackling of the fire, but there was also a *pop, pop, pop* in the fire," Jerry recalled. "And then I heard this loud explosion, and like a tenth of a second later, my eyes went to the left and I saw the electrical fire come out of the wires and it went down the light pole and I said, 'That's the transformer.'"

Then the Gulenchyn house exploded.

"The flames went up in the air above the trees and then went back down," Jerry said. "Cinders and debris were falling everywhere. It was catching the grass on fire."

It was now 11:22 p.m.

Jerry called 911 and told them his address and that there was a house on fire behind him. "And the lady said: 'Yes, we've had other calls from your area and members are on their way.' That's all she said. The light bulb went on. There's something going on here tonight and that's not what I think it is, right?"

What Jerry didn't know was that an hour and twenty-one minutes earlier—at 10:01 p.m.—the first 911 call had been placed by Jamie Blair. During that brief call, the terrified woman described the assailant as a "denturist" and "neighbour," someone who could only be Wortman, and said that he appeared to be driving the RCMP cruiser parked in her driveway. Wortman executed her while she was on the phone. Fifteen minutes after that, Blair's twelve-year-old son, on his own 911 call, reiterated that the shooter was their neighbour and that he was driving a police car.

If Jerry and Florie had known all this, they might not have done what they did next. Instead of locking the doors and hiding in the basement, snuggled up to a shotgun, they went out to investigate. Everything was deadly quiet. There was no one on the road. No flashing lights. No fire-fighters. Nothing. With the grass fire creeping toward other properties, they were worried about their next-door neighbour, Cate Rector. The adventurous Florie cut through the bushes to go to Rector's house, while Jerry jumped into their Mitsubishi and headed out to catch up to her.

"When I backed out of the driveway and came around on the road, I could see the glow of another fire on the other side of the cemetery," Jerry said. "Wortman's chalet was on fire, too."

The Murphys couldn't find Rector but were now curious about what was happening south on Portapique Beach Road. They drove 400 metres down the road to look at Wortman's "chalet," which was by then a hollow, glowing shell. They could see right through it. One of his cars was burning in the driveway. The Murphys continued another 600 metres toward the beach to check on the Griffons, who lived at 4 Faris Lane, at the corner of Portapique Beach Road. It was approaching 11:30 p.m. The only other house on that stretch was a large A-frame on the left that was owned by John Zahl and his wife, Jo Thomas. It was also in flames.

"My God," Jerry said to Florie, "if there is anybody in there, there's no way we can help them."

On the other side of the intersection at Faris Lane, all seemed quiet at the house of Alan and Joanne Griffon, who lived with their thirty-nine-year-old son, Peter.

After moving to Portapique, the Murphys had struck up a relationship with the Griffons. Alan had retired from his factory job at Michelin Tire and was a volunteer firefighter. He had cut the Murphys' lawn until they bought their own riding mower. He also looked after their property when they travelled. Alan did the same for Wortman, as well as other odd jobs, like hauling fifteen truckloads of door cutouts and other items when Wortman was building the warehouse.

The Murphys drove up the Griffons' driveway. Florie knocked on the front door. Jerry was right behind her, looking over her shoulder. There were two dogs in the house, one of them belonging to Peter. One of the dogs slammed against the door, barking madly, but despite the racket, no one answered. The Murphys didn't know it, but the Griffons were hiding inside their house, having called 911 to report the fire at

Wortman's cottage, which they could see farther north up the riverbank. (Afterwards, the knocking by the Murphys would be construed as Wortman banging on the Griffons' door, a mistake that was not corrected until more than a year later.)

The Murphys got back in their car and Florie called 911. It was 11:36 p.m. They headed home, driving north on Portapique Beach Road, driving a little faster now as they poked their way through the inexplicable madness. "I was looking mainly to see if there was anybody around or whatever," Jerry said, when they noticed a "SWAT team" in the ditch. "I could see the yellow stripe on one pants leg. My car was kind of noisy—the muffler was going—so they probably knew I wasn't the guy they were looking for."

He stopped the car and Florie rolled down the window. One of the Mounties approached with a flashlight in his hand and asked who they were. In retrospect, Jerry thought that was a dangerous thing for them to do. "They were going down this dark road, where you couldn't see your hand in front of your face, looking for someone who was killing people, and they were using a flashlight, because they didn't have night-vision or anything. They were easy targets if someone was out there hiding in the bush," he said.

After identifying themselves, the Murphys were allowed to go into their house to get medications and clothes. "You guys get out of here, get out of here now, go, go, don't stop. Don't come back. Don't stop for anybody or anything," the Mountie said.

The Mountie, however, did have one question for the Murphys. They were on a mission to rescue the Griffons, who had called 911 from their hiding place, fearing that Wortman was the one at their door.

"Where is Faris Lane?" the Mountie asked.

"Down at the end of the road," Florie told them. Later she remarked, "They're the police. You'd think they'd know that."

The Murphys ended up driving out of the neighbourhood unescorted, only to find that the Mounties had used their parked vehicles to create a maze near the intersection with Highway 2.

"A female corporal came over to us with a gun in her hand," Jerry remembered. "They searched the car and sent us on our way."

The Murphys headed to Debert, to a family member's house, unaware of the scope of what had taken place in Portapique.

Six days after the massacres, on April 25, 2020, the Murphys were interviewed by two Mounties from the Major Crimes Unit. Constable Michael Townsend first interviewed Florie for thirty-seven minutes while Constable Colin Shaw sat in as a witness. They reversed roles for Jerry's interview, which lasted thirty-four minutes.

In both brief interviews, the Mounties seemed to be going through the motions, focusing more on what the Murphys might know about Wortman than on what had happened in Portapique that night. Even then, they didn't seem all that interested in the details.

For example, the issue of when Wortman had his replica police car up and running was a critical one. The RCMP originally stated that Wortman had specifically designed the car to be used in the massacres, and that was the first and only time it had been on the road. In the two-year gap between the massacres and the commission hearings, bit by bit, information came out showing that Wortman had completed the car and had it on the road in mid-2019. So when Florie described in her interview with the Mounties the sighting of the police car without a licence plate at Wortman's cottage, the natural next question for any investigator would be: "When did that happen?" Instead, this is what followed in her interview with the Mounties:

"Yeah," Townsend said.

"You know, kind of thinking, in talking," Florie mused to me. She then told the interviewers, "I don't think he's a police officer . . . I don't see many police . . . cars here . . . You know. And we don't get into people's business. It's a quiet neighbourhood."

"Yes," Townsend said. "So you're originally from Ontario or . . ."

Over time it came out that the car had been anything but a secret. It had been operational since the previous fall or earlier and without question had been driven on the highways and roads of Nova Scotia, and maybe even New Brunswick. But the Mounties seemed uninterested in pursuing that line of questioning.

In his interview that day, the loquacious Jerry was allowed to talk and talk. He and Florie considered themselves to be pro-police. Between their families, they had at least ten relatives who were or had been police officers, some of them Mounties.

"I have no animosity with the RCMP, the people here, the people on the ground doing their jobs," Jerry told Shaw. "But somebody really dropped the ball on this one, I got to tell you."

One of the many lasting mysteries about the massacres is the precise time when Zahl and Thomas were murdered and their house at 293 Portapique Beach Road was set afire. The Murphys seemed to have been the only people who passed by the house while it was ablaze, but the Mounties weren't interested in what they had seen and when they had seen it.

After that interview, Jerry kept playing over in his head how much he could have told them that he never got the opportunity to say. He felt that they had subtly rushed him through his version of events, said thank you and hit the road. He also forgot to mention the April 2019 accident with Lisa Banfield's car. Jerry expected them to do a follow-up, but like so many others, he never heard back from them.

Flash forward to September 26, 2021, seventeen months after the massacres. The MCC was running an open house at the Debert Hospitality Centre prior to the delayed public hearings, and Jerry was in attendance.

The Debert Hospitality Centre, on Ventura Drive, was just across the street from where Wortman purportedly hid behind a welding shop in the interlude between the two massacres. He had tossed a host of items into the bushes, which were later found. A few hundred metres away was where Wortman shot and killed Kristen Beaton and then Heather O'Brien on the second day of his spree. The two Victorian Order of Nurses employees, who had been driving in separate vehicles, were Wortman's eighteenth and nineteenth victims.

Jerry wasn't impressed by what the commission was doing that night. "It was set up like a work fair, with placards all over the place about what they were going to do," he told me when I sought him out prior to the commission's hearings. "It was bullshit."

But he was determined to get his testimony on the record. He found Commissioner Leanne Fitch. She steered him to a pair of commission investigators, retired Toronto police detectives Dwayne King and Scott

Spicer, who took him into a quiet room and turned on the tape recorder. In the seventy minutes that he talked to the two investigators, Jerry told a more complete version of events, but again forgot to mention a few things, like the car-in-the-ditch story.

In its initial statements about the massacres, the RCMP gave the public the impression that it had swarmed the area with "25 or more resources" and had locked it down, as one would expect them to do in such a horrific situation. RCMP commanding officers Chief Superintendent Chris Leather and Superintendent Darren Campbell claimed repeatedly that shortly after arriving in Portapique, the force had hunted for the shooter and gone door to door checking on and evacuating residents. In the RCMP's first press conference, on Sunday evening, April 19, 2020, Leather said, "Our focus was the safety of the residents in the immediate area. We secured the area and began a search for the suspect."

It certainly didn't look like that to the Murphys. From their perspective, everyone was being left to fend for themselves while the Griffons were evacuated from the area by the police. They wondered what made them so special. As I wrote in *22 Murders*, the Griffons' son, Peter Alan Griffon, was a recently paroled ex-con with ties to the Mexican drug cartel La Familia and the ultra-violent Salvadoran street gang MS-13, and family connections to the outlaw biker gang the Hells Angels. He was also one of Wortman's drinking buddies and worked as a handyman at both the cottage and the warehouse. In fact, on April 18, 2020, Griffon had cleared brush and stacked logs on Wortman's properties and was one of the last people to see and talk to Wortman and Lisa Banfield that day. Curiously, Griffon's recent criminal history was ignored by the RCMP and the commission. To a casual observer, he appeared to be just another neighbour who did odd jobs for Wortman and Banfield.

◆

Leon Joudrey was oblivious to the mayhem surrounding him that Saturday night in Portapique. Even if the fifty-two-year-old woodsman had heard the *pop, pop, pop* of gunfire, he likely would have been unfazed. Along with car wheels on gravel and the buzz of all-terrain vehicles, gunshots are the elevator music of rural life in Nova Scotia—just another after-hours hunter buddy plinking a rabbit or jacking a deer. Joudrey didn't know that thirteen of his neighbours had been murdered, eleven of them along the almost two-kilometre-long course of Orchard Beach Drive, or that four properties had burned to the ground. He slept through it all, having been in both the right and wrong places at pre-cisely the wrong time. It was after he awoke that his problems began.

I first met Joudrey more than four months afterwards, in late August 2020, when he took me on a tour of the community. He had been living there for almost two years, having purchased the property at 140 Portapique Crescent from a friend in February 2018. Recently divorced and the father of two young adults, Christopher and Natalie, Joudrey had needed a place to live with his two beloved dogs, Basil and Yzerman. Portapique looked like a perfect fit, with its relative isolation, rugged beauty and proximity to the ocean. Most importantly, it was so damn affordable. He had a full-time job at the Department of Natural Resources, where he worked as a forest technician, but it was tough living on a single income. The modest but well-kept prefabricated house sat on three and a half acres of scrubby land and sold for $121,000. The annual property taxes were just $638—$1.75 a day.

Leon Joudrey was awakened at 3:33 a.m. on April 19 by the smell of smoke wafting through his window. "I remember the time. I was, 'Oh geez.' I wished I could've slept for another hour, because my daughter was supposed to come that day."

The smoke was coming from the house of Frank and Dawn Gulenchyn, Joudrey's next-door neighbours, a couple of hundred metres away. The RCMP had been on the scene since 10:26 p.m. the night before, but no one had knocked on Joudrey's door and no one was evac-uated that night from Orchard Beach Drive, Portapique Crescent or Cobequid Court, near the beach at the end of Orchard Beach Drive.

Being a professional woodsman and a connoisseur of smoke, Joudrey recognized that "it didn't smell like a forest fire. I thought I should go investigate."

He put on his work coat, which identified him as a Natural Resources officer, got into his half-ton truck and drove around the community, trying to find the source of the fire. A kilometre or so from his house, he came across a single police tactical vehicle, known as a TAV, parked in front of 200 Portapique Beach Road, Gabriel Wortman's magnificent log cottage—or, at least, its smouldering remains. In it was RCMP Emergency Response Team (ERT) member Constable Trent Milton.

"So I pulled up beside the SWAT vehicle, and I was trying to get the guy to motion to me, to talk to me. And he was screaming at me through the window. I didn't know what he was saying. I guess he couldn't roll down his window, so he turned his spotlights on me and got on the loudspeaker," Joudrey recalled. "'You in the black truck, turn around, proceed to the entrance point.'"

It was now around 4:17 a.m., according to Constable Milton's radio transmission at the time. Milton alerted those running the checkpoint at the intersection of Highway 2 and Portapique Beach Road that an unknown man in a pickup truck would soon be arriving there. Joudrey ignored the Mountie's order and didn't show up at the checkpoint, and the Mounties made no attempt to track him down.

By then, the Mounties believed there were five to eight people dead, and they had no clue where the suspected shooter, Wortman, might be. Yet they displayed no suspicion of Joudrey. It had been almost six hours since the first calls were made to 911. Jamie Blair had called at 10:01 p.m. the night before, identified a man who could only be Wortman as her husband's killer and described what he was driving. She was executed while on the phone, and the Mounties didn't rush to that scene.

Blair's sons Alex and Jack, aged twelve and ten, had run next door to Lisa McCully's house, where she secreted them in the basement with her own children, daughter Alex, twelve, and son Marcus, ten, before going outside and getting herself shot and killed. At 10:16 p.m., Alex Blair called 911 and explained clearly to the operator the horror of what they had witnessed and that their neighbour was driving what appeared to be an RCMP vehicle. At 10:26 p.m., neighbours Andrew MacDonald and his wife, Kate, called 911 and were shot at by their neighbour "Gabe" while on the phone. MacDonald described the way he was dressed and what he was driving.

The four children were left in the basement for almost three hours before they were eventually rescued.

Joudrey didn't know any of this as he drove around in the dark. The entire scene was bewildering. The fires had all but burned out. The smoke was everywhere. And there was one TAV near where Wortman's cottage had proudly stood.

As the Murphys had done more than four hours earlier, Joudrey was allowed to drive unescorted back through the neighbourhood. He ignored the Mountie's order and headed toward home because he didn't want to leave his dogs alone in the house. Only then did he realize that the Gulenchyn house had been burned to the ground. Whatever was going on, it seemed to be worse than he had imagined.

Instead of turning left to his house on Portapique Crescent, Joudrey continued driving south on the pocky, pothole-ridden dirt road. All was quiet at the Blair house, where he had eaten dinner the night before with Greg and Jamie after helping them clear some brush off their property. Next door, at 135 Orchard Beach Drive, was the house of schoolteacher Lisa McCully, whom he had dated in the past. He didn't see anything there, either. He didn't notice McCully's body on the front lawn, slumped against the rail fence to his left, nor the body of Corrie Ellison, 18 metres away on the other side of the road, just south of the gate to Wortman's warehouse and man cave at 136 Orchard Beach Drive.

The two bodies had been lying there for almost six hours. In that time, three different groups of Mounties had "discovered" them—at 10:49 p.m., 1 a.m. and shortly after 3 a.m. The last group declared them dead, marked their locations with a GPS app, placed a tarp over each of them and moved on. The crime scene was not protected in any other way, and Joudrey was not the only one driving through it; the police were, and by morning, neighbours such as Doug and Judy Myers were, too.

The perplexed Joudrey turned around about halfway down Orchard Beach Drive and headed home. He searched online for information but found nothing, not even the RCMP's tweets.

Shortly before 6:30 a.m., there was a knock at Joudrey's side door. To his surprise, it was Lisa Banfield, wanting to come in. I reported Joudrey's version of their conversation in *22 Murders:*

"Gabriel lost his mind," she said, which served to dislodge any remaining cobwebs in Joudrey's head.

"No shit, Lisa," Joudrey said. "He burned his own house down. What are you doing here? He hates me the most."

"I'm sorry," she said. "I'd better go."

Joudrey shut the door to stop her from leaving. He ushered her into the bathroom to hide her and called 911. It was 6:34 a.m.

"I happened to know the radio dispatcher at 911," Joudrey said. "When I got on the phone with her, I said: 'Get SWAT down here. I know they're looking for Gabriel. I want her out of my house now.'"

That Banfield's instinct was to turn and leave struck Joudrey as counterintuitive. If, as she claimed, she had been outside all night fleeing and hiding from Wortman, one would think she would be eager to find shelter with someone like the well-armed Joudrey.

"She was ready to go back out. I couldn't let her do that," Joudrey said.

Banfield told Joudrey that she had been hiding in the woods since ten the night before—more than eight hours. The temperature that night was hovering around freezing. With the high tides rushing in and out of the Minas Basin, Portapique is perpetually blustery and cold. It had snowed in Halifax, to the south, that night, and the roads there were slippery. As Joudrey assessed the situation and comforted Banfield, he thought she looked underdressed for the elements in yoga pants and a spandex top. She had bare feet and no gloves, yet she was surprisingly intact. Her makeup looked fresh, and she wasn't suffering from hypothermia, which he knew how to identify and treat thanks to his training with the Department of Natural Resources. Her bare feet were not dirty; neither were her clothes. He didn't see so much as a single pine needle on her.

Three minutes after Joudrey called 911, members of the ERT team found their way to his house. Joudrey lent Banfield a pair of running shoes and a jacket, and the Mounties escorted her to their vehicle to take her to the hospital for further examination.

At the time, all Joudrey knew was that there were some fires in the community, that Gabriel Wortman was a suspect and that Lisa Banfield was in his kitchen. But he still had misgivings about Banfield's story. "I told the police who were there that morning that I didn't believe her. I don't know what happened, but I think it isn't what she said happened," Joudrey told me in our first of many interviews. "That woman did not spend the night in the woods. I don't know where she was, but she was not in the woods all night. If you're in the woods all night, the tops of your feet are going to be dirty and covered in pine needles. Look at the woods around here. Look how thick they are. And I said that from the start, and I stand by it. I can picture it right in my head today how clean she was."

But as with the Murphys, the Mounties didn't seem interested in Joudrey's observations about Banfield, nor did they search his house or property for Wortman. Later that day, when Joudrey learned about the murders, he was puzzled by how the Mounties had handled the situation, and particularly that they didn't seem to be treating Banfield as a possible suspect.

To date, Lisa Banfield has, through her lawyers, declined to answer any journalists' questions or grant interviews.

◆

This is how the Mounties saw it—or didn't see it, as the case may be.

After Joudrey called 911, between 6:33:58 a.m. and 6:42:24 a.m., RCMP records show that at least eight ERT members responded to the call from where they were positioned near Highway 2: constables Brent Kelly, Kyle Josey, Ed Clarke, Ben MacLeod, Jason (Jay) Barnhill, Travis Gallant, Josh Davidson and Andrew Ryan.

In an MCC foundational document, MacLeod described Banfield as "distraught" and "in a state of terror." A transcript of the RCMP's radio transmissions reads:

6:39:38 AM—Constable Ben MacLeod: "We're with the female, taking her back to the truck. (Background: L. Banfield inaudible). She says he has an—a rifle. She doesn't know where he's at."

6:39:51 AM—S/Sgt. Jeff West: "Do you want to confirm that, Hotel 1 [the ERT incident commander], ah, he has a rifle; she has no idea where he's at?"

6:39:57 AM—Cpl. Tim Mills (aka Hotel 1): "Yeah, copy that."

6:40:06 AM—Cst. Trent Lafferty: "Time of last sighting?"

6:41:22 AM—Cpl. Mills: "Does she know if—when that went ah—when—when that set fire?"

6:41:49 AM—Cst. Ed Clarke: "Yeah, Tim, she was there when he lit it on fire. (Background Cst. MacLeod: "I know, but . . .)

6:41:56 AM—Cpl. Mills: "Say again."

6:41:59 AM—Cst. Clarke: "She was there when he lit it on fire."

6:42:04 AM—Cpl. Mills: "Copy that. What time was that at?"

6:42:08 AM—Cst. Clarke: "She doesn't know, man. She ah—she was handcuffed and hiding in the woods."

[Note: There is then a two-minute gap.]

6:44:08 AM—Cst. Clarke: "Yeah, Tim, ah, she said that he was gonna go get her sister who lives in Russell Lake [a neighbour-hood in the Dartmouth section of Halifax]."

6:44:59 AM—Cst. Jay Barnhill: "Suspect last seen by Lisa wearing black jeans, black vest, black hat (inaudible)."

Banfield was transported to the head of Portapique Beach Road, where she was assessed by Corporal Duane Ivany and Constable Jeff Mahar of the RCMP's Emergency Medical Response Team (EMRT). Here is their report, from the same foundational document:

The TAV arrived at the staging areas with Lisa BANFIELD and is received by EMRT. Banfield does not appear to have any significant injuries and did not require intervention by the ERT members who advised she was cold and complaining of a sore back (right side) where she had been allegedly kicked by the suspect. BANFIELD was rapidly assessed as she was directed into the back seat of the Jeep Cherokee with Cpl. Ivany while Cst. Mahar drove. BANFIELD was shivering from the exposure to the cold overnight and when asked about the pain in her back, she advised it was on her lower right side (muscular area) from where the perpetrator had kicked her earlier. Cpl. Ivany confirmed there was no pain or injury to the vertebrae/spinal area and could not see any visible bruising or injury at that time. . . .

As she was being transported to the command post in Great Village, Banfield told the Mounties that she had been handcuffed in the back seat of the replica police car while Wortman gathered weapons. She said his plan was to burn everything down and then go after one of her sisters. She said she escaped from the handcuffs, crawled through the narrow hole that divided the front and back seats, and escaped into the woods wearing just a long-sleeve shirt and thin "pants/leggings with no shoes."

Banfield said she hid in a tree hollow, and that her plan was to seek the help of firefighters, but when none came, she stayed there until daybreak, when she could see where she was, then made her way to the closest house—Leon Joudrey's—to call for help.

Among the important things to note from this description is that the observation that Banfield had no serious injuries was redacted and hidden from the media until late 2020. When the black ink was lifted to reveal what had been hidden, the mainstream and alternative media ignored it.

The Mounties treated Banfield as a victim of domestic violence from the moment they found her. The force and government officials protected her and did not identify her by name for eight months. The RCMP portrayed her as a plucky heroine who had helped them identify Wortman, the vehicle he was driving and the guns he had in his possession.

One of the first things Banfield did after being taken to the hospital in Truro was to seek out a criminal lawyer, with the help of Kevin Paul von Bargen, a Toronto lawyer who was a friend. Eventually, she hired multiple lawyers, both civil and criminal. These don't seem like the actions of someone who is a victim, as she and the police claimed.

If Banfield had been in the woods all night without a cellphone, as she said afterwards, the Mounties couldn't have known when they arrived on Joudrey's doorstep that she was a victim of domestic violence the previous night. Meanwhile, normal police procedure would have been to treat her as a possible collaborator until proven otherwise, an avenue which wasn't pursued by the RCMP. The Mounties seemed eager to assume that her story was true, although it defied both logic and science. Skeptics, including the families of the victims and their lawyers, speculated that Banfield might have been somewhere warmer—even out of Portapique for a time—before returning to the scene. Neither the RCMP nor, later, the commission considered that possibility. Banfield stuck to her original story.

Banfield's unchallenged victim story would become a lynchpin in the overall police narrative, while Joudrey's version of events, among those of others, all but disappeared from the record. To reiterate, despite a number of attempts, by me and others, to reach Banfield, she has, as far as I know, declined to answer any journalists' questions, including my own, or grant interviews to inquiring journalists who, like me, contacted her several times for her story. This makes writing about her story somewhat more difficult. While I will endeavour to provide her version of events, I must make it clear that, based upon the totality of the evidence, her statements to the RCMP and the commission do not appear to be enough to confirm the truth or deny alternative scenarios. It seems likely that she would deny anything in this book deemed to be contrary to the established narrative.

After he was interviewed by Constable Fraser Firth, Joudrey told me it appeared to him that the questions were aimed at finding a weakness or hole in his story so that he could be eliminated as a witness. An entire lexicon has developed over the years to describe the various tactics the police use to make a story go the way they want it to: "firming up," "fluffing," "stretching," "tidying up," "testilying."

"They were trying to get me to say I didn't see anything that mattered," Joudrey said. "But I did see things that I think were important. That's not what they wanted to hear."

It wasn't what the media wanted to hear, either. The only story they wanted to tell about Joudrey began and ended with him opening the door for Lisa Banfield and then calling 911 on her behalf. Indeed, he'd been interviewed on CTV in the month after the massacres. But I wanted the public to know the whole story of what Joudrey saw—or rather didn't see—on Lisa.

There was also the issue of the "under-caution" interview of Banfield by Staff Sergeant Greg Vardy. At the time, the RCMP did not disclose what the interview was about, but the heavily redacted publicly disclosed records clearly indicated that Banfield had been warned that she was a suspect in something criminal. But what? The collective media either missed that or, more likely, weren't interested in pursuing an angle that would only serve to muddy the waters about Banfield. When I tried to pitch the story to the *National Post*, for example, I got this message from editor Deborah Stokes on October 16, 2020, a full six months after the massacres:

> Apologies again—endless insanity here. I did grab a few minutes to discuss your stories with [editor-in-chief] Rob [Roberts] and a couple of other senior editors.
>
> On Banfield, the story casts enough doubt on her innocence with the "caution interview" and some of the other details. But the *National Post* isn't comfortable at this stage of the case to name her publicly. The feeling is the outpouring from victims rights groups would overpower the very worthwhile merits of the story. The facts/evidence really speak for themselves. We might change that position later, but for now, Rob would like to go that route. Hope you are agreeable to that and I will send you an edited version and we would publish early next week.
>
> The Portapique story—and how the police didn't secure the scene—we are keen on that one.
>
> I am still on deadline . . . But let me know your thoughts.

In the end, I pulled the story back and forged an alliance with *Frank* magazine, and also documented Joudrey's testimony in *22 Murders*.

Later, a friend of Lisa McCully recounted how McCully had complained that Joudrey was stalking her by lingering outside her house as he was walking his dogs. This was enough for the delicate flowers in the media to turn a deaf ear in Joudrey's direction.

Joudrey's version of these events was that he was concerned about McCully, with whom he had had a recent sexual relationship, which ended, he said, because he didn't want to get married so soon after his divorce. Joudrey said he liked the headstrong McCully but was concerned about her fondness for Wortman, whom she had dated in the past. She was apparently rekindling that flame. Joudrey said Wortman may have recently bought McCully a ring.

"She always spoke highly of Gabriel. I didn't get it," Joudrey told me. "I used to tell her: 'You know he's using you, don't you?'"

By December 2020, Joudrey's life was in shambles. The massacres had taken place just as storm clouds were arising for Joudrey at work. On the surface, he was an affable guy who was loved by many. He had 236 friends on Facebook and was constantly updating that list with the latest pretty woman he had met. His profile photo was of him standing up in his 16-foot aluminum boat, holding an impressive striped bass that he had caught at his favourite fishing hole, at the mouth of the Portapique River in Cobequid Bay. But he believed that there was corruption in his department and that certain people were receiving favourable rulings. His friend Pete MacIsaac, who had worked with him, described Joudrey this way: "We'd be in a meeting and if he heard something that he didn't agree with, he'd just say, 'That's bullshit' or something like that. He didn't hold back his feelings." That attitude, naturally, attracted problems for him.

He was also struggling with his mental health in the wake of the massacres. Between the two, he was "temporarily" off work on stress leave. He couldn't handle living in Portapique, so he rented out his place and lived in a construction work trailer in the woods near Moose River, west of Portapique. But it was too cold to ride out the winter there.

Meanwhile, Joudrey's allegations of corruption at his workplace had caused an irreparable rift. In a fit of temper, he turned into a keyboard warrior, making references to his guns that were perceived as threats by a superior. She called the RCMP.

"I lost my head and said things I shouldn't have, but it was all exaggerated," Joudrey told me later. "I would never shoot anyone."

One thing led to another, and Joudrey's name and photo were circulated on social media.

A few days before Christmas 2020, Joudrey was driving to New Glasgow, about an hour's drive east of Portapique, where he planned to stay in a motel. He had his most important personal items, including his guns, in the pickup. Unable to find the motel, he saw a Mountie parked in a lot and pulled up to ask him for directions. They got into a conversation, which soon turned to Portapique. The Mountie asked for identification. When Joudrey got out of his vehicle to look for it, everything went south. "It didn't seem like much at first," he told me afterwards. "Things were going well, and then all of a sudden there were police cars coming from every direction."

Joudrey was charged with unsafe storage of his guns and put in jail. He was then committed to a psychiatric facility for a thirty-day assessment. Over the Christmas holiday, drugged, worn out and forlorn, he called me, citizen investigator Chad Jones and others, talking our ears off.

"You know who came to see me today?" he said one night. "Addie MacCallum."

Staff Sergeant Allan (Addie) MacCallum was the commanding officer of the RCMP's Pictou detachment and one of the first Mounties who tried to take charge during the chaos of the massacres. He and Joudrey had played hockey together in the beer league.

"It was a nice visit. Addie told me that he was sorry for what happened to me."

Joudrey was released temporarily from the hospital so that he could spend Christmas with his children, but then had to go back. After a month of treatment, he emerged a shadow of his former self. After couch-surfing for months, he returned to his house in Portapique, and the charges were eventually dropped, but he had been effectively and thoroughly discredited as a potential witness. Joudrey was one of many who were never called to the commission hearings because, as he put it, he was being protected from any discomfort or further traumatization. All that appeared on the official record was his first, superficial interview with the RCMP.

◆

In the wee hours of April 19, 2020, there was a third witness, a Mountie, who also saw nothing.

By 6 a.m., as the sun was threatening to come up, the RCMP had no clue where Wortman or Banfield might be. Only a handful of ERT members were in the neighbourhood. One was Constable Trent Milton. He had been a Mountie since 2003, serving his entire career in Nova Scotia. He'd had a variety of roles but for fifteen years had been a member of the ERT—part-time until 2015, when the RCMP established a full-time unit with full- and part-time members scattered around the province. After the 911 calls the previous night, Milton had been one of thirteen ERT members called out. Eleven of them assembled at RCMP headquarters in Dartmouth. Milton left for Portapique in the first group of four at 11:20 p.m.

That group first ended up chasing flashing car lights and other distractions west of Portapique, on the other side of the Portapique River. Once they got back to Portapique, they patrolled the neighbourhood in the overnight hours, eventually making their way to the Blairs' house, where they found Greg Blair's body on the porch. When they entered the house, they were repulsed by the overwhelming odour of propane. Wortman had taken debris from the fireplace, strewn it all over the living room and turned on the gas, which failed to ignite. The Mounties retreated outside, found the propane tank and switched it off. When they returned, they found Jamie Blair's mutilated and smouldering body in the doorway of the master bedroom. Wortman had tried to set her on fire, but her children had moved the burning logs from around her head.

Milton, who had experience as a homicide investigator, was by then suspicious about Banfield's possible whereabouts. He wondered if she, too, had been murdered and incinerated in the fires at Wortman's cottage and warehouse. If not, where was she?

Earlier, a police dog had been unleashed both near Wortman's properties and near where the bodies of Lisa McCully and Corrie Ellison lay, on either side of Orchard Beach Drive, outside the gate to Wortman's warehouse. The dog did not pick up the scent of anyone on foot.

The RCMP was notoriously short on supporting equipment. It did not have a plane or helicopter in Nova Scotia. It called for a helicopter from New Brunswick, but that was being repaired. Milton had the force's only drone in Nova Scotia, in an assault vehicle parked up near the highway. He went and retrieved it, then returned to the area of the warehouse. At 6:15 a.m., Milton put the drone, which had infrared capability, in the air and flew it over the immediate area. One of four deer popped out of the woods. There were no signs of anything else.

By this time, most of the Mounties on the scene had already called it a night or were being sent home. The bodies that had been discovered— Greg Blair, Jamie Blair, Lisa McCully and Corrie Ellison—were left where they had fallen. The RCMP had no idea there were many more bodies. The scene was secured only in the sense that access to the community was blocked at the intersection of Portapique Beach Road and Highway 2. The next shift wasn't due until later that morning.

Then came the call from Joudrey that Lisa Banfield had shown up at his door.

Milton came across Banfield when she was brought up to the highway to be evaluated as he was putting his drone back in a vehicle. In his first statement to investigators, he said: "I remember being shocked . . . that she had surfaced that morning. Seeing that the cottage had burned down, and the warehouse had burned down, I felt pretty strongly that she had probably been in one of those structures . . . You know, the skeptical officer in us is, is she involved? Is this a ruse? What's, what's going on? But I had no direct contact with her, so I didn't have any communication pieces with her. But I remember having those thoughts when she came out."

It was an important point. The RCMP had declared Banfield a victim before she was even located, but experienced police officers (and true crime afficionados) recognize that women are just as capable of participating in heinous crimes as men. Think of Karla Homolka, Rosemary West and Myra Hindley, among a host of others who worked as a murderous team with their husbands or boyfriends.

Although outsiders might think the police all work from the same playbook, that's not necessarily true. Two policemen standing side by side might be part of different silos, not knowing the whole story or plan. If there was a big picture at Portapique, Milton's spot in it was locating and chasing after Wortman. He may not have been privy to anything else going on.

Another curious thing was that Banfield seemed to have come from a position, as Milton put it, 500 to 700 metres north of where he had flown the drone. That would have put her very close to the highway, where various Mounties had been racing back and forth all night. Cruisers and other marked and unmarked police vehicles were parked at the intersection with Highway 2. If Banfield had moved farther east toward Brown Loop, she likely would have been able to see the two Mountie cars positioned there. If she was where she said she was, why did she not try to contact the police officers all around her? Is it possible that she was outside the area, and somehow slipped back in? Those were questions never asked of her or answered by her. The first time anyone would hear from her would be twenty-seven months later, in July 2022, when she appeared before the commission for a couple of hours.

7

THE RCMP VIEW: SATURDAY NIGHT, APRIL 18, 2020

The first the RCMP heard of what was happening in Portapique was Jamie Blair's heartbreaking call for help at 10:01 p.m. She described a nightmarish situation for emergency centre call takers, one that all but paralyzed them and the RCMP.

As I reported in *22 Murders*, a very credible source within the police, whom we dubbed True Blue, leaked us the 911 tapes in June of 2021. We took precautions to warn the families, then released the recordings in *Frank*, noting that the content was graphic. It was a difficult decision, but one we felt was important to make, because they showed that before 10:30 p.m., the RCMP knew the killer was Wortman dressed as a police officer and driving an RCMP car, and yet it wasn't until 8:54 a.m. that they released Wortman's name to the public on Twitter. At 10:17 a.m.— a full twelve hours after Blair's first call—they admitted how he was dressed and what vehicle he was driving.

Below is the transcript from Blair's first call. The sentences in square brackets are my added descriptions.

911: 911. What is your emergency?

JB: (*inaudible*) my neighbour . . . (*garbled*) . . . been shot.

911: I'm sorry, I can't make out what you are saying.

[Jamie tries to calm down and get the tremble out of her voice.]

JB: My neighbour is . . . (*inaudible*). I think he just shot my husband.

911: You think your husband's been shot?

JB: Yes!

911: Okay. Do you have a home phone or land line to that location . . .

JB: I know . . . talking over . . .

911: Where are you? What is your civic address?

JB: 123 Orchard Beach Drive in Portapique.

911: 123 Orchard Beach Drive in Portapique. Is your husband injured?

JB: I don't know, he is laying on my deck, I don't know what the fuck is going on, there is a police car in the fucking driveway.

911: There are police cars in the driveway?

JB: There's a police car, but he drives . . . he a denturist and he drives . . . those police cars—

[The 911 operator cuts Jamie off. She's frantic.]

911: I'm sorry, did you say there was a police car in your driveway?

JB: There is an RCMP . . . it's labelled RCMP . . . I don't know if it's not a police car . . .

[She can be heard moving around and is likely trying to hide her sons Alex, 12, and Jack, 10.]

911: Listen, you're at 123 Orchard Beach Drive in Portapique, Colchester County? You called from 902 --- ----.

JB: Yes.

911: Is your husband injured?

JB: I don't know.

[Blair is obviously frustrated.]

911: Can you see him?

JB: He is lying face down on the deck.

911: Okay. Has he moved?

JB: I went back out to check on him and the man was coming back up on the deck with a big gun.

911: Stay on the line and we're going to the police. Don't hang up.

RCMP: RCMP, *bonjour*. Hull-oh-oh, can you see your husband from where you are?

[The tape cuts off at this point. We do not know what is on the RCMP part of the tape.]

At this point Wortman returned to the house and killed Blair. Under instructions from a supervisor, the operator phoned Blair back, looking for more details, but the call went to the answering machine.

The RCMP sprang into action. Although all leave had been cancelled because of the COVID lockdown and, theoretically, the Bible Hill detachment was at full strength, it was still short on personnel, a perennial RCMP problem. Instead of six members on duty that night, there were four: constables Stuart Beselt, Adam Merchant, Aaron Patton and Vicki Colford. The RCMP would later give the public the impression that it had stormed Portapique with everything it had, but it didn't. When it came to short staffing, the RCMP philosophy was "risk it out." What could possibly go wrong with not having enough personnel in a critical situation?

The RCMP patrol area is enormous. Some days, a Bible Hill cruiser might rack up 1,000 kilometres during a shift. When Blair's call came in, the four on-duty Mounties were in the relative neighbourhood of the detachment. Two were in Salmon River, while the other two were farther east in the hamlet of Valley, east of Truro.

At high speed it would take them twenty-five to thirty minutes to drive to Portapique. As they raced there, more 911 calls came in, reporting fires and shots. Whatever was happening in Portapique, it was unusual.

Meanwhile, Jamie's sons had run over to Lisa McCully's house next door. As I reported in *22 Murders*,

McCully ushered the children into the basement with her daughter and son and then went to check what was happening. It was then that she likely came across Wortman, who shot her in the head on her front lawn.

The next call to 911 was logged in at 10:16:30. It was from Alex Blair. He and Lisa McCully's 12-year-old daughter, also named Alex, were in the basement. Their younger brothers had left the house and gone outside.

On the call, Alex explained where they were and what had happened, and said the killer was in a police car "just like Dave Lilly's." Sergeant Lilly's wife taught at the same school as McCully and a week earlier had performed in a skit at the school dressed in his red serge. (The RCMP immediately began doing an inventory of all its cruisers and tracking down Sergeant Lilly. He was a suspect until he was found at his cottage.)

At 10:25 p.m., Portapique residents Andrew and Kate MacDonald called 911 after they decided to check out the fires in the neighbourhood. During the call, they described an RCMP car pulling up beside them—it was Wortman. The recording captured the sound of him shooting Andrew, and Kate screaming. Andrew said, "It's my neighbour Gabe. He just shot me in the arm," as they raced toward Portapique Beach Road, where they came into contact with the first RCMP officer on the scene, Constable Stuart Beselt. MacDonald told him that Wortman was dressed as a police officer and driving an RCMP car, which Beselt apparently relayed to the dispatcher.

Although the dispatchers were told that the shooter was Wortman in a "police car," they discounted it because they couldn't find evidence of such a car. They did find registrations and licence plate numbers for three *decommissioned* RCMP cars, but the Mounties located those in the overnight hours. What they didn't realize was that Wortman hadn't registered the decommissioned car he had turned into a replica Mountie cruiser.

They made the fatal assumption that Jamie Blair, Alex Blair and Andrew and Kate MacDonald must all have been referring to a decommissioned police car, perhaps with a decal or stripe on it.

◆

The way the Mass Casualty Commission addressed the RCMP response to Portapique that night revealed much about the inquiry's methods and intent. On February 28, 2022, at its third public session, commission counsel Roger Burrill read into the record its foundational document about what it believed had taken place in Portapique. It's important to note that almost two years after the incident, the commission still couldn't be sure. Although the commission had proclaimed that it was determined to get to the truth, the route it chose to take was a twisted and bumpy one, littered with gaping holes.

"The document that will be presented here has been created as a result of an extensive review of subpoenaed materials within the possession now of the Mass Casualty Commission," said Burrill, a veteran and well-respected legal aid defence whiz. "It's the result of independent investigations and inquiries by the Mass Casualty Commission's teams of investigators. It is the result of consultation with participants who have provided information and access to information. It is also the result of information that has been provided by Nova Scotians."

"So, while it may be imperfect, it is, at this stage, the best efforts to present to you information as of February 28th, 2022," Burrill said. "You need to know that this is going to be a lengthy presentation. I'm afraid I'm going to be with you probably all day. But more importantly, it is a detailed investigation. And even more importantly, it's a disturbing presentation. Perhaps as a result of some of the commentary today, there will be more questions raised, leading to more answers. More answers is a good thing . . . As indicated, this is not the final word. We do not state that what is found in the foundational documents present [sic] unquestioned fact. It is the best information known and may result in more information being provided.

"In this presentation we will do our best, or my best, to provide a chronological narrative of the early hours of what took place in Portapique. It's an attempt, as best we can, to reconstruct the events in Portapique. It is an exercise fitting hundreds, if not thousands, of pieces of information to construct a narrative. It is, of course, a reconstruction of a narrative. There is, I will admit, unfortunately, an inexactitude to the information presented in some areas. This cannot be helped. It will cause some stress, some consternation. It will raise questions. All that is a good thing."

Was it? The inexactitude might have had something to do with the fact that the commission still had not interviewed the most senior commanding officers in the RCMP, and wouldn't until months later. Here is that list and the dates they were first interviewed: Colchester County district commander Superintendent Archie Ferguson (June 14, 2022); Superintendent Darren Campbell (June 28 and July 12, 2022); Chief Superintendent Chris Leather (July 6, 2022); and Assistant Commissioner Leona (Lee) Bergerman (August 2, 2022). Bergerman's boss, Commissioner Brenda Lucki, was interviewed on August 4, 2022.

How could Burrill possibly provide the "best information known"? And why did it take so long—more than two years after the event—before the commission talked to senior RCMP officers? It looked as if the commission was allowing the senior officers to hear all the evidence, especially Lisa Banfield's testimony, which was scheduled for July 15, 2022, before they committed themselves to a story.

Of great interest to me was the fact that the two Mounties who had set up the Nova Scotia operation in 2019, and who continued to oversee it after being promoted and moved to Ottawa, were the last two Mounties in the chain of command to be interviewed. Ottawa-based Deputy Commissioner Brian Brennan, the national Criminal Operations officer, was called in on August 10, 2022, while his underling, Assistant Commissioner Dennis Daley, was last on the list—September 15, 2022. Daley would soon return to Halifax to take over command of the RCMP in the province. If anyone knew what was really going on, it was one, some or all of them.

Burrill's "all day" turned out to be a dissertation lasting three hours and one minute, sandwiched around a one-hour lunch break. The day ended at 1:42 p.m.

The next eight days of the commission's hearings were supposed to cover what happened in Portapique in greater detail, but much of the time was spent behind closed doors hearing arguments from lawyers, especially those representing the National Police Federation, which was ferocious in demanding dispensations for its members. Since the commission was on a tight schedule mandated by the federal and provincial governments, the stalling meant there would be less time for it to conduct its inquiry.

When not engaged with lawyers, the commission returned to the story of the massacres, but instead of calling live witnesses connected to Portapique, more foundational documents were read. It was the least effective way of describing the massacre—telling the story, not showing it. On March 9, the last day of that first group of hearings, the commission devoted its time to what Wortman might have been doing in the interlude *between* the two massacres, then took a break.

The order and approach to the hearings was beyond disorienting. The public still hadn't heard a first-hand account of what had happened at Portapique that Saturday night. One might have thought that the story would begin with what Lisa Banfield experienced that day, but as mentioned, her account was scheduled for July.

When it finally returned on March 28, the commission had been sitting for five weeks, and only now was a Mountie making an appearance before it. That morning, the first three Mounties who responded to Portapique sat as a panel at a long table at the Halifax Convention Centre, each wearing a neatly pressed suit and tie. Constable Stuart Beselt, an acting corporal for almost three years, was joined by constables Adam Merchant and Aaron Patton.

The session with the Mounties was not freewheeling by any means. The points of discussion had already been captured in a previous interview that had been transformed into a foundational document, and commission counsel Burrill proceeded to lead the Mounties through their testimony, highlighting what they had said in the past and asking them to elaborate, if necessary.

The entire session felt rehearsed, especially in how Merchant and Patton seemed to defer to their road boss, Beselt, or to confirm their agreement with a glance or a nod. Constable Patton admitted that they had previously discussed as a group what they were going to say. When he tried to recall what he had done with a shell casing he had found, Patton said that he had forgotten: "I'm not sure who I gave it to," he told Burrill. "It was—we were trying to figure that out last night."

"Second corporal," Beselt interjected. "I don't know who it was."

"There's a lot of members there that were in the mix that we're not familiar with," Patton added.

The story the commission was selling was the one about how brave the three Mounties had been. There seemed to be little doubt about that. They had been sent into an extremely dangerous situation in an area many of them had never been, working with other Mounties they didn't know. They didn't have proper, updated equipment, such as night-vision goggles, which had been promised five years earlier after tragedy struck the force.

In June 2014, three Mounties had been shot and killed and two others severely wounded in Moncton, New Brunswick. In an independent report, former RCMP assistant commissioner Alphonse MacNeil, who until recently had been in charge of the Nova Scotia RCMP, was surprisingly tough on the force and its procedures. MacNeil cited a host of institutional failures, including poor training, outdated communications systems, and a disconnect between the force's largely unaccountable white-shirted managers and the overworked, perennially short-staffed members on the front lines. In January 2015, MacNeil issued his report with sixty-four recommendations, all of which were accepted by the RCMP. Commissioner Robert Paulson said the force would soon implement the recommendations, and he even provided a timetable.

Even though the RCMP said it would provide its members with night-vision goggles, the force dragged its feet, as it always had. Cellphone service in the Portapique area was notoriously erratic, but the RCMP never invested in satellite phones, as had been recommended. The RCMP had never contemplated a night-time outdoor murder spree, so it didn't train its members for such an event. In its skimpy playbook, mass shooter scenarios involved indoor settings in daylight.

Since they didn't have night-vision goggles, the three Mounties had to operate in the dark or use flashlights when necessary, making them an easy target for the shooter, if he had been so inclined. They should have had high-quality maps and GPS on their police-issued phones, but they didn't. Some used their personal phones, which were never analyzed.

One of the crucial flaws in the commission's approach was how it elicited testimony. The trio of Mounties testifying together suggested that they had the same story to tell, but they didn't. They weren't together the entire time. But this detail went unnoticed by the media and most of the public.

The official story was that these three Mounties resorted to their Immediate Action Rapid Deployment (IARD) training and did the best they could to make a viable diamond formation, although they were short one person.

Actually, they started out two men short. Beselt was the first to arrive, at 10:26 p.m. He stopped his Chevrolet Tahoe SUV right in the middle of Portapique Beach Road, about 30 metres in from Highway 2, and sprang out of the vehicle. He was armouring up when Andrew and Kate MacDonald pulled up, making their escape from Wortman. That was around 10:28 p.m. Merchant and Patton were right behind Beselt, already geared up, followed by Constable Vicki Colford. Patton stayed behind for a few minutes to help Colford with the MacDonalds, while Beselt and Merchant headed into the darkness down the road, each carrying about 70 pounds of equipment, including their C8 carbines. Patton followed later, but Colford didn't. Although she had been a Mountie for almost twenty-three years, she was not carbine-trained, and even if she had been, she wasn't physically fit enough to join the men on their mission. "She wouldn't have been able to keep up with us, so it was perfect that we had her for containment," Merchant later said in a debriefing interview.

Beselt and Merchant didn't take their vehicles, because every Mountie knew what had happened in Moncton in 2014. The cruisers had attracted the gunman, who picked off the drivers before they had a chance to get out of their vehicles.

Although the three callers to 911 had provided much detail, all the Mounties on the ground knew was that a man named Gabriel who had a "police car" had shot some people. Andrew MacDonald knew Beselt and told him that the shooter was Wortman.

What the Mounties on the scene didn't know was that Portapique resident David Faulkner had been driving behind MacDonald and Wortman and had seen Wortman slam on his brakes at the intersection of Orchard Beach Drive and Portapique Beach Road, then turn south down Portapique Beach Road, away from the flashing lights of the RCMP cars.

The Mounties also didn't know that there were four children at Lisa McCully's house, two twelve-year-olds hiding in the basement and two ten-year-olds roaming around outside somewhere.

About 300 metres down the road and around a slight bend, Beselt and Merchant arrived at the intersection of Orchard Beach Drive. They had to make a decision: Head to where the 911 calls had emanated from or toward the fire ahead of them on Portapique Beach Road?

The following excerpt from the transcript of the commission session captures how testimony was given. The subject was why it took so long to mount a rescue of the four children.

"Our intent was to go there," said Constable Beselt of the McCully house, "but it's like, we kind of got sidetracked by different things."

"Because your focus is on the threat," Constable Merchant interjected.

"It's the threat, right?" Constable Beselt said.

"You're going to that," Constable Merchant continued. "You kind of got to block everything else out and focus on that."

"We're, yeah," Constable Beselt said, collecting his thoughts. "We're chasing the sounds, right?"

"Yeah," Constable Merchant agreed.

They said they heard gunshots in the distance to the south, which could have been munitions blowing up in the fire at Wortman's warehouse on Orchard Beach Drive or Zahl and Thomas being shot in their house a kilometre farther down Portapique Beach Road. About 600 metres straight ahead, they could see the glow from Wortman's burning cottage and chose to head that way, chasing the bullets and the explosions. They moved surprisingly quickly, considering the distance, the terrain and the situation. They passed unseen by the house of Jerry and Florie Murphy on their left.

At 10:40 p.m., Beselt and Merchant arrived at Wortman's flaming cottage on the other side of Portaupique Cemetery. One of Wortman's decommissioned white Ford Taurus Police Interceptors was also on fire.

At this point in the hearing, Burrill stopped to play a recording of Beselt speaking with the dispatcher: "There is a white Taurus in the driveway there, but we heard shots coming from further down the road, so we're continuing on."

By now, Wortman had been down the road for about twelve minutes, based upon the available evidence. During that time, he had likely killed Zahl and Thomas and set their house ablaze.

Beselt and Merchant headed toward the Zahl-Thomas house, but the fires had not yet illuminated the area. Looking back over their left shoulders, they could see the warehouse fire through the trees. As they cut back, looking for a path, Patton came running up to them.

"It was really dark," Constable Merchant said. "I remember when we're going along and I heard footsteps coming up behind me. I didn't realize Patton was coming. I drew up and I just saw him kind of emerge out of the darkness. It was dark enough you couldn't see any distance."

They cut themselves a path through the rough, thick and tangled forest.

The warehouse blaze was massive. The footprint of the wooden building was 3,200 square feet, with a partial second floor. Wortman had about sixteen motorbikes, 4x4s and other gasoline-burning toys and equipment in the building. "There were some very heavy explosions coming out of there," Beselt said. "Like, I know we wanted to stay as far away from that as possible with just having the explosions. Like, you don't know what's in there, right . . . It's like a war zone in there."

Burrill interjected to ask a question that seemed more suited to his legal aid calling than to someone pushing for evidence as a prosecutor might. It seemed more important to emphasize the stress the Mounties were feeling rather than delve into the efficacy of their tactics. "Constable Merchant, any comment with respect to the tonality of the voice and what you are thinking, experiencing, at this time?"

"Well, I don't know. I just remember coming—we came from the woods, and it was just dark, and then you out [sic] to that and it's just white-hot, huge fire and it—yeah, it was crazy. And just explosions and gunshot, so yeah, I'm sure there was some anxiety or, you know, but—yeah."

The Mounties had moved incredibly quickly. Within about fifteen minutes they had walked a kilometre to Wortman's cottage, surveyed the situation, gotten off the road, took the footpath that cut through the woods and made their way back several hundred metres to Wortman's burning warehouse. Their route through the woods would have put them relatively close, perhaps 100 metres at most from the route Wortman had taken. If Wortman was driving on the barely passable one-lane road through the woods, as the RCMP and the commission would later suggest, it seems odd that the Mounties didn't report seeing his headlights or taillights. Likewise, if he was there, wouldn't Wortman have seen them?

They made their way past the burning building and headed east out of the unpaved warehouse driveway to Orchard Beach Drive. McCully's house was straight ahead, across the road. As they got to the road, they looked to their right and saw the body of Corrie Ellison, whose father was Portapique resident Richard Ellison, lying on the ground.

Legally blind in one eye, hampered by an ankle injury and sporting a fibreglass cast on his broken right wrist, Corrie had hobbled about 500 metres up the road from his father's house to check out the fire and had been shot. He was clutching his cellphone, which was still on.

"Looks like we have one deceased here," Beselt radioed to his dispatcher at 10:49:18.

"The kids that we have on the phone over at 135, ah, on that road, they're saying someone's pounding on their door outside, wondering if that's a police officer or someone else," the dispatcher said.

"No, that's not us," Beselt said. "Do you copy? We have one deceased on the ground."

"Copy that," the dispatcher said.

Who was loose in the neighbourhood and knocking on the door? It certainly wasn't Wortman.

The Mounties crossed the road and went up to McCully's house. Beselt knocked on the door, while the other two covered him. He went to another door, and the children came up from the basement and opened it for him. He was shocked that there were four of them. He stowed them back in the basement. As soon as the trio left, the children were back on the line with 911 and said they thought someone was in the house. The three Mounties returned, quickly searched the house and told them to lock the door again. The men hated leaving them there, but there was nothing they could do. Taking the kids out of the neighbourhood had been rejected by their commanding officers as too great a risk with Wortman on the loose. Instead, the children were given a password—"pineapple"—that the police would use when they returned to the house to rescue them.

Back outside, the Mounties got into their positions, with Beselt lying prone while Patton and Merchant hid in the tree line. In the darkness they couldn't see much, but they noticed someone walking up the road with a rather poor flashlight, as they later described it. They wondered if it was the shooter, but held their positions. They couldn't know that that it was Corrie Ellison's brother, Clinton, who had gone out looking for him when he stopped answering his phone.

"We're about to light this guy up," Beselt told the commission.

"Are you able to explain what that expression means?" Burrill asked.

"Shoot him, right?" Beselt said, then explained that they couldn't get a clear visual on the figure, but they were all ready to pull the trigger if he ran. "You know, like my line in the sand at that point of time is . . . I want to challenge him, right? I want to say, 'Please don't move,' right? And hopefully the person gives up. But in, you know, a scenario, if he's going to run, my line in the sand if he runs, I'm going to shoot, right? Because I want to stop the threat."

"Yeah," Burrill said.

"So yeah, we're getting ready to shoot him. Like, we think it's the suspect."

"How close did Clinton Ellison come to being shot that night?"

"Probably 25 feet, 50 feet," Beselt said.

Patton described what happened next. He told Beselt and Merchant to get ready because he was going to turn on the flashlight on his gun. When he did, the beam illuminated Lisa McCully's body, about eight metres away.

When Patton's flashlight went on, the person walking up the road turned and quickly retreated. The Mounties let him go, based, it seemed, upon the poor quality of his flashlight and the fact that he was walking toward the body and not away from it.

Shortly thereafter, they got a call to rescue Peter Griffon and his family, who were calling for help. The trio headed across a private property north of the burning warehouse and through the Murphys' backyard to get back to Portapique Beach Road. That's when they ran into the Murphys, who were driving back from knocking on the Griffons' door.

"We pressed on down the road to the south to try to basically put ourselves on the line to lure this guy out," Constable Patton said. "And obviously we didn't make it all the way down the road."

Patton's watch recorded their every step. They had gone six kilometres, carrying all that weight under all that stress. They were soaked with sweat and freezing at the same time. In their travels, they hadn't come across Lisa Banfield, who said she was hiding in the woods.

As much as the commission touted the three men as heroic, unfortunately for the RCMP, they showed how incompetent the force actually was. At least three people were murdered after they arrived—Corrie Ellison, John Zahl and Joanne Thomas. If the Mounties had gone to Orchard Beach Drive, from which the first three 911 calls originated, they would have been on the scene, and Corrie Ellison would likely still be alive.

If anything, the trio's description of the scene seemed to prove that Wortman wasn't on a suicide-by-cop mission or that he intended to kill police officers—two RCMP theories at the time. If he had wanted to shoot one of them, he had the advantages of knowing the geography, darkness and RCMP unpreparedness. His every action indicated that he was trying to get away.

Near the conclusion of their appearance before the commission, the trio showed that deep down they were company men first.

"Given your activity that night in Portapique, as you look back with all the information that you have, do you have any regrets about your behaviour?" Roger Burrill asked each of them.

"No, I wouldn't have changed anything, from our perspective or our response," said Constable Beselt.

"Yeah, I agree," said Constable Patton. "I mean, with the information we have in the moment, I don't think I would have done anything differently."

"Same," Constable Merchant added. "I mean, you go through this one thousand times and . . . given what I know, I couldn't have changed anything that would have made any difference."

Constable Beselt concluded, "I think the commission has done a good job of telling our story, because I think it was something that wasn't

told at the beginning and led to a lot of conspiracy about, you know—
that the RCMP didn't react in an appropriate way. And, you know, I was
glad to see that we were finally being acknowledged for going in."

The performance by the three Mounties would prove to be the high
point of RCMP testimony at the commission. The force knew the evidence wasn't going to get any better for it. Beselt, Merchant and Patton
were viewed as a positive that the RCMP could build on to help salvage
its severely tarnished reputation.

8

CORRIE ELLISON AND THE KIDS IN THE BASEMENT

Corrie Ellison was shot five times, once through his cast, as if his hand was raised, three times in the face and head, and once in the shoulder. All the bullets passed through his body. According to Beselt's testimony, they discovered Corrie's body near the gate to Wortman's warehouse at 10:49 p.m., then went to the McCully house to check on the children hiding there.

Meanwhile, Corrie's brother, Clinton, went searching for him and found his body. As Clinton was retreating, he saw a flashlight go on and thought it might be his brother's killer. He hurried down the road, turned off his own flashlight and ducked into the woods on his left about 300 metres from where his brother was murdered. (This was just past where Lisa Banfield said she had gone to hide.) He called his father, Richard, told him what was happening and asked him to call 911, which he did at 10:59 p.m. Ellison, well dressed and suffering from mild to moderate hypothermia, wouldn't be rescued until almost four hours later, just before 3 a.m.

Corrie Ellison's death has long been considered an anomaly by some who have studied the case, mainly because of the lack of information provided by the RCMP. The first time the force addressed the time of Ellison's death was at a press conference ten days after the massacres, on April 29, 2020, by then superintendent Darren Campbell. In providing a timeline for the massacres, Campbell said that Ellison was killed at 10:35 p.m. and that Wortman had fled south toward Cobequid Court, killed the Tuck-Oliver family and Peter and Joy Bond, and then escaped the neighbourhood via a little-known dirt path through a blueberry field to the east by around 10:45 p.m. That timeline became a key component of the official narrative, but the story wasn't quite as solid as it first seemed.

In early 2022, the commission released thousands of pages of its foundational papers, which called the RCMP's timeline into question. The documents showed that the final, blurry photo on Corrie Ellison's phone camera was time-stamped 10:40:12 p.m. That changed everything. Ellison had been murdered then, or slightly after that. The time frame may have shrunk a mere five minutes, but it was a critical five minutes—supposedly the last five Wortman had spent in Portapique. This came to light after two years without explanations by the RCMP.

The time on the phone matched reports of gunshots, but the underwhelming and unconvincing forensic report, the shortcomings of which I will soon address, added more confusion. The forensics determined that Ellison had been shot while leaning into Wortman's vehicle, likely from the passenger side, and later while on the ground. Wortman killed just about everyone with a headshot, including Ellison. Why would he have gotten out of the car, walked around, fired two more shots and returned to the car? He didn't have seconds to spare, and this would have pushed his departure time from the scene to even later.

A curious but entirely uninvestigated conundrum was that it appeared someone had tampered with Ellison's phone after he was killed. Who? We know the crime scene was unprotected. The Mounties on site left his and McCully's bodies in the open all night and well into the next day. As stated earlier, they were "discovered" three different times by different Mounties over an almost five-hour period. At 1:50 a.m., a Mountie reported: "The father of these two (*garbled*) . . . they approached (*garbled*) to check out the fire . . . He shot one of them in the head. It's a .40 calibre Smith & Wesson."

The confusion was compounded by the way the commission handled the ballistics analysis. It was dry, technical and jargon-filled, leaving many observers unclear about which guns Wortman had used and how many bullets he had fired. Autopsy reports did not detail the number of shots that hit each individual, merely remarking tersely: "The cause of death was gunshot wounds and the manner of death was homicide."

My podcast partner, lawyer Adam Rodgers, described in his video blog, *The Rodgers Brief*, how the commission's approach to presenting the ballistic evidence on the seventeenth day of its hearings was unusually convoluted. He was particularly critical of commission lawyer Amanda Byrd. Here's what he said:

> After reviewing those incidents, Ms. Byrd reviewed each of the individuals who were killed and outlined the evidence of what was known in each case from a firearms forensics perspective. Most of the deaths could be linked to a particular firearm. Notably, that of Corrie Ellison was not able to be linked to any firearm possessed by Wortman.
>
> I noticed that Ms. Byrd became emotional when going through the forensics report with respect to the death of Kristen Beaton [Wortman's eighteenth victim]. Though these are reports about deaths, the details are somewhat technical and repetitive in nature, and Ms. Byrd's voice and affect had been fairly flat until that point, making the onset of the emotional reaction all the more unexpected when it happened. I do not wish to be unkind to Ms. Byrd, but would note for young lawyers that it is important to control your emotional reactions at such times so as not to detract from your credibility as a professional.
>
> After the first presentation, we received two presentations from commission lawyer Jennifer Cox. These were presentations of expert reports by Saint Mary's professor Blake Brown and University of California Santa Clara professors [Tara] Tober and [Tristan] Bridges. I had expected that we would be hearing from the experts directly, potentially with the chance of them being subjected to follow questions or cross-examination from the counsel for the other participants. This was not to be, and Ms. Cox presented both reports herself.

[Nova Scotia writer] Parker Donham noted on Twitter that the gold standard of inquiries in Nova Scotia (and perhaps Canada) is the Marshall Inquiry, which had only three lawyers, one investigator and one communications person. The Mass Casualty Commission, on the other hand, has at least fifteen lawyers, eight investigators and four communications staff. Perhaps the strategy of having various lawyers conduct presentations is a way of giving each some public speaking parts, but it is not the best way to present an expert report, particularly when it would be so easy to have the expert appear by video to make the presentation themselves, as the witness Benjamin Sampson later appeared from Toronto.

Mr. Sampson was listed as a "technical witness" and lived up to his billing. He testified about the methods used by forensic labs to identify how bullets are linked back to particular firearms. This testimony connected back to some of what Ms. Byrd was presenting in the morning, and hearing it in isolation made me think it would have made sense to have Mr. Sampson analyze the individual details of the casualties and crime scenes while giving his evidence, rather than separating the two sides of the story.

Instead of making this natural connection, we had the disorienting experience of Ms. Byrd listing the forensic details of each deceased in the morning, and Mr. Sampson talking about how conclusions on the forensic evidence for each may have been reached in the afternoon. It almost seemed designed to make it all less interesting.

On top of the confounding presentation, the RCMP-run National Forensic Laboratory Services could not match many of the rounds that killed people to one of Wortman's guns, specifically the Glock 23, which tends not to leave identifiable marks on a projectile passing through its barrel. That report, dated April 10, 2022, two years after the event, was shy on detail. The Mounties and the commission were so determined to put guns in Wortman's hands that they seemed almost incapable of accepting evidence to the contrary. For example, the Mounties found "a .40 calibre handgun with the ammunition clip removed" next to Greg Blair's body. Here is an excerpt from that report:

BLACK 40MM AFTERMATH HANDGUN

The RCMP seized a black 40mm handgun at the Blair residence after the events. This firearm was found on top of the wood pile on the front deck. The firearm had a warning stamp on it that also said it was "Made in Taiwan by Aftermath." On the rubber grips of the firearm, there was a circular imprint with a skull head emblem and the words "Special Operations Command Miami, FL" on both sides. The slide was pulled back and there was no magazine.

The Commission currently does not have evidence to indicate whether the firearm belonged to the perpetrator, whether he fired it during the mass casualty, or whether forensic firearms testing was performed.

It wasn't a gun. Aftermath makes Airsoft toy guns—BB guns. The Blairs had two boys, aged twelve and ten. I wonder who actually owned the "gun" that the commission was still fretting about two years later.

The forensic reports were riddled with a surprising number of typos and outright errors. For example, one document was a map showing the location of the bodies of McCully and Ellison. It placed them both on the east side of Orchard Beach Drive. In fact, Ellison's body was on the west side of the road, as confirmed by GPS and according to eyewitnesses Judy and Doug Myers, who passed by the unguarded bodies the next morning when they drove out of the community. "I saw his feet sticking out from under the tarp," Judy Myers said in an interview. "He was on our left."

Although the RCMP had established a beachhead at Highway 2 and Portapique Beach Road, instead of reinforcing it and moving into the neighbourhood, the Mounties retreated over and over again. Reports from police sources that a distraught female Mountie had left her gun in the woods were never addressed by the commission. And police weapons were not tested after the massacre.

Yet there was this statement by Chief Superintendent Chris Leather in his first two press conferences on April 19 and 20, 2020: "At one point during the course of the evening there was an exchange of gunfire."

Leather said he didn't know where that had taken place, but it appeared to be something that happened in Portapique and not the shooting of RCMP constable Heidi Stevenson the next day. Leather also said the incident would be referred to the Serious Incident Response Team for investigation.

Leather's statement raised the possibility that a Mountie, either alone or as part of a second team, had ventured down Orchard Beach Drive, run into Corrie Ellison and accidentally shot him. No evidence was presented to support that theory, but there was plenty of smoke. Everyone knew the RCMP had destroyed evidence in the weeks and months after the massacres, and it has never revealed what was destroyed. Lisa Banfield was also in that area, she said, hiding in the woods. She told investigators that she had heard occasional shouting and shots but saw nothing.

The commission, however, concluded that Wortman had likely killed Ellison. The children hiding in McCully's house, which featured an almost all-glass front from top to bottom, reported seeing headlights emerging from Wortman's warehouse laneway around the time Ellison was murdered. The commission found that the angle of the shot that killed Ellison appeared to show him leaning into the passenger-side window of a car. It further found that Wortman had gotten out of his car and shot Ellison again while he was on the ground. A speck of Ellison's blood was found on Wortman's boots.

Months later, on July 5, 2022, the commission issued a supplementary report (misdated July 5, 2012) by former Toronto homicide detective Wayne Fowler, who also seemed to struggle to come up with anything conclusive but exonerated any Mounties: "The interior of the barrel of Glock Pistol has smooth arcs rather (than) sharply defined slots. Due to the design of the Glock's barrel, it is extremely difficult for a Forensic Specialist to identify a fired projectile to a Glock Firearm," Fowler wrote. "It is suspected, based on this review, that the projectile located near the decedent [Ellison] is associated to the Glock pistol used by the perpetrator on April 18 and 19, 2020, and not any of the first responders."

The commission also concluded that Corrie Ellison was the thirteenth and last person murdered by Gabriel Wortman in the first massacre, rewriting the RCMP narrative that the Tuck-Olivers and Bonds were killed after. This would open up new questions about Wortman's escape route, which we'll get into in the next chapter. First, let's fill in the rest of the RCMP view of that night.

◆

Shortly after Beselt, Patton, Merchant and Colford arrived on scene, an improvised command centre was set up at the Great Village fire hall, about a seven-minute drive east of Portapique Beach Road. But it was after midnight before anyone in authority arrived on scene and took charge.

The district commander, Superintendent Archie Thompson, all but disappeared that night. He later said he didn't want to get in the way at the fire hall. (A source close to Thompson said he came home in the early-morning hours, grabbed his personal rifle and headed back out.) That left Staff Sergeant Jeffrey West as the designated incident commander. West, who for the past several years had been Nova Scotia's head of traffic services, didn't get to Great Village until almost 1:30 a.m.

At 11:50 p.m., West's traffic services colleague, Staff Sergeant Andy O'Brien, took command from his home. O'Brien had been off on COVID leave, and had been drinking wine and a toot or two of rum, he later admitted to the commission. Nevertheless, he went into a bedroom in his house and began overseeing the first hour of operations, communicating directly with the Mounties on the scene in Portapique. Afterwards, he continued to participate in calling the shots that night, asking his wife to drive him to the RCMP office because he thought he was too tipsy to drive himself.

"I have a very strong sense of responsibility for the members that I'm responsible to. I lost a member in 2017 who worked for me. My nightmare that night was I was going to lose another," O'Brien told the commission via Zoom. Like many others, he was deemed too fragile to appear in public or to be cross-examined. During his appearance, O'Brien said he advised the members to "be very, very cautious; do not be aggressive." Preservation of life is a police officer's first duty, but O'Brien seemed more interested in preserving police lives first. Unfortunately for the four children, who were in a hellish position, modern police thinking seems to discourage selflessness and old-fashioned heroism in favour of safety first.

O'Brien's directions frustrated the Mounties on the ground, a handful of whom later complained about him. One was Constable Nick Dorrington, who had given Wortman a speeding ticket on February 12, 2020. Dorrington was in the second wave of Mounties arriving in Portapique that Saturday night and was assigned to chase the flashing lights in the hamlet of Five Houses, west of the Portapique River.

Dorrington looked like a veteran RCMP member, but he had joined the force in 2015 as he approached the age of fifty. He had spent seventeen years in the military as a soldier in the Balkans, Bosnia and the Persian Gulf War, and another thirteen years as a civilian in the military. In between, he'd studied Internet technology for eighteen months before giving up. "The RCMP wanted broken, retired military people and I said yes."

In an interview with the commission on the thirty-eighth day of the hearings, Dorrington said: "I'm not sure why Sergeant O'Brien was on the air, in all honesty. He wasn't on duty. He wasn't even actively on duty. He was on COVID restrictions. He's not qualified. And what I mean by that is he's not Immediate Action Rapid Deployment qualified. He doesn't have the training on active shooter situations, which is problematic. We all know that. And the directions that we were being given are contrary to IARD doctrine, so that's a challenge. So I'm receiving direction . . . from a superior who's not on scene, who's not on duty, who's not qualified. So that's where we were. So that's what we did."

A further complication was that the incident commander was being overruled by the "risk manager," Staff Sergeant Brian Rehill, whose job, it seemed, was for the RCMP to avoid risk at almost any cost. The RCMP policy was safety first. By the book!

While the first wave of Mounties to the scene might have been enough to secure the area and trap Wortman, everything was placed in a virtual holding pattern until members of the force's Emergency Response Team (ERT)—the equivalent of SWAT teams in the US— arrived. After incidents such as Mayerthorpe and Moncton, heroism had been banned for front-line Mounties. The force had been fined in the past and warned about greater fines and possible imprisonment for future violations. Everyone had to wait for the ERT, who are trained in the use of special weapons and tactics, unlike first responders. Members of the unit were scattered all over the province and had to assemble and gear up in Halifax, then drive to the Great Village fire hall, where they made final preparations. By that time, it was 12:29 p.m. and they were still six kilometres from Portapique.

In the interim, the RCMP positioned about nine units to the west of Portapique, but not to the east, where Wortman would find an escape route while a handful of brave members charged around the decimation in Portapique.

The fact that the children were still in McCully's house and that the Mounties had no idea where Wortman might be created extreme tension between those who wanted to launch a rescue mission and their superiors, who were trying to avoid all risk. The incident commanders refused to send anyone else into the community for fear that there might be a "blue-on-blue" shooting—Mounties shooting Mounties.

To appreciate the roots of the unfolding catastrophe that led to Wortman's roaming around Nova Scotia and killing twenty-two people that night and the next morning, one must first understand what the Mounties were doing after they arrived at the scene, beginning at 10:26 p.m., more than an hour before O'Brien took charge from afar. They didn't seem to realize that they had Wortman cornered in a neighbourhood where there was only one official road in and out and one unofficial laneway several hundred metres to the east—the so-called blueberry field road. While it might have appeared that the Mounties had sealed off the intersection of Portapique Beach Road and Highway 2, the facts suggest otherwise.

When Beselt, Merchant and Patton ventured into the community, they left behind Constable Vicki Colford, who appeared to have been overwhelmed by all that was going on around her. When Constable Travise Dow arrived at 10:43 p.m., he gave Colford his shotgun, while he pulled out his C8 and took a position in a drainage ditch. This is a critical period in the narrative of what ultimately transpired.

GPS records show that Corporal Natasha Jamieson arrived at 11:01 p.m. and was then the officer in charge at the scene. Although she was a supervisor and had joined the force at the same time as Colford, she, too, was not carbine-trained. She said she had missed carbine qualification because of a foot injury she had suffered on the job. The net effect was that the two officers left to seal the community and capture the shooter if necessary were not tactically trained, a persistent problem inside the RCMP.

When the call came in, Jamieson had been sitting in her cruiser having a door-to-door chat—conforming to COVID distancing regulations—with Constable Chris Grund at the Millbrook First Nation detachment. She and Grund raced to Portapique, taking different routes to see what each might notice. Once she became the officer in charge at the scene, some thought Jamieson showed signs of being overwhelmed.

On the radio chatter, Jamieson's superiors were telling her not to take any needless risks, which translated into no risks whatsoever. By then she knew about the children in the house, but she believed they were safe because Beselt, Merchant and Patton were hunkered down somewhere near them. Instead, however, the trio was roaming all over the neighbourhood.

Constable Grund, a Mountie since 2002, arrived soon after Jamieson and found Constable Travise Dow and another Mountie standing in a drainage ditch "protecting" the ambulance in which Andrew MacDonald was being tended. Grund tried to convince them that they should mount an expedition to rescue the four children in McCully's basement. "We should be going down there," Grund recalled saying. The two Mounties didn't respond or even look at him.

Grund felt compelled to go above Jamieson's head; he used one of the two cellphones he was carrying to contact the command centre, likely talking to risk manager Staff Sergeant Brian Rehill. Grund declined to testify at the public hearings but did an interview with commission lead counsel Roger Burrill and two others sixteen months after the incident, in August 2021, and submitted a signed affidavit on June 23, 2022, during the public hearings. The private cellphone records of the Mounties on duty that night and the next morning were not examined by the commission or provided to the public.

When I first pieced this part of the story together for news stories in 2020 and 2021 and for *22 Murders*, it was at a time when the RCMP was refusing to name names or confirm anything that might be controversial. I was determined to put names on the public record. To add to the confusion, when the force did name names, the information wasn't always accurate. In one Information to Obtain (ITO) document, Sergeant Dave Lilly (referred to as a constable) was described by Constable Shawn Stanton as being on scene with Constable Grund when the children were rescued. The ITO was revised many times over the next two years, but that never changed. Supported by interviews with police sources, I wrote in *22 Murders* that Sergeant Lilly was part of the rescue effort. Two years later, the RCMP said Lilly wasn't there at that point. He eventually became involved in the rescue of the children but was not there initially. He was then dropped a rank, to corporal. Why? We don't know.

As Grund was pushing to rescue the children, Constable Dow and the other Mounties on the scene were assigned by the command centre to join a growing contingent that was chasing reports of flashing lights on the other side of the Portapique River, about one and a half kilometres to the west. The Mounties seemed to think Wortman might have crossed the swollen river at the peak of the 12-metre high tide that night.

Constable William (Bill) Neil from Stellarton showed up at the scene and introduced himself to Jamieson. She ignored him, he said in a post-incident interview with the commission. He, too, thought she seemed frozen, so he also jumped the chain of command and made a cellphone call to the command centre: "Who's in charge? I don't know who's in charge." Neil offered to testify before the commission, but he was never called.

Neil and Grund decided to take matters into their own hands. Something had to be done. They were concerned that Wortman might be in the house with the kids, or near enough to set the house on fire. The children needed to be rescued.

Neil and Grund's transcripts imply that they had a confrontation with Jamieson, and as other police sources told me, an RCMP corporal was quoted as saying, "If you go down there, this will be your last shift in the RCMP."

"I was getting pretty pissed off, right?" Neil said. "Here we are—we have an active shooter and three or four, I'm not sure, dead. We have an active shooter moving through the community setting fires, fucking explosions . . . so we really don't know anything at this point. So I said—a little upset—'Fuck this, I'm going to do something.' And Grund was like, 'Yes, let's go do something.'"

Grund recalled: "I don't know if we asked permission or not, but once we, he agreed, we went."

The two Mounties believed it was their sworn duty—preservation of life—to get the children out as expeditiously as possible.

Finally, at 11:50 p.m., Staff Sergeant Andy O'Brien began barking orders. He told Grund and Neil to make their way to McCully's house. A minute later, they started down Orchard Beach Drive. The distance from their position to the house was about 600 to 700 metres. It was pitch-dark and horror-movie scary. Grund had been using his RCMP phone all day, and it was almost out of battery power. The constables couldn't drive in because the risk manager deemed it too risky. (Ironically, the Mounties were telling residents to drive out of the community in their personal vehicles, unprotected.)

Meanwhile, amid all this chaos, a shaken but uninjured Kate MacDonald was being tended to in Constable Vicki Colford's cruiser. MacDonald's husband, Andrew, had been taken to the hospital in an ambulance. In her statement, Jamieson recalled Kate MacDonald mumbling over and over again, "It looked like a police car," describing what Wortman was driving when he shot at them.

As they made their way down Orchard Beach Drive, Grund and Neil came across a man sitting on his porch, drinking beer, as if he were being entertained by all the commotion. The Mounties told him to go inside. About halfway to McCully's house, they ran into another resident, Bjorn Merzbach, who lived across from the Gulenchyns and was carrying a shotgun. The Mounties levelled their guns at Merzbach and ordered him to the ground until it was clear he was not the shooter.

Merzbach told them he had sent his wife, Allison Francis, and their two children out of the community, but he intended to stay with his dog and his shotgun to protect his property. (Recall that he'd met Jerry Murphy at the fence line around 11 p.m., when they had both been out investigating the house fire at the Gulenchyns.) The Mounties thought Merzbach was being belligerent and ordered him to leave. They even threatened him with arrest—though this was just a threat, as they had no time to waste. Merzbach eventually got into his truck to head out. "Take your shotgun with you," Beselt told him, not wanting a weapon left lying around for the shooter, should he come that way.

Before Merzbach left, he told the Mounties that he was familiar with guns and had heard shots: "You know, I'm a sportsman. I shoot regularly. I could tell, you know, there's two different firearms. I heard five or seven shots out of a rifle and four additional gunshots out of a different gun." The shots were quick and almost overlapping, to Merzbach's ears. He thought it sounded like two different shooters. Later, he had also heard the two shots that wounded Andrew MacDonald, and saw him, Wortman and another car (Faulkner) driving north on the road.

The Mounties continued down the road. They passed the Blair house on their left and arrived at McCully's house at 12:07 p.m., where they found the children in the basement. They told the kids to get dressed and then led them out the door. There was no safe way for them all to walk back up to the highway, so they located the keys to McCully's car, a tiny beat-up Suzuki Swift hatchback, which was parked in the driveway. There was only enough room inside for Grund and the children. "Get out of Dodge," Neil told Grund, and stayed behind, later joining up with Beselt and the others.

Grund squeezed into the driver's seat, his C8 carbine between his legs, started the car and backed out of the driveway. It was now 12:25 p.m., two hours and nine minutes since the children had placed their 911 call.

"Is that my mom over there?" one of McCully's children asked, having noticed the body slumped against the rail fence.

"Guys," Grund recalled responding, trying to calm his nerves. "You know . . . I can't tell you. I really don't know. I just need you guys to remain calm. Just try to remain calm and . . . we'll get somewhere safe, because, right now, it's not safe being here. We have to just get out of here."

Orchard Beach Drive had recently been regraded to cover up the pot-holes that form during winter, but that didn't make it much smoother. Rocks poked out of the dirt. Grund had to drive slowly. It was approaching 1 a.m. and the RCMP still had not mustered enough resources or courage to offer the children protection.

Once they got up to Highway 2, Grund kept driving until they reached the command centre at the Great Village fire hall. The children were then taken by ambulance to the Colchester East Hants Health Centre, the hospital in Truro, with Grund and Sergeant Lilly escorting them. They arrived at the hospital around 1:25 a.m., almost three and a half hours after their ordeal had begun.

Some might say that Grund and Neil were the only true Mountie heroes that weekend. Inside the halls of the RCMP, however, others thought they were loose cannons who didn't follow orders. Considering the unusual way in which the two Mounties were interviewed, it seemed the commission felt the same. Grund and Neil were interviewed on August 19 and September 17, 2021, respectively. Normally, such interviews were conducted by the commission's investigators—all those retired Ontario police officers—but Grund and Neil got special treatment. Their primary interrogator was the commission's chief counsel, Roger Burrill.

Two hours and thirty-six minutes into the three-and-a-half-hour interview, Burrill asked why Grund had not contacted Jamieson once he had the children. "You trusted her, obviously, and she was your supervisor?" Burrill asked.

"Yeah," Grund said.

"That might be a person I would call if I was in that situation," Burrill said. "You didn't. I'm trying to figure out why that was."

"I think at that point we . . . we didn't hear a direct response on that, so we just . . ." Grund said, deflecting the question. He clearly wasn't about to throw Jamieson under the bus.

"No, it's clearly your decision, and in the end, it was a good decision," Burrill said. "The kids got out. I guess my question is . . . the risk manager could have directed somebody to bring in a car . . . It's not clear to me why that didn't occur, and I don't know if it's clear to you."

"I don't think it is. I don't know. I don't know," Grund said. "And, once again, I questioned myself why I didn't bring a car in, too, right."

"In that instance, though, you told me, earlier, Moncton was something on your mind."

"Yeah. And I think that was probably looming on everyone's mind, maybe. I don't know."

Both Grund and Neil were unhappy with how the force had handled the situation, including wasting manpower chasing flashing lights on the other side of the high-tide-swollen Portapique River. That was one of the reasons why they weren't called to speak in public like Beselt, Merchant and Patton, each of whom thought they had done their best in the most trying of circumstances. They had tried to draw Wortman out of the woods where they assumed he was hiding, but that didn't work. In their group testimony before the commission, they said they together had assumed that he had committed suicide, after they heard a random shot in the middle of the night.

The alternative Mountie theory was that Wortman had died in the fire at his cottage, which may have suited Wortman's plan to fake his own death but didn't make much sense. After all, he had been seen killing people in the community well after the fire was roaring. The assumption that Wortman had committed suicide was based on two incompatible theories of the events. That alone should have set off more alarm bells. After hours of not making contact with him, the RCMP should have stormed the area with overwhelming force and taken control of the situation. It didn't. The Mounties thought they had Wortman trapped in Portapique, and that he had likely killed himself. Thanks to their false assumptions, he got away to kill nine more people the next day.

9

A KEY RCMP "ALIBI" HUNG BY A ROPE

Wortman was still in Portapique when the first Mounties arrived on scene, but he would elude them and go on to murder nine more people the next day. In the aftermath of the two massacres, the big question was: How did Wortman escape Portapique undetected by the police?

There were only two ways out of the community. One was up Orchard Beach Drive to Portapique Beach Road to Highway 2, where the RCMP units were staging. The other was an informal, almost two-kilometre-long route just to the east of Orchard Beach Drive that ran between a line of trees and a 215-acre blueberry field. It was a rutted dirt and gravel path that connected to Brown Loop, another potholed, barely passable dirt road. A 750-metre-long semicircle, Brown Loop intersected with Highway 2 in two locations east of Portapique Beach Road. Which way did Wortman go?

When the RCMP originally described what had happened at Portapique, it didn't yet know the precise order in which the victims had been killed. The approximate story was that Wortman had raced around like a commando and likely killed his last five victims—Aaron Tuck, Jolene Oliver, Emily Tuck, and Peter and Joy Bond—in their homes on Cobequid Court before scooting out of the neighbourhood via the blueberry field road by 10:45 p.m. With what we knew in April 2020, it appeared that Wortman had plenty of time to take that route.

This escape route would lessen the RCMP's liability. The force could argue that its members had no way of knowing about the blueberry field road and had done its best but had failed to contain a clever madman.

In 2022, after the forensic examination of Ellison's phone came back showing that his last photo was taken at precisely 10:40:12 p.m., the time frame for Wortman's escape narrowed considerably. As a result, the commission concluded that Ellison was the last victim, and that Wortman must have murdered the Tuck-Olivers and the Bonds earlier in the evening. But there are some obstacles to that narrative. As I pointed out in the previous chapter, when Wortman encountered Ellison, he may have exited his vehicle, walked around to the other side and shot Ellison two more times. That would have pushed his departure time to closer to 10:41. The distance from the warehouse to the edge of the blueberry field road was a little more than a kilometre along bumpy Orchard Beach Drive, so if Wortman did head for that escape route, it would likely have taken him around one and a half to two minutes, making it close to 10:43 by the time he got there.

Judy and Doug Myers, who lived down Orchard Beach Drive close to Cobequid Court, did not recall hearing Wortman roar by in his replica police car. "If he killed the Tucks and the Bonds early on, that meant he would have had to pass my house going to and from their houses. Then, if he left by going through the blueberry field, that would have been a third trip," Judy Meyers said in an interview. "We were watching television, and we might not have seen him. That's possible, but unlikely. If he was racing around like that, I think we would have seen or heard him at least one of those times."

Another unforeseen obstacle came from a most unlikely source, one of the RCMP's original incident commanders, Staff Sergeant Allan (Al) Carroll. Carroll had been in the RCMP for forty years. Off the job, he was a well-liked boys' hockey and soccer coach, popular pastimes for many Mounties. On the job, he had done just about everything a Mountie could do in federal and contract policing without going to the next level and earning his white shirt. He was the boss of his area, the district commander, an old-school cop, gruff and by the book.

When the massacres occurred, he was a month away from retirement. It was not a time for him to learn new ways of doing things. One Mountie who had worked with Carroll said his aversion to learning wasn't a recent development: "Al used to say, 'If I don't know about it, it doesn't exist.'" Carroll didn't have updated programs on his computer. Although Twitter was the RCMP's designated medium for communicating with the public, he said he "didn't do Twitter very well." Like most Mounties in Nova Scotia at the time, one of the things he knew nothing about was the Alert Ready warning system, which was operational but had never been used in the province.

Carroll was a proud generational Mountie. His son, Jordan, had joined the RCMP and served in Manitoba before being transferred back to Nova Scotia, where he was assigned to the Cumberland County detachment at Parrsboro. In fact, that Saturday night, Jordan was the one who called his father at his home in Valley, where he was watching a hockey game, to let him know what was going on in Portapique.

"Hey, Dad, you probably want to know about this," Al recalled Jordan saying. "There's something going on in Colchester. We're all responding to a shooting incident."

Jordan had been dispatched to the scene and was one of the Mounties chasing flashing lights in Five Houses, west of Portapique.

On November 10, 2021, seventeen months after the massacres, Al Carroll was finally interviewed by Mass Casualty Commission investigators Wayne Fowler and Chris Lussow. Also in the room were Nasha Nijhawan, the police union lawyer, and Lori Ward from the federal Department of Justice for the Attorney General of Canada. It looked like another routine, no-surprises affair. Carroll was a Mountie loyalist. By the time he was interviewed, much had changed. Carroll was now retired. The stress of what had happened to him and the RCMP that weekend had turned him to drinking, something about which he wasn't proud. Nevertheless, he was a stalwart, not the kind of guy who would consider soiling the serge.

During the fifty-nine-minute interview, Carroll recounted what had happened that night and into the next morning, praising his fellow members and the RCMP, with one notable exception that provided a telling glimpse into the internal workings of the force.

Carroll and his fellow staff sergeants were at the command centre set up at the Great Village fire hall on Sunday morning. After a hectic night, everything had gone quiet. No one knew where Wortman might be. They assumed he was dead and were in the first stages of mopping up and patting themselves on the back when a White Shirt whom Carroll didn't know walked into the room. Everyone, including Carroll, ignored him.

The White Shirt was Inspector Robert (Rob) Bell, who had taken a Sunday drive from RCMP Nova Scotia headquarters in Dartmouth to the Great Village fire hall. His business card read: "Officer in Charge: Career Development and Resources." Why he was at the command centre was anyone's guess, but his presence said more about the RCMP than it probably would like the world to know.

After graduating from Depot in 1995, Bell had spent six years in Indigenous policing before gravitating toward the job that all but guarantees a favourable career inside the force: banging his butt against the back of a horse for a couple of years in the RCMP's entertainment division, the Musical Ride. The Ride is a nostalgia-driven barnstorming spectacle featuring up to thirty-two horse-riding Mounties recreating the earliest days of the force. After dismounting, Bell moved into the administrative and command stream in Manitoba. A year before the massacres, he had earned his white shirt and was transferred to Halifax. He didn't know much about the province, it seems, and his fellow Mounties didn't know much about him.

While everyone else in the command centre was working that Sunday morning, Bell appeared to be a wallflower. He made thirty-nine pages of notes, including this one at 12:44 p.m., after it appeared that it was all over:

When I arrived at the [command post], I expected it to be chaotic, but it wasn't what I expected. It was organized. Radio channels managed. Two projector screens up with maps. Everyone composed and everyone doing their job. There was some misinformation coming in, but not a lot. It was easily navigated in this instance. On a personal level, I was confused by some of the locations, highways, directions, as I was unfamiliar with the area. Everyone else seemed more comfortable with information coming in. I was the ranking member in the room, but no one was looking to me to take over control, and I wasn't in a position to take over. The situation was under control. . . . The gravity of what had taken place did not hit me until much later. My only thoughts were of Heidi and her family and doing what needed to be done to piece everything together.

Carroll, who continued to be in a command position, wanted to check things out, hand out assignments and deliver some food and drinks to the Mounties who were in Portapique. It was a neighbourhood that he had visited only once before. He recalled how he drove to the community that morning along with Staff Sergeant Andy O'Brien, who had overseen the response in its first hours from a distance and by now had purged the wine and rum he had been drinking the night before from his system.

At the conclusion of the interview, Carroll described how devasting it had all been. "It's the worst . . . one of the worst nights of my life . . . I want to say something more before we finish off . . . Every commander, your biggest fear is losing a member. And I was scared. I've been involved in a lot of situations in the forty years . . . I went home, hugged my wife and cried. And I never had that response before. So, yeah, it's affected all of us, incredibly."

The recorder was shut off, but the parties stayed in the room and continue to chit-chat.

One hour and five minutes after the interview had ended, Fowler and Lussow switched the recording equipment back on to capture an afterthought that had come to Carroll while he was talking with Nijhawan and Ward. He thought he should put it on the record because it might be helpful.

Carroll described dropping off O'Brien and then driving down to "Cobequid Road," actually Cobequid Court. At 10:48 p.m. the night before, Constable Colford had alerted everyone about the blueberry field road, but by then Wortman was likely gone. Now Carroll was facing east, toward the blueberry field. On their imprecise aerial maps at the command centre the previous night, he and his colleagues hadn't seen the dirt road that ran behind the tree line north to Brown Loop and then Highway 2.

As Carroll studied the scene, he noted the well-kept ranch-style bungalow with three garages on his left, at 2 Cobequid Court. To his and the RCMP's everlasting shame, he didn't realize that behind him, across the intersection with Orchard Beach Drive, were five more dead bodies: Aaron Tuck, Jolene Oliver and Emily Tuck at 41 Cobequid Court, and Peter and Joy Bond at 46 Cobequid Court. They wouldn't be discovered until just before 5 p.m. later that day.

Carroll was focused on what was ahead of him. He was trying to understand how Wortman had slipped away unseen. "There was a nice house on the left-hand side and the end of that road was a . . . an entryway into the field, into a blueberry hay field, or blueberry field. And that morning, when I was there, I said, 'Oh, there's a barrier up.' There was a chain . . . a chain barrier, a chain or wire across the top, and there was some type of marking thing to identify the chain was there. That was in place when I was there in the morning, would have been sometime between 10 and 10:30 (a.m.), 10 and 12 (noon). So that chain was definitely in place, and if that was the egress point that Wortman used, I'm saying he would have had to stop, take the chain out . . . take the wire off, drive through and . . . put the chain back in place, put it back up. Otherwise, the height would have cleaned the lightbar or anything off the roof of a car."

"Just a note on that question," Lussow said. "Did you know: Was it locked, or did you make a note of like . . . ?"

"No, I didn't," Carroll said.

Carroll's contemporaneous notes from that day had not mentioned the chain at all. It never crossed his mind that it was important. He was asked repeatedly if he remembered anyone at the house at 2 Cobequid Court. He thought he might have, but it was such a long time ago, he couldn't accurately recall.

The addendum to the interview took a mere two minutes and thirty-one seconds, and then the recorder was turned off for good. Carroll's afterthought was a product of his lifelong training to do the right thing. Everything mattered, no matter how small it might be. That might well be, but Carroll had forgotten the unspoken creed of the RCMP: "Protect the Buffalo." His story about the chain would complicate the RCMP's original, albeit sketchy, narrative.

When it came time for the commission to address the blueberry field road, they didn't lead with Carroll's statement, as one might expect, but with the testimony of the owner of 2 Cobequid Court: Debra Thibeault—a name that had not come up in the previous two years.

◆

On March 30, 2022, two days after the commission heard from constables Beselt, Merchant and Patton, Commissioner MacDonald opened the session by thanking them for adding "to our understanding of what happened and why, building on the factual record we are assembling through our foundational documents."

The next witness was Debra Thibeault, who lived at 2 Cobequid Court along with her husband, Peter.

"Ms. Thibeault has offered to provide relevant information regarding the—what has been referred to as the 'blueberry field road,'" MacDonald said.

Remember, Carroll's statement was still under wraps. He wouldn't be coming before the commission for another fifty-seven days, so the public had no sense of that background as Thibeault spoke (which seems like an odd way of getting at the truth, as the inquiry said it would do).

Thibeault quickly established that it was not a chain or wire across the road, but a length of fisherman's nylon rope with a sign that read either "Private Property" or "Emergency Access." As Carroll remembered, it was hung about waist high across the opening to the blueberry field.

"When you were living at 2 Cobequid Court, how often would you observe this entranceway?" commission counsel Jamie Van Wart asked.

"Every day, because when I'm on my verandah, doorstep, I just look—it's—I'm in that direction looking," Thibeault said, adding, "And when I park my car, it's right there, so all the time."

Thibeault said she and her husband left Portapique around noon on Saturday, April 18, and drove to Halifax.

Van Wart wanted to know if the rope was in place when they left.

"Like any other day," she said. "Nothing was out of place."

"If it had been out of place, what would you have done?"

"I'd go over and put it back together," Thibeault said.

"When did you return to Portapique after the eighteenth of April 2020?" Van Wart asked.

"It was within three days," she said. "I was thinking that maybe it was the second, but they wouldn't let me down there. And then they did. I think it—maybe it was a Wednesday, and only I was allowed down to check my property because they told me that my house burnt."

"And when you say 'they', who are you talking about?"

"The RCMP . . . I wasn't allowed to stay. Just allowed to go down and see what was left of my property."

As it turned out, she was escorted to her property by the RCMP and was "pleasantly surprised" to find that it was entirely unaffected.

"Okay," Van Wart said, "did you make any observations with regards to the entranceway to the blueberry field when you returned?"

"Well, I didn't have much time," Thibeault said. "Like, I had to see my property and get out of there. So it looked like the rope was down, but there's people, like, you know, everywhere . . . I've only got so many minutes and I have to go."

Thibeault then recalled returning to the property about a week later with her husband and taking a closer look at the entrance to the blueberry field. "We returned that way, and I noticed that half of the top of the post was gone; like, the bottom part was gone, like, split off . . . 'Holy, what happened there? Someone drove through there. Where's the rope? Where's that?' So I walked over to it and the rope was still . . . attached to the top and it was swung over . . ." The rope was lying on the ground beside the road.

In response to a later question from commissioner Leanne Fitch about the broken post, Thibeault said: "It took a banging. The post took a banging. And so you could see that."

Thibeault's testimony, coming as it did so early in the process, seemed inexplicable. It wasn't clear what the commission lawyers were trying to prove. Thibeault said the rope had been up just before the massacres and that when she got home—days afterwards—the post was smashed and the rope was down.

If the commission was suggesting that Wortman stopped his vehicle, got out, unfastened the rope, got back into his car, drove forward past the gate, got out of his car, reattached the rope, returned to his car and then drove through up the blueberry field road, that created a problem with timing. In order for the RCMP story to hold up, he had a little more than four minutes from the time Corrie Ellison was killed to the time they said he got to Brown Loop. With the road conditions, it would take him about two minutes to get to the blueberry field fence. It would take him about two to three minutes to navigate the blueberry field road. He couldn't afford seconds here and there. And what about the smashed post? Were they suggesting that he crashed through the barrier, cutting down on the timeline? And if he hadn't crashed through, then who had?

In her testimony, Thibeault said that when she returned to her house on those days, she noticed that the RCMP had set up tents in the blueberry patch for its members who were investigating the multiple scenes. No one else was in the community. The logical inference was that someone in the RCMP had knocked down the post. Was it an accident? Or was it part of the force's strategy to firm up its preferred narrative? At that time, it might have looked convenient to blame Wortman for everything.

When it was Carroll's turn to speak to the commission on May 26, 2022, Commissioner Leanne Fitch introduced him with the usual fanfare: "Today, we continue our work by hearing from Staff Sergeant Al Carroll, who, like all witnesses we have heard so far, will be asked questions developed by commission counsel in the public interest. The commission counsel are impartial and tasked with vigorously seeking the truth."

What transpired was a lesson in how adept lawyers are at pretending to be pursuing the truth when they are really doing the opposite—asking questions designed to *not* get to the truth.

The once tough and brusque Carroll had been reduced to yet another delicate flower. He was so traumatized by events, the commission had ruled earlier, that he could testify only via Zoom. He could ask for a break any time. The commission's "vigorous" search for the truth would not include a rigorous cross-examination. Lawyer Josh Bryson was designated as the only representative of the victims' families to ask questions, but he wasn't allowed to roam very far.

The issue of the rope, which had been important enough to be the focus of one of the earliest sessions in the inquiry, had faded in its importance two months later. After Carroll had answered questions for about two and a half hours, commission counsel Burrill casually asked him about driving down to Cobequid Court that Sunday morning.

"I remember driving down there. That was heading towards the blueberry field, where the egress was," Carroll said. "I see basically—I believe it was a chain. I think it was a chain barrier or a wire barrier across the top of a couple fence posts . . ."

"Okay," Burrill continued, "are you able to estimate or give us some sense of what time that would have been when you made that observation?"

"Between ten and twelve," Carroll said.

"And when you made that observation, was it of any significance to you, given your knowledge of the area at that point?"

"At that point, I looked in," Carroll said. He recalled thinking, "Okay, here's a road into the blueberry field that we hadn't found before."

One would think that Burrill might probe deeper at that point, but he immediately shifted gears: "Now, that's a description of what you saw on the east side of Cobequid Court. Did you attend the western side of Cobequid Court? The other end?"

"No, I don't think so," Carroll said.

And that was that. The commission wasn't interested in how and where the fence was smashed, just the theory that Wortman had gone through the blueberry field. Within the foundational documents, there were other witness statements that mentioned a car driving through the field.

Ronald and Patricia Zimmerman were home that night with their reclusive son Patrick, who lived with them, and their daughter Marybeth, and her husband, Connor Laughren, who were visiting from Ontario. Their house was about three-quarters of the way up the blueberry field road, south of Leon Joudrey's house at 140 Portapique Crescent. At 10:33 p.m., Patricia called 911 to report the fire at Wortman's warehouse to the west.

In interviews after the massacres, each of the family members said they had seen a vehicle moving north on the blueberry field road after Patricia called 911, sometime between 10 and 11 p.m. It wasn't a clear view because the vehicle lights were on the other side of the thick tree line and they couldn't identify the vehicle. Some of them thought it was white; one thought it was a truck because it rode high and was rather noisy. There seemed little doubt that they had seen *something*, but the questions remained: What did they see and when did they see it?

Ronald Zimmerman declined to give a second statement to the commission. His wife and son did provide statements, but they were never called as witnesses.

In April 2022, I had this to say about the stories of the Zimmermans and Laughrens: "I have seen their house from the vantage point of the blueberry field. It would be all but impossible to make out anything, and the timeline is problematic."

In fact, the noisy vehicle was heard on the other side of the neighbourhood by Constable Aaron Patton well after 11 p.m. He was near the McCully house at the time and heard it to the east, which would place it around the Zimmermans' house. "We heard it in the woods," Patton said. "It had a really loud exhaust. Like, uh, an old beater car or something like that, but it wasn't a rumbling exhaust. It was like someone romping on, uh, a vehicle."

Patton's observation aside, the Zimmermans' story was good enough for the RCMP and the commission to accept that Wortman had escaped via the blueberry field.

However, there was one more witness.

10

A PHONE CALL FROM BEYOND

Dean Dillman worked as a forester at the Department of Lands and Forests with Leon Joudrey. He had a background in wildland firefighting, in both Alberta and Nova Scotia. After the fires broke out that Saturday night, his mother, Autumn Doucette, called him at 10:25 p.m. and 10:32 p.m. to tell him what was going on. She then left her home on Five Houses Road and made her way to the west bank of the Portapique River. She found a spot with a clear view of the other side and took photos of the fires blazing there. One was Wortman's cottage and the other the Zahl-Thomas house.

Dillman, who lived nearby, had already packed up his firefighting gear—a Nomex jacket, boots and a hard hat—hopped into his white Subaru Outback and driven east on Highway 2. He noticed four or five Mountie cruisers assembled about 50 metres down Portapique Beach Road. About 200 metres later along Highway 2, Dillman was about to turn right into the western entrance to Brown Loop when he called his mother with an update. "I'm just turning into Brown Loop," he told her.

It would have taken Dillman a minute or more to navigate around the potholes along the 350-metre-long western arm of the dirt lane. He came to a stop at the southwest corner of the road, where it bent to the east. He was parked at the top of the blueberry field road. Dillman turned off his lights and got out of the car, leaned against the hood and tried to assess the situation. He used an azimuth to get his directional bearings. Joudrey's house was on the other side of a meadow. Dillman tried to locate it in the dark. It appeared to line up perfectly with one of the multiple fires he could see, likely the one from Wortman's warehouse. Dillman said he phoned Joudrey to check on him, but he got no answer.

Dillman left after talking to a friend for three minutes and then getting a message from his mother that she had been frightened by someone lurking in the woods near her.

Nobody knew that Dillman had been on Brown Loop until April 30, 2020, eleven days after the massacre and one day after Superintendent Darren Campbell had given his press conference, in which he said the force had received more recent reports that Wortman may have driven across a field and escaped to the east of Portapique, but they were still unsure.

Being the police, the RCMP were trusted to provide accurate and truthful information on a matter that was clearly in the public interest. When Campbell called the press conference on April 29, the RCMP had had ten full days to digest what had happened. It had access to all the information, especially the times when its own members and the public had seen things. It had to know the time when the children reported seeing a vehicle leave the warehouse and the time stamp on Corrie Ellison's phone showing that he was alive as late as 10:40 p.m., though these facts wouldn't be revealed to the public until the commission two years later. At the time of the press conference, though, there was no plan to hold a public inquiry, merely a review conducted behind closed doors. The RCMP was clearly making assumptions—making the narrative fit the available facts, which were not all the facts.

The next day, April 30, Dillman walked into an RCMP field office set up on Brown Loop and told the Mountie manning the desk that he was worried someone might have seen him there. He didn't want investigators wasting time chasing a false lead.

This must have hit the Mounties like a bolt out of the blue. Dillman was interviewed the next day by Constable Kevin Ashley. Sitting in was Staff Sergeant Greg Vardy, who seemed to be a gatekeeper of key information. Vardy was the non-commissioned officer in charge of the Truth Verification Section, one of the RCMP's experts on interviewing and polygraphs, and the main contact for Lisa Banfield. In 2018, Vardy and Sergeant Fraser Firth, another polygrapher, who interviewed both Leon Joudrey and Peter Griffon, had developed a "business plan" for a new system of interviewing to be used by the RCMP in Nova Scotia. It was called the Interview Assistance Team. They would develop standards for interviewers, train them and help with major investigations. With mini detachments everywhere and local constables responsible for doing every kind of investigation, Vardy and Firth thought it would be a good idea to make every Mountie operate at a higher level when it came to questioning suspects and witnesses. They planned to seek out and train strong interrogators and interviewers for their team. Their main tool would be the recently developed Phased Interview Model for Suspects, an alternative to the Reid model used by many police forces since the 1950s. The Reid model creates a high-pressure environment for the person being interviewed, which is followed by sympathy, offers of understanding and help. We've all seen it in hard-nosed TV police series and in the movies. Over the years, the approach has been criticized for inducing false confessions from juveniles and people with mental impairments. Eager to improve, the RCMP liked what it saw and bought into Vardy and Firth's model.

In the new RCMP version, after preparation and the introduction of legal and other obligations to a subject, there is a dialogue phase. The interviewer sits back and prods the subject to talk. This is called "the pure version" interview. That story is then challenged, leading to an accusation and persuasion phase and finally a post-interview phase.

In a later interview conducted by the commission, Vardy described what he did, saying: "Pure version interviewing is when you ask open-ended questions to elicit as much information as possible from their words and no one else's. Right. So we use open-ended questions. You revisit the facts. I used their terms and language to communicate, and you basically funnel down on information they provide. So the idea in a pure version statement is that they will do a large percentage of the talking. I'll have very few questions and any question that I ask should be in an open format. And then you funnel down the information they provide to get further details."

In his own interview with commission investigators, Firth said: "When I'm doing an investigation, I'm in a canoe on a river. I have no paddles. I let the evidence take me where I need to go. I interview with the same principle . . . Using pure version interviewing is often a tool, sorry, an outcome, rather, that will take care of itself. So I'm not going into an interview looking to discredit anyone or to add credibility. You know, the truth is the truth is the truth, whatever they have to say."

When it came time to interview Dillman, Vardy sat back and let Ashley conduct what seemed to be an innocuous sixteen-minute pure version interview.

"I want you to be as detailed as possible," Constable Ashley told Dillman. "'Cause, like I said before this recording started, you know, everything is important . . . and something that may seem small can actually be very big when you have other pieces of the puzzle."

"Um, like I said, I don't have a whole lot," Dillman said, as he laid out how his mother had told him about the fires. "I was there probably ten minutes. I would say 10:45 to 10:55 p.m. Um, left, drove out the same way I went in, and that was all. That's all I really have for you guys . . . I don't have any information beyond that . . . I probably drove over his tire tracks."

Almost eighteen months later, the commission brought him back for another interview, this time with its investigators Dwayne King and Chris Lussow. They spent fifty minutes with him. Dillman told the same story. From his point of view, he just wanted the commission to know that he wasn't Wortman, nothing more. He clearly didn't appreciate his importance in the scheme of things. He was anything but specific. Once again, he guessed that he had had been parked on Brown Loop from 10:45 p.m. to about 10:55 p.m.

"When I left, I can't remember if it was as I was leaving or if I . . . when I was still sitting outside on Brown Loop, but at that approximate time, my mother had called me and she was over on Bay Shore Road, which is on the west side of the Portapique Marsh." He suggested that his mother would know better from her phone records. "I don't have specific times. She likely does."

In both interviews with Dillman, his interrogators emphasized, as they usually do, that every piece of information, no matter how small, could be important. Vardy's pure version interview was all about detail, they said, but then they didn't follow up for more details, a common police tactic. Leon Joudrey had complained about the same thing happening to him when he was interviewed by Vardy's partner, Sergeant Fraser Firth. The pure version interview, as conducted by the Mounties, left such gaps in the story that "the truth" could be interpreted any which way.

Like the Zimmermans before him, anyone could see that Dillman was annoyingly vague and needed to be prodded toward exactitude—anything but a "pure version." He wasn't sure of the times, but neither was the RCMP. He repeated that he believed he was on Brown Loop at 10:45 p.m. for ten minutes, but his phone records—which the Mounties also had—showed that he called his mother at 10:38 p.m. (to tell her he was turning onto Brown Loop) and that she called him at 10:58 (which is when he left to go meet her). He was there for just shy of twenty minutes.

Not only did the investigators fail to ask Dillman about the 10:38 call, they also didn't bother to ask his mother, even though Dillman specifically told them they should check with her. Only she could corroborate his story. Instead, based on their pure version interview, the Mounties were satisfied that Dillman did not get to the top of the blueberry field road until 10:45 or later, and that he must have just missed Wortman.

The first problem with that assumption involves geography. The road from Highway 2 to the blueberry field road is dead straight. I know that from personal experience. During my investigation, I turtled my rental car and got stuck 400 metres down the blueberry field road. I had to walk out and wait for a tow truck at the top of the road, right where Dillman said he had stopped. During that hour, I almost froze to death, but while I waited, I had a perfect view up to Highway 2, which

I guessed was at least three football field lengths away. I saw the tow truck make its right turn onto Brown Loop to rescue me.

Likewise, when Dillman turned onto Brown Loop, he would have been able to see a car's headlights emerging from the blueberry field road to the south. It was unavoidable. Hypothetically, since it would take a minute or more for Dillman to drive down Brown Loop, that alone effectively shaved at least a minute off Wortman's window for escape. If, as the Mounties assumed, Dillman got to Brown Loop at 10:45 p.m. (which he didn't), Wortman would have to have made it to the top of the blueberry field by 10:43:30 at the latest for Dillman not to have seen him. Was that even possible?

But the Mounties and the commission were only interested in what Dillman did after 10:45 p.m., the time he *thought* he had arrived at Brown Loop. They had it all on tape—twice! It fit the story the RCMP wanted to tell. There was no need for Dillman to testify at the commission. Case closed.

I first learned about Dillman's story in late 2020, but he wouldn't talk to me. I did, however, speak with his mother, Autumn Doucette, whose phone records and testimony confirmed that Dillman had called her at 10:38 p.m. to say he was turning onto Brown Loop. In an article in *Frank* magazine for the first anniversary of the massacre, I wrote about a witness who did not want to be identified but who had been on Brown Loop from 10:38 until at least 10:55 p.m. At the time, the RCMP and the media ignored the article—*conspiracy theory*.

It was only when the commission released its report that I discovered the full story about Dillman and his interviews—and saw his phone records. As I pored over the exhibits, which had been released piecemeal, I noticed one other call in Dillman's records that neither set of investigators had shown any interest in. It was made at 10:42 p.m. In the commission's disclosures, the records were partially redacted, so the entire number wasn't there. The call appeared to originate not in Portapique but in Kennetcook, almost 25 kilometres to the south, on the other side of Cobequid Bay in Hants County. It was received in Truro. The phone number Dillman had called ended in 533.

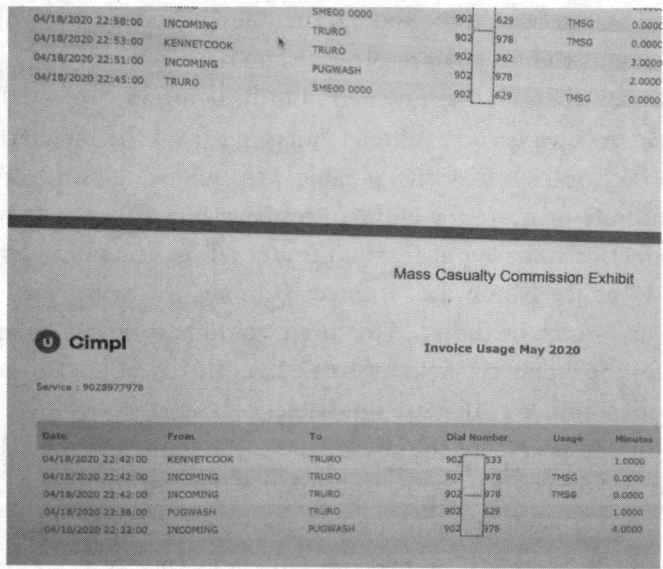

Dean Dillman's phone records from April 18, 2020. (MCC)

In his interviews with investigators, Dillman clearly stated that after he arrived at the top of the blueberry field road, he had tried to call Leon Joudrey but had received no answer. Joudrey was asleep. I had Joudrey's number stored in my cellphone, but it didn't match any in Dillman's records. Why?

Unfortunately, I couldn't ask Joudrey to confirm.

◆

On October 30, 2022, I was recording the *Nighttime* podcast with Jordan Bonaparte and lawyer Adam Rodgers, discussing *Deficits of Trust*, a book that Rodgers had self-published about the Mass Casualty Commission. Before we got into his book, we showed a few clips from a television news story about Leon Joudrey that had run four nights earlier on CTV Atlantic.

The interview opened with a shot of Joudrey standing with reporter Heidi Petracek outside his house at 140 Portapique Crescent. There was a barbecue on the deck. In the middle of the yard near him rested a portable generator with a red gas can on top. Wearing a crisp button-down, predominantly blue plaid shirt, Joudrey might have looked normal to people who didn't know him, but he was vastly different from the man I first met in 2020.

He spoke to Petracek about how haunted he was by what had happened in his community and how he no longer wanted to live in Portapique, where all he could see was his friends who had died.

> PETRACEK: Joudrey doesn't want to be here, but he doesn't know what other choice he has. He's been left to manage this all on his own.
> JOUDREY: They kind of forgot about me. I fell through the cracks of the mental health system and after four months they didn't even follow up with checks on me . . . it's been hell.
> PETRACEK: It's been almost two years since Joudrey was able to work. He wants nothing more than to leave but says he can't afford to. If staying, it means he won't escape the past. Heidi Petracek, CTV News, Portapique, Nova Scotia.

Petracek also interviewed Sandra McCulloch, a lawyer who was part of the team representing a majority of families at the MCC hearings and in a separate class-action lawsuit. McCulloch, who did not represent Joudrey, said she recognized that "there does seem to be those people," like Joudrey, whose experiences are "unique." Local politician Tom Taggart was allowed to mouth a few worn platitudes.

Finally, Petracek interviewed Canadian Red Cross spokesperson Bill Lawlor about the $6.2 million that had been raised for the survivors. He pointed out that the money was designated, as he put it in rather convoluted English, "in particular, with a focus on those who had dependants who relied upon someone who is no longer with us. But certainly, if anyone had an injury, we could encourage them to reach out to us."

We all knew Joudrey and felt bad for him. In *22 Murders*, I reported how, when Joudrey was initially interviewed by Global, they omitted the parts of his statement that referred to his observations about Lisa

Banfield's appearance, which cast doubt on her story about staying in the woods all night. When asked, Global defended its decision, saying they were "advised that parts of his testimony may not be verified. And the police had a different account."

Petracek's superficial pass at the story was maddening because she glossed over, once again, the very thing that had helped propel Joudrey's downward spiral: what he had really seen and experienced. Joudrey wasn't given the opportunity to testify at the commission, something that might have helped him process his trauma.

As we continued chatting on the podcast, my office phone rang. I could see on the call display that it was Pete MacIsaac, who had worked with Joudrey. "Why would he be calling now, in the middle of the podcast?" I wondered to myself. Sharon answered the phone in the living room.

A few seconds later, a notification popped up on my computer screen. The name attached to the message was vaguely familiar. "This has to remain anonymous, as it is a huge breach of confidentiality," the writer said. "But if Leon lived at 140 Portapique Crescent, he killed himself today . . . I hope this can lead you to more truth."

"Oh no, that's where he lived," I replied.

"I thought you should know . . . he committed suicide today."

"How do you know that?"

"I saw Jordan share the video from CTV and when the shot of the generator and the gas can came up. My gut dropped," they wrote.

"When did it happen? Do you have any details?"

"He was found late this morning. He was in the bedroom with a generator running."

"You sure it's him?"

"Yes, it's him."

"What about his two dogs?" I asked.

"They were locked in another room maybe enough to keep them alive."

As this was going on, Jordan could see that I was distracted. I heard the phone ring in the other room and Sharon answering it.

A few seconds later, another notification popped up on my screen. It was an email to me from *my* cellphone, which I could see on my desktop computer. I was momentarily confused, then realized what was going on.

Sharon didn't want to come into my office while I was on camera, so she had sent me an email from the living room on my phone.

"Pete called. Leon killed himself," Sharon wrote.

I quickly went back through my records and located my contact information for the person who had messaged me. Now I remembered who they were; they were solid. I messaged MacIsaac. He told me how he knew about what had happened. I believed him.

Now I faced a dilemma. Convention and privacy considerations dictated that I say nothing until Joudrey's family decided whether to announce his death. Since his body had been discovered almost twelve hours earlier and MacIsaac knew about it, it stood to reason the family knew. I was convinced by the details the contact had imparted to me that Joudrey had committed suicide, but suicide is not something families typically care to acknowledge. It's embarrassing to them. Maybe, I thought for a moment, I should hold my fire and say nothing.

However, Joudrey had documented his mental decline, mostly with Bonaparte, citizen investigator Chad Jones and me. We tried our best but, sadly, none of us appreciated how precarious his position had become. He had always been a victim of the massacres, but he seemed to be stronger than that. In the trauma-informed, post-Portapique world, Joudrey got lost in a crowded sea of bobbing victims.

The obvious victims were the dead and a few people who were either shot at or came close to being killed. Their families, be they close or estranged, were also victims, as were people living in the community, the county, the region, the province and the country. The police declared themselves to be victims, including those who didn't catch Wortman, those who cowered or ran away, and supervisors who chose not to get involved. The 911 call handlers adopted victimhood even though they were just doing their job. Politicians agreed not to talk about the issue, out of respect for the victims, and many of the victims thanked them for their consideration, such as it was. There were so many victims, no one was left to take care of Joudrey as he slid nearer and nearer to the precipice.

I felt I had to say something. I looked into the camera, mulling over what I was going to say as Rodgers explained why he had written his book the way he did: ". . . I wanted an interested citizen to understand what I'm saying."

I could read Bonaparte's face as he struggled to figure out why I seemed so distracted. He recapped some of what Rodgers had said, then threw it to me: "What do you think, Paul?"

I fumbled to find the right words: "There's stuff going on now. I've had a phone call here, um . . ." I paused for a solid three or four seconds. "Apparently, um, I have word that Leon Joudrey killed himself."

"Whoa," Bonaparte gasped.

"I have two sources on it right now," I said. "Two different sources, um, two who don't know each other. One was at the scene, and one was law enforcement. I hope it's not true. I feel very badly having had this happen."

"I heard your phone ring," Bonaparte said.

"Everything we just said about him a few minutes ago is all the more meaningful," Rodgers added.

"I feel awful with that coming live on air," Bonaparte said, his angst palpable.

Bonaparte began checking his records. Joudrey had contacted him after the CTV interview and had left a twenty-five-second message on his phone that Jordan hadn't got to. It was like the old Leon, quick and deliberate, but dark and desperate: "Hey, Jordan, I left you a Facebook message there. I don't know if there's anything you can do or not, but if there is any organizations that want to help me out to get me the fuck out of Portapique, but I can't afford another house. I don't know. I don't want to beg for money, but . . ." There was a slight pause. You could almost sense Joudrey shaking his head before he continued: "It's hell living here, so . . . I sent you a Facebook message, anyway, so, if you get a chance, have a look at it, but . . . I will be talking to you. Take care. Bye."

And that was it. He was gone. The twenty-third victim—or the twenty-fourth if you count the pregnant Kristen Beaton as two people.

Joudrey's death made me more determined to wrestle this beast of a story to the ground. Like many people, Joudrey had a misperception about how the world works. He had faith that the country's institutions were committed to finding the truth. Faith is believing in something in the absence of facts. By the time he chose to end his life, Joudrey had lost that faith. His character had been brutally assassinated. He was left isolated and shunned. He ended up on antidepressants.

"It's been fucked up from the beginning," a frustrated Joudrey told me once. "Nothing has gone the way it should go. It's not normal."

I couldn't agree more.

◆

On February 22, 2024—exactly two years after the commission held its first day of hearings—I set out to find the name behind the 533 number in Dillman's records. I was hoping against hope that Dillman would co-operate and that I could track down who he had called, to see if they remembered the conversation. Autumn Doucette agreed to ask her son about it. The next day, he sent her the contact information from his phone, which she relayed to me.

Dean Dillman's stored contact information for Leon Joudrey.

The 533 number was in Dillman's phone under Joudrey's name, and I realized it was Joudrey's work number. He had two phones!

Even if the RCMP ignored the 10:38 p.m. call, the phone logs proved that Dillman was at Brown Loop by 10:42 p.m., still earlier than 10:45. The RCMP said Wortman had shot Corrie Ellison at 10:40:12 and may have lingered there for a few more seconds. Short of a rocket car, there was no way he could have made it to Brown Loop before Dillman.

Leon Joudrey had come back from the grave to exact his revenge.

The RCMP and the commission concluded that Wortman escaped via the blueberry field road, but the evidence shows that didn't happen in the time frame they were focused on. Recall the forensic report that showed a map with Ellison's body erroneously on the east side of Orchard Beach Drive. Were they trying to make it appear that Wortman was heading south toward the blueberry field entrance when Ellison was murdered?

Regardless, there was a bigger fundamental flaw in the RCMP's story. If Wortman didn't have time to shoot Ellison at 10:40:12 *and* escape through the blueberry field, that meant he must have left by driving up to Highway 2 and going right past the Mountie or Mounties who were standing guard there. Constable Colford was tending to Kate MacDonald at the time. Constable Travise Dow had arrived at around 10:43 p.m., given Colford his shotgun, and then taken up a position in the drainage ditch. Police cars from various detachments were arriving from both directions. Mounties were being forced to work with other Mounties they'd never met. Who knew who was real?

A single blurry frame from the security camera at the Wilsons gas station in Great Village appeared to capture Wortman passing by at 10:50:59, and then he disappeared into the night. The RCMP never showed the whole video. Why not? What did it show? Who was driving? Was there a passenger?

The video matched a story I reported in *22 Murders*. Days after the massacres, Sergeant Bill Raaymakers visited Portapique resident Nathan Staples and apologized for the scary visit he had received from a Mountie dressed in camouflage the previous Saturday night. "He drove right past us," Staples quoted Raaymakers as saying, which later seemed entirely plausible. Here and there in the foundational papers, a number of Mounties stated that a car that might have been Wortman's had driven past them as they headed toward Portapique. Moreover, all through the night, Mounties in cruisers were driving through checkpoints without stopping and identifying themselves.

"I know, like, when we left, we drove past the checkpoint," Constable Patton said in his debriefing interview. "We didn't stop to talk to people at the checkpoints or whatever . . . Just waved at them."

Wortman likely did the same.

Was that too big an embarrassment for the Mounties to admit, or was something more nefarious going on?

The RCMP's story was that Wortman had crossed over from the Zahl-Thomas residence through the field and arrived back on Orchard Beach Drive via the laneway to his warehouse and killed Corrie Ellison. He then left via the blueberry field road. But why would Wortman return to the area where Lisa McCully's body was lying in full view, and where he would expect Mounties to be? That would be brazen unless he had a radio and was monitoring where the police were—but the RCMP and the commission found that he didn't.

With the blueberry field story a non-starter, it raises the possibility that, after killing Zahl and Thomas, Wortman drove straight up Portapique Beach Road and out of the neighbourhood. This could have happened just after Beselt, Merchant and Patton ducked into the woods, shortly after 10:40 p.m. It seems possible. Colford had her hands full at the checkpoint; she wouldn't necessarily have noticed another stranger in a somewhat strange cruiser, with its old-school whip antenna and a push bumper that wasn't typical of a Nova Scotia RCMP cruiser.

That scenario leaves open the question asked by retired detective Tim Kavanagh: "Who killed Corrie Ellison?" Or this more specific one from Clinton Ellison: "Did the RCMP kill my brother?"

I hate to go all conspiracy theorist here, but since there was so much secrecy and I, as an ordinary citizen, can't get or execute search warrants, the only deductive tools I have are observations, questions and words. When it comes down to it, the only solid evidence against Wortman for Ellison's murder is a speck of Ellison's DNA that the RCMP said it found on Wortman's boot. That might sound convincing to an audience raised on *CSI* shows, but the logic of the situation is more problematic. If Wortman was in the driver's seat of his car when he first fired at Ellison out the passenger-side window, how did a speck of blood land on his boot?

Consider the scenario described by the Mounties. The forensic analysis said that after Ellison was shot three times in the head while standing and leaning into the car, he was then shot twice while on the ground. The speculation was that Wortman got out of the car, walked around it and finished him off. After shooting Ellison multiple times in the head—Wortman's preferred target with his other victims—why would he bother getting out of the car and finishing him off when the place was swarming with police and he was trying to make his getaway?

The forensic investigation also did not conclusively tie the bullets to any of Wortman's guns. As we saw from Wayne Fowler's report, the ballistics evidence was inconclusive. In fact, Ellison's was the only one of the twenty-two murders in which that was the case.

There is also the fact that someone appears to have fiddled with Ellison's phone afterwards. The RCMP says it wasn't them.

Remember that Bjorn Merzbach thought he heard two shooters firing different guns at the same time. The children in McCully's house reported someone banging on the door not long after those shots were fired. The RCMP said it wasn't them.

The only other people known to be in the general vicinity at the time were Ellison's brother, Clinton, who was hiding in the woods several hundred metres south of the McCully house, and Lisa Banfield.

In her statements, Banfield said that at one point after she escaped from Wortman, she heard two men talking. "It was like, 'Hey, boys' or something. And *bang, bang*, and then there was nothing," Banfield said, when describing how she hid in an unknown area of the woods somewhere south of McCully's house. It sounds like something someone would say to the police in that situation, but where did that conversation happen? Bjorn Merzbach might have greeted Grund and Neil that way, but he lived several hundred metres to the north of where Banfield was supposedly hiding, and there were no shots fired during the time he was talking to them. If it was Ellison meeting the police, the Mounties said they weren't yet at the scene of his murder at 10:40 p.m. Were there other Mounties that we don't know about? Were there other people wandering around the neighbourhood that we don't know about? After all, there was that noisy car that Patton and the Zimmerman family heard going through the woods east of the community.

Based upon the known evidence, what Banfield heard seemed to relate to Ellison. He was the only victim who was anywhere near where she said she was. The problem with her story is that it doesn't fit the facts. Banfield said in a statement to the RCMP that she heard two shots. Ellison was shot five times. Was she talking about another murder?

There is still much we don't know, in part because none of the police weapons appear to have been seized and inspected afterwards. And as Corporal Trent Milton observed, Banfield was not treated as a possible murder suspect in the Portapique shootings and did not undergo any type of forensic examination. But one thing is certain: the question of who killed Corrie Ellison is still unanswered, despite the conclusions of the RCMP and the MCC.

If the RCMP tripping over itself on Saturday night in Portapique seems out of the ordinary, what happened on April 19, 2020, the second day of the massacres, should disabuse anyone of that fantasy.

11

POLICING FOR DUMMIES?

The first evidence for the RCMP that Wortman wasn't dead was when Lisa Banfield suddenly appeared at Leon Joudrey's door just before 6:30 a.m. She told them what Wortman was wearing, what he was driving and what his plans might be. That still didn't jolt the RCMP into panic mode. It didn't set up a roadblock. It didn't call other police forces for help. It didn't call in its own members, perhaps because that would mean having to pay overtime.

Many of the Mounties who had been sent home before 6:30 a.m. were snuggled in their beds. In Portapique, the handful of remaining officers were going about their tasks. Some were arranging to take the Blairs' wounded dog to a veterinary clinic in Truro. They had no idea where Wortman was or what he was up to.

Just before the sun came up, a vehicle resembling Wortman's cruiser was captured on security cameras leaving the Debert Air Park, where he had apparently been hiding out for the night behind a welding shop on Ventura Drive. The Mounties didn't know that, however, until days later. Wortman headed out of Debert and turned right onto Highway 4, the old two-lane Trans-Canada Highway route that crosses Nova Scotia. He drove into Wentworth, an even larger county than Colchester, and the only one in Nova Scotia that borders another province, New Brunswick.

At 2328 Hunter Road, Alanna Jenkins was already up, texting a friend. It was 6:26 a.m. Jenkins and her fellow federal corrections officer Sean McLeod lived in a well-appointed chalet-style house situated in a park-like setting next to the Wallace River. As I reported in *22 Murders*, both McLeod and Jenkins had a past with Wortman:

> After his first marriage broke up, McLeod had moved in with a friend who owned a place in Great Village. His friend eventually bought another house on Portapique Beach Road, north of Wortman's cottage at number 200. McLeod had two daughters from his first marriage: Amielia, who was his biological daughter, and Taylor, who was fathered by another man. He had raised Taylor as his own and acted as her official guardian.
>
> In the confines of the tiny Portapique community, it didn't take long for Wortman and McLeod to meet. They were both into fishing and hunting, and especially the guns that come with the latter. McLeod was in law enforcement and Wortman was fascinated by anyone in the vocation. McLeod became part of the Portapique Beach drinking club circle. It was a curious relationship. Over the previous twenty years Wortman had barely concealed the fact that he had made loads of money smuggling and selling illegal cigarettes and prescription drugs as well as other illegal contraband across the border from Maine into New Brunswick. For whatever reason, McLeod gave some law enforcement paraphernalia to his new friend, who was an avid collector. One of the items was a set of real handcuffs.
>
> After McLeod met and married his second wife, they purchased the house on Hunter Road. McLeod and Wortman remained friends throughout the intervening years, although McLeod's father, Dale, and his brothers, Scott and Chris, said in interviews that Sean had not brought up Wortman's name until recently.
>
> "He had offered to make some dentures for my father," Scott said in an interview. "He promised him a better price, but at the end of the day, he got them from someone else."

Meanwhile, Jenkins appears to have met Wortman in 2013, after leaving her first husband.

There are two distinct views about whether they started a relationship of their own. Some say it happened; others say it didn't. Jenkins's family members, including her father, Dan, her brother, Josh, and McLeod's daughter, Taylor, are adamant that she never had a relationship with Wortman.

"Alanna would have had nothing to do with someone like him," said Dan Jenkins. "She was an absolutely beautiful person. We know everything she did. She never did anything without us. To say anything like that about her is pure innuendo. If you say that, I will hire a lawyer and sue you." Josh Jenkins's remarks were somewhat more colourful.

There is no question that many people liked Alanna Jenkins. She was always organizing events, and ever mindful of birthdays and special occasions. She spent wads of money on McLeod's daughters and was more their friend and drinking buddy than a parental figure. . . .

But others—members of the McLeod family, friends and acquaintances of Jenkins and confidential sources inside policing—say Jenkins had an undeniable wild side and was a bit of a risk-taker. Many of them believe Jenkins did have a previous, hidden relationship with Wortman. In 2013, for example, police officers from Amherst, Nova Scotia, who were on vacation in Cuba found themselves staying at the same resort as Jenkins. They knew her from work and noticed that she was with a man wearing an RCMP T-shirt. That man was Wortman, they say. Naturally, they approached Wortman and tried to chat him up. He was reticent about talking to real police officers and left without speaking to them. He then made himself virtually invisible for the rest of the week. . . .

In the days and weeks leading up to April 19, McLeod and Jenkins were in contact with Wortman, as they had long been occasional visitors to 200 Portapique Beach Road. Jenkins had lost a tooth and Wortman had offered to build a replacement for her. McLeod eventually became angry with what he believed was Wortman's open flirting with Jenkins. "Sean thought that Wortman was trying to hook up with Alanna, so he confronted him and told him to piss off and stay away from us," Scott McLeod says.

On the morning of April 19, Wortman briefly stopped behind the Wentworth Market, then headed to Hunter Road and drove five kilometres up the dirt road to their house. He turned right into their long driveway and parked his fake cruiser near the house, right beside the river. Remarkably, his gleaming white car still wasn't very dirty.

All this time later, we still don't know exactly what happened after he entered the house. We do know he shot and killed McLeod in his bed. Jenkins's remains were found in roughly the same location.

Why did Wortman go there? Early on, some thought he might have been looking for guns or ammunition, but the commission reported that all of McLeod's guns, most of them unregistered rifles he had inherited from his father, were left untouched. None of the ammunition for them fit Wortman's guns. So he didn't go there for the guns.

Was it for revenge? One of Wortman's neighbours told the RCMP that McLeod and Jenkins had been involved in smuggling marijuana, and likely other drugs, into the federal prisons in which they worked. Was this all a falling-out over business? Was it part of a blown police operation? Had McLeod or Jenkins ratted out Wortman? We don't know. Both the RCMP and Correctional Services Canada denied that there were any ongoing investigations, and Jenkins's phone and email records were not released by the commission.

McLeod's brother, Scott, told me in an interview that, in the days before he was killed, Sean had told their mother that "he wasn't happy with himself" and was going to change his life. We don't know what was bothering him.

Did Wortman go to see Jenkins and McLeod because he was killing those he'd had a relationship with? He and Jenkins had a past, and Jenkins was now seeing him for work on her tooth. McLeod had apparently warned Wortman to stay away from her. Again, we don't know.

Maybe Wortman needed to charge Greg Blair's phone or get one from McLeod and Jenkins. Did he go there because he needed either a phone or a secluded place with Internet service so that he could catch up on the news—about him? If he had gone online immediately, he might have been shocked to find out how little was being said. That changed after 8 a.m., when the RCMP began to acknowledge publicly whom they were hunting.

Or did Wortman just want McLeod's identification and uniform, to give him a different look? If his original plan had been to fake his own death as part of a massive conflagration, that was no longer viable. He was known to be alive. By then he had to be keenly aware that he was wanted and that there was no easy way out. He had to come up with a new plan.

Perhaps Wortman had gone there to hide out, though he didn't do anything to conceal his presence. His car attracted the attention of neighbour Tom Bagley, who was out for his morning constitutional. Noticing the "police car" parked near the house, Bagley went to investigate. Wortman shot him. His body was found just outside the side door of the house. Wortman torched the house before he left. He was now up to sixteen victims.

At 9:23 a.m., Wortman was caught leaving Hunter Road on the same security camera that captured him coming up the road at 6:29 a.m.

Back in Portapique, the Mounties knew about none of this—even after a call came in about the fire on Hunter Road and the sound of gunshots, because it was all on the force's Wentworth County channel. One might think the RCMP would have everyone on a provincial channel by then, but that was not how it did things.

The connection between Wortman and McLeod and Jenkins seems like it should have been a priority for the commission to investigate thoroughly, but it was hamstrung by its convoluted mandate. It couldn't discuss anything of a criminal nature, even if all the parties were dead. It couldn't talk about intimate relationships, because that would be victim shaming. So it pretty well skipped over Hunter Road, to the frustration of Scott McLeod.

"We wanted to know why Wortman targeted my brother and Alanna," he said. "If Sean was up to no good, we wanted to know that. We wanted an explanation, but the commission didn't give us anything."

Instead, the day after Debra Thibeault's testimony, commission counsel Roger Burrill reminded the commission of Wortman's escape via the blueberry field road the night before and picked up the narrative *after*

Bagley's murder: "Today, we continue with difficult subject matter. Commission counsel will present two more foundational documents, on the events at Highway 4, Glenholme, and Plains Road, Debert . . ."

◆

The foundational paper on Glenholme was already in the media's hands, which made what Burrill did that morning appear redundant. He began reading from the document, a mind-numbing experience highlighted with the occasional still photo or brief video. The events in Glenholme boiled down to this: a Mountie corporal drove past Wortman on Highway 4, but lost him when he tried to pursue him. A couple said he was at their property. The RCMP assembled its troops but got to the property just after Wortman escaped. They missed him by just that much! It took Burrill a mere fifty minutes to blast through the details, and not one person connected to the scene was called upon to speak publicly.

When the story about Wortman driving along Highway 4 in Glenholme was reported in the days, months and years after the massacres, it was clear to me that many of the journalists had never been to the area. I've always been a Hieronymus Bosch kind of journalist—not the artist, but Michael Connelly's fictional detective, whose motto is: "Get off your ass and knock on doors." If more reporters covering this story had done that, they might have been able to provide context and challenge the RCMP's flawed version of events.

Individually and together, Chad Jones, Ryan Potter and I visited all the key crime scenes numerous times, some as many as a dozen. I took measurements. Took photos. Talked to people. I tried to match the RCMP and witness stories with what all the witnesses said and with the geography. Here's what I learned, and what Burrill's reading of the commission's foundational paper left out.

At 9:42:30 a.m., the Colchester RCMP got the call that sent a collective chill through the moribund force: "Uh, Colchester members . . . we have just had a shooting on Highway 4 in Wentworth. A female is deceased on the side of the road. Um, unknown if she's been shot or hit by a vehicle. Uh, they heard a loud bang, saw an RCMP vehicle, left towards Truro."

The victim was sixty-four-year-old Lillian Campbell Hyslop, who had gone out for a Sunday walk dressed in an orange reflective vest, sunglasses, mittens, hat and scarf. Campbell Hyslop lived with her husband, Michael Hyslop, a few doors down from the intersection with Highway 4. She had walked west to the highway and turned south when Wortman drove by her on his way from Hunter Road. He didn't know her. He made a U-turn, pulled up beside her and shot her in the head from inside his car. She was collateral damage: another murder scene for the RCMP to investigate, using up its resources. Wortman made another U-turn and continued driving south down Highway 4.

It was only after Campbell Hyslop's murder that the Mounties realized that the fire at Jenkins and McLeod's place and the shootings in Portapique were likely connected. The RCMP still had no idea how many people had been killed in Portapique, but now it knew that Wortman certainly was not dead and was adding to the total carnage.

One of the Mounties who responded to the Campbell shooting was Corporal Rodney Peterson. A Mountie for almost twenty-four years and proudly Indigenous, Peterson had spent almost his entire career in the First Nations and Inuit Policing Program. He was gassing up his cruiser when he heard the call. He had been planning to go to the Tim Hortons drive-through to pick up a snack but realized that would have to wait. He put on his hard body armour but was confused about what was going on.

"So, in my head right now . . . Knowing that they had a shooting and we're looking for a police car, which in my head doesn't make sense. Why are we looking for a police car?" Peterson said in his interview with commission investigators eighteen months after the incident. "So, in my head, it's, you see these decommissioned [stripped-down former] police cars, you know, you see them all over the place. That's what I'm looking for."

It was now almost twelve hours since the first 911 call from Jamie Blair. Lisa Banfield had been in police custody for more than three hours, and the RCMP had photos of Wortman's fake cruiser in hand. Although a number of Mounties were asking for a public alert to be issued, the force's brain trust didn't want to say that Wortman was driving what appeared to be a real police car. They rationalized that the information would confuse people and could create a dangerous situation for real Mounties, who might get shot by a vigilante. Even after the RCMP admitted that Wortman's vehicle looked like a real police cruiser, they still didn't want to set up roadblocks, because that might create a dangerous situation for other drivers should a gun battle ensue. There were so many variables, all of which led to a dangerous conclusion. One could almost hear the White Shirts whinging as they envisioned their curated career paths being truncated—because no matter which way they stepped, it would be into a cow-pie.

At 9:44 a.m., Corporal Peterson headed north from Masstown on Highway 4 in his marked Tahoe SUV. He said he had tried to log in his vehicle but couldn't, so RCMP dispatchers had no idea where he was. Driving at 160 kilometres per hour with lights and sirens, he headed over a hill and noticed a construction site where Nova Scotia Power crews and their vehicles were congregated. He saw a car coming in the other direction, driving slowly. As he got closer, he recognized that it was a Mountie cruiser.

"I just saw an RCMP offic— uh, car going towards Masstown on number 4 there, guys. Is that fully marked, like, or is it an ex-police car?" Peterson asked the dispatcher at 9:47:24.

"The car we're looking for is a fully marked PC, 28-Bravo-11, ID on it," replied another corporal.

"Yeah, he just passed me going to Masstown, I think," Peterson said at 9:47:43. "He's got a reflective vest on, guys." Seconds later, he added, "The guy, uh, was driving slow, smiled as he went by. Uh, white Caucasian male, uh, looked like brownish hair. He's got a reflective, uh, vest or jacket on . . . I'm not sure if he went on the highway [104] or not."

It was a critical moment in the pursuit of Wortman. He was in Glenholme, where he could be contained easily. There weren't that many roads, and there were few cars out, given that it was Sunday morning during the COVID lockdown. One would think, after what had happened the previous night, that the area would be swarming with police, but it wasn't. Everyone had to stick to the playbook and follow orders and rules and regulations.

There are brave and courageous Mounties, as we've already seen. Some were chomping at the bit to go after Wortman, confront him and take him down if necessary. For example, Constable Nick Dorrington was one of five members assigned with protecting the crime scenes in Portapique, but as events unfolded Sunday morning, Dorrington, who had an unmarked car, begged Staff Sergeant O'Brien to free him from Portapique, arguing "we don't need five people guarding bodies."

"I go to O'Brien and request that he allow me to go," Dorrington recalled. "I tell them that, realistically, I'm one of the only ones that stands a chance to get close enough to him in an unmarked car. I said: 'Every cop car he sees, he knows it's the enemy.' I said: 'By the time we get close enough and try to figure out if his cop car is the real one or not . . . we're done. At least in the unmarked I may stand a chance to get close enough to take him off the road and do what needs to be done . . . I got no problem doing it . . . just let me go.'"

"No," O'Brien told him.

The frustrated Dorrington also said he didn't have much confidence in Peterson, who was his immediate superior, describing him as "not tactically sound." His concerns seem on point, considering how Peterson described what he was thinking that Sunday morning when he spotted Wortman heading in the other direction on Highway 4: "I'm trying to decide, should I stop, slow down, talk to this person, or keep going? So, and this is very quick. It's not like I had a lot of time. We're like bam, pass each other. So I said, if I, if I stop, this is the bad guy. I'm going to get shot here. I'm going to get killed. If I continue on, that will give me a chance to turn around and pursue him or to do something right. So, as I'm getting closer to the vehicle, this is very fast. So, as I get closer, I don't as much pay attention to the vehicle as I do to the person inside, right . . . Part of me is saying: Why is this police car coming away from a call that I am going to? But it is possible if they're coming from other jurisdictions or they're on like the tactical radio channel that they can't, they won't, wouldn't hear that. They would have missed . . . I guess the long story short is I'm looking at the danger, which is a person in the police car which I perceive could be a danger or could be a friend. I don't know . . . I believe this is the guy we're looking for . . . So, all this time while doing this, I'm trying to be tactical about it, too, which means that I'm trying not to get myself killed here. In my head, he's got a gun, he's going to use it. You know, usually those don't end too well for the person . . . So, your heart goes in your throat."

Instead of pursuing Wortman and calling for help, Peterson continued to drive north for about 1.3 kilometres before turning around. A key reason, he admitted, was that his carbine wasn't prepared for an engagement. He also couldn't explain precisely where he was on Highway 4, and dispatchers couldn't geolocate his cruiser with GPS because he wasn't signed in.

As three dozen Mounties converged on Glenholme, 18 kilometres east of Portapique, they believed they had an advantage. There were no roads east or west out of the area. Peterson raced down the highway well behind Wortman, but by the time he reached Highway 104, Wortman was nowhere in sight. Peterson looked both ways down the expressway and couldn't see him. He thought Wortman might have continued east toward Masstown, not realizing that he had slipped up the driveway of Adam and Carole Fisher, 1.2 kilometres north of Highway 104 and still in Glenholme.

Wortman knew them both. They had been to each other's homes. That morning, they were lolling about in their pyjamas when Carole saw on Facebook that Wortman had been identified as the shooter.

"Adam, it's fucking Gabe," Carole said. "Gabe's the shooter."

About ten minutes before Wortman approached the Fishers' house, Adam had called 911 to report what he knew about Wortman. He, too, had seen the replica police car at Wortman's warehouse.

A sensor at the base of their long driveway alerted the Fishers that someone had come onto their 28-acre property. When they saw the police car speeding up to the house, they thought the RCMP was responding to Adam's call. But then Wortman emerged from the car. He was wearing a reflective jacket and a black baseball cap, and was carrying a semi-automatic rifle in his right hand and something dark and boxy in his left hand. It looked like a radio. As he rang the doorbell and knocked on a set of locked French doors, Carole and Adam both called 911 again.

"The shooter is here that shot everyone in . . . Portapique," Carole told the call taker, beginning at 9:48:49. She gave her address, saying, "Please, please get here!"

"Gabriel Wortman is at my house," Adam told 911 at about 9:49 a.m.

Afterwards, Adam told RCMP constable Mike Townsend it was like watching a *Terminator* movie. "When he got out of the car, he was stone-cold and collected. He was in no hurry."

Despite the vows to be transparent, the RCMP and the commission were not forthcoming about the details of Wortman's visit to the Fishers. In the transcripts the commission released, the times of Adam's and Carole's individual calls to 911 were stripped out, leaving only a transcript of the conversation between them and their call takers. Anyone could see *what* they said, but not *when* they said it. To determine those times, I had to go through police logs and radio transmissions, which had time stamps. Putting the times in would have made it easier to compare them against Corporal Peterson's movements while he was being "tactical."

According to the Colchester RCMP call logs, Peterson first asked for a description of Wortman at 9:47:24. He then told dispatchers thirty-two seconds later, at 9:47:56, that he had seen Wortman. This would have been mere seconds before Wortman turned right into the Fishers' driveway. The GPS records for Peterson's SUV, accessed later, indicated that Peterson and Wortman likely passed each other about 300 metres north of the Fishers' driveway. It appears that Peterson did not alert his dispatcher until *after* he had turned around, about 1.6 kilometres from the Fishers' driveway, somewhere between the Hidden Hilltop campground and Plains Road. He passed the campground heading south at 9:48:36. Peterson hadn't immediately called it in.

Once he had turned around and headed south, Peterson couldn't see Wortman ahead, although the road in that area is straight and Wortman had likely kicked up dust racing up the Fishers' driveway. The GPS records for Peterson's vehicle indicate that he passed the driveway while both Fishers were on the line with 911, around 9:49:50. But Wortman had parked his car behind the Fishers' two vehicles so that it was not visible from the highway.

The Fishers were terrified. "He's driving a police car," Adam Fisher told 911. "I seen him pull over in the yard. He got out dressed like a police officer."

"Are you sure it was him?" the call taker responded.

"I'm positive."

Fisher hurried to his gun cabinet, took out his 12-gauge shotgun and ran upstairs to join his wife, who was hiding in their shower. "If he comes up to my house, I'm going to blow his fucking head off," he said.

"Okay, I don't want you to use that right now, okay?" the operator replied, urging him to find his wife, take his gun and hide in a closet— which would make them sitting ducks if Wortman got into the house. The police were on scene, the call taker said, and they would take care of it.

Was it pure coincidence that Wortman drove to the Fishers' house shortly after Adam called 911? Or did he know about the call? Was that the reason he wanted to see them? Or did he plan to kill them and steal a vehicle because his was too hot?

In *22 Murders*, I reported that Carole Fisher told friends that, when she called 911, she could hear her call outside the window, near Wortman's police car. She later went silent about that. The Fishers were reportedly also "cottage friends" at Folly Lake with Corporal Natasha Jamieson.

Even a Mountie was suspicious about what was in Wortman's left hand. When he reviewed the Fishers' security video, Constable Mike Townsend wrote: ". . . can't tell from the video, however [I] believe it to be a magazine or maybe a radio." Why would Wortman be carrying a magazine for his gun when he had high-capacity magazines, as the commission had already pointed out? He didn't need more bullets.

A still photo captured by the Fishers' security camera,
showing Wortman's replica police car parked behind the Fishers' vehicles.
The entire video shows Wortman carrying a semi-automatic rifle in
his right hand as he walks toward their house. In his left hand is a dark
rectangular device that appears to be a radio. (MCC)

The RCMP and the commission consistently denied that Wortman had a working radio, although it would have helped explain his incredible luck in avoiding the Mounties over the course of his spree. But if he did have a radio, and the commission admitted it, that would have opened the door to the notion that Wortman had a special relationship with the RCMP. Who would have given him a radio and the regularly changing encryption codes? Any such connection could unravel a hidden story—perhaps that Wortman was an RCMP confidential informant or agent. The RCMP and the commission were bound by law to never reveal anything that might cause a confidential informant or agent to be identified. But the sequence of events at the Fishers' residence that morning strongly suggests that Wortman did have a working police radio.

After Corporal Peterson lost sight of Wortman, Mounties rallied at a parking lot on the east side of Highway 4, a few hundred metres north of Highway 104. The records appear to indicate that the 911 operator didn't pass on the Fishers' frantic messages about Wortman being at their door until 9:50:23, more than two minutes after the call was initiated.

"Break for dispatch," the dispatcher said, cutting into the chatter. "We have the SOC [Subject of Complaint] at 2896 Highway 4 in Glenholme at the residence. Just called in."

The Mounties were confident they had Wortman pinned down—which they might have if they had immediately raced to the Fishers' house. But once again, RCMP tactical training—make sure no one gets hurt—kicked into gear. Even when seconds counted, even when citizens believed they were about to be murdered by a known killer, the Mounties weren't about to be rushed. Like many police forces, they appeared to have forgotten that their duty in a dangerous situation was to put their lives on the line and preserve civilian life.

"Stage before we get there," Corporal Peterson ordered at 9:52:11. The staging point was about a kilometre south of the Fisher residence, just above the exit ramp from the 104. It was on the other side of both a crest and a bend in the road. The Mounties were safe from any gunfire. They had convinced themselves that they were about to spring the perfect trap. They were amassing bodies, dogs, tactical vehicles and snipers with their deadliest weaponry. There was even a helicopter, finally commandeered from the Department of Natural Resources, headed their way. There were no roads going east or west for 3.2 kilometres from Highway 104 to Plains Road. It looked like a cinch.

There were several major flaws with the set-up, however. The helicopter was nowhere near the scene, but rather hovering around Portapique. But even if it had been in the area, there was another issue: there were dozens of marked police cars without rooftop identifiers. Since the penny-pinching Nova Scotia government would not pay for a helicopter—a frill, it deemed—identifiers that could be seen from the air seemed a waste. The only feature that readily identified Wortman's cruiser was the push bar.

Another flaw was that there were no Mounties at the north end of Highway 4, near Plains Road, and none would be coming from that direction. They were tied up at the Campbell Hyslop murder scene, a twenty-five-minute drive to the north. And the Mounties didn't put up a drone or place a spy at the top of the crest so they could monitor the Fishers' driveway and Highway 4. Constables Terry Brown and Dave Melanson volunteered to sneak over to the other side of the Fisher property in their unmarked car, but Corporal Peterson nixed the idea.

Wortman, once again, was either psychic or had a radio or telephone—or both. He seemed to know where the Mounties were and what they were doing. There's no other explanation for what he did next: he abruptly got back into his vehicle, seconds after the dispatcher broadcasted the Fishers' calls for help at 9:50:23. Was he monitoring their calls? Did he know Adam Fisher was armed and waiting for him? At the end of their driveway, he turned left and drove north back up Highway 4, unseen and unpursued.

Thirty-six seconds after Corporal Peterson gave the order to stage, an RCMP plainclothes team thought they had Wortman in their sights and were ready to take him down.

"Break! Break! We got eyes on him," Constable Brown radioed at 9:52:47. "Marked PC on the side of the highway up ahead of us." Brown was travelling with his partner, Constable Melanson, in an unmarked Nissan Altima. They were part of a quickly assembled designated "cut-off" team, whose job it was to catch up and get ahead of Wortman while ERT members chased from behind in their less agile vehicles.

"Guys," Staff Sergeant Andy O'Brien interjected from the command post, "that's [Constable Rodney] MacDonald. MacDonald. We're just trying to log in to find out where the fuck we're at. We're pulling back out right in front of ya."

"Copy. Copy. Uh, Peterson, uh, Brown and Melanson are behind you."

"Just stage right here, guys," Peterson said.

At 9:53:39 a.m., Staff Sergeant Jeff West announced: "Members attending set up containment but wait for ERT. We got a bunch of ERT guys—should be there shortly."

At 9:55:10 a.m., the Mounties were still deciding whether to set up a roadblock.

"Are we going to block off the road by that van?" Corporal Peterson asked Constable MacDonald.

At 9:58 a.m., ten minutes after the Fishers called 911, the Mounties were trying to figure out precisely which was their property. There was a row of houses on the west side of the highway, but the Fisher property was over the hill, a large tract of land sitting almost on its own.

"Can we confirm . . . that it is the property with the excavators?" ERT constable Trent Milton asked. It was. Milton and the ERT contingent that had been in Portapique overnight were now back on the hunt for Wortman.

At 10:00:11 a.m., Corporal Tim Mills (who was an acting sergeant that day) announced that the ERT was now on scene and that he had a special request: "Looking for permission to move up to the house with compromised authority," he asked Staff Sergeant West, who had been on the job as incident commander for almost nine hours at that point.

"Go again, Tim, please. I missed that," West said. He asked a few questions to clarify the situation, and finally agreed at 10:00:50: "You have permission to move, uh, from the highway to the res, with compromised authority. You have control."

"Copy that," Mills said. "I have control."

"Compromised authority" means that ERT members can make situational decisions without having to seek permission, even if it means shooting a suspect. In the circumstances, it appears that this was interpreted as a shoot-to-kill order, which set in motion what was to come over the next eighty-six minutes. The RCMP had assembled a de facto hit team of members who would attempt to catch up to Wortman and kill him, as you shall see in chapter 21.

Shortly thereafter, a strange call came in to 911, reporting a woman's body in a car at the campground north of the Fishers' place. That incident disappeared from the public record, and the commission never addressed it. Why? Was it Wortman, using the phone or radio he supposedly didn't have to slow down his pursuers?

At 10:05, seventeen minutes after Adam and Carole Fisher had first called to report that Wortman was armed and at their door, the Mounties had finally built up their resources and courage and were sneaking up on the Fisher residence. Constable Brent Kelly, the sniper, was creeping through the woods on the property, along with Staff Sergeant Addie MacCallum. Kelly had, earlier that morning, been at Leon Joudrey's house to rescue Lisa Banfield.

Even then, confusion continued inside the RCMP. Minutes earlier, Chief Superintendent Chris Leather had emailed Truro police chief Dave MacNeil and confidently told him the RCMP didn't need any help, thank you, because it had Wortman "pinned down" in Glenholme. In his notes for that time, RCMP sergeant Marc Rose wrote that the risk manager, Staff Sergeant Bruce Briers, "advised that Wortman could be in a white pickup truck." The truck had come out of a driveway 700 metres from the Fisher residence, with a man and a woman inside. It was full-blown Panic City for the Mounties, who weren't even close to pinning down Wortman.

At the Fisher residence, sniper Kelly came up behind an excavator. He later described what happened next: "I crawled around the excavator, fully expected to see the PC [police cruiser], or at least him out there. Nothing! There was nothing there. I was using my optic. Looked all around the yard. It's a fairly large yard. Look all around. I couldn't see anything. There's nothing going on."

While Kelly was busy seeing nothing, Wortman was a nine-minute drive away. A video security camera caught him casually driving along Plains Road in Debert, steps from the welding shop he had visited the night before. He was on his way to kill two of his last five victims.

Meanwhile, the Mounties continued to be confused about the white truck. "Heading westbound on, uh, the Plains Road, about five or ten minutes ago on the way to this. Is that a possible vehicle?" Corporal Al Comeau asked at 10:17:50. He had recently arrived from New Brunswick and was roaming the unfamiliar area.

"Everything leads us to believe it's a marked PC, 28-Delta-11," Corporal Tim Mills replied at 10:18:16. Actually, the number on Wortman's car was 28-Bravo-11.

Another Mountie then reported that the white truck was "off the shoulder in the ditch in tree line. Came out to the, uh, off-ramp and went back into the woods."

Wortman had escaped the RCMP once again.

◆

Much of what I have just shared was not covered by the Mass Casualty Commission. When it came to what happened in Glenholme, the commission downplayed the gravity of the RCMP's failures and the Fishers' fear by having commission counsel Burrill give a dry fifty-minute PowerPoint-like dissertation dressed up here and there with static pictures and snippets of police communications audio to illustrate his points.

For those paying attention, the RCMP's credibility was shot, but it had the National Police Federation on its side—and in the media's ears. As RCMP union boss Brian Sauvé worked tirelessly to protect his members from serious scrutiny or accountability, he spent a lot of time promoting their bravery and heroism—sometimes overstating the competence and quality of his members' actions, and perhaps also the trauma that some of them felt as a result of those events. Unlike ordinary citizens, Sauvé could say just about anything he wanted to and the media would publish it. He could assert a narrative and then be proven wrong, and the media seemed to forget the mistake. Reporters were hungry for a quotable quote—even sans context.

While the commission was hearing the recital of the foundational papers about the second day of massacres, the union reached out to the Globe and Mail's Greg Mercer, who had been reliably deferential to the

Mounties in his coverage. The multi-award-winning reporter had also established that he was sensitive to women's, Indigenous and other issues. He and his colleagues never expressed an ounce of skepticism about Lisa Banfield's woeful tale.

On April 4, 2022, Mercer published a story accompanied by a large photo of a resolute Sauvé standing in front of a row of parked RCMP cruisers. Here are the first eight of the story's twenty-four paragraphs:

POLICE RESPONSE TO NOVA SCOTIA MASS SHOOTING WAS 'TEXTBOOK,' RCMP UNION BOSS SAYS

Brian Sauvé, the head of the RCMP's national union, says criticism of police actions connected to the Nova Scotia mass shooting that left 22 people dead in April 2020 have been unfair, and that the force's handling of the initial attack was an "almost textbook response."

Mr. Sauvé, president of the National Police Federation, was pushing back against those who say RCMP mistakes may have contributed to the shooting, during which a killer went on a 13-hour rampage while dressed as a Mountie and driving a look-alike RCMP vehicle.

"The average Canadian today has the benefit of hindsight. If we look at all the information available to us, we are going to armchair quarterback," he said in an interview with the *Globe and Mail.*

Last month, the union was criticized for arguing, in a motion at an ongoing inquiry into the killings, that forcing RCMP officers to testify publicly at the inquiry would be too retraumatizing for them. Mr. Sauvé said he understood why families of victims opposed the motion, but he argued that the union has been co-operative with the inquiry process and that its position on the testimony had been mischaracterized.

The inquiry, known as the Mass Casualty Commission, rejected the union's motion, and three RCMP officers testified and were cross-examined last week. The commission began public hearings on Feb. 22.

"There's no pound of flesh to be had here," Mr. Sauvé said. "The perpetrator was killed. There's no trial, there's nobody going to jail.

So it's totally understandable that Nova Scotians and Canadians want some closure. And part of that closure is the ability to ask in public hard questions of those who responded that night."

Mr. Sauvé said the Mounties who responded to the shootings dealt with "a career's worth" of traumatic events in the span of two days. Anyone who doesn't understand the impact of post-traumatic stress disorder on police likely won't ever be convinced, he added.

"If a reasonable Canadian looks at this and says 'well, that's what they signed up for,' then they're not paying attention," he said. "The evidence is abundantly clear that public safety personnel are over-whelmingly overrepresented in mental health injuries."

In the second half of his report, Mercer mentioned the plight of murder victim Heather O'Brien and the complaints by Nick Beaton about the force, which we will examine in the next chapter. He included a boiler-plate paragraph on a lawsuit filed by the victims' families about the RCMP's failure to put out a public alert or call out other forces to help.

At the bottom of his story, Mercer did provide an obligatory "bal-ance" by quoting law professor Wayne MacKay, from Dalhousie University, who repeated what he had been saying regularly on talk radio in Halifax:

"I think a lot of people in Nova Scotia have many legitimate ques-tions about how the RCMP handled this," Dr. MacKay said. "I think they've been badly hurt by this. I think the lustre of the RCMP, and their image has taken a hit here, because they're not really delivering on that promise of going above and beyond all other police forces. There were system failures up and down the line . . . This screams out for a clear explanation as to how this happened."

Almost every one of the 117 *Globe and Mail* readers who bothered to comment on the piece had much the same opinion I did. "Who wrote the textbook? Dr. Seuss?" one said. "Was the textbook 'Springfield PD Police Procedures by Chief Clancy Wiggum'?" another asked, referring to the satirical animated TV series *The Simpsons*. Others seriously addressed the issue at hand. A Mr. Atoz wrote: "Every sentence is something along the lines of: what about root causes, what about PTSD, what about other failures in the justice system and government policy. We can never get the truth and hold people accountable because it is all hindsight and armchair quarterbacking. This attitude just demonstrates a lack of good faith, and this inflexible position only diminishes the RCMP."

For the RCMP and its union, the story was the perfect execution of a blue lie. They achieved a win by getting that phrase—"textbook response"—into the esteemed *Globe and Mail*. All that most people would remember was the headline, and it served to reinforce and stoke the emotional attachment some have to the police, especially the Mounties.

But the sickening facts were still the sickening facts. It was getting more difficult for the media to sugar-coat the failures of the RCMP—at least for those who were paying attention to the commission and were willing to dig a little deeper into the documents.

12

WHOOPS! COLLATERAL
TRAUMATIZATION

When the time came for the Mass Casualty Commission to deal with what happened after Gabriel Wortman escaped the clutches of the RCMP for a second time, it revealed to the world both its strategy and just how flawed its trauma-informed approach was. The commission had to explain, without upsetting anyone, how the RCMP had fumbled its way around Nova Scotia for twelve hours after the first 911 call from Jamie Blair and still hadn't put out a public alert about Gabriel Wortman, his shiny replica police car, and the fact that he was murdering people.

By 10 a.m. on Sunday morning, the RCMP suspected Wortman of killing only six people: Greg and Jamie Blair, Lisa McCully, Corrie Ellison, Frank Gulenchyn and Dawn Gulenchyn. They suspected he had shot Lillian Campbell Hyslop, but they were just arriving at the scene. The truth was that Wortman had already killed seventeen people. His eighteenth and nineteenth victims would be Kristen Beaton and Heather O'Brien, two home nurses employed by the Victorian Order of Nurses (VON).

After speaking for less than an hour about Glenholme, commission counsel Roger Burrill took a half-hour break, then continued with what happened next, on Plains Road in Debert. This time, he took a mere forty minutes for his encapsulation, complete with a few photos and audio clips to spice things up. It was emotional control at all costs.

"The foundational document goes into a great deal of detail with respect to forensic and physical evidence," Burrill said in a grave tone of voice. "I will not be doing that this morning. I will not be going into descriptors of crime scene particulars. This is a high-level introduction of the known facts, and as with other foundational documents involving fatalities, the details are indeed troublesome and disturbing. You need to know that, obviously, before I commence my presentation."

As was the case earlier with his Glenholme presentation, Burrill barely scratched the surface of the real story. The O'Brien family had also planted a time bomb in the commission files that would soon detonate in the faces of the RCMP and the commissioners.

Let us begin with the murder of Kristen Beaton. At the time of her death, Beaton was pregnant with her second child. When she went to work that morning, dressed in scrubs, she knew there had been murders the night before in Portapique, but there had been no public warning. The reports were vague. Sometime after 9:30 a.m., Beaton left a client's home in Masstown and headed toward Debert in her silver-grey 2017 Honda CR-V. Before she did, she texted her husband, Nick, and told him that she had learned from a co-worker that Greg and Jamie Blair were among those murdered in Portapique. She stopped at a gravel parking spot on the west side of Plains Road. She and Nick then exchanged a series of texts.

"Apparently 9 ppl were shot and 4 houses were lit on fire. Crazzzy," Kristen wrote.

"Still on the loose," Nick replied.

"Oh, wow, really? That's scary . . . Know what colour?"

"But not many Crown Vic on the road . . . lol," Nick said. "And it was in four different places."

"Wow," Kristen wrote. "That's insane. . . . Ya true I'm headed to Masstown and Debert for the next few visits."

"If you see someone walking don't stop," Nick said.

"They released who buddy is?" Kristen asked.

"No, not yet," Nick wrote. "They try to get in ur rig ram them or run them over and we will deal with it later."

Seconds later, Nick told her they had just released the name of the shooter—Gabriel Wortman. He then called his wife, and they talked for one minute and forty-four seconds.

After she hung up, Wortman pulled up parallel to but slightly behind her car. He walked up to the driver's-side door and shot her dead.

In his presentation, commission counsel Burrill spent almost the entire time tracing Wortman's movements through the eyes of witnesses and security cameras. He devoted what was effectively one paragraph to the shooting and another, later, as a mini biography of Kristen Beaton, as if he wanted to strip any possible emotion out of his presentation. Burrill didn't dare delve into what had been going on behind the scenes, which infuriated her husband.

In the days and weeks after the massacres, Nick Beaton had become one of the faces of the families' anguish. He seemed perpetually angry. He marched. He protested. He made it clear that he trusted neither the RCMP nor the government. He wouldn't talk to reporters unless he was trying to make a point, usually about Lisa Banfield. He was even fed up with the Red Cross, which had used the massacres to fundraise $6.2 million, purportedly for distribution to the families of the victims. Beaton grew so testy, he didn't even trust his newspaper carrier, because he drove a decommissioned police car. Beaton didn't testify at the commission. Some discounted him because of his negative attitude. Why was he so angry all the time? Here are some of the reasons why.

The morning that Kristen was shot, it took eight hours for two Mounties to pay Beaton a visit and officially tell him that his wife was dead.

"You'll be happy to know you're the first one to be notified," Nick recalled the Mounties saying. They left quickly, he added.

"If Nick wasn't so numb, he thinks he would have punched the officer" is how Beaton's reaction was described in a commission summary of the situation.

The Mounties called a "family meeting" on June 26, 2020, with Nick Beaton and Kristen's brother, Rick Roode. Sitting in for the RCMP were Superintendent Darren Campbell; Inspector Murray Marcichiw, who was in charge of the Major Crimes and Human Trafficking units; Sergeant Glen Bonvie of the Northeast Nova Major Crime Unit; lead investigator Corporal Gerard (Gerry) Rose-Berthiaume; and Constable Wayne "Skipper" Bent, the family liaison officer. The commission reduced the interview to a lengthy summary on July 19, 2021, likely because it deemed Beaton's raw and emotional language to be "harmful" and in need of tempering. Near the end of the commission's hearings, on September 14, 2022, Beaton submitted a statutory declaration for the commission to put his thoughts on record.

Beaton's frustration with the Mounties had a sound foundation. After Kristen was shot, her body was allowed to lie outside, uncovered, for hours while Mounties milled around guarding the scene and "investigating." Her brother went to the scene, but the police prevented him from getting close to her body. Beaton complained that the Mounties didn't properly process Kristen's car. They had the vehicle towed to the Bible Hill RCMP detachment, where it was left outside, parked and unlocked, next to Mounties' personal vehicles. It was exposed to the elements, including a late-spring snowfall. "There were no cameras or gates in the parking lot. The parking lot is by a main road for anyone to see," stated the summary, which was never read aloud. "Nick discovered that the driver's window and passenger-side window were shot out of the car. All of Kristen's personal items (like her VON ID) were just sitting in the car . . . nothing was cleaned up or hidden. There were signs of Kristen's trauma in the car."

A telling excerpt from the summary described the scene on Plains Road the day after Kristen's murder: "An RCMP member in red serge came over and hugged [Nick's mother, Bev Beaton], bawling. He explained that he was in Portapique on the Saturday night. On Sunday morning he was sent home . . . at 6 a.m. . . . because they understood that Gabriel was dead in his cottage. Nick does not know that officer's name. He knows that the officer attended the memorial for Lisa McCully at Debert School dressed in red serge."

The officer was likely Sergeant Dave Lilly, who spoke to *Globe and Mail* reporter Lindsay Jones at the time. Lilly was later demoted for unknown reasons, and subsequently retired from the force.

All this pales in comparison to something else that was festering inside Beaton. The RCMP had received a tip that Kristen knew Wortman through an elderly couple she had treated. Their names were Elson and Jill Sutherland. They had lived across the road from Wortman on Portapique Beach Road. Before Elson died in 2017, he had received home care from the VON nurses, visits that Wortman sometimes monitored. It was supposedly then that he met Beaton and struck up a relationship with her. The RCMP wouldn't give Beaton back his wife's phone for about three months, and later told him she had three phones: her own, her work phone and an old cellphone. Later they told him that they did not believe Kristen had had a secret relationship with Wortman, but they couldn't give him some items back because he was suing the force.

"What is the RCMP trying to hide?" Nick asked in frustration.

He wondered why the RCMP seemed to be spending more time investigating his late wife than Lisa Banfield and her past, a subject about which he had been vocal, much to the commission's dismay.

◆

Heather O'Brien had heard there was a killer on the loose in Portapique, 18 kilometres to the west. The fifty-five-year-old had worked for the VON for the past sixteen years, but she was off that day. She felt she needed to get out of the house to clear her head, so she got in her car and headed to the nearby Tim Hortons. She planned to stop by one of her daughter's houses and wave through the window at her grandchildren, the best she could do during the COVID lockdown.

As she headed east on Plains Road in her Volkswagen Jetta, O'Brien was chatting on the phone with a friend, fellow VON nurse Leona Allen, who had just finished seeing a client. As they talked, O'Brien came upon a crime scene to her right, not knowing that another one of her colleagues, Kristen Beaton, was being murdered.

Allen described what happened next to 911 operators: "Hi, um, uh, I was just on the phone, and my friend, who is out in Debert, she said she was near Lancaster Drive in her car. She said she heard gunshots, and there was a police vehicle, and then all I could hear was her scream, and I can't get through to her."

It appears that, after hearing the shots, O'Brien pulled over about 320 metres down the road and stopped with her foot on the brake while she continued to chat with Allen. Having killed Beaton, Wortman raced down to where O'Brien was parked, exited the car and shot O'Brien a number of times in the head through the driver's-side window, shattering it. O'Brien's car then rolled about 60 metres, into a wooded ditch area, ending up against a tree.

At 10:07:53, the RCMP dispatcher said: "Break! Break! Break for dispatch. We have another shooting on Plains Road in Debert."

The Mounties were just getting in position to storm the Fisher residence. They were mobilizing to deal with the false report of a shooting a kilometre up the road at the Hidden Hilltop campground. The Campbell Hyslop murder scene, farther up Highway 4 in Wentworth, was still fresh. Now there were reports of two shootings on Plains Road. The Mounties found themselves going in every which direction.

When the Mounties finally got to O'Brien, they found a pulse and called for an air ambulance for her, which they soon cancelled. They deemed the area to be unsafe and would not allow paramedics or anyone else in. When one of O'Brien's daughters, Michaella, tried to enter the scene, a Mountie told her to "fuck off." The Mounties placed a blanket over O'Brien and declared her dead.

The O'Brien family knew otherwise. Soon after the incident, they went into Heather's computer and found the data from her Fitbit, a wristwatch device that tracked her heartbeat in real time and stored the information on her home computer. It showed her heart beating for eight hours after she was shot. The family captured the image from that day:

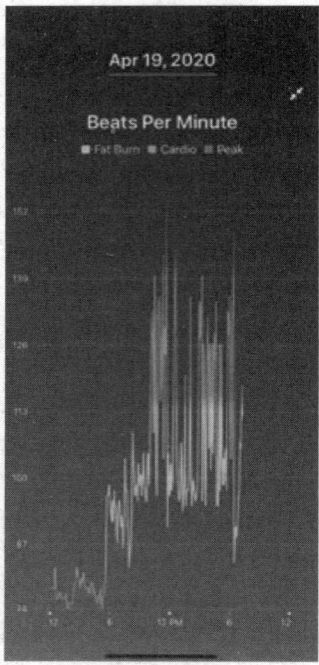

Heather O'Brien's Fitbit readout showed a spike in her heart rate shortly after 10 a.m., when she was shot, and that her heart was beating for eight more hours.

The Fitbit information was raised by the family at an emotional meeting with the RCMP on May 28, 2020, almost six weeks after O'Brien's murder. Its existence was first recorded that day in the handwritten notes of Constable Skipper Bent, the RCMP's designated family liaison officer. Present at the meeting were Heather's husband, Andrew "Teddy" O'Brien, and his four daughters: Kathleen Devine, Darcy Dobson, Molly O'Brien and Michaella O'Brien. The RCMP was represented by case manager Corporal Angela McKay and Constable Bent.

The O'Briens had many questions, which the Mounties seemed unable or unwilling to answer. Teddy O'Brien accused them of hiding Banfield in protective custody. "No one has even seen her," he said.

"The others were screaming Lisa must have known, that she should be charged, knew about the car, knew what he was doing," Bent wrote in his notes. "Numerous times they said they were unable to heal until they get answers. Want details. Will get a lawyer if needed to get answers."

Like many others who had been interviewed, Teddy O'Brien accused the Mounties of using their skills to avoid getting to the bottom of the story. As Constable Bent noted about the atmosphere in the room, "They told us they had questions but every time they asked a question they would interrupt, say we were going around in circles, not telling the truth, that we were trained that way. Andrew told me I would be a good politician because I danced around. Andrew told me we don't have hearts."

For the O'Briens, the big issue was the Fitbit information. Over the next nineteen months, as the opening date for the commission loomed, the family waited for follow-up from the Mounties or the commission. There was none. They sent the commission a New Year's gift on January 1, 2022: the Fitbit printout. And yet Burrill didn't address it in his presentation. Like his summary of Kristen Beaton's murder, his description of events surrounding Heather O'Brien's death was slim.

Then, thanks to the delaying tactics of Sauvé and his union, there was an almost five-week gap between the examination of what happened to O'Brien and the testimony of Corporal Duane Ivany and Constable Ian Fahie, the two officers who arrived on the scene first. When they finally did appear before the commission, they were treated with kid gloves. However, what they had to say largely confirmed the contradictions noted by the O'Briens, who, that night, released the Fitbit information on Facebook with an accompanying message:

As a family we have decided that our best course of action, after today's disappointing hearing at the Mass Casualty Commission, is to make a statement regarding the death of our Mother, Heather O'Brien. Many months ago, we were given earth shattering information. Information that we never knew, or even imagined possible.

When Cst. Ian Fahie approached the scene of our Mother's homicide, he felt a pulse, and she was making slight noises. You can read this information online through Mass Casualty Commission's website. You will have to search for it, but it's there. Cpl. Duane Ivany also attended the scene of our Mother's homicide. Nearly two (2) years after her death he made a statement to the Mass Casualty Commission stating that, initially, he felt a pulse, but later determined, this was just his own adrenaline. In his statement he says she was dead.

During the same time, Cst. Fahie's Statement reads "So we . . . I say, we had to let her die, but you know, we had to let her just pass on. We knew she . . . like to . . . I don't think she was going to make it anyways. So, we got a blanket, covered her up and then we just went to the road and guarded". We are gobsmacked, for many reasons, but mostly because this information was not presented to the public today.

Cst. Ian Fahie is the lower ranking officer in this situation, he has nothing to gain by lying. More likely he has a lot to lose for telling the truth. Life Flight (Nova Scotia air ambulance) was called in for our Mother. They never arrived. Many things about Cpl. Duane Ivany's statement to the commission do not line up with the facts we have on paper. It is in the public's best interest to know how first responders will or will not act in the face of a life-or-death situation. The truth is EVERYTHING is so contradicting. The commission has filled its Plains Road Foundational Document, with many contradicting statements. None more contradicting than the statements of Fahie and Ivany. Compare the two (2) and you will know exactly what we mean. How is it that Fahie (who was there first) is trying to put her car in park, and then Ivany needs to break the windows to get inside? The same windows that were shot out 60 metres from where her car landed. These things, and many others, do not add up.

We are not pretending to know everything that happened, what we do know, however, is we have supporting evidence. We have all the Fitbit information from our Mother's computer that day. Information we did share with the Commission, but they neglected to include in their document. This information records our Mother having a heart beat until 6:00 p.m.

We know this information is controversial, we also know that it has been used in cases in the U.S. to pinpoint time of death. Once again, we are disappointed that the public is not getting this information, and instead being forced to read through thousands of documents to find anything. If it does not fit their narrative, it is not published. Our

Mother deserves better than this and so do the people of this province. There are members of the RCMP who were on scene and never interviewed, nor were the members of our local Fire Department, who were on scene that day. This is unacceptable work in every way. We deserve the best chance to know what happened that day.

Thank you,

The O'Brien Family

Given the extent of her injuries, Heather O'Brien would not have survived even if she had received treatment. Her family knew that, but that wasn't the point. She deserved to be treated with hope and dignity. To add insult to injury, when they took back Heather's Jetta, they discovered that it had not been cleaned. Inside they found body fragments and a spent shell casing, a devastating experience that mirrored Nick Beaton's.

The way the commission handled the Fitbit story was a perfect example of how it favoured the RCMP's official narrative despite contradictory evidence. First, by its own definition, the only truth the commission would consider was the information in the foundational documents, which had been compiled behind closed doors by its lawyers, investigators and other staff. Many of the interviews were soft, unfocused and often superficial. Nothing was tested by cross-examination. Lawyers for the families of the victims or others could ask questions only about facts contained within the foundational documents, and the questions had to be approved in advance by the commission. Everything else was out of bounds. In his opening statement, commission counsel Burrill opined that he was giving "a high-level introduction of the known facts." The Fitbit evidence wasn't in the foundational documents; therefore, it wasn't a fact.

Another commission tactic was spreading out testimony about an incident over a long period of time or in an illogical or non-chronological sequence, as it did when examining the rope across the road at the mouth of the blueberry field, and as it would do for the Onslow Belmont fire hall shooting.

After the Fitbit controversy, the commission took eleven days off, then returned on April 11, 2022, to deal with the events at the Onslow Belmont fire hall.

◆

After murdering Heather O'Brien, Wortman headed south on Plains Road and turned left on Belmont Road, which passed over the expressway, allowing him to see what the Mounties were doing there. He was on his way down to two-lane Highway 2 in Onslow, headed toward Truro.

The Mounties, meanwhile, were scrambling to throw up roadblocks— behind Wortman. Teams that had assembled for the assault on the Fisher residence were now frantically trying to catch up to him. They had heard the compromised authority order given to Corporal Mills and passed it along. Their orders were now to shoot to kill.

Ahead of Wortman on Highway 2 was the Onslow Belmont fire hall, which had been designated as a centre for victims, though few had gone there. Inside were Fire Chief Greg Muise, Deputy Fire Chief Darrell Currie and Richard Ellison, Corrie Ellison's dad. Two other Portapique residents who had been evacuated had just left to get breakfast.

Outside the fire hall, a Mountie cruiser was backed up to the eastern end of the building, with safety cones placed around it. Constable Dave Gagnon was inside the vehicle talking to David Westlake, the regional emergency management coordinator for Colchester County, who was standing outside.

Wortman drove by the fire hall, unnoticed by Gagnon. The RCMP had not alerted the public to the fact that Wortman was driving what appeared to be a marked police car, and even some individual Mounties still weren't sure about that.

About twelve minutes behind Wortman were constables Terry Brown and David Melanson, one of the cut-off teams who, just a little while earlier, thought they had found Wortman on their way to Glenholme but then learned it was a fellow Mountie. Now they were nearing the fire hall in their unmarked Nissan Altima. When they saw Westlake by Gagnon's cruiser, they mistook him for Wortman—an honest mistake in a pressure-packed situation, they said later.

I reported the full story in *22 Murders*, but Brown and Melanson would testify that when they saw Westlake, they identified themselves as police and ordered him to show his hands, which he did not do, which is when they began shooting. When I later took the same route as Brown and Melanson, the fire hall appeared out of nowhere, being hidden by a large hedgerow and an LED sign, which raises questions about how they could have recognized the situation so quickly. Moreover, several witnesses saw Brown and Melanson stop *short* of the fire hall, get out of their vehicle and run toward the building, firing their carbines as they ran and hitting the LED sign on the western edge of the property. One witness, Jerome Breau, who was closest to the officers and had his window down—he had driven up to them thinking it was a traffic stop—didn't hear them shout any commands. Some bullets pierced the wall of the fire hall and became embedded in a fire truck. Others narrowly missed those hiding inside. Mountie Gagnon exited the vehicle and literally waved a white flag, trying to show them that he was a real police officer.

After the shoot-up, Brown casually walked around the building with his C8 on his shoulder, while Melanson peeked inside the fire hall. They did not immediately report the shooting to their superiors; instead, they jumped back in their vehicle and picked up their pursuit of Wortman, who by then had driven through Truro and was headed south toward Halifax. Only after a 911 call came in about the fire hall shooting did they admit, "That was us."

Around this time, there was another strange call to the Mounties. An unknown person reported that Wortman had left Onslow and was on Highway 104 heading west, away from Halifax. The call drew some Mounties in that direction. Remember, the RCMP and the commission insisted that Wortman did not have access to a phone or a radio capable of working on the RCMP's encrypted network. They said the only phone he had was at his warehouse, and that it didn't have a SIM card because it was used only to play music.

The Onslow Belmont fire hall debacle was reviewed afterwards by the police watchdog, the Serious Incident Response Team (SIRT). Its director at the time, former judge Felix Cacchione, accepted the RCMP's version of events and entirely ignored what civilian witnesses had seen.

Here's what the SIRT report by Cacchione, issued March 2, 2021, stated about the actions of the two officers (SO1 and SO2):

As they neared the Onslow Fire Hall, they saw AP2 [Westlake], a man wearing a yellow and orange reflective vest standing by the driver's side door of a fully marked RCMP vehicle parked in front of the fire hall. Attempts made by SO2 [Melanson], using both the mobile and portable radios, to notify other officers of what SO1 [Brown] and SO2 were seeing were unsuccessful due to the heavy volume of radio traffic. When SO1 identified themself as police and ordered AP2 to show his hands, [he] did not do as ordered but instead ducked behind the police vehicle and then popped up before running into the fire hall.

Based on everything SO1 and SO2 had seen and heard since coming on duty and what they had just observed, they had reasonable grounds to believe that AP2 was the killer and someone who would continue his killing rampage. They discharged their weapons in order to prevent deaths or serious injuries.

In its fire hall foundational paper, the commission adopted the SIRT report as authoritative. The MCC listed eight "key witnesses" to the event, seven of whom were outside the fire hall and saw what Brown and Melanson did that day: Sharon McLellan (whose husband, Tim, could also have been called, but wasn't), Jerome Breau, Martin Foley, Charles Hoyt, Joy McCabe, Violet O'Reilly and Joan Van Gestel. However, the only witness the commission called to speak in public about what happened was Richard Ellison, who was *inside* the fire hall and saw only the result of Brown and Melanson's actions—their bullets coming through the wall.

Ellison was on a panel along with firefighters Muise and Currie, who had attended almost all of the public hearings. (On many days, they were the only ones from the public there.) After Burrill completed his typically dry presentation of events, his colleague Jamie Van Wart led the three men through their almost-victim stories. Currie defiantly turned the session on its head, daring to describe the shortcomings and inadequacies of the RCMP and its members. He said those inside the building were not immediately told it had been RCMP members shooting at them, and not Wortman. They were forced to cower in the fire hall, fearing they could be shot dead any second. Afterwards, the RCMP never offered them help. Two years later, Currie was still off work from his regular job at Bell Canada.

After Van Wart finished asking his questions, Muise voiced his own criticisms, stating that it took eleven months before anyone even talked to him about what had happened on April 19, 2020. "I don't think that the RCMP wanted anything to do with the fire hall. I think they were shoving us under the table, hoping this would go away, but I don't think they realized what they put us through," he said, then passed the torch to Currie: "You can go for it now if you want to."

"I only had a couple of things that didn't fit into any of your questions," Currie said to Van Wart. "I found the whole commission, the inquiry, has for me been . . . nothing near trauma-informed. It's been, you know, not transparent. You know, my legal counsel has to fight to get witnesses, people that are important. Important documents are buried, you know, deep within thousands of pages of reference material that don't seem to fit a nice PowerPoint presentation. That has all added to my stress. The least stressful day, probably, so far with this inquiry, is today and me sitting here, because I think there should be more of me and more of Greg and more of Mr. Ellison sitting here. PowerPoint presentations are nice, but there's so much missing and people don't have time to sift through foundational documents and reference material to get the real story, so that's been troubling for me."

Then Currie turned to the RCMP. "And the only other thing I have to say, because I've said it in all my interviews: I don't believe the story that's been told by at least one of the RCMP officers on the outside. My opinion, obviously, but based on witness testimony from other witnesses, the stories don't line up . . . I have been really troubled by that, because it really bothers me that a member of the RCMP may have lied. I can't obviously confirm that . . . I didn't question them, but I've read lot of witness statements and things don't line up."

Van Wart was disinclined to ask the obvious follow-up questions. "Well, thank you, Deputy Chief Currie, for sharing that part of your experience as well," he said. "I think at this point what I would propose we do is to take a break for lunch."

The three dour commissioners just took it on the chin, expressing no commiseration with the firefighters. That wasn't in their trauma-informed game plan.

In a public inquiry in which there was no criminal risk to any of the parties, one might have expected everyone involved in the incident to relate their story in chronological order. First would be the Mounties, followed by the witnesses. But in the tightly controlled MCC process, Ellison, Currie and Muise spoke first, and then, *twenty-four days later*, after several other events were covered, the Mounties were called. Like Ivany and Fahie, Brown and Melanson were treated with kid gloves. In preliminary interviews, Brown had been allowed to have a support person—his wife—by his side. In front of the commission, Brown and Melanson testified together. Both said they saw a man in a safety vest who they thought was Wortman. They said they stopped on the highway and shouted orders, and when they were ignored, they opened fire. And that was the end of the commission's probe into the Onslow Belmont fire hall shooting.

Meanwhile, the growing controversy, over who was being called to speak at the commission and who wasn't, flushed a most unlikely witness out of the woodwork.

13

WHEN ASSUMPTIONS TURN BAD

It was 10:15 on Sunday morning, April 19, 2020. The Mounties were at the murder scenes of nurses Kristen Beaton and Heather O'Brien on Plains Road in Debert. It had been eight minutes since Gabriel Wortman had passed unnoticed—except for images on a security camera—by the Onslow Belmont fire hall, and the RCMP was scrambling to catch up to him. Constables Brown and Melanson, in their unmarked Nissan Altima, were now bearing down on the fire hall and would soon shoot up the place. Other Mounties were chasing another false lead, that Wortman had headed west on Highway 104. In Portapique, Constable Dorrington was guarding bodies but begging to participate in the cut-off team hunting Wortman.

Meanwhile, Wortman was entering the town of Truro, where almost everyone was either only vaguely informed or entirely unaware of the ongoing havoc. Despite pleas from some on the ground to announce that Wortman was in his own replica RCMP cruiser, RCMP commanders were dragging their feet, hoping to catch Wortman before anyone found out the embarrassing truth. At 10:15 a.m., a call came in to the 911 call centre that sent shivers down the yellow-striped pants of every Mountie who heard it. The transcript was included in the Mass Casualty Commission's foundational papers.

"What is the emergency?" Elaine, the 911 operator asked.

"Right," the man said. "You guys have an active shooter in Portapique, Gabriel Wortman?"

"Right?" Elaine responded.

"I'm just wondering if you guys are aware of what weapons he does have," the man said, discombobulating the 911 operator.

"Um, can you, uh, why, how you, how would you know, sir, how many weapons he has?" she asked.

"I know he has an AR-15. He has a Barrett .50-calibre sniper rifle. I know he's got a Glock 40 and he's got an assault 12-gauge shotgun . . . he's probably got enough ammunition to hold you guys off for four or five days," the caller said.

"Do you know if these are all legally obtained?" Elaine asked.

"No, they're all brought across the border. He's been smuggling out of Maine for probably the last twenty years," the man said, adding a few seconds later, "He also has two cases of nail grenades."

"Nail grenades?"

"Yeah."

"Okay, one second here," Elaine said. "And you said you [sic] had enough ammo to last three or four days?"

"Oh, yeah. Easy," the man said.

"What's your name, sir?"

"Robert Doucette," he replied.

Doucette, who is no relation to Autumn Doucette, spoke to the operator for nine minutes. Two minutes into the call, at 10:17 a.m., rather than triggering the Alert Ready public warning system, the RCMP fired off a photo of Wortman's replica police car on its Twitter account. Reporters and social media picked it up and alerted those who were paying attention to what was unfolding.

At that exact time, Wortman was captured calmly driving by Jimolly's Bakery Café and Murphy's Fish & Chips at the corner of Inglis Place and Esplanade Street, making his way through Truro as if he was a regular cop on patrol. There wasn't a real police car in sight because RCMP chief superintendent Chris Leather had told Truro police chief Dave MacNeil a few minutes earlier that the Mounties had everything in hand outside the town's limits. Nothing to worry about, Leather had assured him.

If Wortman had shot someone in Truro, such as the couple shown in the security camera video walking down the sidewalk away from him, we'd likely be telling a different story now. The Truro Police Service would have become involved, sparking an independent investigation that the RCMP would not have been able to fully control.

It was only as Wortman was leaving Truro that the RCMP called to ask MacNeil to lock down the town. MacNeil later described the move as "a Hail Mary pass." The Mounties still had no idea where Wortman was.

As for Doucette, the next thing the fifty-six-year-old knew, he was sitting at RCMP headquarters at 80 Garland Boulevard in Dartmouth, being interviewed by Halifax police detective Constable Anthony (Tony) McGrath, who worked with the RCMP in an integrated forces unit in the Halifax region.

Doucette told McGrath that the last time he had seen Wortman, about eleven months earlier, Wortman had ten cases of .50-calibre and two cases of .40-calibre ammunition. He said Wortman had a stockpile of official decals from the RCMP, Halifax Police, fire chiefs and postal vans. Doucette talked about stolen property and secret compartments in Wortman's properties and vehicles. He described Wortman's cross-border smuggling and his criminal associates.

How did he know all this? Doucette was Wortman's long-time right-hand man. In *22 Murders*, I could identify him only as "the Carpenter." At the time, nobody was certain of his surname, but it was well known that he had worked on Wortman's residential and commercial properties in Dartmouth and Portapique. I had heard many tales about him. He had lived on Wortman's warehouse property. He drank and womanized with Wortman. He was a scary guy in his own right, a legendary thug whom people were afraid to go near. Even though Wortman towered over him, he, too, was afraid of Doucette.

There were tales about Rob the Carpenter getting into arguments and threatening to throw people off a roof. Others talked about him carrying a gun. I was told the best place to look for him would be Dorchester, the federal penitentiary in New Brunswick. Of all the people in Wortman's circle—second only to Lisa Banfield, perhaps—Doucette enjoyed the widest vista. He knew what made Wortman tick.

Over the next little while, the Mounties seemed keen to learn everything Doucette knew, and he didn't disappoint. He described Wortman as "meticulous . . . he's the type of man that planned out everything," right down to how many screws he would need to fasten down a metal roof. He was a "money guy . . . money, money, money . . . The code to his garage at the house was GOLD."

According to Doucette, Wortman was also a sexual predator and had made advances to at least seven of the female victims. He was a drug dealer in cocaine, oxycodone and fentanyl, and Doucette had seen him with 10,000 oxycodone tablets at his cottage and 200,000 at his denturist office. Having once been an undertaker, Wortman would boast about the best ways to dispose of bodies. He always had lime and muriatic acid on hand. Doucette had never seen him with an RCMP uniform, but he had seen a Halifax Regional Police uniform on a hanger.

Doucette also told McGrath about Wortman's jealousy and temper. He described how he had mowed down a 25-metre-long fence with his pickup truck after a fight with his uncle over the property that Lisa McCully eventually bought.

He talked about Wortman and Banfield's life together. "I always wondered about him and Lisa having separate bedrooms," Doucette said, "both at the cottage . . . I call it, well, a fucking mansion . . . and at the house on Portland Street."

Years earlier, he had witnessed some epic fights between Banfield and Wortman. "I know he's had a gun to her head a few times. It was something that I heard them arguing about. At both places I heard them have that argument . . . And when he started throwing a fit about it, she just asked him, like, 'What are you going to do, put a gun to my head again?' And then he'd do stupid stuff like take the tires off her car so she couldn't go anywhere."

The transcript of the interview ran to forty pages. At the bottom of page thirty-eight there is a noteworthy moment, the significance of which seems to have been missed. Police interviews are typically conducted by a detective or two while supervisors monitor everything from another room and can follow up on pertinent information, allowing the interviewers to stay engaged. But during the interview with Doucette, McGrath asked him to think about anything else he might want to say and then left the room. When he returned, Doucette said he had indeed remembered something else. This is how the interview continued:

"He can watch every one of his properties from his phone," Doucette said.

McGrath immediately got up and left the room for another five minutes. Bad kidneys, or bad information they didn't want on record?

"All right, Rob," McGrath said upon his return. "Anything else?"

"You know, he can watch every one of his properties from his phone," Doucette reiterated.

"Okay, all right," McGrath said. Was he was trying to steer Doucette off the subject?

"Some of them you can see over two blocks away," Doucette said, trying to be helpful. "So . . ."

"Yeah," McGrath said. "He's got cameras all through there."

"He can see every inch of his property from his cameras," Doucette continued.

"Up in Portapique?"

"In Portapique and Portland Street," Doucette said.

"All right," McGrath said, then asked, "Anything else?"

Doucette shook his head.

"No. All right. That's, those are all the questions I got for you now."

Four days later, Constable Dayle Burris and Corporal Kathryn MacLeod of the RCMP conducted a thirty-one-minute follow-up interview with Doucette. The drastically under-schooled Doucette immediately spotted something he didn't like about the Mounties' pure version approach.

"What I would like you to do is tell us that information in as great a detail as you can, Rob. Every little detail is important," Burris said. "Don't leave anything out."

"I kind of liked Tony's questions," Doucette replied. "It's easier to talk when you have questions."

Burris chuckled. "Well . . ."

The Mounties reverted to their usual technique and nudged Doucette along, which in the end was not much different from what McGrath had done.

Strangely, neither the Mounties nor Halifax's McGrath seemed all that interested in chasing down the final resting place of the Barrett .50-calibre sniper gun, the grenades or all that ammunition. Wortman certainly didn't use it up for target practice. Neither did the Mounties pursue with Doucette the information about Wortman's phone, which one might have thought was important, considering that everyone said Wortman didn't have a phone and had relied on Banfield to take messages for him.

Doucette was useful to the RCMP in the days and weeks after the massacres, a period during which the force was confident that there would be a mere internal review of its performance. For journalists like me, the truth would be found in Information to Obtain documents (ITOs), in which the police use gathered statements and data to make the case for a search warrant. ITOs are supposed to be public information, but Sergeant Angela Hawryluk, who was the affiant, redacted Doucette's name and other identifiers. However, the juiciest claims were still there for the public to see.

In June 2020, I co-wrote a story for *Maclean's* about how Wortman may have had a special relationship of some sort with the RCMP, raising doubts about the veracity of the force's original version of events. After the story broke, Superintendent Darren Campbell emerged as the point man for the RCMP, telling the CBC's Elizabeth McMillan: "Recent media articles painting him as some underworld organized crime figure— nothing has been uncovered whatsoever that would suggest that."

After the internal review was upgraded to a public inquiry, which meant some of the RCMP's dirty laundry was in danger of being exposed, the force quickly moved to batten down the hatches for the coming storm. On July 30, 2020, the force put out a statement that it had found no evidence that Wortman had illegally disposed of bodies. It read, in part:

Some of the information that was unsealed and released from the ITOs on July 27, 2020, is from one individual who was interviewed and provided information which described the gunman as someone who was involved in the importation and trafficking of illicit drugs and firearms.

As part of H-Strong, investigators have conducted close to 700 witness interviews and only this one witness has come forward with information that the gunman was actively and recently involved in the importation and trafficking of illegal drugs. No other persons interviewed of the close to 700, including those closest to the gunman, have provided similar information that proves the gunman was an illegal drug smuggler and or drug trafficker. Therefore, we cannot corroborate this information. . . .

The one same witness is the only witness who described the gunman as having been involved in other murders and the disposal of bodies prior to April 18, 2020. The RCMP has not received credible or actionable information that the gunman was involved in any other murders.

The statement was not attributed to anyone in the force and was passed off as mere housekeeping, but sources said it was issued at Campbell's direction, and the 1,600-word news release was anything but ho-hum. It was aimed directly at Doucette and almost everything he had told the police.

But the public didn't even know Doucette's name, because it had always been redacted. Like Leon Joudrey before him, he got tossed overboard, along with much of what he had told the Mounties. It was as though the RCMP was editing the official narrative in plain sight.

When it came to the Mass Casualty Commission, one would think Doucette would have been a perfect candidate to testify, but he fell into the same category as many others who were deemed too close to the killer and who, perhaps, knew too much about his criminal activities. There was no mention by the RCMP or the commission about the security cameras on Wortman's properties and what might be on them.

The grenades were clearly real; other witnesses, as you'll learn, talked about their existence. Without Doucette's story, the sniper rifle, the boxes of ammunition and Wortman's myriad other sordid activities disappeared into the ether. The commission was bound not to tread down that path.

◆

After the massacres, most people were still defending the Mounties—"our brave first responders"—and critics like me were being shouted down, but by the summer of 2022, the tone had changed. The MCC had been limping along for over three months, and increasingly, people were complaining about what looked like a sloppy cover-up. But there was virtually nothing new being done by legacy and alternative-media journalists. They tended to take what the commission doled out to them and publish it.

Andrew Douglas and I were still busting new stories in *Frank* magazine, hoping to draw out even more information. We expanded *Frank*'s bullpen of loyal but hidden mainstream sources. We even came up with colourful names for some, such as White Knight and Red Horse, to go along with the original True Blue. They had all helped us to uncover some of the commission's deepest secrets, weeks and even months before it was set to reveal them.

In early April 2022, commission insiders, whom we dubbed "reviewers," had described almost frame by frame a video re-enactment that the RCMP had done with Lisa Banfield about the beginnings of the massacre. I wrote that "the RCMP and the inquiry have signalled that they are married to Banfield's story," but one of the problems with the video was that Banfield didn't seem to remember all the details, not even where Leon Joudrey's house was located. At another point in the video, Banfield is depicted trying to find a safe place but seems indecisive. "One of the police officers there points to where she should go," the reviewer said.

We put it all on the record to test how the commission might try to spin it when the time came. Would they still run with it? Would they tinker with it? One story opened up leads to another, and then another. That's how investigative journalism works—in increments. The trick is to keep digging up new information and expeditiously publishing it.

Our work led to an invitation into Gabriel Wortman's inner world. It began with a telephone call on June 2, 2022, to *Frank* editor Andrew Douglas. He emailed me the news: "Robert Doucette: 'I was Gabriel Wortman's best friend for a number of years.' He says he spent three hours being interviewed by police on April 20, 2020. Sounds like he has a lot to say, and he wants you to call him."

Of course I wanted to talk to Doucette, but I had to take some precautions first, to try to ascertain if he was on the level. That he had reached out to me was flattering, but I was still suspicious. I called him.

"What can I do for you?" I asked, after introducing myself.

"You're the only one who understands the story," he said.

I had expected a tough guy, but through the phone I heard someone who seemed hurt, even vulnerable. The injured child in his psyche wasn't that far beneath the skin. Like so many who had dealings with the commission, Doucette didn't like the way he had been treated. Even he thought there was something wrong with the way the commission was going about its business. "You'd think that they would want to talk to someone like me," he said.

He told me about his call to 911 on April 19, 2020. "I was warning them to look out for the others," Doucette said. "Heidi Stevenson was still alive when I called. I knew they were approaching him with caution, but I was saying that they should be approaching with even more caution."

Now, more than two years later, Doucette wanted to see what was in the commission records. He didn't have a computer, so he asked me if I could get him printouts of his statements. Douglas printed them, and citizen investigator Chad Jones delivered them to the front desk of the Dartmouth motel where Doucette was living. After Doucette and his lawyer had read them, we talked again.

"I'm guessing that there's probably 42 percent missing," Doucette said, adding that he had recently given the documents to his lawyer in an ongoing matter. "I just gave her a copy as reading material. I didn't tell her anything was missing until she told me. She told me there must be a lot missing because you get sentences and then there is a comment. There just seems that there's something missed out. She said it ends nowhere."

Doucette complained that his interviews, as published by the MCC on its website, were misleading. "The statements appear to indicate that I spoke with them two or three times. In fact, investigators came to see me seven times. They came so often that I was kicked out of my apartment in Halifax by my landlord. He had some tax issues and the neighbour across the street was a cocaine dealer who complained about all the police hanging around."

There was no question that Doucette lived on the edge and had a relatively minor criminal record for assault and threatening, but he had been close to Wortman for two decades. Whatever anyone might think of him, he was worth an investment of time and energy.

Over the next three weeks, I, and then Jones, established a telephone relationship with Doucette. We had to make him feel comfortable with us, and vice versa. Once, he texted me just as my phone battery died; I texted him back on Sharon's phone, a slip that would eventually lead to a story in and of itself.

He told me his full name: Robert Arthur Mitchell Crowdog Taylor Doucette.

"Rob Doucette is an illusion," he said. "People think I am a biker when all I am is a fucking Indian. I look like a pretty intimidating guy. I've looked this way since I was sixteen years old. People see me coming and they cross the street, but that's not who I am. It's just my protection. I'm the total opposite. I go to work. I come home. I do crafts. I carve peace pipes. I do leatherwork."

Crowdog, as he liked to be called, to acknowledge his proud Mi'kmaq heritage, was born and raised in the Yarmouth, Nova Scotia, area. He and his brother, David Andrew Doucette, spent much of their childhood in the foster care system. He told me about his miserable early life, how he and his brother bedded down in a dog cage, starving, getting by on a stash of pickled cucumbers. I told him about some of my adventures in journalism. He boasted that in the nineties he was a prolific hit man for the Hells Angels. I told him about my dealings with other hit men over the course of my life. He had a Hells Angels entrance tattoo "smudged out" on the underside of his left bicep. He said he was sixteen at the time and his outlaw-biker father had inducted him.

"Are you a Hells Angel?" I asked.

"No, I am not a Hells Angel, but I do have acquaintances who are Hells Angels."

He told me that his brother had been shot and killed by Toronto police on Spadina Road in February 2015 in a suicide-by-cop.

I countered by relating the gruesome and violent way in which one of my cousins had died.

The biggest surprise was that, like Wortman, Doucette had many police officers in his family. His maternal grandfather had been a police chief somewhere in Nova Scotia, perhaps Lunenburg, but he wasn't sure about the locale. His great-uncle had also been a police chief, somewhere out west. First there was Wortman's extended family of police and now Doucette. Birds of a feather? Had I slipped into a bizarro real-life version of the movie *The Departed*? I checked out that part of his story, and it was even wilder than I could have imagined.

Doucette's grandfather had been a police chief in Nova Scotia, all right, but not just any garden-variety one. He was Verdun Mitchell, the Halifax police chief from 1950 to 1968, when he committed suicide. The truth about Mitchell was hidden for fifty-two years, until veteran Halifax reporter Bev Keddy broke the real story on December 8, 2020, in *Frank* magazine. He wrote, in part:

> Verdun Mitchell became Chief Verdun Mitchell of the Halifax Police Department in January of 1950, at the age of 33, and remained in that position until early in the evening of Tuesday, October 22, 1968, when he went into the bathroom of police headquarters, probably sat on one of the toilets, and ate his service revolver. The Dennis-owned newspapers of the day, the Chronicle Herald and the Mail Star, only reported that his death had been "sudden."
>
> That sudden death came nearly 13 years after another sudden death, the December 8, 1955, murder of Michael Leo Resk, the Gottingen Street grocer whose murder is the oldest cold case registered with the province's Rewards for Major Unsolved Crimes program.
>
> Although it will almost certainly never be proven definitively, sources say it was known in the police department as far back as the late 1950s that Verdun Mitchell killed Michael Resk. The motive varies, depending on who's telling the story.
>
> There are persistent reports, going back decades, that Resk's store was little more than a front for illegal gambling. . . .

Yes, the police chief was believed to be a murderer, a suspicion that was covered up for more than half a century in tightly controlled Halifax.

As is so often the case, the beatification of Verdun Mitchell began immediately after his death. He was saluted by politician after politician for his supposedly great contributions to the community. The two Halifax daily newspapers at the time were dogmatically slavish to power. Their approach to journalism was summed up by their joint owner and publisher, Graham Dennis, who died in 2011. At a July 2014 reunion of *The 4th Estate*, veteran journalist Ralph Surrette recounted what Dennis had told him years earlier: "It's not our job to question the government. It's the opposition's job to question the government, and it's our job to report what they each said." Dennis's thinking echoed that of the long-deceased John Muir, my old *Hamilton Spectator* publisher from the same era: "Nobody elected the press to do anything."

In Halifax, at least, some were beginning to challenge that philosophy. In 1968, the investigative magazine *The Last Post* was created, followed a year later by the similarly-minded bimonthly newspaper *The 4th Estate*. After Mitchell's death, *The 4th Estate*, created by journalist Nick Fillmore and his father, Frank, began poking around the edges of the story.

"I just know that he shot himself while on the job in his office," Nick Fillmore recalled in 2023. "The *Herald* had the story three or four days before *The 4th Estate*, but they didn't cover it right away. When the *Herald* did report it, the story was a simple one column on an inside page. We obviously gave it more coverage: Why would a police chief commit suicide? We never got an answer. The assumption in the community was for personal or family reasons. My father and I were criticized for asking impolite questions."

I sent Doucette a photo of Mitchell, which put him into a bit of a tailspin. He didn't know the story and had never seen a photo of his grandfather.

A few weeks later, I had a book signing event at the Chapters outlet on Micmac Boulevard in Dartmouth, not far from where Doucette was living. He wanted to come over and get an autographed copy of my book. I was sitting at a table near the front of the store when he walked in, accompanied by a pleasant-looking woman. He was shorter than I expected, but at age fifty-six, he was still as muscular as I had been told.

"A lot of people say I look just like Woody Harrelson," he said.

Well, Woody Harrelson with a long grey braid that went halfway down his back. He wore a leather vest adorned with Native patches and symbols. He said it was a handed-down family treasure that his great-great-grandfather had begun wearing in 1897.

We shook hands and he wandered off into the store while I finished up. Sharon had come to the bookstore with me and was somewhere out of sight.

"There's a scary guy at the back of the store," she said when she returned.

"That's Rob the Carpenter," I told her.

When the event was over, Doucette and his companion drove off to her apartment so that she could get a sweater, and then met us at Finbar's Irish Pub, where we were joined by Chad Jones, who laughed out loud over the Woody Harrelson comparison.

The woman with Doucette seemed accomplished, but I'd learned long ago to take nothing for granted. There was something about her story that didn't make sense to me. I later found a Halifax Regional Police news release announcing that she had been charged with stealing a flight attendant's uniform from Halifax's Stanfield International Airport. The police said that she planned to use it to sneak onto an international flight, track down Elon Musk and have a baby with him. (I don't know the outcome and she can't now be reached.)

What I didn't know was that Doucette had been charged with assaulting her and that there was a no-contact order between them. Doucette later told me that he didn't assault her; it all had to do with her dog attacking him, biting him seventeen times and inflicting fifty-four wounds to his head, face, chest and arms. She had charged Doucette with assault, he said, because she didn't want the dog taken away. They both seemed fine with the arrangement.

In court documents from that case, Doucette was described as "a police hater" and "an associate of Gabriel Wortman" and "violent."

"They call me an associate of Wortman's," Doucette said. "I was trying to save lives and they [the police] make it look like I was fucking involved. They call me a police hater, but one of my best friends is a cop in Toronto."

I needed to record him. Chad Jones would help conduct the interview, while Jordan Bonaparte would tape and film it for the YouTube version of the *Nighttime* podcast. We didn't know what to expect, so we also brought along the brains and martial arts expertise of Ryan Potter, just in case. The four of us spent the sunny afternoon of July 1, on the Canada Day long weekend, inside the dumpy motel that Doucette called home.

In his spartan room, he had a shrine of Native artifacts on the dresser and a purloined U-Haul moving blanket for a bedspread. As Bonaparte set up one of his phones on the dresser to film the interview from that angle, Doucette startled him: "Hey, you got that camera sitting on my 300-year-old beads!" He showed us a bag of "diamonds" that he called his "retirement fund."

Doucette was clearly mindful of being on his best behaviour. He drank a dealcoholized blonde lager, while we each had a real craft beer or two from Tanner & Co Brewing, which is just down the road from where Sharon and I live. We even smoked a few cigarettes to help make him comfortable while I gently asked him questions and allowed him to regale us with his stories.

From left to right: "Rob the Carpenter" Doucette,
Chad Jones, Ryan Potter and Jordan Bonaparte on July 1, 2022,
in Doucette's motel room. (Palango)

We were hardly settled in when Doucette, a grin on his face, pulled out his phone. He had something he wanted us to hear. He said that he didn't hate the police, but he didn't trust them, which was one of the reasons he carried a mini recorder in his pants pocket that he could switch on when times became interesting for him. He played a short blurb from one of those moments. We listened to it a couple of times. It seemed intriguing, but I didn't know how long we could hold his attention and I wanted to capture as much as we could before dealing with that recording.

Doucette talked about how he had built secret compartments for Wortman in all of his properties—places where he could hide guns, money and drugs—and how Wortman's warehouse was filled with stolen goods. He described his suspicions about Wortman's being a killer who was expert at disposing of bodies. His smuggling. His associations with outlaw bikers. He even told us about how he shot Wortman's pet wild bear after it had gone after a friend's dog.

I wanted to talk about Wortman's secret phone. It seemed implausible in this day and age that a wheeler-dealer like Wortman could get through life phone-surfing and never having one of his own. Doucette believed that, although Wortman hadn't told him where the phone had come from, it was somehow linked to the police. He said Wortman was disciplined about his secret phone: "He hid it in the door panel of the truck. It was always in silent mode. Lisa didn't even know about it. I saw it. It was an Android phone, like a Samsung. He never called me on it, and I didn't know the number to it."

He repeated what he had told Halifax constable Tony McGrath: that Wortman had used the phone to monitor his home, business and warehouse security cameras.

Although the police and the commission and just about everyone associated with Wortman said he didn't have a telephone, in the May 27, 2021, version of the information to obtain a search warrant, there was an unredacted reference to such a phone being listed in Lisa Banfield's phone records, along with his verified email address.

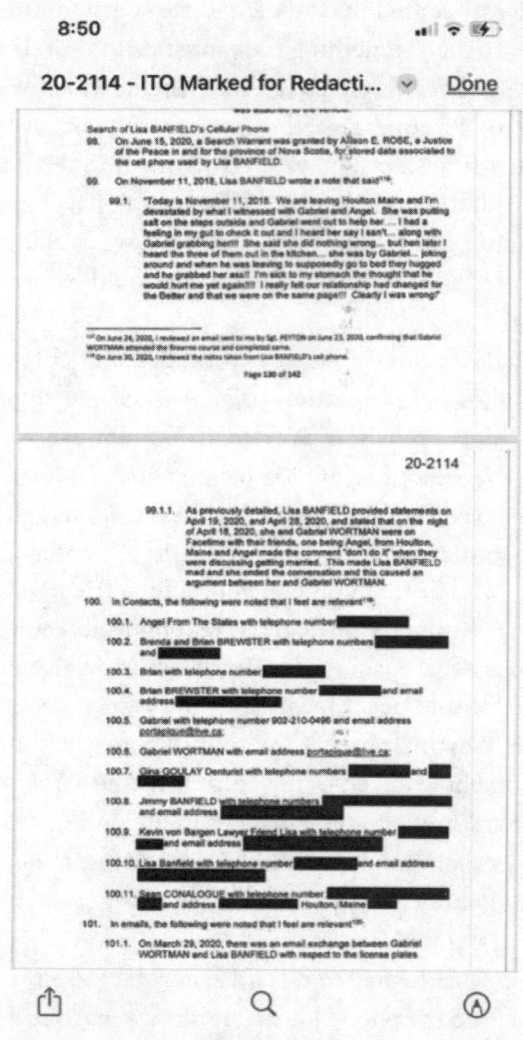

Paragraph 100.5 of the May 17, 2021, ITO showed a reference to what was described as Gabriel Wortman's telephone number.

The ITOs were constantly evolving and changing. Ryan Potter, among others, vigilantly scrutinized each one to detect even the most subtle changes. When he saw the number, he suspected that the

Mounties had made another mistake. "I found it odd," Potter told me. "It wasn't redacted in any of the ITOs, unlike almost everyone else's phone number."

Potter did some research and learned that it was a Telus system phone number, but it didn't appear to belong to Banfield or to Wortman's clinic. He called it, but there was never an answer.

When the commission published its foundational documents, any mention of that phone seemed to have been erased from the record.

Doucette said Wortman was driven by money, sex and love of Portapique. I later paraphrased Doucette's comments in one of three articles we published in *Frank*. "He wanted to own the entire area. The people he liked, he liked a lot, almost to the point of taking ownership over them. He would give dentures away to people who needed them but if he thought a customer could afford to pay, Wortman wanted every last cent owing to him."

He described Wortman as being on a never-ending hunt for sex. "Gabriel would chase everything from eighteen to eighty," he said. "He was a pig that way. He would just go up to women and say: 'I would like to fuck you.'"

He also described attending hot-tub parties at Brenda Forbes's house on Portapique Beach Road, which John Zahl and Joanne Thomas eventually bought and were murdered in. I'd heard about the parties from others, but Doucette provided even more detail. "He'd just go with a bunch of booze, strip off and climb in the hot tub. Everybody else would just shoo . . . and get out of the hot tub. Gabriel was built like a donkey. Wasn't a whole lot of women who wanted that near them," he said.

As it turned out, Doucette was the one who had prompted the police to nose around in Kristen Beaton's life. He had told the Mounties about Wortman's close relationship with the elderly Elson and Jill Sutherland across the road, and how he had come to know the VON nurses, in particular Beaton. It was all an incredible stew of information. (To repeat, the RCMP said that it found no evidence of such a relationship.)

We all wanted to know more about Lisa Banfield. "She was always chilly and even on a nice day needed a blanket at the cottage," Doucette remembered. I wrote the following in *Frank* about that part of the conversation:

> In December 2020 Lisa Banfield, her brother James and brother-in-law Brian Brewster were each charged with illegally supplying ammunition to Wortman, some of which he used in the 22 murders that were committed that weekend.
>
> His finances exhausted by the legal battle, James Banfield eventually pleaded guilty to a charge. Earlier this year, as her case was set to go to trial, Banfield's case was transferred to Restorative Justice, as was Brewster's. [After that process was completed, both Lisa and Brian's charges were dropped. James Banfield successfully withdrew his guilty plea.] This meant everything would be hidden away in a closed and odd process, considering the facts. Restorative justice means the two sides in an alleged crime come together, talk things over and work out a resolution, as if it were a dispute that could ever be resolved.
>
> Doucette said he told the MCC investigators that Banfield had been purchasing ammunition for Wortman "since around 2010 or 2011. She wasn't around Portapique all that much but when she did come up, I saw her bring ammunition. I don't know if she had a PAL (Possession and Acquisition Licence). She got ammunition for everything except the Barrett. I don't think it's easy to get .50 calibres in Canada. I think Gabe brought a bunch of those in from the States."
>
> Doucette said he and Wortman used to shoot the guns, especially at the warehouse property with its long, cleared fields.
>
> He said Wortman liked shooting the Barrett but wasn't a very good shot at first. Doucette said that after he coached Wortman "he could take the top off a beer bottle from 500 yards or so."
>
> Doucette said he twice saw Banfield firing a Glock 40 pistol outside the cottage at 200 Portapique Beach Road. He said she was inexperienced at the time and that the gun was too much for her.
>
> "She almost lost the gun over her head . . . and she handed it to me and shook her head," Doucette said. . . .

Doucette said that Lisa Banfield didn't like him hanging around, but that he wasn't all that fond of her either.

"To my mind she was the controlling one," Doucette said, echoing comments made by others, as reported previously.

"She didn't like anyone hanging around that Gabe liked. One time Gabe, me and some guys were sitting around having a beer and Lisa marched in and said to Gabe: 'You, come with me, right now.' He jumped up and went with her."

Doucette said that he witnessed moments of friction between the two but didn't ever witness Wortman hitting or abusing Banfield. He did see him jack up her Mercedes, remove all the wheels and throw them into the river in one fit of pique.

Another time he heard Lisa say through a closed door: "Don't you ever put a gun to my head again."

On the other hand, the day after one row between the couple, Doucette said that it was Wortman who was sporting a black eye.

We don't know who gave him that black eye, and Doucette acknowledged that "there were a lot of people who didn't like Wortman." I have tried to reach Banfield for her comment on this matter through her lawyer, but at the time of writing I haven't received a response.

◆

It looked as if we were on a roll, but then we dealt with the recording that Doucette had us listen to soon after we entered his motel room on Canada Day. So much of what he told us had been confirmed by my own interviews with other witnesses or police statements from witness interviews. As quirky as he might have been, Doucette seemed honest enough. The recording he gave us seemed a bit odd, but we rolled the dice and ran with it. I wrote a story about it for *Frank* magazine. Andrew Douglas published it online immediately. Bonaparte and I featured it on the *Nighttime* podcast. Here is the first part of the magazine piece:

WORTMAN WAS INVESTIGATED BY THE RCMP
AS EARLY AS 2004 FOR A MURDER

By Paul Palango

A 34-second snippet of audio tape recorded in the spring of 2004 shows that Gabriel Wortman was being investigated in a still unsolved murder by the Royal Canadian Mounted Police.

The murder victim was Kevin James Petrie, a 50-year-old career criminal who had been charged more than a dozen times with drug trafficking, various thefts and assaults between 1993 and 2000. At the time police said Petrie had been assaulted during an apparent home invasion at 269 Pleasant Street in Dartmouth. He died 11 days later after being found in medical distress at 7132 Spruce Street near the intersection of Joseph Howe Drive and Highway 102. An autopsy showed he had died from the effects of a blunt force trauma to the head.

In March 2019, the fifteenth anniversary of Petrie's murder, the Nova Scotia Department of Justice offered a $150,000 reward to help solve the murder.

Robert Doucette, who worked as Wortman's carpenter and side-kick for almost 20 years, says he was with Wortman at his denturist business at 193 Portland Street in Dartmouth when two plain-clothes RCMP investigators walked through the door and intro-duced themselves.

The Mounties were likely assigned to the Halifax Regional Police/RCMP Integrated Major Crime Unit.

Doucette said the mood was casual and informal and they had come to see him about a person they described as "Kevin." Doucette knew of "a booster" named Kevin who did "business" with Wortman but didn't know Kevin's last name.

"Kevin was just a little common thief . . . that used to hang around with us quite a bit. He used to pop in and sell stuff to Gabriel," Doucette said in an interview with me, *Nighttime* podcast host

Jordan Bonaparte and citizen investigators Chad Jones and Ryan Potter. "The only time I ever seen Kevin was when I happened to be there and he would come and sell stolen stuff for 40 per cent of the cost. He sold meat for half the cost. I always wondered what happened to Kevin, myself."

At one point during their 35–40-minute conversation with Wortman, the Mounties honed in on the big question all murder detectives ask: when did you last see the victim?

It was at this point Doucette reached into his pocket and activated the mini tape recorder he always carried with him. He captured about 36 seconds of what was being said before he thinks he accidentally turned off the device hidden in his pocket.

The 36 seconds captured this exchange just after Doucette said the police mentioned Kevin's name:

Mountie: . . . he's also dead.

Wortman: Ahhhhhhh.

Mountie: You don't seem too surprised to hear that. Why is that?

Wortman: I had a vision that it was so.

Mountie: So when was the last time you saw him, I mean, other than your dream?

(At this point there is a six to seven second delay as Wortman considers his response and then Wortman does what might be described as an almost disembodied sing-songy mantra for another six seconds. It is difficult to decipher exactly what he is saying but it sounds like this).

Wortman: "I got it I got it I got it I got it I got it I got it I got it . . ."

There is an indecipherable last comment after Wortman's chant at which point Doucette believes he may have accidentally turned off the tape.

Even to the untrained ear, Wortman appeared to zone out—dissemble—when asked about Petrie, like a little child being caught stealing from the cookie jar.

Doucette said that he played the tape for RCMP investigators questioning him about Wortman but that the Mounties showed no interest in pursuing its possible importance nor do they appear to have released anything about the tape to the Mass Casualty Commission investigating Wortman's deadly rampage on April 18 and 19, 2020, which left 22 Nova Scotians dead.

It was a great story until it blew up in our faces.

A podcast listener thought there was something familiar about it. He did some research. It was a clip from the television show *CSI*. We had all been had. It was an embarrassing mistake.

The next day Douglas and I went to the Dartmouth Court House, where Doucette was making an appearance regarding the assault charges against his friend Michelle, which ended up being dismissed.

Doucette was standing outside the courthouse. "Hey, brother," he said, seemingly oblivious to the havoc he had caused.

"What the hell did you do?" I asked.

He seemed genuinely flummoxed.

I played the audio from the *CSI* scene for him and said: "You said you taped this. It's from a *CSI* episode."

"It sounds similar," Doucette said.

"It's not similar," I said. "It's exactly the same."

Doucette said he couldn't explain what had happened. He said that he had played the tape for RCMP officers during his first interviews with them.

He said the Mounties had taken both his cellphone and the recorder and didn't return them for ten days. In our interview with him at the motel, he did say that he had thought things were missing from his phone when he got it back. He didn't mention anything like that about his tape recorder until that moment.

There was a record of the police taking the phone on April 19, 2020.

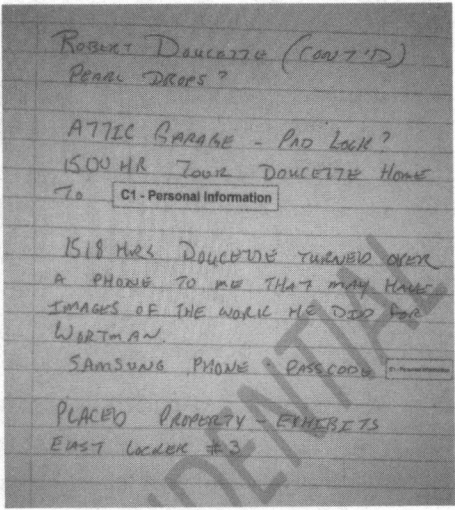

From Constable Tony McGrath's handwritten
notes: 3:18 p.m., April 19, 2020. (MCC)

"I thought the original tape was longer, but I hadn't listened to it for years. It was in my drawer," Doucette said.

"Are you suggesting that the RCMP deleted the original tape and replaced it with a conversation from *CSI*?"

"I don't know."

"So the question remains," I said. "Did two RCMP detectives really come to Wortman's denturist office when you were there and ask him about Kevin Petrie?"

"They did," he said. "I was there when it happened. I can't explain what happened on the recorder."

Were we set up? Who knows. It didn't matter. It was a humbling and embarrassing moment for all of us, an undeniably stupid, rookie mistake. It's what happens when you are on the front lines, taking chances, and get careless. It's not the kind of thing that happens to those who always play it safe and never take a risk.

"I guess we're going to have to do a big shit-eater," Douglas said glumly as we put together a piece in which we would admit our transgression. The next cover of the magazine featured a headline that read:

"When *Frank* and Palango Got Duped," complete with a photo of me, Doucette and a couple of sheriffs at the courthouse.

We also prostrated ourselves on the next *Nighttime* podcast—no doubt to the delight of our media competitors.

"I'm done with that guy," an angry Bonaparte said that night.

Sharon and I weren't, as you shall learn.

Doucette had now been thoroughly discredited, but like many people who spend their lives living on the edge, he certainly wasn't all bad. There was much truth in what he had told us. I wasn't really all that angry. In fact, I felt a little bad for him.

If there was an upside, it was that we had done something the RCMP and the commission wouldn't do: provide a glimpse of those with whom Wortman had been closely associated and what they knew about him and Banfield.

Another positive was that our wrong assumption didn't get anyone killed. We picked ourselves up and continued to pursue the story. It was just another bump in a bumpy road.

14

TWENTY-SEVEN WITNESSES TO A MOUNTIE'S MURDER

While Rob "the Carpenter" Doucette was on the phone trying to alert the RCMP to how dangerous Wortman might be, Wortman was still driving through Truro. As he left town, the RCMP received another tip about where he might be. This time, it was the Sobeys supermarket in Lower Truro. RCMP and Truro police raced to the scene. By now, even some Mounties were beginning to suspect there was something fishy about all these bogus calls.

"Can we be sure that it's not him calling to throw us off the trail?" Constable Blake DeCoste, a traffic cop at Bible Hill, radioed.

"We're going to try and get confirmation," said dispatcher Tara Dill. "We're wondering if it's possible. They were just told to move to the back of the building, uh, by Truro police, who we've asked to shut down the town."

Wortman was long gone.

Sergeant Darren Bernard was in the Millbrook RCMP office, entirely unaware that Wortman was entering his jurisdiction. A proud Mi'kmaq, Bernard was Corporal Natasha Jamieson's supervisor at the Millbrook First Nation federal detachment near Truro. His day had begun at home with an early-morning call from Jamieson. Unclear about what was going on, Bernard contacted one of his juniors, Constable Jared Daley, who told him how crazy things were getting: "Holy fuck, man. Turn your radio on. It's fucking chaos. He's shooting people again. I don't know what to do," Bernard recalled Daley telling him. "It doesn't seem there's anybody in charge. No one's telling me what to do."

As the situation sunk in, the outspoken Bernard couldn't believe what was happening, but he wasn't all *that* surprised. Considering the force's neglected and decrepit state, a catastrophe like this one was inevitable, he later told commission investigators. In the world of the RCMP, where anyone can do any job, people were in charge who had no clue about street policing. The top dogs were in the Major Crimes Unit, which investigated homicides, attempted homicides, suspicious disappearances, drug trafficking activities and sexual assaults. In Nova Scotia, the unit had a well-earned reputation among rank-and-file Mounties as being anything but expert when it came to building successful cases. Bernard didn't have evidence, but he suspected this was another Major Crimes screw-up. He could sense it. He called them "the usual suspects."

At 10:23 a.m., Wortman stopped at the Millbrook trading post. It was time for a costume change. He got out of his car, peeled off his blue RCMP jacket and put on a yellow safety vest, then headed south toward Brookfield on old Highway 2, which was not being patrolled. It wasn't as if the RCMP were trying to lock down all roads leading in and out of Los Angeles; there were only three roads connecting Colchester County to points south. Groups of Mounties were congregating at various points along the Highway 102 and 104 expressways, but there was no one positioned along the secondary route, Highway 2. Once again, there were no roadblocks in front of Wortman—only behind him.

Meanwhile, a rumour began circulating in the media and on social media that Wortman had a hit list of people he intended to kill. This was later found not to be true; it was later revealed in court documents that the Mounties themselves had initiated the false story. But back in Portapique, Constable Nick Dorrington, who was still guarding the crime scene, feared he might be on that list. As far as he knew, he was the last Mountie to have had official dealings with Wortman, having given him a speeding ticket the previous February 12.

Dorrington called his wife, Dawn, to warn her that Wortman might be in the Truro area, where they resided. Dawn then called her friend Lynn, who lived farther south on Highway 2, near Brookfield. "I just happened to be talking to her," Dawn Dorrington later told investigators. "She was standing in front of her picture window . . . maybe that's not the best place to stand. . . and she spoke out loud: 'Should there be an RCMP vehicle that just drove past my house?'"

Alarmed, Dawn texted her husband: "Hey, Lynn just saw a RCMP vehicle drive by her house on the number 2 highway in Brookfield. Should there be a cop car here?"

"Tell her to call me right now," Dorrington replied.

At 10:41 a.m., Dorrington tried to break into the cacophony on the radio: "Do we have any members in Brookfield area?"

One minute and twenty-two seconds later, the channel cleared and he got through: "Bravo-9 is looking for confirmation if we have any marked units in Brookfield right now. I have information that a marked unit just passed through Brookfield."

Sixty-six seconds later, a dispatcher said the call centre had just received another tip about a car with B11 on it, likely Wortman's 28B11.

Wortman was heading south from Brookfield, either on Highway 2 or on the parallel Highway 102 expressway. Instead of trying to block his progress, Mounties began hustling to the Brookfield area.

◆

Until recently, Constable Heidi Stevenson had been working out of the Cole Harbour detachment, on the east side of Halifax. On April 19, she picked up cruiser 15B1—an old-school Ford Taurus similar to the 2017 model Wortman was driving—and headed to the deeply suburban Enfield detachment at 6:35 a.m. Her GPS log showed that she hit speeds of as high as 162 kilometres per hour before she pulled into Fall River, where she stopped for almost ten minutes. Was she chasing someone, or getting a bite to eat at one of the fast-food outlets there? She left Fall

River, driving up to 120 kilometres an hour before arriving at the Enfield detachment at 7 a.m. Enfield was one highway exit north of Halifax Stanfield International Airport and about 44 kilometres from Brookfield, where Dawn Dorrington's friend would later see Wortman passing by her picture window.

That Sunday morning, there were four Mounties on duty at the Enfield detachment, all constables: Chad Morrison, who was in on overtime, Chris Gibson, Austin Comeau and Stevenson. Stevenson was the shift boss, the acting corporal, because of her seniority, but without the pay. She was still getting constable wages.

Although she was well-liked, Stevenson was anything but a well-rounded cop. While the RCMP and the commission released the work and training histories of more than 200 Mounties involved in the massacres, it did not do so for Stevenson and a handful of others. We do know that she had spent thirteen of her twenty-three years with the RCMP in its travelling circus, the Musical Ride, an unusually long stint—members typically spend three seasons with the Ride. After finally dismounting, Stevenson served as a school liaison officer and press spokesperson. Now she was pushing a cruiser around rural Nova Scotia.

Comeau was a rookie with a mere eleven months on the job. When he arrived for work at 7 a.m. that day, he remembered that there was scuttlebutt about something going on in Colchester County, but there wasn't much information available except for a BOLO (Be on the Lookout) for "a wanted male for times eight homicide." There were no details. No one was given orders. There was no grand plan being formulated.

"So me being a fairly new member, I called one of the guys I was working with and kind of asked him what was going on, and none of us were really sure," Comeau later told investigators. "So we're trying to make some inquiries, make some phone calls, gather more information . . . I called one of my buddies, Adrian Solarino. He was working the night before and kind of gave me a rundown of what happened . . . I called another buddy of mine that works in Sackville, New Brunswick, just seeing if he had any different information."

Stevenson also tried to get a reading on what was going on in Colchester County, but wasn't having much success either. Having been a media relations officer, she valued the importance of communications. "Has there been discussion about a media release in regard to that vehicle?" she radioed Staff Sergeant Briers at 8:44:22 a.m. "Just for the public to be on the lookout for that and to also be aware that he may . . . it . . . we don't know if he's got a uniform or access to anything else but just to, uh, keep an eye out for that car."

Briers passed it to the command centre, where Staff Sergeant Al Carroll, who had been up all night, rejected Stevenson's suggestion in his name and that of staff sergeants Addie MacCallum and Steve Halliday. Once again, it was obvious to Stevenson and others that there was a clear move to be made—put out an alert and block the roads—but those in command were refusing to do that. Why?

"They rejected her suggestion because they weren't going to take orders from a 'junior' female member," retired Mountie Cathy Mansley said, drawing on her own disappointing experiences within the force. Mansley and Stevenson had been at Depot as recruits at the same time, a troop apart. In the women's dorm, there were two beds and a shared closet in each pit. Mansley and Stevenson spent seven months together as "pit partners" while in training. Both served in detachments in the Halifax area once they got their yellow-striped pants. Mansley became one of the thousands of women who eventually left the RCMP, complaining about sexual harassment and bullying. She took a settlement and signed a non-disclosure agreement not to disparage the force.

"If they had put out a BOLO when Heidi suggested it, it likely would have saved all those lives, including her own," Mansley said. "Dorrington proved it, later. His wife's friend put them on the trail. If they had engaged the public earlier, they would have had eyes everywhere."

Stevenson's job was to set up a perimeter to contain Wortman. In such a dangerous situation, one might have expected a massive number of police officers to be called in to work, but the force had never been big on going overboard, preferring to "risk it out" and save money whenever it could. Other members from the nearby Indian Brook detachment showed up at Enfield, and Stevenson assigned her Mounties to various locations to monitor the three roads leading into their county from Colchester.

Twelve-year veteran Constable Morrison checked out cruiser 15B06, a newer Ford SUV Police Interceptor, headed north to Shubenacadie, about 23 kilometres away, and took a position on Highway 224, also known as the Gays River Road, on the north side of the Shubenacadie River. He got there at 10:22:05, five minutes after the RCMP finally put out its public BOLO stating that Wortman was in what appeared to be a fully marked RCMP cruiser.

Gibson and Comeau were in their cars when the call came in for two carbine-trained members to head up to Colchester. They volunteered for the assignment. All of the Mounties were monitoring two RCMP channels at once, one on their portable and the other on their car radio. Some were also using their cellphones because the radio was jammed.

Stevenson couldn't go to Colchester because she was not carbine-trained. In fact, this is how her carbine training report, written by Superintendent Robert Doyle, read: "Heidi attended the Carbine operators Course from June 4–8, 2018. However, she was removed from the course due to repeated safety violations. Heidi was talked to regarding not putting the safety on the carbine after three violations. Unfortunately, after the fourth violation, she was dismissed."

When I wrote *22 Murders*, I did not have access to that report. I instead quoted another former Mountie, Chris Williams, who had been in the same platoon as Stevenson at Depot: "She was a wonderful person. I liked her a lot. She was a good police officer. I had tactical training. I was in the ERT team. You never know when you are going to get into a life-and-death situation. At times like that you have to have that killer instinct. As much as I liked her . . . Heidi didn't have an ounce of killer instinct."

Carbine training is a must for any police officer who might find themselves in a life-threatening situation. In the RCMP, a carbine is typically a Colt C8, which is an adaptation of the M4 military assault weapon. A C8 can be used as a semi-automatic or fully automatic rifle, capable of firing 750 to 950 rounds per minute. Mounties sometimes fail carbine training because they just don't have the aptitude for it. Sources say, however, that there is a suspicion that many fail on purpose. If they do not have carbine training, then they can't be called to dangerous situations. These Mounties tend to gravitate to the softer office and nine-to-five jobs, but they receive the same pay and promotions. The higher they rise within the organization, the less they need a gun. Meanwhile, carbine-trained members cannot rely upon their non-carbine-trained members in difficult situations. That makes their work more dangerous. This is just one of the institutional problems within the RCMP, and many other police forces, as well.

Brian Sauvé and his National Police Federation have reinforced the myth within the force that any Mountie can do any job because all of them are so well trained. After the massacres, he even made the argument that carbine training wasn't an issue for Stevenson when she encountered Wortman and that she would have had to rely on her handgun training first.

"Carbine training is the issue," Mansley said. "If Brian Sauvé was sitting there and someone was shooting at him, is he saying he wouldn't want to have a carbine to defend himself? A mass killer had been on the loose for thirteen hours. He was headed Stevenson's way with an AR-15. She was alone in her car! He's got forty-five rounds and she's got fifteen in her Smith & Wesson. You don't bring a sandwich to a banquet."

At 9:55:39, Stevenson made her way up Highway 102 to Exit 10, on the southwest side of the Shubenacadie River. She took up a stationary position there with a couple of other Mounties for the next thirty-two minutes. The radio channels were jammed. It was all but impossible to figure out what was going on. The RCMP still had no idea where Wortman might be as he wended his way south. The cut-off teams were racing around Nova Scotia, drifting south, but hadn't yet come close to him.

At 10:44:31, after hearing Dorrington's message about Wortman possibly heading south, Stevenson radioed Morrison, who had been alone for twenty-two minutes. "Chad, if there's anything to that last one, I'm gonna make my way to your position."

Stevenson headed down Highway 215 south and east to Shubenacadie. It is a paved two-lane roadway. The speed limit was 80 kilometres per hour. Stevenson's GPS records show that she was in no hurry, driving about 62 kilometres per hour. She seemed to have no sense of the scope of the danger that lay ahead of her.

At 10:47:41, Constable Dorrington, still a forty-five-minute drive away to the north in Portapique, was perplexed by what he was hearing over his radio channel. The Mounties were now converging on Brookfield, trying to catch Wortman in a place where he had been, not where he was going—south toward Halifax. "In regards to the Highway 2 sighting, it was seven minutes ago," Dorrington reminded them, but it was now too late.

Forty-three seconds later, Morrison saw a marked Ford Taurus cruiser coming his way from the north. He knew that's what Stevenson was driving that day, and didn't notice that this one had a push bar on the front. "Who's approaching 224 and 2 there now?" Morrison asked.

"That's me," Stevenson said, unfamiliar with the area. The time was 10:48:29 a.m. She was wrong about her positioning: she was just about to turn left onto Highway 2, about a minute away from the Cloverleaf Circle interchange and even farther from where Morrison was waiting.

Morrison made a U-turn, and as he did, Wortman turned left and came toward him for a door-to-door meetup. As Wortman aimed a handgun with a laser beam at him, Morrison recognized what was happening and gunned the car. Wortman fired three shots, one of which hit the Mountie's portable radio. Morrison was also wounded in both arms. In his panic, Morrison accelerated his cruiser around the turn onto Highway 2, hitting the guardrails on both sides of the road. Wortman pulled out behind him.

At 10:49:05, Morrison was speeding across the Shubenacadie River bridge: "I'm shot. I'm shot. Southbound on number 2—southbound 2 taking the Shubie. I'm shot."

At precisely that time, Stevenson was passing beneath him, under the bridge. "The Shubie" was the exit ramp on Morrison's right. It would take him down to the south extension of Highway 2. If he had driven straight, he would have been back on Highway 224. As Morrison got closer to the exit, he radioed: "Turning southbound on Highway 2." He then drove to the Milford EMS ambulance station, where he arrived six minutes later.

Morrison and Stevenson didn't see each other. It's not known if she even heard him. If she had, one would think she would have had the situational awareness to recognize how dangerous things had become.

In that case, the wisest thing would have been for her to immediately pull over and call for reinforcements. She didn't do that.

Stevenson came around and up the ramp, and as she was about to reach the pavement of Highway 2, Wortman came across the highway and slammed his vehicle into hers. Seconds later, Joey Webber arrived at the scene.

The noise of the crash grabbed the attention of people in nearby houses. When gunshots sounded, more looked out. People driving by also witnessed the wreckage. Every witness who could see Stevenson's crashed cruiser during the unfolding event seemed certain that she was in the driver's seat, sitting behind the wheel, when Wortman shot her the first time.

Witness Craig Vanderkooi, then a sixty-year-old handyman, had a face-on view through his telephoto lens from a distance of about a football field length across the Cloverleaf Circle interchange.

Wortman's replica cruiser, 28B11, is at left, parallel to the guardrail. Heidi Stevenson's cruiser sits nose to the guardrail, to the right. In the background is Joey Webber's Ford Escape. Note that Wortman's vehicle has no bullet damage. (Craig Vanderkooi)

In an interview with RCMP sergeants Dave Legge and Bill Raaymakers, conducted five hours after Stevenson's murder, Vanderkooi said this: "I heard three shots, or thought they were shots, wasn't sure. So I got up,

I went to the window . . : and then I heard three more, uh, *boom, boom, boom.* So I said, well, those are gunshots. So I went to my kitchen window and then I realized that there was two police vehicles up there, crashed. Um, obviously, one, one person was hiding behind, has a yellow vest on, he's ducked behind the front fender of the car."

Vanderkooi thought he could see Stevenson slumped over the steering wheel, still wearing her sunglasses. A technical report for the commission suggested that her car's airbag likely went off with the original impact and that Stevenson might have been dazed or even knocked out, but there was no conclusive proof of that.

Meanwhile, Joey Webber had arrived, likely stopping to see if he could help. Allow me to reprise what I wrote for *22 Murders.*

That morning, Webber knew Wortman was out there somewhere in Nova Scotia, thanks to the vague RCMP alerts, but he needed to get some errands out of the way. Darren Bezanson, a neighbour and long-time family friend, told the CBC's Haley Ryan what Webber was thinking. In rural Nova Scotia, wood stoves are the standard, with oil, propane or electric as a backup. Webber needed some furnace oil. Buying the oil a couple of jugs at a time is a rural Nova Scotia tradition. No one wants to tie all their money up in a 1,000-litre tank in the basement.

Webber drove in his silver Ford Escape along the winding, country roads to Milford Station to get the oil. As Bezanson told Ryan, he wanted to do it "before that crazy guy" came closer.

On his return home, Webber came upon a confounding scene at Cloverleaf Circle. Two RCMP cruisers were crashed together up against the guardrail at the top of the ramp. One Mountie was outside his car. Webber, wearing a hoodie, pulled up next to the cruisers, stopped and got out of his vehicle. He walked over to the side of Constable Stevenson's car, which had its nose in the guardrail.

"He walked around to the rear quarter panel and then started walking back to his vehicle," said witness Craig Vanderkooi in one of several interviews. "He had his hand in his pocket. He wasn't panicking, just walking. I moved to get a better view . . . there were one or two more shots."

As Vanderkooi was looking for a better position from which to photograph the evolving scene, Wortman ushered the lanky Webber into the back seat of his crashed fake cruiser and shot him in the back of the head.

In his interview with the RCMP, Vanderkooi described what he saw next. "Uh, at that point, I went upstairs 'cause I could get a better view. Uh, at that time, he had gone around to the vehicle, the other vehicle, that was facing towards my house, opened up the door and he pulled something out of the car. I couldn't tell what it was at that time. So . . . I ran back downstairs and got my binoculars. I went back upstairs and then when I looked, I could see that the person laying on the ground was obviously a police officer."

Wortman had shot Heidi again through the driver's door window and pulled her out of the car. A few witnesses thought he had shot her while she was on the ground, while others thought she was already dead in the car. Although forensic reports did not detail her injuries, Stevenson was grazed once and hit five or six times with bullets or shrapnel, likely after a bullet pierced the "silent patrolman," the plexiglass divider between the front and back seats.

Stevenson and Webber were Wortman's twentieth and twenty-first victims.

◆

The RCMP would later say there had been a shootout between Stevenson and Wortman, but that wasn't supported by the majority of witness statements, of which there were many. In all, twenty-seven witnesses stepped forward to tell the RCMP what they thought had happened. No two people remember seeing exactly the same thing, which is not uncommon for eyewitness evidence, but most agreed on at least one thing: Stevenson was never seen lying, kneeling or standing outside her cruiser firing her gun.

One witness said that, immediately after the crash, Stevenson rolled out of the car. Another said she got out of the car and stumbled to the ground. One said they saw her fire a single shot at Wortman. A few thought Wortman was using both a rifle and a handgun, which was not implausible. One woman thought there had been three people with guns, and that there had been a gunfight, but she admitted that she had a bad memory and deferred to her husband as having better recall. Unfortunately, her husband's first view of the scene was of Heidi Stevenson lying dead beside her vehicle. As for his wife, she had left her vantage point in the middle of everything to give her phone to her husband so that he could call 911.

There were no photographs of Stevenson or Webber being killed, but some heard those two or three shots. There was no recording that captured the sound of all the gunshots, but we can add up the witness statements, starting with Vanderkooi, who heard seven or eight shots in total from his position north of the cloverleaf.

South of Cloverleaf Circle, Eric Fisher was even closer to the scene. He called 911 at 10:53:19 to report "multiple shots fired out on the circle . . . there appears to be a police car . . . One looks like a police officer, somebody walking back and forth."

Two days later, Fisher and his wife, Rosalie, were walking their dog in the area, which had previously been searched by a large team of Mounties. The photos of the Mounties combing the crime scene area were well used by the media. Nevertheless, the Fishers found bits and pieces of car parts and other melted metal in the gravel—and a pair of handcuffs, which we'll return to in the next chapter.

The Fishers called the RCMP and told their story to Staff Sergeant Greg Vardy. They began with what they had seen take place at the cloverleaf the previous Sunday morning. "I heard . . . approximately three shots or so, not ju— exactly sure . . . I'd say about three shots and, um, and I, and as I looked out the window, this guy was running . . . I'm not sure whether he went back to the car and then came back around again and or not . . . I'm kind of assuming or thinking that there was two episodes like that," Eric Fisher told Vardy. "These first three shots and then [he] ran back around his car for some reason, come back and fired more shots. And then, as that all was taking place, that's when the other gentleman [Webber] . . . ran up . . . I think figured he was assisting somebody in trouble."

Rosalie Fisher then said: "I heard the shots. I was upstairs and heard the shots. I heard, like, *bang, bang, bang, bang.*"

Then Eric described what he believed was the murder of Stevenson: "Like I said, there were three shots and then, um, when I looked out, I saw him running, coming up around the back end of . . . of Constable Stevens[on]'s, I guess it was, car or what I assumed was her car, around the back and come up and fire a bunch of more shots."

"Okay," Vardy said, "and what direction were those, were those shots fired?"

"Well, right at the side of the car . . . Like he was shooting right, right point-blank, right at . . . the driver's, round the driver's door, somewhere there."

Around this time, RCMP sergeant Marc Rose heard a radio call from an unidentified male voice, which said: "Member is okay." Rose asked the man to identify himself, but he didn't. Rose suspected it was Wortman, but how could Wortman have been on the RCMP's encrypted system without his radio registering on the network? Each detachment had its own band and network within the larger network. Part of the problem was that Mounties were on different bands. It raised the question: Did Wortman have a New Brunswick–based RCMP radio?

Every witness heard approximately the same number of shots: eight, or maybe nine or ten. Some saw slightly different things. Tanis Witt was among about a half-dozen witnesses who were in their vehicles, viewing the scene from various angles. On May 6, 2020, seventeen days after the massacres, Witt contacted the Mounties to tell them what she had witnessed. She had just gone to Tim Hortons in Milford and was talking to a friend near Ettinger's Home Hardware, on the west side of Cloverleaf Circle. They heard three shots. Instead of running the other way, Witt hopped into her car and went up to the interchange to see what was going on for herself. "Both of the police cars were there, smashed," she told the Mounties. "There was a police officer sitting on the ground, leaning back against the front seat. The door was open. At the time, it looked almost like a mannequin, and in my head, I assumed that it was the gunman that had been shot, and there was another man there, not in uniform . . . So there was another vehicle in front of me. They drove over the grass and around. I drove over the grass to go around . . . because I have first aid." Witt soon changed her mind about getting out of her car.

She then said something that one would think would be of extreme interest to investigators and the commission: "I rolled down my window to offer, um, help, but by then, the man that was there had walked over to the other police car, which I now believe is the gunman's car. It looked to me like he had a phone up to his ear. He had his back to me and he was far away. I decided to not yell to him, and I continued on my way."

Who could Wortman have been talking to? What would they be saying? Whatever it was, Wortman almost robotically changed course. He used some of Joey Webber's furnace oil to start a fire in the trunk of his own vehicle. It was an uncharacteristic thing for him to do. Not the fire; he had proven that he was practised at that. But he left a stash of $20,000 or more in his car and let it burn. That was not his style. It was like he was admitting to himself that it was over. He had gone too far by killing Stevenson. If he was chasing some kind of deal, he had crossed the line and the deal was long gone. Is that what he was told by whomever he was talking to on the phone or radio?

Wortman then left in Webber's Ford Escape and headed south on Highway 224.

Wortman had just lit a fire in the trunk of his replica police car. In this photo released by the MCC, he was photographed about to get into Joey Webber's Ford Escape. Behind the redacted area to the left lay the body of Heidi Stevenson. (Photo by Elaine Mosher-Whitman provided to the MCC)

The first Mounties, an ERT team, arrived on the scene at 10:56 a.m., three minutes after Eric Fisher had called 911. The cut-off team was close on Wortman's heels, but not close enough. The fire began to rage, engulfing both vehicles. The police let it burn, but they dragged Stevenson's body away from the flames.

By that time, Sergeant Darren Bernard from Millbrook had arrived in his powder-blue Ford Taurus cruiser, which looked better suited to the Maine State Police. Bernard went to Stevenson. He liked and respected her, and was determined to try to save her. He struggled to get her soft and hard armour off. "It was hard to get the chest clear," he said afterwards. "I remember looking for a pulse, and I couldn't find one anywhere. Armpit, I looked everywhere, and I couldn't find one . . . Nothing seemed to make sense."

While he tended to her, the grass caught fire and black smoke blew over him, but he refused to leave her side. "In my culture," he said, "when there's a deceased person, you have to stay with them. So I stayed with her and just sat in the dirt for I don't know how long."

As he surveyed the scene, his radio was a scramble of voices; then Bernard heard dog handler Constable Craig Hubley frantically shouting: "Pump six. Pump six. Pump six." Something was happening.

Bernard's anger at his own organization welled up. He thought he saw Major Crimes sergeant Fraser Firth in the growing crowd of onlookers around the circle and wondered to himself: "What's he doing here?"

As shocking as Stevenson's death was for the Mounties, you could all but read what they were thinking from their conversations, like this exchange between Staff Sergeant Steve Ettinger and Corporal Calvin Beers:

"Does Stevenson have a carbine in her car, or did she?" Ettinger asked.

"Negative," Beers replied. "Stevenson is not carbine-trained."

"That's what I thought," Ettinger said.

Bernard, like all the other witnesses who had critical things to say about the RCMP, was not called to tell his story before the commission. Criticizing the force was deemed to be victim shaming or too traumatizing.

15

NOT ENOUGH HOLES IN THE FORENSIC REPORT

At 3:45 p.m. on April 19th, the news that a Mountie had been shot and killed near Shubenacadie was confirmed. Just after 4 p.m., the public learned Heidi Stevenson's name via a tweet by Prime Minister Trudeau. We still didn't know how many people had been killed by Wortman, so Stevenson instantly became the face of the massacre and was the focus of the first press conference, at 6 p.m., by Assistant Commissioner Lee Bergerman and Chief Superintendent Chris Leather.

"Today is a devastating day for Nova Scotia and it will remain etched in the minds for many years to come," Bergerman began flatly. "What has unfolded overnight and into this morning is incomprehensible and many families have experienced the loss of a loved one. That includes our own RCMP family. It is with tremendous sadness that I share with you that we have lost Constable Heidi Stevenson, a twenty-three-year veteran of the force, who was killed this morning while responding to an active shooter incident. Heidi answered the call of duty and lost her life while protecting those she cared for."

Bergerman continued for a minute more, noting that there was one other injured officer and "many victims outside of the RCMP," then concluded that Nova Scotians needed to come together to support one another.

It was Leather's turn. As the person in charge of RCMP criminal investigation operations in Nova Scotia, he should have known everything. His was considered a voice of authority. He began by offering his condolences to Stevenson's family and the families of all the victims. "We are in the early stages of an incredibly detailed and complex investigation that has forever changed countless lives and left multiple victims," Leather continued, adding that the "focus right now is to gather all evidence and information about these incidents and to get answers to many unanswered questions."

He summarized the police response to the initial firearms call in Portapique the previous night, noting that the "search for the suspect ended this morning when the suspect was located, and I can confirm that he is deceased, and I can also confirm that the matter has been referred to SIRT." His four-minute speech was light on facts—he couldn't even confirm the total number of victims. Instead, he doubled down on the fact that the investigation was ongoing, which meant he couldn't provide further details on portions of it.

In his second press conference, the next day, Leather said he had made *three* referrals for SIRT to investigate. As a reminder, the Serious Incident Response Team is an independent investigative agency "tasked with the investigations of serious incidents involving police in Nova Scotia." One referral to SIRT was obviously about the shooting of Gabriel Wortman at the Irving Big Stop, which we'll discuss in Chapter 22. Leather didn't elaborate on the other two at the time, but a second was likely the Onslow Belmont fire hall shoot-up. Leather described the third one this way: "At one point during the course of the evening there was an exchange of gunfire." But he said he didn't know where it had taken place. The mention of "evening" implies it was something that happened in Portapique, perhaps the shooting of Corrie Ellison, or something entirely unknown.

Leather had been well briefed before making this initial statement about the "exchange of gunfire" and the third referral to SIRT, but over the next two days, a new version of events emerged. Behind the scenes, the RCMP quietly raised concerns that one of Stevenson's bullets may have errantly hit Joey Webber. What shots were they referring to? No one had seen Stevenson fire her gun. Of the twenty-seven witnesses who came forward, only a handful said they saw Stevenson outside the car. Among the others, most had heard between seven and nine shots fired, importantly in three separate bursts: presumably Wortman's initial shots at Stevenson, his shots at Webber, then his second burst at Stevenson.

There was a single outlier on the number of gunshots fired. When I asked around, I was told that "somebody with the RCMP had seen it all," but I could never figure out who that Mountie was until the commission hearings.

Colleen Nesseth worked as a communications manager at the Shubenacadie Radio Communications Centre, the provincial dispatch centre for its trunked mobile radio system. The system served as an alternative emergency communications network and linked various entities, including the federal and provincial governments and their various agencies. In other words, Nesseth worked closely with the RCMP, and she appeared to be the mysterious "RCMP" witness I had long heard about.

Nesseth lived about 125 metres to the south of Cloverleaf Circle, in a dark-blue sidesplit with a partially obstructed view of the scene from her rear windows and deck. She and her husband, Clayton Willis, were in the kitchen that Sunday morning. Willis was baking bread. They were far enough away that they couldn't determine whether Wortman was using a handgun or a rifle—his Ruger Mini-14 assault rifle, which fired .223-calibre bullets.

Nesseth had called 911 at 10:50:30: "I see two police cars that have hit each other on the Cloverleaf in Shubenacadie, and I believe there's been shots fired."

"Do you see anybody outside of the vehicles?"

"I do," Nesseth said. "Appears to be a police officer. He's wearing high-vis yellow . . . it can't be shots fired because he's too calm . . . I mean, there was at least thirty!"

"At least thirty shots, you heard?" the operator asked.

"Yes."

In her husband's interview four days later, with Sergeant Fraser Firth, Willis said: "He was shooting into the back window [the driver's-side back window] because I seen the back window when it popped out, right? I could see the glass was gone . . . when he fired because he . . . was walking this way." Willis continued: "Then he walked over, went up to the front of the car, the person that was in the car, he reached in, undone her belt, to her, whatever, I don't know . . . Took the person out of the car . . . dropped them on the ground and shot them on the ground, and then reached down and picked something up . . . No rush whatsoever. He just walked back . . ."

At this point, Willis couldn't see what Wortman was doing, because a house closer to the scene obstructed his view to the right. At that moment, Wortman killed Joey Webber. Then he came back into view. Willis saw him open the trunk of his replica police car and start a fire.

Nesseth said she had heard about thirty shots, but Willis stated that there were between fifteen and eighteen. Everyone else heard seven to nine. One explanation given for Nesseth's hearing so many shots was that other witnesses had heard explosions, likely bullets bursting inside Wortman's burning car. Another explanation for the discrepancy was that Nesseth and Willis lived relatively far from the scene. Houses obstructed their view. The gun was loud. Echoes?

In a later interview, Nesseth recanted the number of shots she had actually heard, but that didn't matter to the RCMP. Her initial statement was a pure version of the events. And with her shirttail connections to the force, she was deemed to be a more credible witness than the others who were much closer to the scene. None of the statements would be tested by cross-examination.

A later analysis of Stevenson's GPS log compared to the 911 call log from the RCMP's star witness, Colleen Nesseth, showed that there was likely about fifty-five seconds at most between Stevenson's car coming to a stop at 10:49:35 and Nesseth's call at 10:50:30. If the RCMP story were to be believed, that meant the accident occurred, Stevenson was not stunned by either the collision or an airbag crashing into her forehead, and she managed to get out of her car, exchange more than a dozen shots, return to her car and then be murdered through the window—a succession of events that seems unlikely given the time frame.

When Constable Heidi Stevenson was murdered, Gabriel Wortman was almost thirteen hours into his spree and had already taken nineteen lives. That Stevenson was alone in her cruiser when Wortman literally ran into her and killed her wasn't a good look for the force. As beloved as Stevenson was, any thorough and objective investigation would reveal just how poorly the circumstances leading up to and including her death would reflect on the RCMP. A question I posed in *22 Murders* was: Who sent an unprepared Heidi Stevenson to her death? Instead of looking inward at their own flaws, the RCMP focused their messaging on making Stevenson a heroine. The force glossed over the fact that Nesseth and Willis had seen Stevenson killed inside her cruiser and dragged out of it, which was corroborated by several other witnesses. Instead, the Mounties homed in on the thirty gunshots that Nesseth said she had heard, as evidence that there was a shootout between Stevenson and Wortman.

◆

The story-shaping began a day after Stevenson's death, long before all the witnesses had been interviewed and a forensic examination completed. As we know, on April 20, Leather made a public reference to three SIRT referrals, which came as news to acting SIRT director Pat Curran. At the time of the massacres, Curran was sitting in for Felix Cacchione, who was off work on medical leave from October 17, 2019, to June 1, 2020. Cacchione's record, as previously noted, showed that he had moments during his career, as a Nova Scotia Supreme Court judge and as SIRT director, of being less than even-handed.

Curran, too, was one of the province's elites. Not only was he a former chief justice of the Nova Scotia provincial court system, he also was chief executive officer of the Art Gallery of Nova Scotia. While those with similar pedigrees could usually be counted on to be team players and think like everyone else, Curran was no such pushover. When he heard Leather make his comments about SIRT, Curran and his colleagues were shocked. "Chris, all of us at SIRT were startled when you mentioned two additional referrals," Curran wrote to Leather in an email. "None of us had any idea what the second additional matter might be."

The next afternoon, the RCMP officially asked Curran to investigate Stevenson's murder because it was concerned that, in trying to defend herself, one of her shots may have struck and killed Webber. However, it wasn't until 7 p.m. that same day that the forensic examination of Stevenson's vehicle was completed. All of the ballistic evidence was placed in an evidence storage locker, and the forensic examination of the shell casings would not be completed for another two weeks. Was the RCMP psychic?

As I was drafting this chapter, I stopped to search the commission's website for a certain document and once again found myself sidetracked as I surfed through a bunch more files. At one point I typed "Stevenson" in the search engine. Up came seventy-seven documents, of which fifty-five were sequentially numbered photographs of a charred and rusted pair of handcuffs, found in a pile of rubble near a makeshift memorial at Stevenson's murder scene by Eric and Rosalie Fisher two days after the incident. Only one of the photographs showed what appeared to be the same handcuffs lying flat in their entirety. All the rest were close-ups of various parts of the handcuffs, which essentially showed nothing.

Recall that Lisa Banfield said that she'd escaped from handcuffs in Portapique. The Mounties couldn't find them in Portapique but now seemed eager to prove that these were the set used on Banfield. They learned that the handcuffs were manufactured by the Peerless Handcuff Company in West Springfield, Massachusetts, but there was nothing the lab could do to link them to Wortman. The Mounties continued to assume they were the ones used on Banfield, and that became the default truth.

I wondered why so much space in the Stevenson documents was being given to the handcuffs. It triggered my Spidey sense. Was the commission trying to distract people from something else on the list? It was an old trick, many times seen. Then I noticed something intriguing—a document named COMM0018258, headlined: "Response to Stevenson Referral."

Inside was a letter, dated April 22, 2020, from Pat Curran. It was a reply to Leather's referral to SIRT, submitted the day before. It read, in part:

> It is inconceivable, and utterly incompatible with the mandate, that SIRT would investigate the apparent murder of a police officer unless there was reason to believe the death was caused by the actions of another officer.
>
> In this case, not only was there an apparent murder, but, as you said to me by telephone on Sunday afternoon, the officer was "executed" by the suspect who later died at Enfield. SIRT most definitely does not, and will not, investigate executions of police officers by civilians.
>
> Although you mentioned the officer's death to me that day, you made no request that SIRT take part in, let alone take on, the investigation of it. I did not know who was conducting that investigation, but I believed it was either the RCMP, HRP or both. . . .
>
> It was not until receipt of your "formal referral" mid-afternoon on Tuesday April 21, well over two days after Cst. Stevenson's death, that SIRT was asked to investigate Cst. Stevenson's death. If SIRT had concluded this was otherwise an appropriate referral to accept, it would have been pointless to do so. Nearly all the significant investigative decisions had been made and acted upon already.
>
> SIRT does not accept the referral. Those who have started and carried out the investigation to this point should complete it or find some other police agency to do so.
>
> Pat Curran
>
> Interim Director

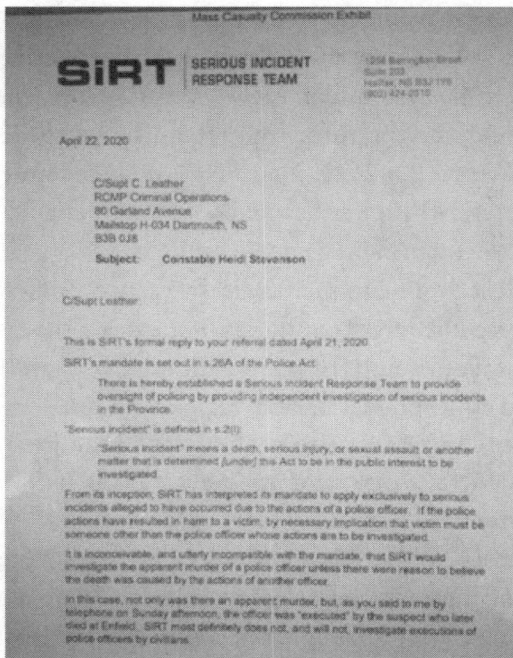

The first page of the two-page letter from Pat Curran to Chris Leather. (MCC)

When I discovered this document, I had been working this story for almost four years. Although I had always suspected that the Mounties were being duplicitous, finding proof wasn't all that easy. But here was COMM0018258, hidden in plain sight, one document in a mountain of them—transparency, as the commission would call it—and it raised real questions about what the RCMP was trying to accomplish.

Note Curran's outraged tone, which alone made it a highly unusual institution-to-institution missive. One can almost hear him calling the Mounties' bluff that there had been a shootout and that the disingenuous way to "prove" it was by suggesting that Stevenson had inadvertently killed Joey Webber before she was shot, although there was not a stitch of evidence to suggest that happened. Curran reminded Leather that he had said two days earlier that Stevenson had been "executed." That description fit the evidence.

However, Leather and the red-serge gang seemed undaunted by Curran's rebuff. While they couldn't say anything publicly themselves, because everything was under investigation, there was one person who could speak for the force by pretending to speak only for its members. On April 25, 2020, National Police Federation president Brian Sauvé stepped forward to make a statement. It was six days after Gabriel Wortman's spree ended, and Nova Scotia and the rest of Canada were just coming to their collective senses. Newspapers across the country were filled with obituaries of the dead, the cost subsidized by the government. Emotions were running sky high. It was in this highly charged atmosphere that Sauvé spoke to Canadian Press reporters Kevin Bissett and Adina Bresge. *CityNews* headlined their version of the story: "Nova Scotia Mountie Saved Lives by Stopping Mock Police Car: Union."

"She was a hero," Sauvé was quoted as saying. "She realized it was the bad guy, and she rammed him, from my understanding. I recognize that she did something that probably saved countless lives. I don't know, five, ten, twenty, how far this guy was going to go."

Those few words created a vivid image in the memories of those who read them. Heidi Stevenson was not just murdered; she went down with a fight. As stirring as the story might be, there was no proof that Stevenson had rammed Wortman's fake police car. Any objective analysis of the collision between their cars showed that didn't happen. Sauvé's false description was so indefensible, in fact, that nine days later, on June 4, 2020, Superintendent Darren Campbell batted it down in a situational update for the media. "I can provide . . . a few details based on the evidence," Campbell said. "While Constable Stevenson's and the gunman's vehicle collided, we do not believe that Constable Stevenson rammed the gunman's vehicle. We can also tell you that the gunman's vehicle sustained more damage than Constable Stevenson's vehicle."

The message that Stevenson didn't ram Wortman fell on mostly deaf ears. It wasn't the kind of statement that left an indelible impression, and Campbell followed it with a new description of Stevenson's last seconds. "She bravely engaged the gunman and there was an exchange of gunfire between Constable Stevenson and the gunman."

It was the first time they had announced that Stevenson fired at Wortman before she was killed, and they didn't provide any evidence to back up their version of events, even though credible witnesses had since come forward. But this was when the federal and provincial governments were promoting the notion that an internal RCMP review was all that was needed, not a public inquiry.

As for Sauvé, after he was caught out by his own force telling a fib about Stevenson ramming Wortman with her cruiser, it would seem logical that reporters and editors would be wary of any of his subsequent musings. But Sauvé was a designated official source. And with the RCMP seeming to hide behind the ongoing investigation, he continued to speak on behalf of the force, often in ways that promoted a preferred narrative.

In the ensuing days and weeks, Sauvé began to shill an expanded version of the heroine story across the country. On June 23, 2020, he wrote an opinion piece that was published in the Halifax *Chronicle Herald* and elsewhere, headlined: "BRIAN SAUVÉ: RCMP Acted Heroically to Stop Gunman's Nova Scotia Rampage." He wrote, in part:

> There have been some reports alleging that the RCMP did not correspond with neighbouring Nova Scotia police agencies during this time. The detailed information that I have reviewed very clearly refutes these claims. The RCMP was, in fact, in close contact with other Nova Scotia police agencies throughout the response, sharing information and resources as required.
>
> I cannot address this incident without reserving a special place for the heroics of Const. Heidi Stevenson. After a vehicle collision with the gunman, Const. Stevenson bravely engaged him. An exchange of gunfire ensued, and Const. Stevenson, who was wearing both soft and hard body armour, was shot and killed.
>
> A devoted mother, wife, and daughter, Const. Stevenson spent 23 years as an active member of the force, and notably spent time working at RCMP headquarters as a drug recognition expert.
>
> It is extremely difficult to convey how incredibly brave a person must be to engage an active shooter, no less on your own. She did not

take these actions to protect herself. Her sacrifice was to put her life on the line to protect the lives of innocent civilians. Members of the RCMP will never forget her sacrifice, honouring her memory each and every day that they are on the job.

On behalf of his employers, union leader Sauvé was establishing the new default truth in the minds of the public. It was an uplifting story in a greater tragic tale. That Stevenson had gone down fighting wasn't quite a dream ending, but it was better than her being outmanoeuvred and coldly gunned down without getting off a shot of her own.

The embellished narrative flushed out a witness who was willing to whisper a protest.

◆

Bernard Myra had seen more than anyone at the Cloverleaf Circle scene, but he had kept quiet for almost three months. After contacting the RCMP, Myra was interviewed at his home on July 13, 2020.

A few minutes prior to shooting Stevenson, Wortman had wounded RCMP constable Chad Morrison on Highway 224. Myra and his wheelchair-bound wife, Elizabeth Small, had been driving south from Mastodon Ridge, a park just north of Shubenacadie, and were passing the entrance to the Shubenacadie Wildlife Park when they saw two police cars race out from Highway 224, turn left in front of them and head toward the bridge. The first car (Morrison's) was nearly out of control and was "fishtailing and then he got straightened out."

According to Myra, Morrison crossed the bridge over the river, and then the bridge over southbound Highway 2, and entered the Cloverleaf Circle exchange. The exit to southbound Highway 2 was about 100 metres ahead on the right, almost directly across the highway from the ramp where people who are headed north on Highway 2 get dumped out. After Morrison took the exit, Myra said, Wortman slowed down for a moment as he, too, approached the exit. It was then that Myra noticed another Mountie cruiser coming up the ramp on the other side of the road.

Cloverleaf Circle: According to the MCC final report, "After being shot by Wortman, Cst. Morrison drove south. As he crossed the bridge, Stevenson (route in yellow) was passing under the bridge and didn't see him. Morrison exited to the right and Stevenson came around the ramp. Wortman saw her coming, crossed the lane and rammed her. Joey Webber (yellow dot) then stopped to help and was killed by Wortman." (MCC)

"I don't know if she tried to hit him or she tried to block him, but anyway they hit head-on and then her car turned sideways and her door flew open, and all I saw was, like, a pair of feet come out of the car and it was police, uh, shoes 'cause they have the yellow," Myra said. "I think they have the yellow on the bottom . . . Next thing I see was him coming from the other side from where his car was and he was walking standing straight up. And I've seen it, I think it was an assault rifle you call it. And when he got to the back of her car, he bent down, looked around and she must have been laying flat over whatever and he just stood back up, walked up and just shot her, gradually turned around and walked back.

Wortman then returned to Stevenson, Myra said, bouncing from one image to another. "I think it was two shots that he fired into her when she was laying there," before he shoved her with his foot, causing her to come to rest partially under the rocker panel of her car. Wortman took Stevenson's Smith & Wesson Model 5946, with its distinctive silver body and black grip, as well as the extra ammunition clips she had with her.

Myra was stopped in the middle of the road. He had put his car in park. Other cars moved around him. He then saw a silver Ford Escape pull up to his left and stop parallel to Wortman's crashed vehicle and to the right rear of Stevenson's car, which was nose into the guardrail.

"The gunman motioned [Webber] . . . between the two cars and I don't know if he threw him in the back seat or just shot him standing up, because you couldn't see, right?" Myra said. "He took him back there and shot him like it was nothing."

Myra said Wortman opened a door to Webber's SUV, loaded it with a bunch of guns and started a fire in the trunk of his own car. He then got into Webber's vehicle, made a U-turn and headed off south on Highway 224.

It was July 13, 2020, when Myra provided the RCMP with this compelling evidence about exactly what had happened. He saw and heard three bursts of gunshots. He didn't see a gun battle. Stevenson was never out of her vehicle until she was pulled out by Wortman, as other witnesses had said.

Despite Myra's and other corroborating statements, the RCMP stuck to its story that Stevenson had bravely fought back. "She's our hero," retired RCMP sergeant Joe Taplin said later. He had worked with Stevenson for years. "I just have the total, utmost respect for her; I think of her quite a bit, all the time."

But former Mountie Cathy Mansley was angered by how the Mounties were treating Stevenson's death. "One female corporal said that after Heidi died that 'it is too bad that she died, but that's part of the job that we face every day,'" she told me. "It was sickening to hear that. I know that member. She's always been a brown-nosing bitch. She spent most of her career doing paperwork—a desk jockey. She probably never worked a day in her life where she faced real danger."

Like many ex-Mounties and some current members, Mansley was also astounded by how the media had failed to hold Sauvé accountable for the fictions he had spoken, among them the false story that Stevenson had rammed Wortman's vehicle, his defence of outmoded RCMP training standards and his empty claims about the force's ethics, integrity and professionalism. "It's all bullshit," Mansley said. "Heidi died because she was a victim of the RCMP's incompetence. You'd think the union would have raised issues about the poor communications, the lack of proper equipment, the failure to implement recommendations from the past and the dangerous work conditions. No, they tried to make Heidi a hero instead. That was demeaning to her. She wouldn't have wanted that. I can't believe that Brian Sauvé would have done that to Heidi. He just threw her under the bus just to make the Mounties look better. Heidi didn't deserve a fairy tale, she deserved to have the truth be told about what happened to her."

Mansley said what many other Mounties allow themselves to think or say only off the record, for fear of retribution or shunning by the force. She spoke from her heart, not knowing that her strong opinion was overwhelmingly supported by the facts.

◆

For nearly two years, the purported gunfight between Stevenson and Wortman continued to be a vague but still potent symbol of the massacres, until April 11, 2022. That day, the Mass Casualty Commission spent the morning on the Onslow Belmont fire hall shoot-up by RCMP constables Terry Brown and Dave Melanson. Recall how Deputy Fire Chief Darrell Currie lambasted the RCMP and the commission afterwards, described in Chapter 12.

Then, during the afternoon session, the commission released RCMP-generated forensic documents that purported to add meat to the bones of the Stevenson "exchange of shots" story. The commission invited no discussion or cross-examination that might challenge the report.

RCMP forensic investigators said they had found eleven rifle casings and two rifle rounds—Wortman's, since Stevenson didn't have a carbine—on the roadway around Stevenson's and Wortman's vehicles. They also reported finding nine 9mm shell casings, which were also likely Wortman's, as he had a gun capable of firing 9mm rounds. The most spectacular finding, though, was bullet casings "possibly coming" from Stevenson's handgun, found not only outside her vehicle but in the grass on the other side of the guardrail. This finding suggested that she had positioned herself there, fired a shot or two, and then got back into her car to be murdered by Wortman. Not one witness reported seeing Stevenson—under fire—get back into her car. Perhaps the shell casings threw themselves onto the grass?

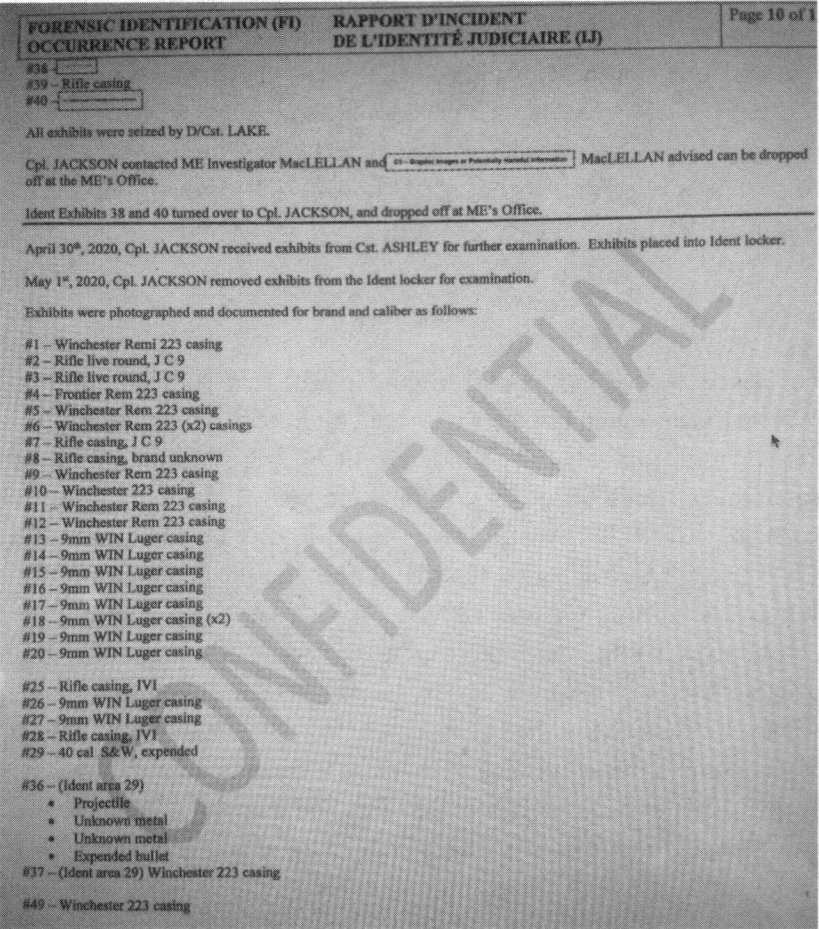

A list of shell casings found at the scene, according to the RCMP forensic report. Unlike typical forensic reports, it is lacking in important details, like linking the shell casings to specific guns. (MCC)

After Stevenson's car was placed on a flatbed and taken to the coroner's office for examination, investigators found another rifle casing and two more 9mm casings in the front footwell. More 9mm and rifle casings were found burnt in Wortman's replica car. According to the investigators, a total of thirty-two rifle and 9mm shell casings was found at the scene.

One of the complications in identifying the shell casings was that Wortman had three different brands for one gun—a sign that he didn't exactly have a prodigious stockpile of ammo. Some of his ammunition was the same as what the Mounties used in their standard-issue Smith & Wesson Model 5946 service pistols. There were also indications that Wortman had a bug-out bag or crate in the trunk of his cruiser that held scattered ammunition, which exploded as his vehicle burned. But the forensic report was anything but conclusive.

However, the RCMP claimed that fourteen of the casings found were Stevenson's, and even went so far as to say they had proved that one of Stevenson's bullets had grazed Wortman's upper right forehead area and that fragments had embedded in his scalp, causing a skull fracture. The Mounties would later say that this welt helped them identify the killer. The media didn't question that story: a female Mountie who had exacted her revenge from beyond the grave was far too irresistible a headline. (Matthew Bowes, the provincial medical examiner, provided a more likely explanation for the welt, which we'll get to in Chapter 22.)

The RCMP story was that Stevenson had fired her gun fourteen times, at least twice while she was in the car, since they found two shell casings in the burnt-out floorboards beneath her steering wheel. I talked to many police officers who were familiar with RCMP weaponry, and they all agreed that the story was pure fancy. It seemed like the force had figured out how to spin forensic evidence during an era when public perception was skewed by fictionalized TV series like CSI, in which forensic work is both quick and conclusive. It's not that way in the real world, but the RCMP presented its forensic work as if it were thorough and conclusive. How could anyone prove otherwise?

Ex-Mountie Cathy Mansley continues to be torn about what actually happened. On the one hand, she wants to believe that her late friend heroically engaged in a gunfight with Wortman but ran out of bullets. On the other, she doesn't buy the RCMP's version of events. "That gun ejects its casings out the side and they fall immediately to the floor," she said. "You have to ask yourself: Where was Heidi holding the gun when she was supposedly shooting? Over the steering wheel? What was she aiming at? Wortman was behind her. She didn't break any of the windows of her car. The only windows broken were by Wortman's bullets. Witnesses saw that. Was she strapped into her seat belt and firing over her shoulder and not hitting anything, even her own car? The whole story is a crock. This isn't their first rodeo, you know. They've had a lot of practice doing this kind of thing."

Mansley was also critical of the forensic report itself. "It's amateurish," she said. "There are few specifics. There are references to things like 'projectiles,' but no explanation about what they might be. Files are missing. Things are redacted. Why?"

The RCMP story suggested that Wortman hid behind the front end of his car while he and Stevenson exchanged shots, but Wortman's car had no bullet damage and there was only a single exiting bullet hole in Stevenson's front passenger-door skin. If Stevenson fired shots from inside the car at Wortman, how did the bullets get out of the car? What was she aiming at? She certainly wasn't aiming through the door to shoot Wortman in the knee. No, that exiting bullet hole was likely created by Wortman when he shot downward through the driver's-door window at Stevenson.

The commission, though, didn't think Stevenson's gunfight was fantasy. In its final report, the MCC twisted itself into knots to endorse the RCMP's version of events:

> At some point after the collision, Acting Cpl. Stevenson exited her vehicle from the driver's door and came to be on the ground. There is conflicting witness evidence about whether this was done under her own power or due to the interference of the perpetrator. Several

The forensic report found that, other than the bullet that exited the front passenger door of Stevenson's vehicle, the only other bullet holes entered the vehicle from the left rear, precisely where witnesses said Wortman was seen crouched down and firing at Stevenson while she was still behind the steering wheel. (MCC)

community members witnessed the cloverleaf scene, and their accounts of the incident are summarized in the following section of this chapter. Here, we summarize forensic evidence and other information that sheds light on the course of events.

We find that Acting Cpl. Stevenson exchanged gunfire with the perpetrator before and after she exited her vehicle.

Acting Cpl. Stevenson's portable radio was activated on four occasions between 10:49:40 and 10:52:57 a.m. During the middle two activations, there are gunshot sounds but no communication from Acting Cpl. Stevenson. On the first and last activations, no audio was transmitted. Forensic evidence later seized from the scene included fourteen casings that were consistent with having been fired from Acting Cpl. Stevenson's RCMP-issued Smith & Wesson pistol. Several of the expended casings were recovered in and around the driver-side floor of Acting Cpl. Stevenson's vehicle. A bullet hole was located on the passenger-side door of Acting Cpl. Stevenson's vehicle; three bullet entry holes were located in a rear panel of the vehicle, on the driver's side. At least two casings from Acting Cpl. Stevenson's gun were found on the roadway and in nearby grass, suggesting that she continued to shoot after exiting her vehicle.

During the exchange of gunfire, the perpetrator fired several shots toward Acting Cpl. Stevenson's vehicle. He then approached Acting Cpl. Stevenson and shot her at close range before taking her pistol and ammunition. He did not take her radio. Those shots killed Acting Cpl. Stevenson. The perpetrator sustained a head wound from bullet fragments shot from Acting Cpl. Stevenson's firearm during the exchange . . ."

It was a neat summation of what the commission wanted people to believe. Notice how it highlighted "conflicting witness evidence," the lack of communication by Stevenson during the "shootout" and the single bullet hole in the front passenger-side door of her car. The only conflict in the evidence was between what credible witnesses said they saw and the RCMP's undeniably dubious "forensic findings." But the commission didn't delve into any of the supposed conflicts in witness stories. During its hearings it carefully danced around the facts, highlighting only what helped its ultimate version of events.

There was no clear explanation given for where Stevenson might have been positioned when she was doing all that shooting. Since she supposedly missed Wortman thirteen times, where did those bullets land? None of them hit or were heard by any of the witnesses who were arriving on the scene. There were also allegedly fifteen bullets in Stevenson's gun. The forensics lab could account for only fourteen of them and couldn't seem to find the fifteenth, even at other crime scenes; that fifteenth bullet would turn out to be a key component of the RCMP's tale.

One way to get to the truth would have been to have SIRT director Felix Cacchione and interim director Pat Curran appear before the commission to answer questions. But neither man was interviewed by commission investigators until everyone else in the inquiry had given statements or testified. Curran wasn't interviewed until September 2, 2022, the Friday before the Labour Day long weekend. A transcript of the interview was dumped on the public and disappeared long after the public hearings were over. Cacchione was interviewed on September 9, the same day as the last public witness, Deputy Commissioner Brian Brennan, who had set up the RCMP operations in Nova Scotia and was ultimately in charge. By the time Brennan appeared, the commission had successfully put most of the public and the media to sleep—and the heroic story of Constable Heidi Stevenson was already cemented in their minds.

But as these last two chapters have shown, the evidence for the gunfight is weak, at best. Even Chris Leather described the interaction between Wortman and Stevenson as an execution, according to Pat Curran's email. Stevenson's fellow Mounties knew she wasn't carbine-trained. The long and the short of it is that she never should have been there. The RCMP failed her and then failed to be accountable.

I found it odd that the RCMP had Wortman's police car towed, with Webber's charred body inside, not to the coroner's office but to the RCMP's Bible Hill detachment. Were the Mounties removing evidence from the car that might tie Wortman to them? I had long suspected that Wortman might have been an undercover informant for the RCMP in their fledging battle against the outlaw biker gangs that ruled the Maritimes. I voiced this in *22 Murders*, where I described the seemingly symbiotic relationship between the RCMP and the Hells Angels. From top to bottom inside the RCMP, the force was focused almost exclusively on the biker gangs, at the expense of just about everything else. As report after report over the decades has determined, federal policing of fraud, other financial crimes and national security, for example, were at best back-burner concerns for the Mounties.

Nova Scotia is perceived as a bucolic land in the North Atlantic, sparsely populated with personable dancing and singing denizens, and some of that is true. What is also true is that there has always been a well-entrenched criminal element in the province, particularly in the

Truro area, which includes Portapique. Now, with the inquiry under way, I had access to a whole new slew of documentation that pointed to connections between Wortman and the RCMP's war on outlaw biker gangs, especially the Hells Angels.

16
FARGO, NOVA SCOTIA

On the night of April 18, 2020, the RCMP were thinking about the Hells Angels, the most prolific outlaw biker gang, as early as the first 911 calls from Portapique, according to documents released by the Mass Casualty Commission.

Jennifer MacCallum, the acting supervisor on duty that night in the Operational Communications Centre, called her husband, Staff Sergeant Addie MacCallum, the commanding officer of the RCMP's Pictou detachment, an hour east of Portapique. He was the top-ranking non–White Shirt in the area, known as the DANCO (district advisory non-commissioned officer), and within hours would be working in tandem with staff sergeants Al Carroll, Bruce Briers, Steve Halliday and others to bring some control to the chaos unfolding in Portapique.

"Uh, it's Jen at dispatch," Jennifer said, playing the professional and not acknowledging her husband personally. "Just wanted to make sure that you're aware of what's going on in Colchester."

"No," Addie replied.

"Okay," she said. "We have, um, an incident where there's been possibly multiple people shot in Portapique in a residence."

"Okay."

"The original caller was believed to be Jamie Gratto, who's in PROS [the Police Reporting and Occurrence System] in 2007 as a witness to the Mersereau murder," Jen said.

"Yup," Addie replied.

"Uh, and apparently a suspect did leave the area and we have possible multiple fatalities, so, we don't know who exactly at this point. After she disconnected the line, we got another caller who we believe is her child. Um, the members are there. They're just trying to figure out who, what, where and when. And now there's multiple house fires in the area, including possibly the neighbour's house."

"Okay."

"Okay?" Jen said.

"Who's there on scene?" Addie asked.

By "the Mersereau murder," Jen was referring to the killing of Randy Mersereau, a former Hells Angels boss in Nova Scotia. Although Mersereau had been murdered almost twenty-one years earlier, in 1999—that one incident had led to a long line of revenge killings among Hells Angels members. It took more than a decade for the RCMP to solve the case, during which Jamie Gratto emerged as a key witness. Gratto would go on to marry Greg Blair, change her name, and settle in Portapique with their two kids.

We will return to the commission hearings in due course, but first we need to take a colourful digression back in time to Truro, Nova Scotia—a place that might better be called Fargo, Nova Scotia—to understand the connections between Mersereau, the Hells Angels, the RCMP, Jamie Blair (née Gratto) and Gabriel Wortman.

◆

Truro, with a population of about 13,000, has long been known as "the Hub" of Nova Scotia, a transportation crossroads that was an important cog for regional and national business. In the late 1990s and early 2000s, the single largest criminal threat in the province was land pirates on two wheels—outlaw bikers—and they made Truro their hub, too. It was a logical choice: Truro is somewhat remote, a way station between various points on the map, under-policed and surprisingly welcoming, in part thanks to the demise of the Ports Canada Police in 1997.

In the 1990s, Prime Minister Jean Chrétien and his finance minister, Paul Martin, were determined to balance the federal budget. One way to do so was to deal with mounting problems, restructure and institute lasting and meaningful change. Another was to pretend to do this by rationalizing services and pushing responsibilities and costs down to the provincial and municipal levels, thereby shifting the tax burden from taxpayers' right pockets to their left. Chrétien and Martin, along with Justice Minister Anne McLellan, chose the latter. McLellan, you might remember, stepped down from the commission when it became a public inquiry.

In the name of austerity and modernization, Chrétien announced that the Ports Canada Police would be disbanded and its responsibilities absorbed by local police services and the federal RCMP. But all police services are not interchangeable. Progressive Conservative MP Elsie Wayne, who was the first female mayor of Saint John, New Brunswick, before being elected to Parliament in 1993, recognized the problems that would be created and raised the issue in Question Period. She asked this question of David Collenette, the minister of transport: "Ports Canada police officers are specialists in their field. They are trained in national and international crimes such as drug trafficking, illegal immigration and terrorist activities, as well as gun running. Security guards and local police forces are not. Why is the minister of transport subjecting our communities to the possibility of increased crime by disbanding the Ports Canada Police? Does the minister realize that a lack of national standards for policing our ports will make them much more inviting to criminal elements?"

Collenette replied: "Mr. Speaker, I think the honourable member, for whom I have great respect, is being very irresponsible to suggest that there will be an increase in crime. This is about the devolution of authority to local organizations, councils and communities. It is a policy that the former Conservative government talked about quite a bit but never did anything about it. We put this regime in place. I can assure the member that the quality of policing will not suffer and crime will not increase. It is going quite well across the country, including the Atlantic and the port of Vancouver."

Elsie Wayne was entirely prescient about the consequences of the government's actions. The RCMP was given an expanded federal role, but it was more work than the force could handle and it struggled to fulfill the requirements of its contract policing duties in the provinces and territories outside Ontario and Quebec. The unintended consequence of the dissolution of the Ports Canada Police signalled that it was open season for criminality in Canada. Canada's major ports were effectively unguarded. Money laundering became so pervasive that the term "snow washing" was being used to describe how lax Canada had become in dealing with international ill-gotten gains. White-collar crime was all but normalized. And a ferocious battle waged among criminal gangs over access to this money spigot for smuggling drugs, guns and more.

Although Nova Scotia is more than 1,000 kilometres to the east of Quebec, it falls under the umbrella of the Quebec criminal franchise's real estate—the shipping and receiving department, as it were. The Quebec Biker Wars between the Hells Angels and their rivals, the Rock Machine, which began in 1994, escalated with the "opening" of the country's ports for smuggling and led to 162 murders by 2002, when the war ended.

Under the leadership of Walter Stadnik from Hamilton, Ontario, and Maurice "Mom" Boucher from Quebec, the Canadian Hells Angels were transformed from a ragtag group to a powerful criminal enterprise that controlled the illegal drug trade in Eastern Canada, generating enormous profits for the gang. In 1995, Stadnik and Boucher founded the elite Nomad chapter of the Hells Angels. The Nomads had no clubhouse but oversaw Hells Angels operations across the country. Although most of the Nomads were from Ontario or Quebec, a Nova Scotian biker, David "Wolf" Carroll (no relation to Al Carroll), had risen to the top of the organization. Stadnik and Boucher controlled Nomad operations with an executive council known as La Table or the Table of Five.

Journalist Julian Sher, who has written extensively about the Hells Angels, described the Nomads in an interview with the *Globe and Mail* in 2008: "In Quebec, the Nomads were just the toughest and meanest and most powerful. Stadnick and his partners were able to build a pyramid structure that put the Nomads on top of all the other clubs, which you don't see anywhere else. And La Table was a powerful clique, which is why they amassed such huge fortunes."

Wolf Carroll led the 13th Tribe, a Dartmouth, Nova Scotia, outlaw motorcycle gang that answered to the Hells Angels in Quebec and eventually morphed into a full-blown Hells Angels operation. The Dartmouth crew was a deadly one. Carroll and three other Halifax club members—Randy Mersereau, Patrick "Frenchy" Guernier and Michael "Speedy" Christiansen—were charged but acquitted in the 1985 Lennoxville massacre, in which five unruly Hells Angels were murdered. Carroll, Mersereau and Guernier were subsequently convicted of living off the proceeds of prostitution and received one-year prison terms.

In 1998, Mersereau broke away from the club with the intention of setting up his own drug trafficking operation. His insubordination and betrayal incensed Carroll, who put out a contract on Mersereau's life.

Enter Dany Kane, the Hells Angel hit man, who, along with his lover Aimé Simard, had been arrested for the 1997 murder of former Hells Angel Robert MacFarlane. RCMP constable Gilles Blinn and auxiliary constable Dale Hutley had pulled Kane and Simard over in a traffic stop in the days before the murder. They were called to testify, as they could conclusively place the defendants in a white car heading toward Halifax. But Blinn couldn't pick Kane out of a rather dubious photo lineup, and the judge in the case, Nova Scotia justice Felix Cacchione, dismissed the charges. Cacchione went as far as suggesting that Blinn was "a liar." What was possibly unknown and entirely unaddressed by the court was that at the time, Kane was the RCMP's top confidential informant— code number C-2994—inside the Hells Angels organization.

According to a former Nova Scotia police officer, whom I've dubbed Jimmy McNulty, "The RCMP wanted Kane back on the streets because he had a direct line to Stadnik and Mom Boucher. That's who they really wanted."

Kane, who was also an informant for the Sûreté du Québec, told his handlers that he and Carroll were on their way to Halifax to take out Randy Mersereau. Unlike the RCMP, which showed no interest in Kane's murderous ways, the Sûreté thought it would be unethical of them to allow Kane to commit a murder while working for them. Kane and Carroll were stopped and arrested near Rivière du Loup, Quebec, after guns were found in their car. But that didn't kill the plot; the Hells Angels got some local Colchester County men to lend a hand.

The designated hit man was Leslie Greenwood, who had grown up with Carroll and called him "my uncle" because Carroll had once dated Greenwood's aunt. Greenwood lived on a messy property squeezed into a triangle of land where Pictou Road meets East Mountain Road in Valley, a Truro "suburb." Addicted to crack cocaine and a host of other drugs, the shifty-eyed man was seen by some as harmless, except that he was a magnet for violence.

After Carroll had moved west to Quebec, Greenwood stayed tight with another long-time friend from the Truro area, Jeffery Lynds, who, after serving stints at chapters in Ontario and Quebec, took control of the Angels' Nova Scotia operations. The Lynds family owned most of the property on Hiram Lynds Road, just north of Valley, which is where Leon Joudrey and one of Wortman's first victims, Greg Blair, who was related to Lynds, had once lived.

Death seemed to follow the group around. In 1998, nineteen-year-old Troy Cook disappeared from Truro. His last contact was a call to his employer begging off work, from a pay phone booth at the Tim Hortons on Pictou Road in Bible Hill. The geography was interesting. It was just up the road from Greenwood's place and steps from Randy Mersereau's used-car business, Auto Scout Car Sales, at 28 Jennifer Drive. Some in Truro said that Cook owed drug money, while others said he was dating the daughter of a Hells Angel who didn't like him. A knowledgeable police source said the RCMP had conducted a raid and arrested Cook, but "he was the wrong Troy." Since he had been in custody, the bikers feared that he had spilled the beans. Cook's body was never found. Local legend has it that he was dumped into an already-dug grave at the nearby century-old Muslim cemetery on Pictou Road. The grave was sealed the next day, after a planned funeral. Cook's roommate apparently left Truro and also hasn't been seen since.

By 1999, Greenwood owed Lynds a considerable amount of money for drugs. Lynds took over the contract for Mersereau's life from Carroll and promised Greenwood that he would cancel his debt once he had murdered Mersereau.

On September 24, 1999, Greenwood built and planted a bomb at Randy Mersereau's used-car business on Jennifer Drive, which was not far from the RCMP detachment in Bible Hill. The bomb blew a hole in the side wall of the building. Seven people, including Mersereau, were injured, but no one was killed.

Five weeks later, on Sunday, October 31, 1999, Halloween night, Mersereau went out on a date with Jamie Gratto. During the evening, they went to a house on Peppard Drive in Onslow Mountain, which was owned by an acquaintance. A surprise party of sorts was planned. In the basement recreation room, Jeffery Lynds was waiting. When Mersereau came downstairs, Lynds shot him five times, killing him. Mersereau's body was then buried in a shallow grave. Gratto didn't say a word about what had happened, at least not to the police.

Life went on in Colchester County—which is to say, so did crime.

Mersereau's brother, Barry Kirk Mersereau, who went by his middle name, sought revenge, which proved to be rather unwise. In September 2000, Kirk Mersereau and his wife, Nancy Christensen, were found shot to death in their home on Cogmagun Road in Centre Burlington, just north of Windsor, Nova Scotia. Their eighteen-month-old son and three dogs were found unharmed.

At any other time, a likely suspect would have been hit man Dany Kane, but he had mysteriously died a month before the murders, overcome by carbon monoxide in his Montreal-area garage. His lover/partner in crime, Aimé Simard, was in prison in Saskatchewan, where he would be murdered in 2003, stabbed 187 times.

All this violence helped the RCMP concentrate their efforts, and in 2001, after a series of successful police raids and prosecutions, the Hells Angels seemed to be effectively out of business in Nova Scotia and elsewhere in Canada.

But the impact from the Mersereau murders would reverberate for years as the Mounties scuffled around Nova Scotia trying to find Randy's body. Although the RCMP had its suspicions about who was responsible for the brothers' deaths, there were no solid leads in the case for a decade. According to RCMP records released by the MCC, Jamie Gratto's role in Randy Mersereau's murder was uncovered by the Mounties in 2007, after Jeffery Lynds was arrested on drug charges, but that connection went nowhere. She was seen as a witness to a murder that she didn't want to admit she had witnessed.

It took a double murder in Montreal in 2010 to finally unravel the Mersereau mystery. Jeffery Lynds hired brothers Robert and Timothy Simpson to kill two men: organized-crime hit man Kirk "Cowboy" Murray and his occasional driver Antonio Onesi. Lynds wanted Murray dead because he had botched a hit on a drug dealer; he promised to pay the Simpson brothers $20,000 for each body, and that he would get Robert into the Hells Angels afterwards. Les Greenwood, who was back in debt to Lynds for drugs, was the designated delivery and getaway driver. He drove the Simpsons from Nova Scotia to Montreal for the kill, and then back.

Five months later, Lynds and the Simpsons were arrested in Nova Scotia for the two murders—as well as another—and taken back to Montreal. Fearing that he would be poisoned in prison and that his brother might be killed, Robert Simpson became a police informant. He fingered Jeffery Lynds as the man who had hired them to kill Murray.

The Quebec revelations kicked the RCMP investigation in Nova Scotia out of its stupor and into high gear. In November 2010, eleven years after he had gone missing, the RCMP found the body of Randy Mersereau buried in a field on Hiram Lynds Road. The police were assisted by the imprisoned Jeffery Lynds, who had angered the Angels with his reckless behaviour and felt that his days were numbered.

Kirk Mersereau and Nancy Christensen's murders were solved a month later.

The renewed investigation focused on another Portapique resident, twenty-five-year-old Michael John Lawrence, who, like Greenwood, blew through crack, cocaine, hash, LSD and marijuana like a madman and in 2000 had run up a tab of $28,600 to Jeffery Lynds's nephew, Curtis Blair Lynds. Curtis Lynds had an innovative and potentially lucrative plan for Lawrence to pay off that debt: a Brink's truck robbery.

In the early-morning hours of Friday, September 8, 2000, Curtis Lynds gave Lawrence a .357 Magnum handgun and dropped him off at the eight-unit Sunrise Motel in Brookfield, south of Truro, where Lawrence was living. The motel is on the east side of Highway 102, heading to Halifax. Lawrence had to get to Halifax to complete his mission but didn't have a car. He crossed over the highway on the bridge, walked down the ramp and began hitchhiking.

Charles Maddison had left his Portapique home at 7 a.m. that morning in his 1989 blue Dodge Dakota truck and was headed to Halifax for several doctors' appointments when he pulled over to pick up his neighbour Lawrence. After they had driven a few kilometres, Lawrence pulled out the big gun and forced Maddison to leave the highway near Shubenacadie. They drove west to a remote area along Panuke Road in lightly populated East Hants. There, Lawrence walked Maddison into the woods and shot him twice, leaving his body where it fell. Lawrence then drove to the Bayers Lake shopping centre, in the west end of Halifax, to rendezvous with Curtis Lynds and another man, Jason Lindsay. The plan was for them to rob the Brink's armoured truck making a cash delivery to the Atlantic Superstore at the shopping centre.

"I just killed a guy," Lawrence said to Lynds upon his arrival.

Because of Lawrence's lengthy diversion, it was too late to jump the Brink's guard, who was just about to get into his truck. The armed robbery was called off, which angered Curtis Lynds even more. Now, he said, Lawrence owed him even more money. To pay off his debt, Lawrence was given the contract on Kirk Mersereau and Nancy Christensen.

As bad fortune would have it, Leslie Greenwood continued to be in hock to Jeffery Lynds and was also called on to join the cabal in return for having his latest debt cancelled. Lynds chose Greenwood because he knew that Kirk Mersereau trusted him and would open the door for him.

When Lawrence and Greenwood arrived at Mersereau's secluded house, Lawrence hid in the truck. He said Greenwood knocked, Mersereau answered, and Greenwood immediately shot him and Christensen. Lawrence heard the shots and hurried to the house. He fired two bullets at Mersereau's Rottweilers on the porch, missing them.

A third dog, likely the vicious one, was tethered to a chain. When he got into the house, Mersereau was face down on the floor. Christensen was sitting in a chair with a cup of tea in her hand and a bullet hole in her head. Neither of them was moving.

According to Lawrence, Greenwood said, "Hurry, get in there. I shot them . . . Make sure they're dead."

Lawrence said he fired two shots into Mersereau's head and one into Christensen's. Afterwards, Curtis Lynds told Lawrence that his debt was retired. All was good—until it wasn't.

At the time of his arrest in December 2010, Lawrence was easy for the police to find. He was already in the Springhill federal penitentiary, serving a sentence for armed robbery, one of the fourteen criminal convictions he had earned in his adult life. When the police came to him about the Mersereau-Christensen murders, Lawrence said he had recently learned that he had cancer, and he had found religion. Feeling guilty, he confessed to murdering Charles Maddison and agreed to help the Mounties. His handler was Bruce Briers, then a sergeant. Lawrence took the RCMP to where he had left Maddison's body, but it was no longer there and has yet to be found.

There was one hole left in the overall story: the Mounties needed more evidence against Les Greenwood; they couldn't just take the word of Lawrence or Lynds or any of their other informants who were trolling around the community. It was time for a sting operation known as Mr. Big, which involves undercover officers or informants posing as members of a criminal organization to elicit a confession. Soon "outlaw bikers" were sidling up to Greenwood and befriending him, trying to get him to trip up and confess what he had done. Court records indicate that at least two informants, posing as drug dealers, were used in the case. We do not know who they were.

In the end, Jeffery Lynds was charged and convicted in the Montreal murders and agreed to co-operate with the police investigation. In return, he was not charged in the Nova Scotia cases, although he admitted to pulling the trigger on Randy Mersereau. Before his case came to trial, Lynds died in prison in 2012 of a suspected suicide. But the story in Truro is that his death was faked, and that he is alive and well somewhere deep inside the witness protection program. It was a variation of Wolf Carroll's fate. Carroll is a legend in criminal circles. In 2001, he was charged with thirteen murders but narrowly escaped being arrested in Mexico. He hasn't been seen since and is believed to be living under an assumed name, likely in South America.

Greenwood, who was convicted and imprisoned over the Montreal murders, was twice convicted of the Mersereau-Christensen murders, but both convictions were overturned on appeal. At the time of writing, he was facing a third trial.

Curtis Lynds was already in prison on drug trafficking charges when he was charged with the two murders. In 2014, he pleaded guilty and was handed a life sentence.

◆

Like many elite criminal organizations, the Hells Angels is run like a business, and its business is to provide extraordinarily profitable prohibited services to the public operating outside the regulatory, justice and tax system structures. The job of the police is to interrupt that business, seize ill-gotten gains and punish or imprison the controlling minds and other participants. It's a never-ending, almost symbiotic cycle: The bikers commit the crimes. The police solve some crimes and dismantle the bikers' operations. The bikers go to jail. The police get promoted. The bikers send new people, usually members who have recently gotten out of jail, to reboot their franchise operations. The police investigate. They charge and "dismantle" the organization. And so on. It's a deadly game of Whac-A-Mole, played with real people.

Over the years, the criminals have gained some significant advantages. Each time the police succeed in thwarting their operations, the Hells Angels study what went wrong and mount another attack, carefully watching for repeated patterns by the police.

The police, on the other hand, are constrained in what they can do by defendant-friendly laws in Canada, such as the landmark decision in the 1991 Supreme Court case *R v Stinchcombe*. William Stinchcombe was a lawyer charged with theft and fraud. The Crown denied the defence access to some of the evidence against him, which the judge allowed, and Stinchcombe was convicted. The case was then brought to the Supreme Court, where Justice John Sopinka, a former Hamilton, Ontario, defence lawyer, writing on behalf of the unanimous court, ruled that all information gathered by the police in a case, relevant or not, must be disclosed to the defence, whether or not the Crown uses it at trial. Sopinka argued that imposing an obligation of full disclosure would further, rather than impede, the pursuit of truth, and that denying the accused full disclosure was a violation of the Charter of Rights and Freedoms, which ensures that individuals' rights are respected over those of the collective. Criminals are individuals, too. As a career defence lawyer, Sopinka clearly viewed the world through the eyes of an accused criminal determined to know everything that the police knew—especially everyone they might have talked to along the way.

Stinchcombe and other, similar rulings tipped the balance of the justice system toward the criminals. The perpetrators of crime are treated more like victims of crimes, and the perpetrators of the crimes against *them* are the police, who need to be controlled. Consequently, the police have little room to manoeuvre in investigations. They must follow strict guidelines. There are limits on wiretapping and surveillance. One slip-up and an investigation is toast. They must be creative in their investigations.

When it comes to infiltrating outlaw biker gangs and other organized crime groups, gone are the days of slipping an undercover officer into a clubhouse. To conduct a successful investigation, the police must rely on luck and ingenuity in some cases, but mostly on members or associates whom they can squeeze into co-operating with their investigations. The only alternative is suitable outsiders who have street cred with the bikers, a.k.a. informants. But that is an extremely shallow pool.

As for the criminals, the Hells Angels and their lawyers have weaponized *Stinchcombe*. They watch and analyze everything the police do. If the police come into contact with someone in any way, they study what happened, or didn't happen. If they suspect a rat, they invest in exposing or exterminating them. They know that every dead rat discourages others from taking the police cheese. Their counter-surveillance even extends to infiltrating police departments and government agencies.

As serene as Portapique might have seemed to an outsider, its dark side was hidden just beneath the surface. The message to the community from the Mersereau and related murders was an implicit one: Don't mess around with the bikers. Wrong them and you, and maybe your family, will end up dead. In the twisted, upside-down vernacular of rural Colchester County, Nova Scotia, it was better to accept them, and call them "good people," than to rat them out and risk the inherent dangers. "Snitches get stitches is something children are taught in day care in Nova Scotia," a female customer of our glass business jokingly told me one day, but even so, there were still snitches in Nova Scotia.

17

GABRIEL WORTMAN'S "ATTRACTIVE" CRIMINAL CONNECTIONS

Although the Mass Casualty Commission declined to delve into Wortman's criminal connections, preferring to promote the fiction that he was just a wayward successful businessperson, the Dartmouth denturist was no stranger to the underbelly of the Maritimes. While a student at the University of New Brunswick in the late 1980s, Wortman was often seen with an older gay man who many assumed was a professor. But he wasn't faculty. He was a lawyer and long-time family friend of the Wortmans named Tom Evans. Wortman started out as a junior partner to Evans in a smuggling scheme that involved illegally bringing cigarettes and drugs into Canada across the border with Maine.

Largely known as an ambulance chaser in Fredericton, Evans was a corrupt lawyer whose clients included members of the Medellín drug cartel, whom he had met in the usual way in which lawyers meet their customers. In April 1989, the two Colombians had been the target of a US–Canadian undercover operation. They were flying a twin-engine Aero Commander 1000 so low that it clipped trees, forcing them to land at the Fredericton airport. Once on the ground, they were arrested. On the plane, the RCMP found 500 kilograms of cocaine, whose wholesale value was $25 million before it was cut for distribution on the streets. It was touted as the largest drug seizure in Canadian history. Afterwards, the cartel sent a rescue team to bust out and save the two captured men, which provided another series of colourful stories involving Evans over the years.

Mexican and South American drug cartels operating in Canada seemed rather exotic and rare, but it was no accident. The cartels had long identified Canada as being weak on enforcement and a perfect platform on which to build their international business, along with partners like the Hells Angels and traditional Italian organized crime.

In 2009, Evans unexpectedly died, and though his death was ruled natural, some on both sides of the law suspected that Wortman may have killed him and altered his will, making himself the sole heir to Evans's money and real estate. As executor, he had Evans quickly cremated and sold off two of the lawyer's properties in Fredericton, netting himself $232,000.

After his killing spree, the default truth was that, *before* the massacres, Wortman gravitated toward cops like a groupie, which seemed to be factual. As a boy, he had been belittled and psychologically abused by his father and his seemingly indifferent mother. At the same time, he was surrounded by current and wannabe police officers. One of his childhood friends was Scott Baker, who grew up to become a constable with the Summerside, PEI, police service. Two of his uncles and one of his cousins were Mounties. He even attended his uncle Chris Wortman's graduation at Depot in Regina. As an adult, he partied with Mounties and other police officers. Wortman even carried what appeared to be an RCMP badge in his wallet, which he joked got him better rates at hotels.

Although some folks described him as being a police supporter, Wortman had long been involved in criminal activities, as I detailed in *22 Murders*. The period from 2007 to 2011 was a tumultuous but profitable time for Wortman as he continued his illegal operations, smuggling drugs, guns and motorcycle parts across the border. These activities didn't go entirely unnoticed by the authorities. A few months after Evans's demise, Wortman and Banfield were flagged at the US–Canada border "for drugs," according to a report to the MCC. Over the years, they were also flagged for smuggling, but nothing ever came of it, as with all the other problems Wortman generated for himself during his life. Many believed he escaped scrutiny because of his close relationships with police. Although Banfield said Wortman never smuggled anything when she was with him, she later told the Mounties that on one occasion he had smuggled a gun while she was with him.

The more I looked at the events, the more I wondered if we had things backwards. Maybe Wortman hadn't gravitated toward the police; maybe the police had gravitated toward him, thinking he could help with undercover operations aimed at the Hells Angels. He was a perfect candidate in many ways. He could pass for a professional businessman. He worked as a denturist only two or three days a week at best. He took months off at a time, if he so desired. He travelled extensively. And he had contacts in the underworld.

Sources say that Wortman knew Wolf Carroll and the Mersereau brothers, and was accepted by the Hells Angels and many of their puppet clubs. The old 13th Tribe and Hells Angels clubhouse was at 118 Portland Street, a few blocks south of Wortman's denture clinic on the other side of the downtown street. It's still there, now serving as the home of the Darksiders, a Hells Angels puppet club. Police and knowledgeable sources say that Wortman was also friendly with members of other clubs, including Bacchus, the Red Devils, the Gate Keepers, the Highlanders and the Redneck Mountain Men, among others.

Gabriel Wortman had the ideal credentials to be an informant. He looked respectable but had a proven track record of being a bad boy, and he was always looking for easy ways to get money. Wortman told people he liked using white vehicles when smuggling; the decommissioned police cars gave him an added edge, he thought. A fully decked-out police car would be useful for getting past the border police. Was Wortman using the cars to pursue his criminal ways, or were they part of a sting operation? Numerous police sources concur that Wortman or someone close to him was on the police payroll. He was into motorcycles, which gave him something to talk about with the bikers. He may also have been part of a group of paid informants, which has become rather common in some communities, police sources say. These same source-believe that Wortman was likely considered an invaluable informant. They suspect he might have been employed by a number of forces simultaneously, with or without knowledge of his involvement being shared among them.

And then, of course, there was Wortman's neighbour and friend, Peter Alan Griffon. After the massacres, the police kept Griffon's name out of the media until reporter Stephen Maher from *Maclean's* magazine and I figured out his close relationship to Wortman. I wrote in *22 Murders*:

> The reason Peter Griffon had caught our attention was that on December 11, 2014, he had been arrested by the Edmonton Police Service. The police were conducting an investigation into what is known as a security threat group. Members of two notorious international crime organizations were operating in concert in the city. One was La Familia, the Mexican drug cartel; the other was MS-13, the ultra-violent Salvadoran street gang also known as Mara Salvatrucha. Police identified Griffon as being linked to both groups. When they stopped his car, they found cash, cocaine, a score sheet, a portable hard drive, a camera and multiple cellphones. The warehouse where Griffon was living was later raided. There police found multiple firearms, including two .22-calibre rifles, one with a silencer, ammunition, four kilos of cocaine, $30,000 in cash, and equipment to package and traffic cocaine. Eleven days later, on December 22, the police announced three further arrests and linked Griffon and the others publicly to La Familia and MS-13.
>
> "[La Familia's] presence in Alberta should be of concern to Albertans," Inspector Darcy Strang told CBC News on December 17. "Their connection to Mexican cartels and MS-13 creates a linkage to violence that is incomprehensible to most. I can tell you that Peter Alan Griffon was one of the targets of this investigation."
>
> In his defence Griffon admitted to having a $1,000-a-day cocaine habit, and he downplayed his connections to La Familia and MS-13. As the parole board put it: "You report that you were living in the warehouse part time. In terms of the weapons, you state you held a

party, and found the guns and ammunitions in the warehouse the next day, which you stored in a locker and forgot about."

When he was convicted in 2017 in an Alberta court, Griffon had received a global sentence of six years, four months and one day. He was immediately given credit for time served and other credits, which reduced it to two years, nine months and eight days. The then thirty-eight-year-old Griffon was paroled a year later in 2018 and sent back to Portapique Beach to live with his parents.

Three law enforcement officers who reviewed Griffon's file for me all came back with the same conclusion. Two words were missing, they each said: "Hells Angels."

"The Hells Angels control everything that moves in Alberta," said a senior investigator familiar with the drug trade. "There's no way someone could move in and push around that much weight without the Angels either knowing about it or approving it."

Delving into Griffon's family background, I soon learned that in the 1980s and 1990s, his grandmother was a long-time family friend of the murdered Hells Angel Randy Mersereau, and his uncle was an outlaw biker who had done a long stretch in prison. Griffon was also one of Wortman's drinking buddies and worked as a handyman at both the cottage and the warehouse. Griffon even used a trade he had learned in prison to help Wortman—applying decals to one of Wortman's four decommissioned police cars to make it look like a real police car. And as I mentioned in Chapter 6, he was one of the last people to see and talk to Wortman and Banfield on April 18, 2020. After the fires erupted that night, Griffon tried repeatedly to call Banfield, without success.

Why might the RCMP need Wortman as an informant? Well, they hadn't kicked the Hells Angels out of the Maritimes, as they'd hoped. And so the story of Fargo, Nova Scotia, continued.

◆

After the fallout from the Mersereau murders and the demise of Jeffery Lynds and his crew, the Hells Angels began to fill the vacuum. They designated Nomads Emery "Pit" Martin and Robin Moulton as the new bosses; Martin would take over New Brunswick, while Moulton's task was to rebuild in Nova Scotia. Hells Angels middle managers and soldiers, many from Ontario, moved east and set up shop in mostly rural areas, the jurisdiction of the RCMP. Hells Angels puppet clubs sprung up everywhere, particularly in the Truro and New Glasgow areas.

RCMP commissioner Robert Paulson was obsessed with eradicating the Hells Angels. Every time the police thought they had squashed them, the gang seemed to come back even stronger. This led Paulson to create the Federal Serious and Organized Crime (FSOC) section in 2016. New Brunswick assistant commissioner Larry Tremblay took over command of all such operations in the four Maritime provinces. Reporting to Tremblay, according to RCMP sources, was Inspector Ron Desilva, who was in charge of FSOC operations in New Brunswick.

From 2016 to 2020, Desilva ran a series of often interconnected projects across the Maritimes whose targets were the Hells Angels and their puppet clubs. These projects included Titanium, Touchdown, Tugboat, Thrasher, Objection, Orchestrer [sic], Toast, Tippaul, Trilogy, Thunder, Thunderstruck and Triton. The last three were particularly notable. Operation Thunderstruck targeted Pit Martin and his operations in northern New Brunswick, while Project Thunder was aimed at Marcel Friolet, who was licensed by the Hells Angels to traffic drugs in the area. Project Triton targeted Robin Moulton and his activities in both Nova Scotia and southeastern New Brunswick. After all three men were arrested, Project Trilogy was created to chase down Moulton's replacement, Jesse Logue.

In 2019, the police asked for the public's help. Elderly Dieppe, New Brunswick, residents Bernard and Rose-Marie Saulnier knew their son Sylvio was connected with Hells Angels and, attempting to be good citizens, gave the police information that led to successful raids and the arrest of Logue. But they seemingly paid for it. On the night Logue, Sylvio and others were charged, the Saulniers were murdered. On September 7, 2023, the fourth anniversary of their deaths, the RCMP announced that twenty-seven-year-old Janson Bryan Baker had been arrested and charged with the murders.

Project Triton didn't end with the arrest of Moulton but continued to focus on the Hells Angels, who were still operating in the area. Sources familiar with the investigation say the force likely used the same confidential informants or agents. An informant provides information to the police, while an agent takes direction from them. Overusing informants or agents is a dangerous thing to do: the longer they are undercover, and the more success they have, the more vulnerable they become.

Jimmy McNulty and other police sources I talked to said they noticed a big change on the ground after the RCMP reorganized. "Around 2016, the CFSEU [Combined Forces Special Enforcement Unit] was all over Moulton in Nova Scotia," McNulty said. "We had followed him back to New Brunswick. We had identified some assets and buildings and were closing in on him when we were shut down by Tremblay. He put his guys in place, mostly French-speakers. They took over."

Shortly afterwards, those in the outlaw biker police units were called to a planning meeting in Truro. "There was a new guy sitting at the table with the boss," said McNulty. "We were told that he was a Mountie who was the handler for a hot new informant. We didn't know who the informant was, but the vague description we got suggested that he was from the Portapique area. Over the next little while, we began to see a pattern. Whenever we did a raid, one of the things we always found were pill presses that seemed to be linked to the informant."

Subsequently, I was given a name for the likely handler: Constable Peter Hurley. An RCMP member at the Bible Hill detachment, Hurley had a reputation inside policing for developing and running informants. Some thought he was good at that job, while others felt he pushed the informants too far and risked overexposing them.

"You know," said McNulty, "the bikers aren't dumb. When something goes south, they analyze what happened and look for patterns to see if they can figure out who the rat is. If you use the same trick every time, that makes it easy for them and dangerous for the informant."

Between 2016 and 2019, Wortman's interests seemed to change. In addition to drugs and motorcycle parts, he also was smuggling guns across the border, including at least one Barrett .50-calibre sniper rifle. He had a case or two of grenades, which he proudly showed off to select people. The only customers for such exotic weaponry were outlaw bikers. Coincidentally or otherwise, sniper rifles and grenades became a feature of many of the search warrants involving bikers issued across the country during this time frame, and police recovered sniper rifles, grenades and other weapons in raids on outlaw biker operations in Nova Scotia, Ontario and elsewhere. They were also searching for the kind of hydraulic pill presses that are useful in the world of drug trafficking, and that Wortman, as a denturist, could have supplied.

At the time of the massacres, Moulton had been locked up for almost three years and was serving the end of his sentence in the Springhill penitentiary. Around this same time, Hurley was quietly transferred out of Bible Hill and landed in Ferryland, a remote detachment with a population of 371 on the Avalon Peninsula of Newfoundland. He was never called before the MCC.

So was Wortman a criminal or an informant? If the former, then the RCMP had nothing to hide, but if the latter, then his killing spree didn't reflect very well on them, did it?

Let's take another look at the Les Greenwood sting in 2010. According to the court records, many of the Mounties involved in that operation were intimately involved in the response to the Nova Scotia massacres and the follow-up investigation. These included:

- Sergeant Dave Lilly and Constable Fraser Firth, both of whom were in the Major Crimes Unit at the time.
- Then sergeants Brian Rehill, Al Carroll and Bruce Briers, who was Michael John Lawrence's handler; in Portapique, Rehill and Briers, now staff sergeants, were the risk managers controlling the movements of RCMP officers on the ground. Carroll, also now a staff sergeant, was the original incident commander.
- Corporal Gerard Rose-Berthiaume, who was later the lead investigator into the massacres.
- Sergeant David Legge, who specialized in running informants; he was the human source handler and coordinator from January 2011 to March 2013, and played a role in interviewing key Portapique witnesses.

- Sergeant Steve Halliday, who was running the Combined Forces Special Enforcement Unit from March 2007 to 2011, and was on the ground that night in Portapique.
- Corporal Angela Hawryluk, who was in federal drug enforcement then, and later controlled the collection of information and wrote applications for warrants in the Portapique case.

All of these Mounties had deep experience in dealing with undercover operators and informants. They could be trusted to keep a secret; that was their business. In some ways, it is not surprising that they all were involved in the two separate actions over a decade apart. Nova Scotia is not that big a place, and the RCMP presence is not huge.

Although all of them gave statements after Portapique, most did not testify in public. Those who did, like Carroll, Briers and Rehill, were granted accommodations for undisclosed reasons and were not exposed to hard or deep questions.

If Wortman were indeed an RCMP operative working in New Brunswick, Inspector Ron Desilva would have been involved, likely along with Superintendent Jason Popik of the Nova Scotia Federal Policing Criminal Operations section. Popik was a covert and undercover specialist who ran RCMP general duty operations from 2016 to 2019 and was involved in all outlaw biker operations in Nova Scotia. According to the April 2020 organization chart for the Nova Scotia RCMP, Popik worked with Chief Superintendent Chris Leather, the provincial Criminal Operations officer, but he seemed to operate more in Tremblay's world than Leather's.

Unsurprisingly, neither Popik's nor Desilva's name ever came up with the MCC. The commission wasn't all that interested in this kind of context; neither, it seemed, was the RCMP.

As for Griffon, the RCMP appear to have made a special effort to evacuate him and his parents—ahead of the four children who had been hiding in the basement of Lisa McCully's home and talking to a 911 operator and the RCMP for almost two hours at that point. Knowledgeable sources say Griffon disappeared for two days after he left Portapique. Where did he go? Whom was he with? We don't know.

When RCMP constable Ben Kershaw interviewed Griffon on May 4, 2020, Sergeant Fraser Firth sat in. In an interview later with the commission, Firth said he couldn't recall Griffon's name, which was unusual for a cop in that situation, considering that Griffon was an ex-con on parole, was connected to the Hells Angels and a drug cartel, and was Wortman's buddy who had put the RCMP decals on his car, and one of the last people to see him before he began to kill people. Firth did remember that Griffon was "lying through his teeth" early on in the interview. Griffon was never charged with anything.

Commission investigators said they had difficulty finding Griffon and did not interview him for almost two years. The commission then passed on having him testify and answer questions at its public hearings.

The RCMP acted as if any discussion of cartels operating in Nova Scotia was the product of journalistic hallucinations, but the Mounties inadvertently tipped their hand on June 26, 2020. The scene was the aforementioned "family meeting" with Nick Beaton, husband of murder victim Kristen Beaton; her brother, Rick Roode; and, from the RCMP, Superintendent Darren Campbell; Inspector Murray Marcichiw, who was in charge of the Major Crimes and Human Trafficking units; Sergeant Glenn Bonvie of the Northeast Nova Major Crime Unit; lead investigator Corporal Gerard (Gerry) Rose-Berthiaume; and Constable Wayne Bent, the family liaison officer. What was said at the meeting was described later in a summary produced for the commission. It read: "One of the investigators told Nick that he had been working undercover with high-level members of the drug cartel for the last 12 to 16 years. He said the RCMP brought him on board because of his expertise, and he explained that his specialty was undercover work with the high-level cartel. When he said this Darren kind of perked up and told the investigator to shut up. He and Gerry appeared to be really mad at the investigator. That investigator hasn't been seen since."

The only investigator I could find who appeared to have that background was Marcichiw, who had served in British Columbia, Alberta and Bogotá, Colombia, before coming to Nova Scotia. It was yet another whiff of the likely deeper story, but it was quickly snuffed out.

18

"MAD" MAX AND THE FAKE POLICE CARS

The fact that Wortman had a replica police car and used it to carry out the murders was a major factor in how long it took the RCMP to apprehend him. In the aftermath of the massacres, many asked how he'd gotten his hands on a car in the first place—and if the RCMP had known about it. One of the narratives that circulated was that Wortman had built the replica police car for the purpose of the shooting spree. The problem with that story was that there was some evidence he had been collecting old police cars not only during the previous year but for as long as six years.

On April 25, 2022, the Mass Casualty Commission would turn to this very question. It had been eleven days since the last witnesses—the officers who shot and killed Wortman—were called. (We'll get to that hearing later; for now, we're going to step slightly out of chronological order.) The following week had been dark, to acknowledge the second anniversary of the massacres. But now it was Max Liberatore's turn.

Liberatore must have thought he had one of the least controversial positions in the Canadian public service: the Atlantic branch of

GCSurplus, then located at 13 Akerley Boulevard in Dartmouth's Burnside Industrial Park. The government-run entity disposes of surplus equipment and items that have been legally seized and deemed the proceeds of crime. There are branches in every province, but Prince Edward Island and Newfoundland and Labrador are served from the Halifax location. Of his thirty-one years in public service, Liberatore had worked twelve at GCSurplus.

The day he appeared before the commission, Liberatore was dressed in respectful semi-formal fashion, the top button of his shirt open under a delicately patterned yellow tie. When he took his place at the witness table, Liberatore might have been expecting a softer, gentler ride, given the "trauma-informed" process, but unlike the nine Mounties who had spoken in the weeks and months prior, he had no one there to hold his hand or give him comfort.

Liberatore sat alone at a large table in a meeting room at the Prince George Hotel, the venue of the week. The setting was not at all like a courtroom. My podcast partner, lawyer Adam Rodgers, described how it worked in his daily blog coverage of that day:

> Witnesses are not called to "the stand" as they are in court, but are rather invited to the "witness table." Witnesses are sworn or affirmed, as they are in court. I think it is relevant to identify any distinctions between the MCC proceedings and a court process, and whether those differences have any effect. It may be that witnesses feel less gravity or solemnity being called to a table than to a stand. Another is, unlike with a Judge entering a courtroom, we do not "all rise" when the Commissioners enter, which is disconcerting for lawyers' reflexes.

Liberatore had given three previous interviews. The first was on April 21, 2020, a fifty-one-minute session with RCMP corporals Kathryn MacLeod and Patricia Davis. The second was sixty-seven minutes long and took place twenty months later, on December 17, 2021, with commission investigator Dwayne King, commission counsel Rachel Young, and Krista Smith, who specialized in policy and research for the commission. As the clock ticked down for his commission appearance, an emergency thirty-four-minute interview was conducted on April 21, 2022, by commission investigators Dwayne King and Chris Lussow.

In those three interviews Liberatore laid out how he had first met Wortman. Although he said it had been about eight years earlier, it was more likely ten. In 2009 and 2010, Wortman had opened two different accounts at GCSurplus under his own name. He later deleted those accounts and opened a third one under the name Berkshire Broman Corp. During his first visit to GCSurplus, Wortman was accompanied by two men, one "with long hair," Liberatore said. They were looking at Harley-Davidson motorcycles that had been seized by the Crown. Over the ensuing years, Wortman would become a frequent bidder on everything from office furniture, tools and gadgets to boats and even a helicopter. Why a helicopter? We don't know. The commission didn't seem keen to dig into that one, which we duly noted in *Frank*, writing:

> The helicopter is not the kind of thing that the RCMP or the commission appeared to be eager to discuss in public.
>
> According to the GC Surplus documents, on January 20, 2015, Wortman—operating as buyer 1122342—offered $235,000 for a 1979 Sikorsky S76A helicopter.
>
> The twin-engine medium helicopter is like those used by the coast guard, police in provinces outside Nova Scotia, air ambulances or by executives. It can seat up to 12 passengers. The helicopter can fly 740 kilometres on a tank of fuel.
>
> Wortman didn't win the bid for the helicopter, but the very fact that he had tried to get it raises obvious questions, like why would a Dartmouth denturist be interested in such an exotic machine?
>
> To attempt to answer that question would cause the MCC to veer into a territory it appears determined to assiduously avoid— Wortman's criminal operations and what the police knew and didn't know about them.
>
> Just about everyone who knew Wortman in Nova Scotia and New Brunswick [was] keenly aware that he had long been involved in smuggling cigarettes, alcohol, drugs and guns, among other things,

across the border with Maine. The only ones who didn't seem to know about all this, if you believe their story, are the police, especially the Mounties.

Wortman all but telegraphed what he was doing or intending to do with the more than 350 bids he had made on government surplus items listed with GC Surplus, beginning with his first one.

On July 11, 2010, Wortman—then known as anonymous buyer number 1077145—made a blind bid, as was the practice then, on an inflatable rigid hull Zodiac boat. His offer of $16,333 was not good enough.

Sixteen days later, on July 27, 2010, he made a last-minute bid on another Zodiac. This time for $21,014. He lost again.

Over the next nine years he would bid on 17 other Zodiac or comparable boats. On May 27, 2014, he took a shot at a Catamaran Patrol Vessel, offering $30,500, but again lost.

His final unsuccessful bid on a Zodiac—$16,007.

Over the years, Tom Evans and Wortman had used every means of conveyance to bring drugs over the border, including their own private pilot and an isolated landing strip in southern New Brunswick. Many claimed that Wortman was a purveyor of a wide variety of drugs, including marijuana, methamphetamine and cocaine, though he was never charged with any such offence. That being the case, the helicopter offer made sense. But who would fly it?

In all, Wortman made forty-four purchases from GCSurplus, but he bid on much more. A couple of times he showed up with Banfield in tow. "Wortman lost out on more bids than he won," a source told me for a *Frank* article published in November 2021. "When he lost, he wasn't very happy about it."

Now, in front of the commission, Liberatore would be led through his previous testimony, some of which had already been reported. It looked like it might be another boring day at the commission, full of old news, but it wasn't Roger Burrill who began questioning Liberatore. It was Jamie Van Wart, the only professional prosecutor on the team, the go-to guy when a witness needed to be pummelled.

Under questioning by Van Wart, Liberatore said he was employed as a warehouseman, one of two people also known as storepersons. His job was to organize and prepare items for auction. He said he had been dealing with Wortman for eight years. Wortman struck Liberatore as being both personable and odd. He said the women in the office—of all ages— were leery of Wortman because he was a little too "touchy-touchy."

That was all extraneous information. The primary focus of the hearing was the four decommissioned police cars that Wortman had purchased between March and September 2019, paying a total of $21,596.81. Selling used police vehicles netted the RCMP $8 million a year until the massacres forced the federal government to put an end to that business line.

While he was gathering his cars, Wortman was shopping outside of GCSurplus for the accessories he would need to build his replica police car. On March 26, 2019, he bought a Setina PI Interceptor Push Bumper ram. Ten days later, he purchased rear-window armour bars. On May 7, 2019, it was a Whelen Liberty lightbar. He bought a radar unit and a radar tuning kit. He started to dress up one of the older cars, but it didn't pass muster.

Then the 2017 Ford Taurus Police Interceptor came up for auction. It was almost new, with a relatively minor ding on the front end, yet the government had written it off. It was a steal. Wortman bought it on June 27, 2019, for $13,500, with taxes and transfer fees. He put it on one of his credit cards. Wortman bragged to Liberatore—and many others—about the replica RCMP car he was creating from the 2017 Ford. It even had a fleet number based on real Mountie cruisers from the Oxford, Nova Scotia, detachment: 28B11.

Van Wart read from a section of Liberatore's first interview with the RCMP, two years to the day earlier: "So when he bought the car, he was always coming in then. We would look and all that, and he was telling me about this cop car that he bought in his garage, and he was starting to do as a cop car . . . I said: 'Oh, okay. You have whatever. Right?' So . . . when he came in again, he'd be telling me about the cop car . . . Then he came in and he started showing me pictures of the car, what he did to it after . . . and it's all cleaned up. And then he started showing me the decals he put on the car."

Then Van Wart asked Liberatore if he remembered sharing that information with the police.

"Yes, I actually had a Sunday dinner with my brother-in-law, and my brother-in-law's brother is an RCMP officer," Liberatore answered. "So I was telling him what [Wortman] was telling me at the time."

The RCMP officer in question was no ordinary member but Staff Sergeant Greg Vardy, the head of the Truth Verification Section and the key interviewer for Lisa Banfield. Vardy passed on the information, and Liberatore received a visit from two RCMP officers "so I could tell them what [Wortman] was telling me, I guess."

"Can you remember any other information he told you about the mocked-up police car—cruiser?" Van Wart asked.

"Yes, when I asked him why he was buying cars . . . he actually told me . . . and . . . the girls and employees at work he was building the RCMP car for parades for the fallen cops of New Brunswick . . . He was going to put their name on it."

Liberatore also recalled saying to Wortman: "You can get in that goddamn car and drive down the road and pull people over . . . He goes, 'Yeah . . . you can do it pretty quickly. They can pull over for me. It's no problem at all for me.' . . . He wasn't hiding it, I can tell you that."

Let's pause here and think about what Liberatore told the commission. He said that, albeit indirectly, he had reported the car to the RCMP. He said two Mounties had visited him about it. He went on to say that Wortman had told him he was driving the car and possibly pulling people over with it.

Liberatore wasn't the only one. In their mountain of interviews, the RCMP and the commission had statements from others who said they had seen the car on the road.

Lisa Banfield's older sister, Beverley Davidson, knew about the car. She and her husband, Dale, were interviewed by RCMP constables Denis Chartrand and Holly Murphy on April 19, 2020, five hours after Wortman's killing spree ended.

"I knew about the police car," Beverley told them. "You know that's not good news, doing something like that."

"So tell me what you knew about this police car that he had all fitted up," Murphy said. "How long has he had that?"

"I'm trying to think if I saw it or whether it was just pictures that Lisa showed me on her cell. It's in the last year."

"And when you saw it, or saw the pictures of it, did it have, like, the RCMP decals on it?"

"It had all the bells and whistles," Beverley said. "Lisa just told me he always wanted one, so he got one."

Beverley also recalled a 2019 incident that led her to believe that Wortman was driving the car around Nova Scotia and Lisa knew it. "I think he must have, because Lisa said she got caught speeding and it was an RCMP car up riding behind her," Beverley told the constables. "And she thought it was Gabriel, trying to scare her . . . But it wasn't him anyway . . . she got caught for speeding."

Wortman told the Davidsons that he had cleared the car with the "Crown prosecutor" and that it was legal to use in parades. There is no evidence that he was given official permission to drive the car, but is it possible that he had unofficial consent from the RCMP? If so, why?

Another witness insisted that he had seen Wortman and Banfield together in an RCMP cruiser. Immediately after the massacres, Bruce Gilmour responded to the RCMP's appeal for information and called its Major Crimes hotline to report what he knew about Wortman and Banfield. Gilmour worked at O'Regan's Mercedes-Benz, on Kempt Road in Halifax. The dealership regularly serviced Banfield's 2015 Mercedes, and Gilmour was familiar with both her and Wortman, whom he considered to be a "pretty prominent person in our city."

Gilmour's story is a good example of how the commission defined transparency. He was first interviewed by RCMP corporal Ken Parsons on April 23, 2020. He was reinterviewed by commission investigator Dwayne King on August 11, 2021. Both interviews were released along with what seemed like an avalanche of other materials on April 22, 2022, three days before Liberatore testified. In other words, what Gilmour had to say was buried and largely ignored. The CBC's Haley Ryan was one of the few who wrote about it, getting to Gilmour in the twenty-ninth paragraph of a sixty-paragraph omnibus report that covered all the events and documents of the day.

Gilmour said he had seen Wortman and Banfield together in Halifax in what appeared to be an RCMP cruiser. The problem was that he couldn't recall the exact date. In his first, nine-minute interview, he thought it was sometime in April 2019. Banfield's Royal Bank Visa record showed she paid $638.49 to the dealership on April 1, 2019. Gilmour waffled in his interview, in that he recalled seeing her again on January 30, 2020, which was confirmed by a $33.52 charge posted the next day to the same credit card. He couldn't remember which day it was that he saw the car, and Corporal Parsons didn't press him.

In the second interview, which lasted twenty-four minutes, Gilmour had the benefit of paperwork in hand to refresh his memory. He said he still wasn't certain about which day the incident happened, but he was leaning toward January 30, 2020.

In both interviews, Gilmour described the interaction in the same way: "When Miss Banfield showed up with the paperwork, I noticed an RCMP—what looked like an RCMP car outside the door. I casually asked Lisa, because I knew they dealt in dental work . . . 'Are you guys doing dental work for the RCMP now?'" He said Banfield responded, "No, that's just Gabe picking me up."

"Well, I have to go have a look at this," Gilmour recalled saying. He poked his head through an open window and asked Wortman, "What's the deal with the police car?"

According to Gilmour, Wortman replied that restoring decommissioned police cars was his hobby. "He said he picked up two of these cars from Crown assets and [it was] just a hobby of his, making it look this way. And at the time, it looked fully decaled like an RCMP car, roof lights and all. The only discernible difference I could see, 'cause I had a visual inside the car, is that . . . the rear seats look like, you know, what you see in a police car, like not cloth . . . but the rest of the car inside did not look done up like a police car with computers or anything like that. But the outward appearance of it looked very much like an actual cruiser. Like, it had all the decals like the police, like the reflective stuff on the back, roof lightbar, like, the whole deal, you know. If I were to see it going, I probably wouldn't take a second glance, 'cause it looked just like one of the RCMP cruisers."

Gilmour said that a minute or two later, Banfield "jumped in and they left."

Although Banfield denied Gilmour's story in its entirety, there were elements in his version of events that had not been previously reported. For example, in his first interview, immediately after the massacres, Gilmour quoted Wortman as saying that he had recently purchased "two cars from Crown assets." That was not only true, it was also something the public didn't yet know. The source of Wortman's decommissioned police cars—GCSurplus—and the timing of his purchases had not been reported. How could Gilmour have known these facts without Wortman having told him?

The mocked-up police car Gilmour described appeared to be a first try by Wortman, before his more successful attempt with the 2017 Ford Taurus. But the RCMP and the commission didn't seem interested in the possibility that Wortman had created a previous replica police car. Did they believe Gilmour had imagined that he saw a fully decked-out fake police car when it was really just a decommissioned one?

Gilmour's story also put Banfield in the passenger seat of Wortman's RCMP cruiser, which she denied.

Although the commission did not give Gilmour's story its due, there is a reference in the notebook of RCMP constable Troy Maxwell to Wortman's allegedly driving a decommissioned police car as early as 2013. Maxwell had responded to a complaint by neighbour Richard Ellison that Wortman was racing around Portapique in the vehicle. And there was a mention of another fake cruiser in one of Banfield's emails to Wortman in September 2019: "The stuff is out of the other cop car."

Was the Ford Taurus Wortman's second replica cruiser? If so, what had he been doing with the first one? And how could the RCMP not know about it?

Whatever the case, Wortman appeared to be so confident in the days leading up to the massacres that he was unafraid to drive the replica car past RCMP detachments or real Mounties. On the day before the massacres, RCMP constable Wayne Tingley remembered that he had seen "a new-looking RCMP vehicle with a black push bumper on the front and no licence plate on the back of the vehicle in Elmsdale on Friday April 17, 2020 . . . I thought this was strange but assumed the Enfield detachment may have gotten a new vehicle."

Others came forward to say that they thought they had been pulled over on Highway 104 by Wortman.

Lisa Banfield told investigators in her first interview after the massacres that Wortman had never driven the vehicle on public roads, but multiple witnesses reported seeing it, which contradicts the narrative that Wortman built the replica car specifically for the massacres.

The commissioners knew all this background, and now Max Liberatore was in front of them, testifying. It was an opportunity to dig deep into what the RCMP knew and when it knew it, but did the MCC do so? No. Counsel Van Wart did not pursue that line of questioning. In fact, it seemed like he was just trying to make it all go away, and Liberatore helped him to do just that. The deeper Liberatore got into his version of events, the more his memory began to fail him, particularly at potentially incriminating moments.

In her statements to the RCMP, Lisa Banfield had described Wortman and Liberatore as friends, which Liberatore denied. He said he had never been to Wortman's cottage, although sources close to the investigation believed that he had been. Liberatore also could not recall a half-hour call that registered on Lisa Banfield's phone on November 19, 2019. Remember, the story was that Wortman didn't have a phone and Lisa took all his calls for him.

"Yeah, I don't have no memory of that at all," Liberatore said.

"Do you have any memory of phone conversations you had with the perpetrator?" Van Wart asked.

"No, not on the phone."

Van Wart then pressed Liberatore about work that Wortman had done on one of Liberatore's teeth in September 2019. Wortman had also made a set of dentures for Liberatore's father, who didn't have a health plan.

"Okay, are you aware of whether or not your father paid for the services he received from the perpetrator?" Van Wart asked.

"I was told that he asked to pay for it and [Wortman] said he didn't have to pay for it. He said that I was good to him when he came there, talk to him and stuff like that at my job."

The clear inference was that Liberatore had given Wortman preferential treatment in exchange for under-the-table benefits—which accurately describes how Wortman liked to conduct both his legal and illegal businesses.

Lawyer Tara Miller, acting for the family of murder victim Kristen Beaton, later asked a particularly pointed series of questions focused on Liberatore's earlier statements about the first time he had met Wortman at GCSurplus.

"In your April [2020] statement to the RCMP . . . you talk about how [Wortman] came in knowing that there were these Harley-Davidsons and they were there as proceeds of crime . . . Do you remember how he would have known that?"

"They were on for—they were up for sale," Liberatore replied.

"Yes, I appreciate they were up for sale, but do you have any understanding how the perpetrator would have known at that point that those were the proceeds of crime versus some other means of having been there for sale?"

"I don't recollect how he would know," Liberatore said.

Once again, the inference was that Wortman was being fed information by either the police or the bikers—or both.

In the end, Liberatore didn't come off well as a witness, thanks to Van Wart. *Halifax Examiner* editor Tim Bousquet later remarked that, by that point, nine police officers had testified at the commission. "My own observation is . . . seven of them were allowed to testify as part of panels, and not individually, and even the cross-examinations were restrained. The only truly aggressive interrogation of a witness was that of Max Liberatore, a manager at the GCSurplus warehouse in Dartmouth, who knew the killer was piecing together a look-alike police car."

Liberatore's wife, Trish, messaged me one night to complain about how her husband had been traumatized by his experience at the commission and by the way he was being treated in the media. She said she wanted to restore his reputation, writing: "Paul, I'm really upset that you are putting untrue info about his case. I would like to clarify his relationship with the perpetrator to you. I don't want fake news to carry on."

"If he wants to talk and tell his side of the story, I'm here," I messaged her back at around midnight. "I'm doing my best in a difficult situation. Few people want to talk on the record about [such] an important story. Like I said, I'll talk to him on or off the record. Let's talk tomorrow, if you wish. It's late and I've had a long day and night. Thank you. Paul P."

"You say he is definitely a scapegoat, but you talk about him like he's an accomplice," she replied. "He is a victim. He will not speak, but I will for him."

"There are questions, many questions," I wrote. "That he did not come across well at the MCC is not my fault. If you are going to speak for him, it will not carry as much weight as him speaking for himself."

"I seen a totally different person when he was being questioned," she said. "Max is such an outgoing person, so very friendly. He had no idea this guy whom he gave totally great customer service to was this awful hateful person . . . Max has no dentures and neither do I. He is suffering, too, from this experience."

"Trish," I replied. "The reference to work by Wortman on Max and his father came up at the MCC and was widely reported. It's easy to shout Fake News and accuse me of being responsible, but those facts came from the testimony. If he wants to correct the record, fine. I'm here. I'll listen but I'll have questions, lots of questions. It's your choice. I have no doubt he's suffering. One way to deal with that is to take control of the situation, tell the truth and let the chips fall where they may."

I never heard back from either her or her husband.

Perhaps the most revealing lesson learned from Liberatore's day of being grilled was that there was another, more active GCSurplus customer who might have been very helpful to the commission.

◆

RCMP assistant commissioner Larry Tremblay and I had a couple of things in common. One was that both our wives were glass artists. Although we had never been introduced, I had a sense that we had run into each other in the glass world, either at a trade show or at our old store in Chester. Then there was the RCMP. I had written my books about the force, and since 2016, Tremblay had been the commanding officer in New Brunswick, as well as for all major federal investigations in the Maritime provinces. That alone would have made me interested in his actions, but something further caught my eye along the way, something I found out just as I was completing *22 Murders*: Tremblay was also a frequent flyer at GCSurplus auctions. I squeezed a few paragraphs into the final pages of that book to put it on the public record.

Tremblay had opened his account in 2013. Sometimes he showed up in Dartmouth in plainclothes and other times in uniform. It was a four-hour or longer drive from the RCMP's New Brunswick headquarters on Regent Street in Fredericton. Like Wortman's, his final purchase was on March 11, 2020—the last day GCSurplus was open before shutting down because of COVID restrictions. It's not known if the two men met each other there, but they had plenty of opportunity to at least rub shoulders over the years.

As I wrote in *22 Murders*, a source wondered if "GCSurplus was being used as a meeting place between Tremblay and confidential informants or agents. We had no proof that this was the case or whether Tremblay or Wortman met there, but in light of what happened with Wortman, it seemed like a possibility."

Over the years, Wortman made forty-four purchases; Tremblay made seventy-seven, with a flurry of purchases from late 2017 to his last one. He seemed unusually focused on industrial equipment, such as lathes, industrial fuel pumps and industrial thermometers. It certainly wasn't for his wife's glasswork. Was he speculating and flipping the equipment to someone else? Was the RCMP using it as props for a fake business? A fake drug lab? These were questions that no one was about to answer.

Behind the scenes, things got weird. Citizen investigator Chad Jones and I were intrigued by the role the New Brunswick RCMP may have played in the lead-up to the Nova Scotia massacres. We knew that the Nova Scotia RCMP said it had called on its New Brunswick wing for help, rather than any of the closer, well-equipped local municipal police forces, which seemed strange. But what if New Brunswick had actually been running the show from the beginning? If so, then it would be on the financial hook.

In late 2020, Jones filed a Freedom of Information request asking about any expenditures the New Brunswick RCMP had made relating to the Nova Scotia massacres. Instead of receiving an answer in thirty days, as legislated, Jones got one almost two years later. It was largely gobbledygook, pointing us to Inspector Dustine Rodier, one of Tremblay's Nova Scotia acolytes, who had overseen communications at the time of the massacres.

Meanwhile, I had been told by a source about the activities of a New Brunswick–based RCMP superintendent who had suddenly appeared at Nova Scotia headquarters as the right-hand man to the Criminal Operations officer, Chief Superintendent Chris Leather. The superintendent was known only as Cosmo, and he travelled with his own coffee maker and beans. Cosmo who? I put out a journalistic all-points bulletin on the *Nighttime* podcast of November 21, 2021. The next day, I got an email that read, in part:

Greetings Paul

It has come to my attention that you are looking to identify an RCMP officer that was seconded to the RCMP in Nova Scotia in the aftermath of the mass murders in Portapique. The RCMP officer whom you identify as "Cosmo" is in fact me.

My name is Costa Dimopoulos. . . .

The reason I was seconded to NS was to provide assistance in the aftermath of the murders there, as the senior command wanted to draw upon my experience in dealing with some of the issues that surfaced in the NB homicides, and their aftermath.

I was in NS from the end of April to about the beginning of September which is when I found out I was suffering from a serious illness. I have not been to work since, and as I said I am now retired. All of my involvement in NS has been disclosed, and my notes turned over and now form part of the record.

And yes, I do love a good cup of properly brewed espresso, and brought my own machine. Life is too short to drink bad coffee.

Regards

Costa Dimopoulos

I soon realized that, between Rodier and Dimopoulous, we were dealing with a tight-knit interconnected group of Mounties.

Rodier had been Staff Sergeant Bruce Reid's immediate superior when Reid dramatically committed suicide in October 2019 on a baseball diamond in Rothesay, north of Saint John, New Brunswick. He called 911 before shooting himself. Reid had chosen the spot because it was in the jurisdiction of the Kennebecasis Regional Police and not the RCMP. He didn't want his colleagues finding his body. Although the RCMP said he didn't leave a suicide note, one of his family members said he did. He was despondent over his drinking, which he attributed largely to the working conditions he was dealing with. Reid had been a well-respected member involved in motorcycle gang investigations and undercover operations. Stationed at the Hampton, New Brunswick, RCMP detachment, he had become disenchanted with what he believed was the dysfunction and unprofessionalism of his superiors, up to and including Tremblay. Among other things, Reid believed that an informant recruited by the RCMP was out of control and that the force had generally mishandled and overexposed informants, leading to people being killed. Two other RCMP members familiar with the Hampton detachment confirmed that there were significant management problems there. Reid committed suicide in October 2019, weeks after the Saulniers were murdered.

Dimopoulous had been the district commander when Rodier ran the Hampton detachment, before moving to Nova Scotia. The 2014 murders in Moncton of three Mounties, constables Douglas Larche, Dave Ross and Fabrice Gévaudan, happened on Dimopoulous's watch. The subsequent report by retired RCMP assistant commissioner Alphonse MacNeil had been thorough, and damning of the RCMP's actions. MacNeil's recommendations had been almost entirely ignored by the force, and after the Nova Scotia massacres, Dimopoulous came to Halifax to guide the Mountie bosses there with the "experience" he had gained from a similar tragedy. It all fit with what I suspected was going on.

Dimopoulous didn't testify at the commission, but among his records was something I found very interesting: New Brunswick paid for his time in Nova Scotia. That was a very un-RCMP-like move. Why him? Why only him?

Deep in the shadows of the post-massacre investigation, other high-ranking New Brunswick Mounties seemed to be unusually involved in the proceedings in Nova Scotia. One was Inspector Ron Desilva, who you'll recall oversaw Federal Serious and Organized Crime operations in New Brunswick, including multiple operations against the Hells Angels. Another was Superintendent Derek Santosuosso, who gave Nova Scotia RCMP communications boss Lia Scanlan "talking points" five weeks after the massacres. Santosuosso's email to Scanlan on May 26, 2020, read: "As discussed here are some points. I can elaborate or address others if you'd like. Let me know. D." The rest of the email is blank, with a giant "CONFIDENTIAL" running diagonally across the page. Unfortunately, we have no idea for whom the talking points were intended, but it's likely they were for Superintendent Darren Campbell's press briefing eight days later, on June 4, 2020.

Something else dramatic happened that year. As my band of investigators and I were sniffing around New Brunswick, Public Safety Minister Carl Urquhart, a former Mountie and Fredericton police officer, unexpectedly announced that he was stepping down. The new public safety minister, Ted Flemming, then petitioned RCMP commissioner Brenda Lucki to have Tremblay removed from office. It was an unprecedented action. No real reason was given. I couldn't help but wonder, in the circumstances, if the New Brunswick government was shocked to find out that it was paying for the RCMP investigation in Nova Scotia. Or perhaps the RCMP was trying to distract from its operations under Tremblay during the period from 2016 to 2020.

After such a spectacular disaster, an institution will normally bring in fresh blood to oversee things. Not in Nova Scotia and New Brunswick. Every important senior position was filled with people who were instrumental in what had happened. This is striking when we recall that the RCMP is famous for moving members under fire to other locales and out of harm's way.

Whatever the reason for Tremblay's ousting, afterwards the same group of Mounties was still entirely in charge in New Brunswick and elsewhere across the Maritimes. Ron Desilva was promoted and made the head of the RCMP's Codiac detachment, which provided municipal policing in Moncton and its suburbs. Tremblay's protege DeAnna Hill was brought back from Newfoundland and elevated to assistant commissioner in charge of New Brunswick. Another protege, Superintendent Jennifer Ebert, went from PEI to Newfoundland and was also made an assistant commissioner. Santosuosso was put in charge of the Mounties' tiny operation in Prince Edward Island, where he was promoted to chief superintendent. Nova Scotia's Darren Campbell was promoted and became the Criminal Operations officer in New Brunswick, under Hill. They were either the best available from the RCMP's 20,000-person bench, or they were there to keep a lid on things. Or both.

19

WORTMAN'S COP FRIEND
AND THE BRINK'S MONEY

In the diverse constellation of people associated with Gabriel Wortman, one of the most fascinating was a mysterious Halifax Regional Police constable whom he was rumoured to be friends with. Various people recalled seeing the two of them together. "I remember going to his place and this old cop was sitting at the kitchen table," said one associate of Wortman's. "I never got his name, but I know he was always there."

His name was Barry Warnell. At the time of the massacres, he had spent almost five decades on the force—its longest-serving member. Warnell was interviewed only once, on June 1, 2020, six weeks after the massacres, by RCMP constables Mike Willcock and Jeff MacFarlane from the Southwest Nova Major Crime Unit. The perfunctory sixty-four-minute interview was conducted at a Dartmouth community centre.

Warnell said he had first met Wortman eighteen years earlier, around 2002, when Warnell was doing a paid-duty security job at a Nova Scotia Liquor Corporation outlet on Tacoma Drive in Dartmouth. Wortman came over to him and chatted him up, and eventually the two men became friends, sharing an interest in real estate. Over the years, they spent considerable time together.

Warnell's lucrative sideline was buying rental buildings and operating them through his property management company; he had assembled an impressive portfolio of buildings believed to be valued at several million dollars *before* the real estate boom of the early 2020s. After he met Wortman, they worked on each other's buildings. Wortman was an electrician and a carpenter. "He was a really talented guy, right, and he does beautiful work," Warnell said. Warnell even bought Wortman's house at 26 Pine Street in Dartmouth after Wortman's first marriage ended in divorce.

At the time Warnell met him, the denturist had begun his relationship with Banfield, who was living with him in the apartment above the clinic. Wortman had coveted the two buildings next to his office. In 2000, there had been a suspicious fire at 191 Portland Street, the building next door. In 2001, three weeks apart, there were two more suspected arsons, at 189 Portland Street, two doors away. Then thirty-three years old, Wortman bought the two buildings for a reduced price on October 29, 2001. A fourth and final fire in 2003 rendered 191 Portland unhabitable. Both buildings were eventually razed, and Wortman created a parking lot for his denturist business.

Although Warnell was not specific about the date of the following conversation, he described to the Mounties how Wortman had slyly bragged to him about burning down one of the buildings.

According to Warnell, Wortman said, "You know the place burnt down, eh?"

"Did it?" Warnell replied.

"Yeah. A legal electrical fire."

Warnell said, "Really?"

"Yeah. And a good job nobody was there and around there."

To the Mounties, Warnell concluded, "I never thought nothing about it that he set the fire, right."

In the months before the massacres, as reported in *22 Murders*, Wortman seemed flush with money and eager to invest. He looked at buying a small strip mall in Bass River, west of Portapique. He sniffed around a septic tank and portable toilet business in Onslow, near Truro, but demurred.

Warnell added that Wortman told him much about what he was doing with his money, such as becoming a silent partner in an excavation business, which was never disclosed elsewhere. The two men were so close that when Wortman reminisced about how much he liked the house on Pine Street, Warnell said he would leave it to him in his will because he had no kids. "We had a few laughs about it, right."

With all his experience with and insights into Wortman, one might presume that Warnell would be more than qualified to testify before the Mass Casualty Commission. Nope.

The first time the public learned about Warnell's interview was after it was released as a foundational document by the commission almost two years later, on May 6, 2022. By that time, the commission had been sitting for seventy-two days, having held just nineteen public hearings, more than half of them panel discussions or presentations. Along the way, it seemed to be stage-managing perceptions and emotions by putting the focus back onto Wortman when evidence or witnesses challenged the official narrative. As had become its wont when releasing potentially controversial information, the commission packaged Warnell's statement with a group of other interviews, including emails between Wortman, Banfield and a lawyer named Kevin Paul von Bargen, which we will return to later.

Another interview in the package was with Wortman's first wife, Corinna Kincaid-Lowe. "He could be very compassionate. And I know that sounds completely off the wall, given what has happened, but he had a very kind side to him," she told her Mountie interrogator. "But he also had a very chippy side . . . If someone slighted him, it would upset him."

Although Warnell had been in sporadic contact with Wortman until several weeks before the massacres, what he had to say presented a dilemma for the commission. While it touted itself as an inquiry in search of the truth, it had shown with its selection and treatment of previous witnesses that it was in search of only *approved* truths. It was willing to beat the bushes high and low for evidence that fit its prescribed priorities: coercive control and violence against women. When it came to the perpetrator, as it referred to Wortman, the commission wasn't at all interested in discovering the still unrevealed factors that might have served to push him over the edge. In other words, the commission was about as keen to hear Warnell's story as one would be to put their bare hand on a hot burner, but he couldn't be ignored, because his name and their relationship were known. Therefore, the sixty-four-minute interview conducted by the RCMP almost two years earlier was dusted off and sprung on the media at a propitious time, in the hopes that no one would notice Warnell's potentially explosive police insider view of what had likely happened to Wortman.

◆

Warnell had had an incredibly long forty-seven-year career, all as a constable, beginning with the Dartmouth Police Department, which in 1996 was absorbed by the Halifax Regional Police. In his interview with the Mounties, Warnell portrayed himself as a dedicated and fearless cop who took solo assignments that others wouldn't without a partner riding along with them. He had spent five years on the drug squad and had been seconded to the RCMP for a three-year stint. He joked about his scruffy, working-man appearance and how people didn't believe that he was a police officer. "I look like a bum, eh?" The "janitor" look, as he called it, would prove useful for the undercover work he did.

Sources from the Halifax police told me that, as a Dartmouth constable, Warnell was a legend—the first municipal police officer to get deep inside the outlaw biker world as an undercover operative. "Me and my buddy sat with him one night and it was unbelievable the stories that he told us," said one source, whom I'll call Ranny Gillis. "Then something happened inside the UC [undercover] world and he was removed. He spent the remainder of his career on patrol—but he still ran snitches."

In his interview with the Mounties, Warnell didn't discuss his time running informants—and they didn't ask. Instead, the effectively self-propelled Warnell rambled along, drifting from one thing to another, usually without being asked a question, like when he speculated on whether Wortman was a cop hater. "I never, ever, ever seen anything like he was a cop hater, right?" Warnell said, adding, "Never seen him with a gun or anything like that, yeah."

The two Mounties said little: "Okay . . . okay . . . No? Hmm . . . Hmm . . . Hmm . . . Hmm. Uh-hmm . . . Hmm, that was a couple of months before this happened, you say? Okay. Yeah. That was it, eh?"

Occasionally they would steer the conversation with a question: "As long as you've known him, how would you generally describe Gabriel's personality?" Constable Willcock asked.

"I thought he was always in good spirits, eh?" Warnell answered. "I never seen him mad . . . I never seen him violent or anything like that, you know. He was always the same way, pretty well, to me . . . He was a really mild guy, you know."

Warnell recalled how a mutual acquaintance who operated an Esso station where Wortman hung out with the locals described Wortman: "He's just fucking laughing all the time. I can't fucking believe that he did that."

Warnell wasn't soft-pedalling Wortman. Many others said the same thing. For example, his neighbour Alan Griffon described Wortman as "The nicest guy I could ever meet, honestly. He, he was nothing but nice and polite to us. And if I was around and I happened to be out on the deck, he'd come in and . . . and say 'hi' and 'how's your wife doing' and stuff, or he'd stop you on the side of the road. Nicest guy. He had me do all kinds of little things for him . . . never had a problem with him, never ever showed any type of disrespect or any type of hostility."

Warnell knew that Wortman was no angel. In addition to the property fires that seemed to follow Wortman, Warnell caught him stealing from Kent Building Supplies in Bayers Lake after they had begun working on projects together. Wortman had slipped a $150 roll of lead chimney flashing into a length of four-inch diameter ABS pipe and finessed it past the cashier. "I can't deal with this," Warnell said. "I thought about it for a couple of days and . . . I said, 'I'm not gonna be a suspect or accused [of stealing]. I spend a lot of money over there, right. In six months, like, I spent a hundred thousand there—in six months at Kent's . . . I was like their best customer. I went to . . . security . . . there one day and told them: 'That guy that comes in with me is stealing.

And it seems like he steals a lot up here.' And I told him how he does it; I showed him how he does it. From that day on, I never seen him at Kent's for years and years."

Despite Wortman's wayward ways, the two men stayed friends. Warnell said he thought Wortman's new-found interest in buying, refurbishing and reselling decommissioned police cars was a potentially lucrative business. But when Wortman told him he was going to build one out to look like an authentic RCMP cruiser, Warnell thought that might not be such a good idea. "What do you mean you're going to put signs [decals] on it, Gabe?" he recalled asking Wortman.

"Yeah," Wortman replied.

"Where do you get the signs at?"

"You buy them over the counter."

"Holy Jesus," Warnell remembered saying. "What a waste of money that is, right? . . . Anyway, I never thought anything about it."

Warnell also discussed the curious and well-reported incident involving Wortman that took place on February 12, 2020. That day, Wortman found an unmarked grey Halifax Police car parked in the fenced lot of his denturist office. Considering his friendly past relationships with police officers, one might expect Wortman to invite the officers in for a coffee or something stronger, but that's not what he did. In an entirely out-of-character moment, he went ballistic. He locked a chain across the entrance to the lot, and when the police returned from the nearby Tim Hortons, he didn't allow them to take their vehicle out. He had a patient in the chair, receiving treatment, while at the same time he was leaning out a window and lambasting them. Eventually, Halifax police sergeant Tanya Chambers-Spriggs was called in to mediate the beef. The entire episode was photographed by Banfield.

Wortman drove to Portapique later that afternoon in one of his white decommissioned police cars and was stopped by RCMP constable Nick Dorrington; Constable Vicki Colford also joined the scene. What happened is unclear because Dorrington's and Colford's versions of events didn't match. In any event, Dorrington said Wortman was aggressive but calmed down. The Mountie took a photo of Wortman's vehicle and issued him the ground-level ticket for speeding—15 kilometres over the limit. (Wortman filed an appeal, which was in the courts at the time he died.)

The oddest thing about all this was that Wortman immediately contacted *Frank* magazine and provided Andrew Douglas with the photos that Banfield took of the incident. He wanted the all-but-insane interaction and his speeding ticket publicized, which seemed counterintuitive for a man who had spent most of his life assiduously avoiding the limelight. Even Warnell wondered why Wortman had done that. It looked like he was trying to draw public attention to his *not* getting along with the police. Why?

In his interview, Warnell told the Mounties he recalled telling Sergeant Chambers-Spriggs that he thought he could have resolved the situation at the clinic, had he been called that day.

Wortman and Warnell's final conversation took place one night in early April 2020. Wortman called Warnell and asked him to meet at his office. When Warnell got there, Wortman told him that he was planning to retire and wanted to sell the building and the two vacant lots that served as a parking lot. He was hoping to get $1.2 million for it. A consortium of six Dartmouth real estate investors had offered him "one million and fifty thousand," but Wortman was holding out for more. He wanted to know if Warnell was interested, but he wasn't.

"I know he wanted me to have the property, but I said, 'You know, Gabe . . . the problem is, down here it's too congested, you can't get in and out of here.'"

Wortman didn't deny that. Warnell quoting him as saying: "You're fucking right. You're fucking right. There's days I fucking can't get out of here because of the fucking buses."

Before they parted, Wortman reminded Warnell about his promise to return the Pine Street property to Wortman in his will, so that he could make some money off it.

"Geez," Warnell said, "this guy should be doing quite well for himself, right. He's in his early fifties . . . he's gonna make a million dollars off this property . . . Girlfriend's doing good. He's retiring. He's got money."

When he first learned about the massacres, Warnell was taking a day off. "I sit here and hang around with this guy and there's . . . nothing ever—there was no red flag that this guy, there's something wrong with him. I tell you, it ate away at me so much for a couple of days. I couldn't sleep and I couldn't eat."

Warnell was uncharacteristically still in bed a few days later when the phone rang around 6 a.m. It was Sergeant Chambers-Spriggs, calling him in to work. "She told me that about the money, right? About seven hundred and seventy thousand delivered to him by a Brink's truck . . . Tanya asked me to do that report, right?"

Ah, yes, the infamous Brink's truck.

◆

It all began in June 2020. I had been using *The Rick Howe Show*, a local Halifax morning talk show, not only to discuss the twists and turns of the evolving story but also as an instrument to ferret out leads. There were persistent tips about Wortman withdrawing a large sum of money and having it delivered to him in a Brink's armoured car. It was not the kind of story that could easily be corroborated using conventional journalistic techniques. On the morning of June 11, I was looking for information, which I described in *22 Murders* this way:

> I needed to know more about Peter Alan Griffon, so I introduced him to the public as one of Wortman's regular drinking buddies. I felt that Griffon, with his heavy-duty criminal background, might be a key to the real story. With the province in a COVID lockdown, I could use radio to speak directly to anyone stuck in quarantine who might know something useful.
>
> Peter Griffon aside, what I really wanted to know was the Brink's story. In the days and weeks prior to the massacres, I told Howe, it appeared Wortman had been acting erratically. And then I dug into it. "There are reports of him withdrawing large amounts of money—$500,000 some say, $1 million others say. The money was said to be delivered to his denturist operation on Portland Street in Dartmouth. What was he doing? Did he owe money to the Hells Angels?" I asked.

"Heavy stuff," Michael Marshall wrote on [his blog] *40 Gallons and a Mule*. "Is Paul just dropping bad acid and spinning this stuff out of his butt—or what?"

By the time I hung up the phone with Howe, I was kicking myself. I had forgotten to mention Brink's. Seconds later, I got the shock of my life. My appeal to the public had worked. Someone I didn't really know but who was connected to our business in Chester contacted me. "I can give you the scoop on the whole thing," they told me.

"I'm all ears," I said.

"The amount he got was $475,000."

"Delivered to his business by Brink's?"

"No, he picked it all up in Burnside."

"How can you prove this?"

"I have the videos."

"The videos?"

"Yeah," the person said. "The two videos I have are of him arriving at Brink's in an unmarked car and driving into the garage. The other one I have is him in the 'man trap' waiting for his bag of money, and then he is seen putting the bag of 475K in hundreds into his trunk and driving away."

"Is there any chance that there was a second delivery by Brink's?"

"No, that was the only one."

"How can I get these tapes?" I asked, admittedly a little surprised by what might be a legitimate journalistic scoop.

The source wasn't just going to hand them to me. They didn't ask for money, but they wanted an assurance of anonymity.

I worked with Stephen Maher and Shannon Gormley on the story, which was published with the accompanying videos in *Maclean's* on June 19 and 20 under our names. We detailed the information we'd learned: that the pickup at Brink's was unusual and had the hallmarks of an undercover operation. No other scenario really made sense. There was no reason for retail bank customers to deal directly with Brink's, our sources told us.

As we were going to press, Maher was contacted by Jessica Davis, a former CSIS agent who was becoming a prominent go-to source for journalists for stories about security and intelligence. Maher said Davis assured him that nothing untoward was happening; people picking up money at a Brink's depot in "small towns" like Halifax was a common practice, she said. I smelled a Smurf, my nickname for a camouflaged fixer trying to patch a hole in the RCMP armour.

The day after our second story, RCMP superintendent Darren Campbell said in an interview with the *Toronto Star* that "the gunman had no special relationship with the RCMP whatsoever. The investigation has not uncovered any relationship between the gunman and the RCMP outside of an estranged familial relationship and two retired RCMP members." Campbell added that the reason for the large cash withdrawal was unknown, but he linked it to Wortman's belief that, because of the worldwide pandemic, his financial assets "were safer under his control."

That was enough to spook *Maclean's* editors, who were concerned that the reputation of the magazine had been besmirched. They didn't trust me to write another story. That's how easy it can be for those in power to neutralize someone who won't play their game.

Thirty months later, commission investigator Stephen Henkel, a retired Toronto detective, issued a seven-page report on the Brink's transaction. Among others who covered the story, Chris Lambie reported the following in the Halifax *Chronicle Herald* on September 28, 2022:

"NO EVIDENCE TO LEAD ANY REASONABLE PERSON TO BELIEVE" NOVA SCOTIA MASS SHOOTER WAS A POLICE AGENT

An investigator from the Mass Casualty Commission could find no evidence Gabriel Wortman was an agent for the RCMP, according to a report produced for the public inquiry.

"Due to the persistent rumour that the perpetrator was a police informant or agent for the RCMP, the commission undertook an investigation as to whether there was an evidentiary basis for this rumour," says the Aug. 13 report by Stephen Henkel, an investigator "with extensive experience in the recruitment, handling and debriefing of confidential human sources and police agents" who has worked with Criminal Intelligence Service Ontario and spent more than three decades with the Toronto Police Service.

While he doesn't name the publication, Henkel points to a June 19, 2020, *Maclean's* magazine article written by Paul Palango, Stephen Maher and Shannon Gormley entitled "The Nova Scotia shooter case has hallmarks of an undercover operation," as the root of the rumour.

"The authors of that article relied on 'police sources' who provided information based on, what appears to be, speculation and assumptions," Henkel said in his seven-page report.

"There is no evidence to lead any reasonable person to believe that the perpetrator was an informant or involved in undercover operations for the RCMP."

While Wortman did drive to the Brink's outlet in Burnside to pick up $475,000 in cash weeks before he murdered 22 people in April 2020, Henkel said "the method in which he received such cash is not indicative of him being a police informant."

Confidential sources "are not sent to businesses and asked to produce identification in order to receive payment," Henkel said. "This would go against the methods and practices of source handling and of protecting the confidentiality of a police informant."

I had to laugh out loud. This was shoot-the-messenger character assassination at its finest. It was clearly aimed at me, with "proof" that I was an unreasonable person, as it were, because I continued to insist that something was not right about the Wortman story. If one had looked closely at what Henkel actually said, rather than just copying down his words and publishing them, one would see that he was actually making my case.

Like everyone else who wrote about Henkel's report, Lambie had focused on his statement that there was "no evidence" that Wortman was an informant. The true lede was buried twenty paragraphs deep in his story, in the conclusion to Henkel's report. It read:

By its nature, the recruitment, handling and debriefing of confidential human sources is conducted in a manner that is secretive, with the goal being the protection of the identity of the "informer." This careful handling of source records and related documentation is also strictly controlled from viewing and access. The access is controlled even with the policing agencies to ensure the identity of the informant is known to as few people as possible. Information regarding an informant is something that would not be accessible to Commission investigators.

Lambie captured the last sentence but failed to state the reason that Henkel could not find evidence of Wortman's being an informant: if such evidence existed, Henkel wouldn't be allowed to see it. And if he did happen to see it, he couldn't talk about it.

That nuance was missed by many journalists and commentators, who seemed to ignore Henkel's description of the protocols involved with confidential human sources, not appreciating the roles that agents and uncoded and coded informants play in the modern justice system. Informants are no longer rare birds. Just about every police officer is urged to get into the informant game, with the built-in assurance that if something goes wrong, it will all be hidden. No outsider can pierce their protective armour. There is no room for accountability.

Henckel derided my journalism, calling it mere "speculation." Without supporting documents or admissions, *he* speculated that the only proper conclusion was that Wortman was not a police informant or agent. For me to report otherwise was reckless.

But was it? When it comes to reporting on police informants in Canada, informed speculation is the only useable weapon in a journalist's quiver. Most journalists can't or won't speculate. To do so is potentially dangerous and difficult to defend. It's easier to hide behind the fiction that every single fact must be triple-sourced before it is reported.

As you have seen, there are no concrete clues that Wortman or someone in his close circle was working with the authorities. There are no pay stubs, and there never will be any. Everything is ephemeral—wisps of information here and there. It's the old walk-like-a-duck, talk-like-a-duck thing. And when it came to the Brink's pickup by Wortman, no one seemed flexible enough to consider the possibility that the rules of engagement for informants might have been altered to accommodate Wortman at an unusual point in history: the COVID lockdown.

The commission also released transcripts of interviews with Lisa Banfield and her sister Maureen, who described a dramatic and elaborate three-car manoeuvre to pick up the money that March morning. Wortman drove into the Brink's yard. Lisa was guarding him in another decommissioned police car, while Maureen served as a lookout in another location. The high drama seemed intended to show just how unbalanced and crazed Wortman had become. It was plausible but, I thought, somewhat improbable, even stagey.

He was depicted as a jittery nervous Nellie when he had proven beyond a shadow of a doubt that he had nerves of steel—always confident, cautious and cocky. He had successfully smuggled sniper rifles, grenades, guns, drugs and cigarettes across the border for two decades. He had rubbed shoulders with outlaw bikers, gangsters and police. Eighteen days after the Brink's escapade, he coldly killed twenty-two people over a thirteen-and-a-half-hour spree, blithely driving past real Mounties, coolly waving to some of them as if he were on their team. Near the end of his spree, he took a sunny Sunday drive along the main streets of Truro with the RCMP hot (well, warm) on his tail.

Why, then, would he have been weak-kneed about picking up the money at Brink's and taking it home? Who did he think was going to jump him? If he was hijacked, did he really think the unarmed Banfield sisters, both in their early fifties, would be able to protect him? Couldn't he protect himself? He had all those guns.

To me, it looked scripted to fit with the official narrative about Wortman's growing erratic behaviour. But standing back and looking at the situation objectively, there was evidence that he was leading his normal life, wheeling and dealing right up to that fateful weekend.

On April 3, 2020, fifteen days before the massacres, Wortman cashed in on a load of face masks, which were out of stock in stores because of the pandemic. He sold most of them for $7,500 to Shannex, which operates seniors' homes, and then drove around gleefully distributing free masks to his accountant, his favourite mechanic, Dana Geddes, and others. The Shannex money didn't stay in Wortman's company's bank account for long. It was deposited on April 3 and then withdrawn immediately in three separate tranches, leaving a balance of $66.87 in the account, mirroring what he and Banfield had done with all their accounts.

On the weekend of the massacres, trucker Eddie Creelman was going to be bringing Wortman a package, and they were planning to meet. Hours before the massacres began, Wortman was clearing land that he hoped to develop someday.

Everything looked somewhat normal. Until it wasn't.

20
FOLLOW THE MONEY

It is all but impossible to uncover the identity of a police informant, even after their death, as we all know by now. The next most difficult thing is to learn the details of the specific operation in which they were involved—and even more so if that operation was a failure.

In our *Maclean's* stories, Maher, Gormley and I described the Brink's transaction as having the hallmarks of an undercover operation, referring not just to the amount of money but also to the unusual pickup. Recall that in his interview with the RCMP, Warnell talked about the money Wortman *received* from Brink's. Like many others who seemed to know about the transaction, he said the money had been delivered to Wortman, not picked up. Warnell said he was told it was $770,000, not $475,000. Were there two deliveries? Was the second one made by another armoured car company, called Brink's the way all facial tissue is called Kleenex?

After the massacres, the RCMP found $705,000 hidden in a munitions box in a wall outside, and a bunch of charred bills in a couple of other locations, including Wortman's burned-out replica police car. More money was found stuffed into a hiding place in the apartment above his Dartmouth clinic. The RCMP had a plausible explanation for the cash, complete with emails from various parties inside Wortman's bank. Wortman had cashed in Guaranteed Investment Certificates he had taken out in 2015 that hadn't yet matured. It is important to note that he agreed to pay a $16,100 penalty to do so, something he would not normally do. It's abundantly clear that he was frantic about getting his money. Dean Branton, CIBC's vice-president of marketing for Nova Scotia and Prince Edward Island, tried to convince Wortman that his money would be safer in the bank and that the banks would not collapse. He quoted Wortman as cursing a lot during the conversation: "Well, you let me worry about my fucking safety, buddy." Wortman also balked at paying Brink's a fee for the pickup, so the CIBC covered it.

The bank still couldn't satisfactorily explain why it felt compassion for this one pushy denturist in Dartmouth who was in such a hurry to get his money. Why couldn't he wait in line like everyone else? It wasn't like he would be going anywhere. The borders were closed. Nothing but the essentials was open.

In many ways, it looked like the authorities were using the $475,000 transaction as what film director Alfred Hitchcock called a MacGuffin—a distraction that draws attention away from what is really going on. Whatever that was, the commission seemed to go along with the misdirection. Former Toronto detective Dwayne King wrote two reports for the commission about the money. One was not released until after the first dump of documents hit the street. We'll get to that explosive report later. In the one that was released on July 19, 2022, King found: "The $705,000 in cash is not direct proceeds of street level drug trafficking. The $475,000 in cash picked up by the perpetrator from Brink's is not payment related to a confidential informant."

It was a tune the RCMP had been singing since the news first broke: the force never paid $475,000 to Wortman. Was it a flat truth or a shaded one? The Mounties never did explain the original source of the money.

Once again, my distant cousins in the media ran with that story, confident they could finally put the informant business to rest. They and the commission did not factor any of the following into their findings:

- The CIBC was the bank of the Canadian government and the RCMP.
- Numerous sources said the CIBC was used solely to pay off informants, agents and those in witness protection.
- The amount of $705,000 was not the correct total. The RCMP found that Wortman had $745,919.13 in cash on hand, some of it stashed at the denture clinic. It's not clear if that amount included the estimated $20,000 that burned up. Either way, the total was closer to the $770,000 that Wortman's friend Barry Warnell said he had taken out. The government produced a receipt for the deposit of $705,000 into a trust account, but there was no mention that my colleagues and I could find of where the other $40,919.13 ended up.
- In his report King pegged the excess amount at $268,000 (an approximation), the sources of which were unknown, but did state that when confidential informants are paid, it is usually in cash. Like his colleague Henkel, he added the meaningless codicil that there was "no evidence that Wortman was a confidential informant."
- Contrary to the assertions of former CSIS agent Jessica Davis, we were unable to find anyone in the security industry or in banking who thought the Brink's pickup was a normal practice. As we published in *Frank* magazine, some said the only time they had experienced similar pickups, elsewhere in Canada, was for informants or emergency money for someone in a witness protection program.
- The RCMP and other police forces have been victimized in the past by their own officers ripping off payments intended for informants, according to numerous sources. These crimes are rarely, if ever, reported.
- As is the case with the majority of Canadian financial institutions, the CIBC security department employed many retired RCMP members. Similar relationships exist within security companies such as Brink's. Numerous sources have said over the years that the perception in the policing community is that the Mounties on the inside of the system often continue to work quietly for

the force and protect its interests—an embodiment of the notion that "there is no such thing as an ex-Mountie."

The MCC never released a key document that might have helped to prove conclusively what had transpired.

Five days after the massacres, the RCMP investigated the Brink's transfer. On April 24, 2020, Corporal Kathryn MacLeod and Constable Dayle Burris interviewed Marcel Briand, the manager of the Brink's office in Dartmouth. The interview lasted just twenty-four minutes and was aimed at identifying documents and videos about the transaction.

Briand said that "Joe Muluchy" from CIBC Global Services Division in Ontario called him on March 27 to alert him that a client was coming to pick up cash at the facility, which Briand said was unusual, contrary to ex-CSIS agent Davis's much-quoted assertions.

After Wortman had picked up the money, Briand walked into his operations manager's office and remarked, "That was kinda strange." Then they talked about why someone would pick up that much cash. Briand added that the Wortman pickup was a security exception. "We don't authorize clients to come to our facility to pick up anything. We do have standing exceptions for some clients who hold precious metals . . . that they can come and drop off or pick up any of their product. But a cash transaction is not something that we do on a day-to-day basis. That was a request from our client CIBC."

The last thing Mounties MacLeod and Burris asked of Briand was the location of the manifest signed by Wortman and copies of the video-tapes related to the transaction. They said they would have a search warrant issued to retrieve them. Briand said he had the video on a jump drive, but the documents were in a safe.

Briand was not interviewed by the commission or called as a witness. The documents from the safe were never revealed to the public. There was never an explanation for the source of the extra $268,000 (and likely more) that Wortman had received and stashed. Were these documents destroyed by the RCMP in its purge of files, or were they held back from the commission by the Attorney General of Canada, as the commission complained in its final report?

I found it odd that the commission made the case that Wortman had negotiated the pickup of the money at Brink's on his own. If it were truly committed to transparency, it should have disclosed the relevant documents from the Brink's safe. It seems like that would have cleared up any lingering doubts and quashed further speculation.

Afterwards, I went back to the source who had provided the videos of Wortman picking up the money. I asked them two things.

"If picking up money at Brink's is such a common practice, has anyone used that service since Wortman?"

"No," they replied.

The key document was the release form that Wortman was videotaped signing. No one has seen it to this day.

"On the release, who authorized the pickup?" I asked.

"The RCMP New Brunswick."

Since then, a second source has confirmed the same information.

◆

Wortman's erratic behaviour in the weeks leading up to the massacres seemed to coincide with the COVID lockdown, but as an explanation it wasn't entirely convincing. The initial lockdown temporarily closed his denturist business, but he had only been working there two or three days a week, even in his busiest times. After the massacres, there was much speculation, slyly fuelled by the RCMP, that the closing of the international border had put a crimp in Wortman's illegal activities, as if he were living hand to mouth.

He had more than enough money on hand—bricks of $100 bills—and likely more stashed somewhere. He had a couple of million dollars in real estate assets he was trying to flog. He easily could have ridden out any economic downturn. As Barry Warnell put it, he wasn't the kind of guy who would easily part with his money. In addition, the border-crossing ban was expected to end on April 20, 2020, the day after the massacres ended. For all Wortman knew, the border was about to be opened again (on April 20, the closing was extended another 30 days).

The timing of Wortman's meltdown dovetailed with what the Federal Serious and Organized Crime section was doing on the streets. Led by Superintendent Popik in Nova Scotia and Inspector Desilva in New Brunswick, the Mounties were continuing to disrupt the outlaw bikers. Recall the incident in which Wortman locked the unmarked police car in the lot at his Portland Street office? Here is what I wrote about it in *Frank* magazine:

On February 12, the day of Wortman's two known and public run-ins with the police, the RCMP was in the process of making arrests of more Hell's Angels and their associates in New Brunswick and Nova Scotia.

The first arrest of an unnamed biker was made on Feb. 17 in New Brunswick, the same day the Frank article was published about Wortman's problems with the police. The arrests continued for the next seven weeks, a highlight being a raid on the Red Devils compound on Alma Crescent in the Halifax neighbourhood of Fairview. Not much is known about the details of that raid to date, which is unusual. If Wortman or anyone associated with him was suspected of being the rat, then under the Hell's Angels code his life expectancy was automatically shortened significantly.

Among the items the police and Crown focused on were the [pill] presses they found. Were the bikers getting suspicious? Attempts to find out whether Wortman had contacted those bikers were rebuffed by the lawyer acting for the Hell's Angels.

The conjecture in policing circles is that Wortman's cover as an operative was blown and that his life was likely in danger.

Project Triton, the long and continuing RCMP operation targeting the already-jailed Hells Angels Nomad Robin Moulton, was continuing to sweep up his associates in Nova Scotia and New Brunswick.

Wortman collected his cash from Brink's, and perhaps elsewhere, on March 30, a significant date. As described in *22 Murders*, knowledgeable police sources say that informants are typically paid out ten days before a covert operation is scheduled to come to an end. Multiple police sources also told me the end of a police operation is usually a very dangerous time because, after the suspects learn what has happened, their hunt for informants kicks into high gear.

Eight days before Wortman began killing, on April 10, 2020, the New Brunswick RCMP proudly announced the arrest of two Hells Angels and two Red Devils, the culmination of Project Thunder and Project Triton. The announcement came several days after the end of the operations. The force crowed about how their triumph was linked to the earlier arrests of Assistant Commissioner Tremblay's prime target, Moulton, and his fellow Nomad Emery "Pit" Martin.

While Wortman and Banfield were supposedly shacked up in Portapique, riding out the lockdown, they were doing more than playing "COVID games," as Wortman put it to his neighbour Dana Geddes.

In the days leading up to the massacres, Banfield spent $555.96 at Walmart, according to documents released by the MCC, which were not reported by the media. She also made a series of unexplained purchases at three different Staples Canada outlets. Although it was the early days of the COVID lockdown, Staples stores were open because they were considered an essential service. On April 15, Banfield purchased something for $60.94 in Dartmouth, and then appeared to return it that same day to the Bedford store. She then made another purchase in Bedford for $74.79. Two days later, on April 17, she made five separate purchases at the Staples in Truro, three of them for $50.92, one for $49.98 and the final one for $38.19. I couldn't find any record of her ever making any other purchases at Staples.

Maybe it was all innocent and Banfield was stocking up on gifts. It seems unlikely that she was buying office supplies or doing a massive amount of photocopying, since Wortman was retiring. Maybe they were stocking up on Folgers coffee to ride out the lockdown. But to me, the amounts were indicative of a service she was buying. Assuming that every sale attracted Nova Scotia's 15 percent harmonized sales tax, the base prices of the purchases were $52.99, $65.03, $44.28, $43.46 and $33.21. Those would be extremely odd retail sale prices, ruling out something like US SIM cards for their phones. In my day job as a glass

artist, the only time I've encountered such numbers is for shipping services, which Staples provides for businesses.

What might Banfield have been shipping the day before the massacres?
PPE masks to distant friends? Motorcycle parts to Wortman's customers?
Personal valuables? Money? And to whom would she have shipped it? It
was yet another detail the MCC never explored in depth.

Wortman, meanwhile, was liquidating all his assets as part of his
"retirement plan." The apartment above his clinic was all but bare of
furniture. Based on police records, it appears that Lisa Banfield may not
have been living there full-time, but rather at her sister Maureen's house
near Russell Lake in Dartmouth. The afternoon before the massacres
began, Wortman and Banfield went for a long drive, during which
Banfield chatted on the phone with friends. They stopped by the
Springhill penitentiary, where Robin Moulton was incarcerated, and
Wortman told Banfield he "could never go in there." Then they went to
the liquor store and bought groceries at Foodland. Wortman also
dropped off denturist equipment to a competitor in Springhill. He didn't
sell the equipment; he *gave it away*—a very un-Wortman-like move.

My source Jimmy McNulty speculated that "the Angels linked those
arrests to Wortman, mainly through the hydraulic pill presses they were
using. I firmly believe that he was the original supplier. We know from
the search warrants that the Mounties put cameras or other eavesdrop-
ping devices in those presses. They likely tried to cover the tracks by
using intermediaries, but if you keep doing the same or similar things in
multiple cases, they will eventually figure out what is really going on."

The RCMP, true to its corporate doctrine of "efficiency," apparently
didn't want to give up on what it thought was a good thing. Finding
another informant might take forever. It couldn't accept that the informant in Project Triton and related operations might have been burned.
Police sources believe that the RCMP, or another agency for whom
Wortman may have been working, tried to use him one more time in a
high-stakes operation when he should have been decommissioned, as it
were, or even put in witness protection.

◆

Back to Constable Barry Warnell's interview. After learning about Wortman's money, Warnell suspected that his friend had a desperate grand plan, which he sketched out for the Mounties in June 2020. He suggested that Wortman's fulminations about the imminent collapse of the banking system may well have been an act. From his experience, Wortman just wasn't the kind of person who would devolve into a survivalist holed up at his cottage, armed to the teeth and chowing down on rice and beans for the rest of his life. Others thought much the same. When Wortman told his neighbour Dana Geddes that he would shoot a deer if he needed to survive, Geddes chuckled. "You could do that, but they're not going to taste very good at this time of the year."

Warnell thought the survivalist story was a screen. He believed Wortman was hectically liquidating anything and everything because he was getting ready to make a run for it. He was in a hurry to unload the Portland Street office. He was gathering all his money that wasn't hidden in a safe place, either in an account that couldn't be traced to him or offshore. Whatever was going on, Wortman didn't have time to list and sell his properties. He had enjoyed success in the past with burning buildings down. Warnell intimated that Wortman likely planned to burn his cottage, warehouse and vehicles for the insurance money. Everything, it seemed, except for Banfield's Mercedes, which was parked in the garage on Portland Street, and a decommissioned police car also in that lot.

Why?

In a recording, Warnell recounted to the Mounties the conversation he'd had with Sergeant Chambers-Spriggs about Wortman's money: "Who do you think he's gonna get the money to?" Warnell said, asking a rhetorical question of himself. "I'm gonna tell you something, Tanya. He gave the money to nobody . . . His plan is to get out of here . . . He's [inaudible] in this country and that money's gonna get him out of here. So I tell you, he don't plan on giving that money to nobody. And I don't think he ever planned on dying, either."

In the context of the conversation, there are only a few candidates for the inaudible word: "dead" or "fucked," or their synonyms.

Warnell didn't buy into the RCMP story that Wortman had pre-planned his rampage. He thought Wortman was trying to do something more sophisticated: fake his own death. In his view, the replica police car was not intended as a subterfuge to sneak up on people and murder them, but as a tool for escaping the chaos and going into hiding. He surmised that Wortman planned to pull a "Wolf Carroll."

"Ah, Dave Carroll," Warnell told the Mounties. "Wolf Carroll."

"Hmm," Constable Willcock interjected.

"He's been gone thirty years now [actually about twenty], the Hells Angel. Some bikers think he's hid [in witness protection]. They don't believe he's missing. On the run, right?"

The wily Warnell had planted an offal sandwich in the neat little picnic basket of those who seemed to be trying to cover up what really happened. Both Warnell and Sergeant Chambers-Spriggs were excluded from the Spinquiry's witness list because they might take the commission into places where it didn't have the heart, or government permission, to go. A source later showed me a copy of a mass email sent on August 17, 2020, by Halifax Regional Police Superintendent Andrew Matthews to all Halifax Police officers who might have involvement in the massacres' investigation. Matthews ordered them not to provide their notes to the RCMP for the inquiry, which might also explain why Warnell wasn't questioned further or called to testify.

Warnell seemed to think that Wortman knew he was a dead man walking in Canada. The only possible reason is that he had crossed the wrong people.

In *22 Murders*, I briefly described a telephone conversation that was overheard by one of my sources. I knew the person on the receiving end of the call. In the conversation, they described how Wortman had acted as an intermediary in a $1 million deal that had fallen apart for unknown reasons. It had taken place a week to ten days or so before the massacres. When I and a witness confronted that person and asked them about the call, they played dumb. Being from Colchester County, they were well aware of the likely consequences of saying the wrong thing to the wrong people. They didn't want to end up in a double-decker grave in the Muslim cemetery. I included the anecdote in *22 Murders* as a journalistic fishing expedition.

My first impression of the conversation was that Wortman was somehow involved in a drug deal with major players. But then I was told by another source that Wortman was trying to use the Brink's money and other cash to negotiate for his life, but he had been turned down. Whatever he had done was so egregious, his death was the only option.

Different law enforcement sources with experience in the area told me variations on the story. They were wisps, I admit, but there was an irresistible consistency to them.

One humorous version was about a cross-border undercover operation that involved drug cartels and weapons. In this tale, there had been a meeting at the Maine–New Brunswick border that imploded when the police realized that the people on both ends of the deal were informants—spy versus spy—one RCMP and the other FBI or DEA.

Another version of the story sounded like it could be the real thing: Wortman was pretending to be a major arms dealer, but the buyers had smelled a rat and walked away.

Finally, there was this one from someone in the Portapique area with a connection to outlaw bikers: "I was told that Wortman had three visitors in the nights before the massacres. The first was about a big deal that he was trying to negotiate. The second visitors were the police who were monitoring what was going on. The third was from the original people. They had recorded the police coming and going," my source said.

When asked about it later by the commission, an appearance we will soon get to, Lisa Banfield denied that anyone had visited them in the nights before the massacres. The veracity of her statement should be weighed against, among other things, her other assertions. She appears to have spent much of her time living away from Wortman, in Dartmouth, while he was in Portapique. She claimed to have been a victim of domestic abuse and coercive control by Wortman over the course of their relationship. Although she was never really pressed on these subjects by the RCMP, she also indicated that she knew nothing about Wortman's criminal activities over the nineteen years they were together, including the fires on Portland Street in the early 2000s, his cigarette, drug, gun and grenade smuggling, and his flagrant tax evasion.

To me and others, it looked like Wortman's concern about the border being closed was that he couldn't get across it to escape the deadly quagmire in which he found himself. Why did he feel compelled to cash out, pack up and hop the express out of the country as soon as he possibly could? Who could he have screwed over so badly that fleeing was his only recourse? The Hells Angels? Drug cartels? The RCMP?

The commission wasn't interested in delving into any of this, of course.

And now let's return to the hearings, picking up first with the events in the last moments of Wortman's life.

21

GABRIEL WORTMAN STOPS FOR GAS

As the fire from Wortman's replica RCMP cruiser blazed in Shubenacadie, the Mounties now had a slightly-better-than-vague idea of where he was. He couldn't be northwest or east. There weren't enough roads in the area. He had to be south, but where?

After leaving Cloverleaf Circle, Wortman raced down Highway 224 for about ninety seconds, then turned left at number 198 and drove up the long, elevated gravel driveway, pulling in behind Gina Goulet's house. The vehicle couldn't be seen from the highway.

Goulet had known Wortman for years. One witness said she had taught him at the Nova Scotia Community College in the 1990s. Wortman and Goulet had gone to denturist school at around the same time and eventually dated—in secret. Banfield knew Goulet as well. As part of Wortman's "retirement plan," he had tried to get Goulet to abandon her own practice and work for him, but she declined.

At 9:59 on the morning of the rampage, Goulet had texted her daughter, worried about Wortman's coming to her isolated house. "Gabriel, that denturist that wanted me to work for him, he's running loose with a gun . . . He knows where I live . . . I hope they catch him."

The two texted back and forth for almost an hour. Goulet had said she might go shopping, but her daughter urged her to stay home and lock the doors. It was a fatal mistake for Goulet.

At 10:58 a.m., Gina telephoned her daughter, but when she answered the phone, there was no one there. Panicked, the daughter and her husband headed for Goulet's house. What they didn't know was that Wortman had busted into the house, cutting himself along the way. Goulet hid in her bathroom, but Wortman smashed through the door and shot her repeatedly. He then changed clothes again, loaded everything into Goulet's Mazda 3 and got ready to head off.

But he didn't get far. Goulet was notorious for driving her car with almost no gas, and Wortman must have been dismayed when he looked at the car's gauges and saw the little light shining.

Around this time, another of those strange distractive calls came into the RCMP.

At 11:09:37, the RCMP dispatcher cut in: "Just have an update here; a person called, time delay of five minutes at . . . Highway 2 in Shubie. Heard about seven shots and then someone drove away fast. He didn't see them, and unknown direction of travel."

The RCMP and the commission had no explanation for the origin of the calls, which totalled at least six: that there was a dead woman in a car at Hidden Hilltop campground; that Wortman was parked in front of the Onslow Belmont fire hall; that he was escaping to the west on Highway 104; that he was at Sobeys in Lower Truro; that "the member is okay"; and that gunshots had been heard on Highway 2.

Unlike the other calls, which seemed intended to lure the Mounties to somewhere behind him or in the opposite direction from where he was headed, this one sent the police to Highway 2, which ran parallel to Highway 224 to its west. The distraction would give Wortman an opportunity to elude the Mounties once more.

As a convoy of ERT trucks roared down the Highway 102 expressway toward the airport, other Mounties flooded south, many of them unfamiliar with the area. Along with the Halifax Regional Police, who had finally been drawn into the action, the RCMP were starting to erect roadblocks, but they were still being extremely cautious. At 11:10:43,

Staff Sergeant Steve Halliday, who had been on scene the night before in Portapique, said: "All members make sure you're aware that, uh, take a position of cover there so that you don't get ambushed by this individual. Keep an eye for the car from a position of cover."

A wild card in all this was the cut-off team of constables Terry Brown and Dave Melanson, who had almost gone after one of their own members near the Fishers' house on Highway 4 in Glenholme, then minutes later shot up the Onslow Belmont fire hall. Now they were on Highway 2. When they had heard the fake call that Wortman was at the Sobeys in Lower Truro, they had gone to the Sobeys in Elmsdale, near the 102, to sound the warning. Then they hopped back in their Nissan Altima and returned to Highway 2. Now, as they drove south to an intersection just north of the RCMP's Enfield detachment, they saw something.

"That person has a firearm in their hand," Brown said at 11:17:27 a.m. "We're gonna take him down there."

Jason Shannon, a Halifax police detective constable, shouted: "That person is a HRP officer! The camo guy by the white truck is an HRP officer!"

The camo guy was Blain Lane. A veteran Halifax constable, Lane lived in the neighbourhood and had gone out to the intersection armed with his personal hunting rifle to help his colleagues and protect his neighbours. He didn't know how close he had come to disaster until I showed him the transcript while writing this chapter.

"That was me, all right," Lane said. "I was with the guys on the Number 2 in front of Elmsdale Landscaping. I was just helping with the traffic. They were overwhelmed and undermanned. At no time was I not in the presence of uniformed RCMP members."

Lane summed up how many city police generally felt about the Mounties and specifically regarding that day. "Those clowns have zero tactical or situational awareness. No love lost at all levels."

Three minutes earlier, at 11:14 a.m., Wortman, now in Gina Goulet's Mazda 3, had pulled into the empty Petro-Canada service station in the northwest quadrant of Exit 8 on Highway 102 at Elmsdale Road. He came to a stop at pump seven as an unmarked black RCMP Ford F-250 pickup with a walk-in truck cap wheeled up to pump eight beside him. Three camo-wearing ERT members "dismounted," as the Mounties like to say.

It was one of the ERT teams that had been at the Fishers' house in Glenholme. While Constable Andrew Ryan, the driver, fuelled the vehicle, Constable Jason Barnhill took a position at its front, while Constable Brent Kelly went to the back. Kelly had replaced Constable Ben MacLeod on the team at Glenholme, where an hour earlier he had "popped" out of the woods at the Fishers' residence and realized there was no one there to shoot.

Now the constables at the Petro-Canada station were keeping an eye out for Wortman, who they knew, from all the radio traffic after the murder of Stevenson, must be somewhere in the area. Another seven RCMP vehicles, along with Halifax *Chronicle Herald* photographer Tim Krochak, who had glommed on to the convoy, were waiting in the parking lot of the Atlantic Superstore, where the gas station was located, for Ryan to fill up his truck. No one, including Krochak, noticed anything unusual at the time.

Wortman was inside a hornets' nest. It had been thirteen hours and thirteen minutes since the first 911 call was placed by Jamie Blair the previous night. His name and photograph were finally being circulated. Now there were Mountie snipers armed with C8s on either side of him. But Wortman's luck continued. He remained cool, calm and collected—not the same guy who, twenty days earlier, needed two fifty-year-old women to protect him when he picked up his $475,000 at Brink's.

The situation was made even more awkward by his unfamiliarity with Goulet's car, which had the gas cap on the passenger side; he had driven up to the wrong side of the pump. With the Mounties steps away, Wortman tried to stretch the hose across the back of the vehicle, but it wasn't long enough. He holstered the pump handle, coming quite close to Kelly, then got back into the car and whipped around to pump five, only to find that the pumps had been turned off. It was a lockdown that even the Mounties didn't know about.

Wortman left the station and headed south seven kilometres to the next exit, Enfield, hoping that the Irving Big Stop pumps were still open. The convoy soon followed. And it was there that he was shot and killed, at 11:26 a.m.

As I wrote in *22 Murders*, the RCMP sent out a message that Wortman was in custody.

For Krochak and other photographers at the scene, the RCMP messaging was as confusing as ever. "I had shots of the dead guy beside the Mazda," Krochak said. "I think they shot him dead in the car and then the next wave came and ordered him out of the car. He didn't answer, so they [shot] him again. The CBC camera was shooting the scene and I pointed out to him that the guy was dead. He said: 'Oh, shit,' and they put him on live."

All these photos of Wortman lying dead, and the RCMP continued to insist for almost four hours that he was "in custody." . . .

One of Krochak's photos, distributed around the world, captured Wortman's final moment in the sun, literally and figuratively. It was beating down on him. His hands were bound behind his back. His chin was resting on the pavement. He looked uncomfortable, even unreal—like a mannequin. There was a splotch of blood on his forehead and more had pooled around him. He had been shot in the head and the torso. It had taken thirteen and a half hours, but the killings were done.

In the aftermath, the official narrative was that Wortman had been killed at the Big Stop. Although there were persistent rumours from as early as April 2020 that Wortman had gone to a service station other than at Enfield, there was no way to prove it. Both Irving and Petro-Canada, whose security teams are filled with ex-Mounties, had made employees sign non-disclosure agreements about the respective incidents.

As we know, Wortman's death was one of the incidents referred to SIRT. Now back at work, the SIRT director, former judge Felix Cacchione, showed he was no Pat Curran; his official report aligned with the RCMP narrative. Released on December 15, 2020, it was the first time the public heard an official account of what transpired on the morning of April 19.

I included the following excerpt in *22 Murders*, substituting "Wortman" for the initials "AP" (affected person) used by Cacchione.

. . . Wortman then set fire to both the RCMP officer's police vehicle and the mock police vehicle he had been driving and drove away in the civilian's Chevrolet Tracker.

Unbeknown to the police, Wortman then drove a short distance to the residence of an acquaintance where he entered the residence and killed the acquaintance. Wortman then changed out of the RCMP clothing he had been wearing and into civilian clothes. Wortman then drove away in his latest victim's grey Mazda 3 vehicle leaving behind the Chevrolet Tracker and the discarded RCMP clothing.

Wortman was headed toward Halifax-Dartmouth when he stopped for gas at the Irving Big Stop in Enfield. SO1 [1st Mountie] and SO2 [2nd Mountie] were travelling together and unaware that Wortman was no longer driving the Chevrolet vehicle when they pulled in to refuel at the same Irving Big Stop. SO1 was driving the police vehicle and stopped at a pump adjacent to a pump where a grey Mazda 3 vehicle was parked. SO1 exited the vehicle to begin refueling and as he looked across to the adjoining pump he observed a male with a noticeable hematoma and some blood on his forehead.

SO1 recognized this person as Wortman from photographs he had seen at the command post. SO1 drew his service weapon and alerted SO2 that Wortman was in the vehicle parked next to theirs. SO2, a member of the Emergency Response Team, left the vehicle and moved across the front of the police vehicle. Wortman then raised the pistol he had stolen from the RCMP officer he killed approximately 30 minutes earlier. SO1 and SO2 then began firing their service weapons. Wortman died at the scene.

As you can see, Cacchione's report described the showdown between RCMP Constable Heidi Stevenson and Wortman, and the murder of Gina Goulet that followed, then moved to the Irving Big Stop, where two Mounties killed Wortman in self-defence. Notably it omitted any reference to the Petro-Canada stop.

◆

After Cacchione had published his report, an "accidental" lapse in security in RCMP documents momentarily revealed SO1 to be RCMP dog handler Constable Craig Hubley. Halifax *Chronicle Herald* reporter Chris Lambie was made aware of the "error." Then a secret source inside the RCMP, one unauthorized to speak on the record, filled in the blanks for Lambie, who wrote a story headlined "The Inside Story of How an RCMP Dog Handler Shot N.S. Mass Murderer." Lambie quoted his shy insider as saying "the mass murderer appeared to be making a threatening move when the two officers shot him. . . . They were concerned for their safety. . . . Hubley's observation skills are unique. . . . A lot of people wouldn't have spotted him, and he would have slipped away and gone on killing. That alone speaks volumes to the kind of officer he is. He's smart. He's just switched on, to use one of our phrases. He's just squared away. He's got a big police brain."

It was a great story, made even better by Hubley's pedigree within the justice system. He was the son of a Mountie and had been a Mountie for nineteen years at the time of the massacres. His beloved stepmother was Deborah K. Smith, who had recently been appointed chief justice of the Supreme Court of Nova Scotia.

But it struck me as odd that the police had withheld the information for so long. In an analogous situation, any police force, including the RCMP, would proudly trumpet the name of a hero like Hubley. That's what police tend to do. Hubley was being uncharacteristically shy about publicity, and so were the Mounties. Even after Lambie's story, Hubley stayed in the shadows. Why?

For someone with a police background and a chief justice for a step-mother, Hubley seemed less than enthusiastic about co-operating with the system. Like many of the RCMP members on duty that day, he refused to give his handwritten notes to investigators within the RCMP and the Mass Casualty Commission. It appears the commission did not even attempt to subpoena them.

What the commission released on April 5, 2022, was the "voluntary statement" Hubley had written and submitted for the SIRT investigation on September 4, 2020. The public had since learned that his partner on

April 19 was Constable Ben MacLeod. This is what Hubley wrote about their encounter with Wortman:

> I drove into the Big Stop pump area and saw that a lot of pumps had orange bags over the handles. The pumps run in a line and positioned in a manner that run the length of the building. I pull up at the first pump that didn't have an orange bag on it. The gas cap on my suburban is on the driver's side and set almost to the rear of the truck. I stopped at pump six.
>
> When I stopped short of having the gas cap next to the pump such that the driver's door was about even with the pump. I saw that there was a small grey car parked on the other side of the pump. I didn't notice anyone in the car. I was wearing the operational uniform of a PDS [police dog service] handler. The colour of the uniform is ranger green. . . .
>
> I got out of the driver's side of my Suburban and saw that the gas cap was far from the pump. I was aware that Cst. MacLeod had gotten out of the truck, I assumed to provide security. I looked around the pump at the car and saw a man sitting in the driver's seat. The passenger side window was up. He was wearing a white tee shirt. I had a profile view of him as he looked straight ahead and he didn't seem to notice me. He had a large hematoma on the side of his forehead and there was a small trickle of blood running down his forehead. I thought it odd that this person hadn't addressed the wound or tried to stop the bleeding. The look on his face was one of someone who had just been in a fight. He was breathing heavy with his mouth open and he was worked up. His appearance, injury and demeanour were outside of what I would expect from a person at a gas station. This caused me to pay closer attention and I recognized him from the pictures I had seen in the command post. I recognized that it was Gabriel Wortman and was certain it was him. I stayed behind the pump and called out to Cst. MacLeod: "Benny, it's him." At the same time, I drew my pistol and pointed it at Wortman.

Wortman heard me call out to Cst. MacLeod. He reacted by jerking back while seated and immediately raised a silver coloured pistol in my direction with his right hand. He was looking at me as he did this.

I knew that Wortman was going to shoot me. I feared for my life and Cst. MacLeod's life. I knew that he had already killed a number of people including at least one police officer. I knew that Wortman could have stopped if he chose to and surrender to police, but he didn't. Instead he chose to shoot police officers and murder people.

Wortman did not hesitate at all. As soon as he heard me, he immediately tried to point his pistol at me. There was no doubt in my mind that he was in the process of killing me. I had no time to issue any commands to Wortman. The distance separating me from Wortman was approximately fifteen feet. There was no time to move to cover because Wortman was already in the process of killing me. The closest available concealment was the gas pump. In order to move to cover behind my Suburban, I would have to expose myself more to Wortman.

I shot Wortman through the passenger side window while he was seated . . . while I was shooting Wortman I saw him moving and jerking in the seat . . ."

Hubley's dramatic rendition was perfect for the media, who reported it unquestioningly. No one cared how Wortman had really died. That's what hundreds of people told me over the years. "Give the guy who shot him a medal," they'd say.

But something was off about the RCMP's official story. Why was there no mention of the Petro-Canada—something that eyewitnesses saw—and why did it take so long for Hubley's story to come out? These were just two of the questions I had as the first anniversary of the massacres approached and the public still awaited a full official explanation. That's when a source, whom I've dubbed True Blue, emerged with the 911 tapes from Jamie Blair, Alex Blair and Andrew MacDonald, *and* the security footage from Petro-Canada and the Big Stop, which told a different story.

◆

The gas station tapes, as they became known, showed that Wortman did indeed go the Petro-Canada service station at Elmsdale Road before heading to the Big Stop, as I described above. In the first video, Wortman is just a few feet away from Constable Brent Kelly, who stands at the back of the unmarked car, wearing tactical gear, and appears to be watching Wortman.

It was irrefutable proof that Wortman and the RCMP had come into close contact with each other *before* the Big Stop.

True Blue also released some, but not all, of the Big Stop security tapes to us. Some were deemed "too graphic." Those we did see and publish were enough to show that Cacchione's and Hubley's version of events didn't align with the videotape evidence.

The security video showed Hubley's Suburban lurching to a stop, then Hubley popped open his driver's-side door. MacLeod jumped out of the vehicle to the right and hurried into a position at the right front of the car, with his C8 assault rifle primed and ready to fire. After Hubley exited the Suburban, Wortman's vehicle noticeably shuddered. A split second after that, MacLeod, then Hubley, opened fire. MacLeod targeted Wortman in a bead of eleven shots through the lower right area of the front windshield as Wortman sprawled across the passenger seat. Hubley unloaded twelve shots through the front passenger window.

When Hubley's Sig Sauer handgun was examined later, it had three rounds left, although he may have done a reflexive reload, which he couldn't remember doing.

Most notably, the tapes showed that it was only seconds after Wortman arrived at the Big Stop that Hubley and MacLeod appeared, and seconds later, they began shooting, at 11:26 a.m. It was as if the RCMP had superimposed Constable Kelly's experience onto Constable Hubley's, fusing the two into one, in the process making sniper Kelly disappear. (He was soon promoted to corporal for his efforts.)

Regardless, the tapes exposed that neither the RCMP nor SIRT, the police watchdog, had told the whole truth about what actually happened on April 19, 2020. Why not? There were only two logical explanations:

(1) The RCMP didn't tell Cacchione or SIRT investigators, who were either retired or seconded Mounties, and Halifax police about the Petro-Canada stop; or (2) Cacchione, alone or submitting to political pressure, went along with the concocted story so as not to embarrass the RCMP any further.

When questioned about his report, Cacchione responded that, yes, he had seen the tapes, but he had better and clearer copies that told a different story. Here is what the CBC's Elizabeth McMillan reported on June 10, 2021, in an article headlined: "N.S. Gunman Stopped at Gas Station in Elmsdale Before Heading to Big Stop: SIRT Director Says No Evidence Police Officers at Pumps Recognized Suspect."

SIRT's director, Felix Cacchione, said video from the Petro-Canada was part of the materials he reviewed, but he didn't draw any conclusions from it beyond that it showed the suspect had changed out of a police uniform and was driving the car he stole from Gina Goulet, the last person he killed.

Cacchione said he found no evidence that RCMP officers followed the gunman from the Petro-Canada to the Big Stop about 7.5 kilometres away.

"There was no indication in any of the radio transmissions that indicated he had been recognized and a broadcast made that he was driving a grey Mazda 3 vehicle. There was nothing like that. The officers didn't know—the officers at the Petro-Can—that it was him," said Cacchione.

One of the videos Frank Magazine posted shows that three seconds after opening his door, an officer had his gun drawn. It's not clear at what point he started firing.

Cacchione disputed the suggestion that the officer, a dog handler, got out of the vehicle intending to shoot. He said it only took seconds for the officer to spot a bruise on the gunman's forehead and realize it was the man wanted for murdering several people.

"Getting out of the vehicle, [the officer] would have been looking directly at the affected party and that's when he recognized him. There was no indication that he recognized him while he was in the police vehicle," said Cacchione.

"The quality [of video] we viewed was excellent, it was not grainy. It was typical of surveillance footage but it was not blurry," he said. "What I see on screen from Frank Magazine is very condensed compared to what I saw."

He said viewing snippets of video can change the appearance of the events. However, Cacchione said he could not release the full videos and said SIRT handed over its files to the public inquiry that is now examining the events of April 18 and 19, 2020.

"I would rather that the entire footage be posted than to pick and choose portions," he said.

The Mounties' behaviour wasn't normal. They were being obtuse and confusing. We were starting to believe that perhaps they had no intent to arrest Wortman, that a shoot-to-kill order may have been issued. One reason for such an order might be that Wortman was an undercover informant for the RCMP and something had gone wrong. But of course, there was no way to prove it.

I viewed the video of Wortman in Goulet's car from a point of view looking down and through the front passenger window. It wasn't entirely clear, but I couldn't see a pistol in Wortman's hand. To me, it looked like a white piece of paper, perhaps a napkin or tissue, as if he was holding it up to surrender. If that were the case, "compromised authority" would not be a legal defence for the Mounties who had shot Wortman.

Despite our suspicions, we would have to wait to see if the commission revealed new information that would help everyone make sense of what had happened.

◆

Eighteen months after the massacres, on October 6, 2021, Constable Brent Kelly was finally interviewed by commission investigators Paul Thompson and Will Crews. This is what he told them about the incident: "So, he leans across the passenger seat and he kind of looks up like he's looking back, and I noticed there was, like, a slight bump over his left eye, right," Kelly said. "I really didn't pay much attention to a guy with a shiner. I'm like, that's not that uncommon, right? And there was nothing really of the behaviour to make you think otherwise. He was just like doing the same thing Andrew Ryan was doing. Trying to get the pump to work. But he moves over to another pump."

Kelly's description didn't appear to match his actions and body language in the Petro-Canada security video, in which he seemed to be suspicious of Wortman. In fact, he told the commission that when he watched the version of the video that *Frank* had published on the Internet, he found that his memory of the situation was not accurate. He had thought Wortman's car was facing away from him and not toward him. It isn't just civilian witnesses who have faulty memories!

As we were conducting additional research for this chapter, citizen investigator Ryan Potter noticed what he thought was a discrepancy between Kelly's interview and the three pages of his handwritten notes also released by the commission. "There seems to be a page or two missing between pages 1 and 2," Potter told me. "On page 2 he's talking about things that aren't on page 1. The whole thing at the [Petro-Canada] gas pumps isn't described at all."

I called up Kelly's notes. Potter was right. Kelly wrote at the bottom of the first page: "11:02: Suspect possibly in grey/silver Tracker" [the original erroneous description of Joey Webber's Ford Escape]. The second page began with: "I then got called over [to?] some members near the highway saying there was a [Honda] Civic coming up the ramp [word scratched out] involved. Confirmed not involved . . ."

In his interview, Kelly filled in some of this void, saying that after Wortman left the Petro-Canada station, Constable Ryan moved his vehicle to another pump to try to get gas. Kelly said he had a good view of the highway ramp, and when another officer told him a suspicious car was coming up the ramp, Kelly used his rifle scope to zero in on the driver. "That's not him . . . He looked to be Asian."

Kelly's next entry into his notebook was at 11:25 a.m., as he and the convoy were rolling up to the Irving Big Stop. What happened in between? Kelly's notes and interview don't fully describe what took place, and the key piece that is missing is the two minutes that Wortman and the Mounties were at the Petro-Canada station. I checked the notes of constables Ryan and Barnhill. Neither of them mentioned the incident either. I couldn't help but wonder if this was part of the RCMP editing process that may have involved destroying evidence during the summer of 2020. If police watchdog Cacchione's investigation centred on the RCMP members' handwritten notes and there were none, it was easy to see how he could write a report that didn't include the Petro-Canada visit by Wortman. If it wasn't on paper, it didn't happen.

Once Wortman drove away from the Petro-Canada, did Kelly and/or his colleagues realize too late that they had been face to face with Wortman? If so, they knew what car he was now driving. Did he or they relay that message, not by radio but by phone, WhatsApp or a private ERT radio channel? None of those records were reviewed by the commission.

In *22 Murders*, I reported what witness Jerome Breau told me in an interview. Breau had been at the Onslow Belmont fire hall when the Mounties shot it up and later stopped to talk to Mounties parked on the median of Highway 104. At that time, he heard a transmission: "He's in a Mazda!" Breau estimated that it was about 11:17 a.m., which fits perfectly with the timeline of Wortman's exit from the Petro-Canada. There was no record of that transmission in the RCMP's or the commission's documents. Was it among evidence that was destroyed?

When questioned about it later, SIRT director Cacchione told the media adamantly that the RCMP had *not* identified Wortman at the Petro-Canada station. He stood by his original report, even though its credibility should have been in shreds by then. Once again, Cacchione brushed it all off as conspiracy theory, which was by now the go-to statement for dismissing unfavourable stories.

22

DEATH AT THE BIG STOP

The Irving Big Stop at the Enfield exit on Highway 102 is a very large service centre that serves as a refilling station, truck stop, weigh station and local dining option. It features a long row of twelve gas pumps. With the COVID lockdown in place, there were few people out and about that morning. The parking lot was bare, other than a single motorcycle parked near the front door of the restaurant, though the Mounties and a couple of Halifax police officers were beginning to congregate.

At 11:24 a.m., Wortman drove along the row of pumps, turned right and stopped beside pump five. He turned off the car and seemed to just sit there for twenty-four seconds. There are two versions of what transpired next: the mythical, blue-lie Mountie version and the cold, hard facts on the videotape.

The original RCMP story was typically vague, with a whiff of heroism. An unidentified RCMP dog handler had pulled into the Irving Big Stop to gas up on his way to helping in the search for Wortman. While pumping gas, he happened to look over at the next bay and saw a man standing there with "a thousand-mile stare." The man then returned to his car. The dog handler, sensing that something was off about the man, signalled to his partner. The two Mounties challenged the man, who they now believed was Wortman. Wortman made a threatening move, they said, and they both opened fire and killed him.

As I mentioned in the previous chapter, Hubley told SIRT he had "no time," contrary to this original RCMP version. He also refused to hand over his handwritten notes to either RCMP investigators or the commission, perhaps because his story would not withstand scrutiny.

Contrary to what the RCMP initially implied, Hubley wasn't starting his workday when he ran into Wortman. It happened at the end of his day. He and his ERT partner, Ben MacLeod, had first gone to Portapique. Later, they had been at the Fishers' house in Glenholme when the compromised authority order was given, essentially giving the Mounties a licence to shoot Wortman, without first getting permission from a superior, if they felt at all threatened. They had spent the next ninety-five minutes racing from place to place as part of the designated cut-off team that rumbled through Shubenacadie minutes after Heidi Stevenson and Joey Webber had been murdered.

Although the collective media didn't pay any attention whatsoever to the timeline, Andrew Douglas and I and our band of citizen investigators always did. From our perspective, the RCMP was playing games. On page 42 of the foundational document for the Enfield Big Stop, there was this confusing entry at paragraph seventy:

> The video-surveillance footage from the Enfield Big Stop appears to show a duration of less than 10 seconds between the time the unmarked Suburban stops at pump 6, and the moment that shots are fired towards the Mazda 3. If the surveillance video plays in real-time (e.g. 10 seconds in the video is equivalent to 10 seconds of real time), an apparent incongruity exists between the ERT radio audio (18 seconds from Cst. MacLeod broadcasting "break" to the sound of gunfire), the surveillance video (less than 10 seconds between the Suburban stopping and members firing) and the accounts of Csts. Hubley and MacLeod (as detailed below, both members recall that they did not recognize the perpetrator and take actions towards him until they exited the Suburban at the gas station). The Commission

is therefore investigating whether or not the surveillance video accurately portrays the passage of real time. . . .

The timing was critical to proving the veracity of what the Mounties said had happened. It looked to me like the RCMP needed to stretch the time to provide room for Hubley's version of events, but then shrink it to avoid any evidence that the Mounties' actions were premeditated and, perhaps, technically unlawful.

Recall what Sergeant Darren Bernard said he heard over the radio while he watched over Heidi Stevenson's body: Hubley frantically shouting, "Pump six. Pump six. Pump six." In the context of events, those are words that would likely have been uttered as they were approaching pump six, not once they were stopped there. And they certainly weren't announcing that they were going to pump six to fuel up. Combine Bernard's statement with Jerome Breau's about hearing a Mountie over the radio shouting, "He's in a Mazda!" Taken together, the two radio transmissions suggest that the Mounties knew what Wortman was driving.

But in their statements, Hubley and MacLeod said they didn't know that Wortman was in a Mazda and didn't recognize him when they pulled up to pump six. They insisted that everything Hubley said in his voluntary statement occurred after they had come to a stop.

It looked like the old invisible hand of the RCMP was back on the job, attempting to edit the evidence to suit its preferred narrative. The Mass Casualty Commission had promoted the foundational documents as the single source of accurate information, but the paragraph cited above shows how it was all too willing to shade the truth to help the Mounties get out of the jam they had created for themselves. The key point was the "less than 10 seconds between the Suburban stopping and members firing."

In keeping with its methodology, rather than deal with what happened at the Big Stop in a coherent and integrated fashion, the commission spread the hearing over two consecutive days, April 13 and April 14, 2022. (Constable Kelly, who ran into Wortman at the Petro-Canada station in Elmsdale, was never called as a witness. His evidence was released in a document dump.) The first day of the examination of the shooting of Wortman began with another PowerPoint drill, this time led by commission council Anna Mancini. In her presentation, Mancini did a second-by-second, frame-by-frame breakdown instead of playing the security video and allowing the images to speak for themselves. All this orchestration made the timing and sequence of events more difficult to understand. The presentation wasn't even chronological, which made it seem like the incident took longer to unfold than it actually did, serving to distort the context and the facts. Mancini jumped from video to video and jumbled the times into the following sequence: 11:24:23, when Wortman arrived; 11:24:52, when Hubley and MacLeod pulled to a stop; 11:24:53, 11:24:56 and 11:24:57, as Hubley prepared to fire; 11:25:01; then back almost a minute to 11:24:09; 11:24:15, 11:24:37 and then a jump to 11:24:51; and then another jump to a door opening at 11:31:04.

The security video was slowed down and shown out of sequence, with the time stamps removed. But we clocked it all. The actual amount of time that elapsed from the moment Hubley's vehicle lurched to a stop to the first shots was about five and a half seconds. Mancini and her slide show turned seconds into minutes, and it took her about an hour to explain it. The "less than 10 seconds" in the foundational paper was actually about half that, according to the security tape, something that the commission attempted to rationalize.

Months before the Big Stop hearing, *Frank* published information from commission insiders—as you'll recall, we nicknamed them "reviewers"—who told us that the MCC intended to find that Wortman had committed suicide with Heidi Stevenson's gun before he was shot by Hubley and MacLeod. One reason for this narrative might be to protect the RCMP if evidence turned south; the force could argue that Hubley and MacLeod had done nothing criminal because they were shooting a dead man who had threatened them just before he took his own life.

As Mancini continued with her presentation, she did, in fact, link the murder of Constable Stevenson with Wortman's demise. It seemed as though the commission was trying to prove that Stevenson wounded Wortman, and that Wortman committed suicide with her silver and black Smith & Wesson Model 5946. But it wasn't prepared to show clear video of what was purportedly in Wortman's hand just before he died.

The Heidi Stevenson hero story had three pillars: the Quentin Tarantino–like shootout in Shubenacadie, her wounding Wortman in the head with a shot, and then Wortman using her gun to kill himself. As we saw in Chapter 15, the shootout didn't happen. The RCMP forensics team couldn't match shell casings to guns but had determined that slivers of metal that grazed Wortman were linked to a bullet likely fired by Stevenson. Stevenson's supposed fifteenth bullet was never found. Confirming the suicide would clinch the story. Enter Dr. Matthew Bowes.

Dr. Bowes's appearance looked like it would be another mind-numbing session. No one expected anything dramatic. The forensic evidence had been released to the media, and there wasn't much to be found in it. For those who paid attention only to the first part of the testimony, in which Mancini led Bowes through the evidence, their overall impression would have been that Wortman had committed suicide with Heidi Stevenson's gun. The media loved that story, although compelling evidence to the contrary was presented later that they entirely ignored.

As Mancini pressed Bowes to confirm that Wortman had committed suicide, Bowes would not comply. He said there was stippling on Wortman's forehead that was indicative of a close-in shot. Although Wortman might plausibly have shot himself, he was *killed* by the bullets of Hubley and MacLeod, which "morcellated," or tore apart, every organ in Wortman's body. "His lung was unrecognizable as a lung."

Another default truth that the RCMP had promoted over the previous two years was that Wortman had been shot twenty-three times— once for each victim, including the Beatons' unborn baby. That number fit their poetic end story. But Bowes said he had detected twenty-five discrete entry wounds. That wasn't worth the ink for the media—a single bullet for every victim sounded better than twenty-five.

Lawyer Robert Pineo, acting for most of the families, had to keep his questions within the parameters the commission would allow. Nevertheless, he found an opening and cut to the chase with Bowes, asking him about the report from RCMP forensic examiners that linked shards of metal to a bullet from Stevenson's gun, the "proof" that

Stevenson had wounded Wortman. One crucial flaw in that theory was the fact that, while Wortman had a variety of ammunition for his own gun, some of it was the same as Stevenson's.

Bowes presented a more likely scenario for how Wortman had received the injury to his forehead: that the shards were from a bullet ricocheting off something else before striking him. Bowes suggested glass. It could also have been metal. If Stevenson had been in a gunfight with Wortman and the bullet that injured him was a ricochet from her gun, she would have had to fire that bullet from inside her vehicle. But there were no holes in the vehicle's extant windows. If she had been outside the car, her shot would have had to ricochet off glass or metal before hitting Wortman, but there was absolutely no evidence of that happening. Wortman's car windows were all intact prior to the fire. Again, a gunfight was unlikely.

However, there was clear evidence of a time when Wortman could have been hit by a ricochet *from his own gun*. The photographs from the crime scene showed that he had fired two bullets through the glass and metal from directly behind the rear passenger window of Stevenson's car. Witnesses saw him crouching down when he fired. His head was below the roofline of her car, which would have been immediately to his right. His wound was on the right side of his upper forehead. One of those bullets could easily have shattered and struck him in the head. That made more sense than Stevenson firing a bullet without ever getting out of her vehicle. Pineo had poked a hole in the Mounties' narrative.

He pressed on and struck gold. Here is an excerpt from the transcript of that exchange:

PINEO: Okay, and I don't know if you noticed this or not, but I'll ask you if you did. Did you notice that the only two weapons that were submitted for that ballistics test were the pistol, the Sig Sauer, and the Colt used by the RCMP officers?

BOWES: I did not notice that detail, no.

PINEO: You didn't. Okay.

BOWES: No.

PINEO: Are you aware that the pistol that was formerly Heidi Stevenson's was not submitted for testing? Were you aware of that?

BOWES: No, sir. The decision about how ballistics testing is done
   and what is selected for that testing is not up to me.

PINEO: Okay, you determined the cause of death was—sorry, the
   cause of the perpetrator's death was homicide by multiple shots?

BOWES: Yes, that's correct.

PINEO: Okay.

BOWES: Homicide here is the manner.

PINEO: Okay. So, you—your ultimate conclusion then is that the
   self-inflicted wound was not the cause of death?

BOWES: Ultimately, no. I think that in the grand scheme of things,
   I think that the collection of homicidal gunshot wounds are [*sic*]
   probably of greater importance both in their immediacy and
   their clinical importance.

Bowes and Pineo had single-handedly destroyed the credibility of
the RCMP's forensic report, created by investigators that the public
depends on to be honest and accurate. They also shot down the twin
blue lies about Stevenson's fifteenth bullet and Wortman's suicide. To
reiterate, that shell casing was never found. Stevenson's gun was found
between the seat and the console of the car in which Wortman died. The
RCMP speculated eight months later that it had fallen there after his
body was pulled out onto the pavement at the Big Stop. Stevenson's gun
was never sent for forensic testing. As ex-Mountie Cathy Mansley put it,
"It was all bullshit . . . Heidi deserved the truth."

◆

The next day, commission council Roger Burrill introduced Hubley and
MacLeod to the public for the first and only time. The two constables
were wearing suits, not their uniforms. Hubley sported a short, boxed
beard, while Macleod was clean-shaven. They didn't look or sound all
that delicate, but they were treated as if they were so vulnerable their
next destination might be a straitjacket, and lawyers for the families
weren't allowed to ask them tough, probing questions. Everyone had to
stick to the agenda as laid out in the foundational papers.

They described themselves as being part of a "hybrid team of part-time ERT members." In other words, the RCMP was desperately short-handed and taking a duct-tape approach to its operations. Nothing new there. They stuck to the story, with a slight refreshing here and there. For example, Hubley added that everything from his getting out of the truck to recognizing Wortman took place "in a second."

Andrew Douglas and I believed that the partial tapes we had released to the public showed enough of what had happened at the Big Stop to refute the RCMP's narrative, but when we were able to look at the tape in its entirety during the commission hearings, it raised new questions about Hubley's statement. The video was from the camera on the main building, and it was one of the clips that the commission would not allow to be run at normal speed. It captured Hubley and MacLeod, in the Suburban, racing across the lot toward where Wortman was parked, turning right into pump six and stopping short of where a driver normally would to fill up a large vehicle like a Suburban. That position, however, gave Hubley partial cover from Wortman, who was still sitting in his vehicle on the other side of the pumps. Hubley repeatedly said that he had pulled into the first service bay where the gas pumps were not covered with bags. The videotape showed that pumps eleven and twelve were covered, but pumps one to ten were not. Hubley had raced past four open pumps and turned sharply into pump six.

Hubley also reiterated that before he and MacLeod arrived at the pumps, they didn't know Wortman was in a Mazda 3. So how did he identify that the stranger in the car beside him was Wortman, put his vehicle in park, exit his vehicle, begin to pump gas, see bruising on Wortman's forehead, notice Stevenson's gun in Wortman's hand, alert his partner, pull out his handgun and begin firing, all in five and a half seconds? Although Mancini had parsed the videotapes frame by frame, Burrill showed no interest in challenging Hubley's narrative about the sequence of events in those five and a half seconds.

Under ever-so-gentle questioning, Hubley added a couple of new twists to his already public story that deserve a thorough dissection. He said:

- When he pulled up parallel to the Mazda 3, he saw that the man in the driver's seat had a bleeding wound on his upper forehead. This caused him to wonder why the man hadn't treated the wound. They were beside each other, with their vehicles facing in the same direction. Hubley was in a Chevrolet Suburban, which sits high, while the six-foot-two Wortman was in a low-riding Mazda 3 with tinted windows. How could Hubley see his forehead from there? Also, Hubley had said in his voluntary statement that he was 15 feet away, with Wortman out of his car; now he was saying he was right beside Wortman, who was in the driver's seat.
- He saw a gun in Wortman's right hand and recognized it as Heidi Stevenson's Smith & Wesson service revolver.
- He and MacLeod fired their weapons only after Wortman made threatening moves toward them and they feared for their lives.

Near the end of the hearing, Burrill asked Hubley and MacLeod a question that was obviously aimed at refuting what I had written in *Frank* and in *22 Murders*. "I'm coming to the conclusion of my questions for you," Burrill said. "I wanted to ask you, specifically and pointedly, did either of you recognize the perpetrator before you pulled into those gas pumps at the Big Stop Enfield?"

The two Mounties each responded with "No."

"Did either of you know or have any indication that the perpetrator would have been at that location before you pulled into the gas pumps at Big Stop Enfield?"

Both Mounties each said no again.

"This is going to be a very direct question," Burrill said. "Did either of you get any orders from anybody, or direction from anybody, to execute Gabriel Wortman?"

"No," said Hubley.

"No," said MacLeod.

"Given your knowledge of the situation, the information that you processed [*sic*], your training and experience, would you have done anything differently than you had done on that morning of April 19, 2020?

"No," said MacLeod.

"Constable Hubley?"

"No," he said.

◆

At *Frank*, Andrew Douglas was perplexed by the state of journalism in the country. He had worked at the magazine for seventeen years, the last twelve as its editor. Throughout his career, he was an outsider in the world of journalism who revelled in needling and lampooning reporters, talking heads and their editors. *Frank*'s business model was based on satire, with the occasional scoop. Now, it seemed, the world of journalism had become a dystopian nightmare. Just about every story being published was based on "official" sources or had a political agenda. Not one mainstream or alternative news outlet seemed interested in holding the powerful accountable.

Douglas had a crazy idea. He would bypass *Frank*'s tight-fisted owner and put some of the little money his enterprise had where his mouth was. He thought he could force the commission to release all of the Irving Big Stop security tapes so that the true story could be told once and for all. On April 25, 2022, *Frank*'s lawyer, the well-regarded David Hutt, filed a submission with the commission that argued it was important for all the tapes to be released because they "may suggest a slightly different version of events from the one set out in the Big Stop [foundational document] and evidently adopted by the commission counsel." Over the next several weeks, other legacy media outlets joined in the application: the CBC, CTV, the Canadian Press and Global. Eventually, the arguments by all those lawyers seemed to wear down the commission. After more than a month of fighting to have the tapes released, a date was finally set: Monday, June 13, 2022.

Douglas was confident that we had won a worthy journalistic victory. "Let's see what we get on Monday."

"I don't know," I said. "I've seen this before. What devious trick are they going to pull out of their bag to distract everyone?"

We both laughed.

June 13 came and went.

On June 17, the commission said the videos were displayed on their website. They weren't.

Finally, on June 20, the tapes were released. David Hutt found the commission's announcement of their release astounding. Infuriating, even. "The decision is defensive from the start, pre-emptively justifying each step taken by the commission or its counsel regarding the videos," Hutt wrote to Douglas. "They say their mandate—to 'be guided by restorative principles in order to do no further harm,' and 'be attentive to the needs of and impacts on those most directly affected and harmed'—is an 'important public interest' put at risk by publication of the videos. But this broad argument could justify suppressing ANY exhibit from the killing spree."

And when we looked at the videotapes posted on the commission's website, we realized they were incomplete and clumsily edited. Here's an excerpt of what I wrote in *Frank* on June 22:

OFFICIAL SOURCES OR IT DIDN'T HAPPEN

by Paul Palango

The first thing we noticed was that even though the Commission was supposed to release all the video tapes, some were extremely truncated. Sections were missing. Wortman's Mazda and Hubley's Chev Suburban suddenly show up at the adjacent pumps as if plopped out of the sky. The Commission said there were technical issues with some of the cameras.

But the images from one camera—positioned over Pump 6 at the Enfield Big Stop—married with the images from the others appeared to tell a conclusive, unadulterated story about the final seconds of Gabriel Wortman's life.

He was sitting in the driver's seat of the grey Mazda 3 sedan at Pump 5. He had been sitting there for 26 seconds or so. A tan Chevrolet Suburban pulls into Pump 6. It's wide of the pumps and not lined up with the gas tank. The vehicle stops. The driver, Constable Craig

Hubley, gets out while at the same time reaching for his sidearm. He immediately takes a firing position and unloads at Wortman through the passenger side window of the Mazda 3 in which Wortman was sitting. Ben MacLeod exits the passenger side, comes around to the front of the vehicle and starts shooting. Total elapsed time between the car stopping and the first bullets being fired: between 5 and 6 seconds.

The videos raise obvious apparent inconsistencies in the official narrative. Much of what Hubley and MacLeod said happened, clearly didn't happen and it certainly didn't all happen within 5 or 6 seconds.

So how did the mainstream media handle this?

The television stations ran some of the video but didn't bother to contrast the testimony of Hubley and MacLeod and the findings by Cacchione with what the videotape showed. They didn't comment on the obvious anomalies in the videos.

The CTV report was so poor that the reporter even had the police vehicle already at the gas pumps when Wortman arrived.

The print media and most of the television stations relied on a single report by The Canadian Press to describe what happened, a story which also did not dare challenge the official narrative.

A small but telling point in all the coverage was that all the mainstream media—these paragons of virtue, ethics and accuracy—failed to report that it was Frank Magazine's initiative and dollars that provoked the release of the tapes.

[At this point in the original article, my podcast partner, lawyer Adam Rodgers, made a lengthy legal argument about how it was possible that Hubley, in a spectacular feat of athleticism, did everything he claimed to have done in the short time he had. Rodgers has since reconsidered that opinion, but in the column he did make the other side of the argument.]

Rodgers has lingering questions about the Mountie's version of events. While it might appear that the Mounties knew Wortman was there, a court would require a solid piece of evidence, such as a text or radio message, to prove that point.

"So, the decision to stop for gas at all seems suspect, if indeed the tank was just below half full," Rodgers added. "The decision to go to pump 6 is also suspicious, if the other pumps were available and not covered by orange bags. He definitely did not reach for the pump. His attention was focused immediately on the person in the car. I would suggest that his observation time was extremely short, but not implausible.

"His articulation of what he was thinking at that time may seem too in-depth, considering how short the timeframe had been. It seemed to me like how as a pitcher I would occasionally have to react to a line drive hit back at me. There is far less than a second to react to put your glove up and catch or deflect the ball, but when you think back on it, you can describe the way the ball came off the bat and what you did. It would be an elite recognition and reaction, but in my mind possible under the circumstances."

Wherever the truth might lie, one can remain fairly confident that it won't be uncovered by an industrious, curious and skeptical main-stream media who have long since had those instincts bred from their collective bloodlines.

At the same time Canadian trust in journalists has continued to fade, the mainstream media can't seem to grasp the problem.

The commission could pretend that it was being transparent, but its actions suggested there was something to hide. In the end, Douglas's fight to get the security tapes was only a partial win: our distant cousins in the mainstream and alternative media didn't delve into the signifi-cance of the tapes. And there was a new story to cover. Like the 17:51 from Montreal, it arrived on schedule the next day.

◆

On June 21, the commission released on its website documents that appeared to show that RCMP commissioner Brenda Lucki had inter-fered in her own force's criminal investigation back in 2020.

What criminal investigation? Since the massacres, all the RCMP had seemed to be doing was busywork. There was no plan to charge anyone, and no one was ever charged, with the curious exception of Banfield, her brother and brother-in-law, whose relatively minor charges were eventually dropped. In fact, the RCMP had made it quite clear that it didn't want to charge anyone; if there was a criminal case, it would be forced to disclose what had really been going on.

Lucki's sin was that she had asked, on behalf of the federal government, about the specific guns that Wortman had used in his murder spree. There had been a video conference. Superintendent Darren Campbell had taken notes about Lucki's questions. The notes were released to the commission. When the commission posted them on its website, pages were missing. Now even the Mounties were shouting cover-up! Then the pages were found. And, yes, they were deemed to be incriminating of Lucki.

Reporters flew off to chase the story like a flock of seagulls spotting a child dropping a container of french fries on the other side of the bay. The *Globe and Mail* ran a triple-bylined (Robert Fife, Steven Chase, Greg Mercer) skyscraper headline:

RCMP COMMISSIONER BRENDA LUCKI ACCUSED OF INTERFERING IN N.S. MASS-SHOOTING INVESTIGATION TO HELP LIBERAL GOVERNMENT'S GUN-CONTROL AGENDA

RCMP Commissioner Brenda Lucki pressed the Mounties to disclose the weapons used in the Nova Scotia mass shooting to help advance the Liberal government's gun-control legislation, the public inquiry into the April 2020, killings was told. . . .

In a statement Tuesday evening, Commissioner Lucki said she did not interfere in the investigation. However, she did not address alleged political interference by Mr. Blair and the PMO and only commented on her interaction with Nova Scotia RCMP.

In notes submitted to the inquiry, RCMP Superintendent Darren Campbell described how he was reprimanded at length by the commissioner. He said she was upset because she had "promised the Minister of Public Safety and the Prime Minister's Office" that the RCMP would disclose specifics about the type of firearms used by the gunman.

Supt. Campbell's notes make it clear he was concerned that politics could interfere with a cross-border police investigation.

His notes say Commissioner Lucki explained that the Nova Scotia RCMP needed to understand that the release of the information "was tied to pending gun-control legislation that would make officers and the public safer by or through this legislation." The gunman, however, never had a firearms licence and smuggled three weapons into Canada from Maine.

"The Commissioner accused us (me) of disrespecting her by not following her instructions. I was and remain confused over this," he wrote. "I said we couldn't because to do so would jeopardize ongoing efforts to advance the U.S. side of the case as well as the Canadian components of the investigation. Those are facts and I stand by them."

Lucki was the perfect scapegoat. The end of her five-year term was coming up. She was seen as a flunky for Prime Minister Justin Trudeau. She was unpopular with all ranks. She had made and would continue to make a series of gaffes, including stating that there was no racism within the RCMP.

My phone began ringing off the hook. Talk show hosts wanted to talk to me. Podcasters were eager to Zoom with me.

"Has the RCMP become politicized?" one well-known wag asked.

"It's been politicized since 1984, after the federal government implemented the recommendations of the McDonald Commission and made the RCMP commissioner a deputy minister," I said. "The commissioner is effectively appointed by and serves at the pleasure of the prime minister, like some of the better banana republics."

"Why was Lucki interfering in the investigation?" was another popular question.

"The RCMP is a federal police force, even in its provincial contract role," I would reply. "She is effectively the police chief. A police chief has the right to know what is going on in an investigation."

"Is this the end of Brenda Lucki?"

"Of course it is," I told one interviewer. "She's on her way out anyway. No matter how much the government says to the contrary, she's been a disaster.

This is just a nothingburger. The whole point of it is to distract the media from what the Mass Casualty Commission was forced to do yesterday."

"What's that?"

"They released the Irving Big Stop tapes, which showed that the RCMP was not telling the whole story about how Gabriel Wortman was shot and killed. And then this. The powers-that-be don't want anyone paying attention and thinking too much about what is on those tapes."

I could read the minds of many when I said that: "conspiracy theorist."

In the end, Lucki's term ended with a whimper.

One of her last acts was an appearance before the MCC, out of uniform like all the other Mountie leaders who appeared before and after her. That was important in and of itself. The RCMP likes its members to dress up in public. When they don't, you know things are going badly and they don't want to get stains on the uniform—Protect the Buffalo.

All the brass who appeared before the commission—Superintendent Campbell, Superintendent Dustine Rodier, Chief Superintendent Chris Leather, Assistant Commissioner Lee Bergerman and Deputy Commissioner Brian Brennan—said nothing much and moved on. Those who didn't retire with a full pension stayed in their current jobs or were promoted.

All this brings us to a couple of loose ends in the tale. Let's begin with the only person who was there at the beginning, with Gabriel Wortman in Portapique on Saturday night, April 18, 2020: Lisa Banfield.

23

THEIR EMAILS REVEAL
A PLOT AND A SWOLLY

After the massacres she was, at first, a mystery woman. No one knew her name. She was just Gabriel Wortman's common-law wife. The RCMP invoked privacy considerations and referred to her as a victim. Then *Frank* magazine broke the ice and published her name and photograph on its cover: "Lisa Banfield, Hero . . . How Many Lives Did the Killer's Girlfriend Save?"

It may have looked like Andrew Douglas was gushing about her co-operating with the RCMP by naming Wortman and identifying the replica police car he was driving, but he had pulled a neat dodge: "We decided to call her a hero. Who was going to complain about that?"

The mainstream and alternative media didn't take the bait. From the moment she came out of the woods that April 19th morning, they had decided that Banfield was a victim of domestic violence and that further evidence, good, bad or otherwise, need not be considered. Just naming her was deemed to be damaging to her. The template for the coverage of Banfield was set. She was surrounded by layers of protectors: family, friends, acquaintances, a civil lawyer, top criminal lawyers, feminists, journalists, the RCMP and the commission itself.

To understand the level of deference bestowed upon Banfield, we need to briefly recap what is known about her relationship with Wortman, whom she met in 2001. Here's an excerpt of what I wrote in *22 Murders* about their first years together:

As Banfield moved into Wortman's life in 2001, they shared the apartment above the business. The location was a perfect set-up for Wortman. At the back of the clinic was a series of garages where he could store some of his motorcycles. Meanwhile, Banfield became not only his live-in girlfriend but eventually his full-time personal assistant. Most Wednesday nights, and sometime Tuesdays, he would head out to Portapique for a long weekend, while she remained in Dartmouth running the clinic, serving customers and polishing and tinkering with dentures. Much of the business was conducted in cash.

Before long all telephone calls to Wortman went through Banfield. He told people that he valued his private time away from work and didn't want to be bothered. That's one way of looking at it. By then it was already known in the criminal world that cellphones and vehicles with GPS systems were trackable by the police. That was why career criminals didn't use phones that could be linked to them and why they disconnected GPS systems in their new vehicles. General Motors' OnStar roadside service and similar systems from other companies functioned as both cellphone and GPS—a fink to be avoided.

Taking his calls, Banfield got to know everyone who was in contact with Wortman. With her permanently installed in his life and business, the neighbourhood fires continued, and crazier and crazier situations continued to pop up around the couple. On September 14, 2001, flames erupted at 189 Portland Street, two doors down from the denture clinic. Three weeks later, another fire was set in the same building. It makes one wonder if Banfield was oblivious to all this or whether she was getting a little nervous going to bed at night.

The latest fire came at a time when the police were ramping up their efforts against the Hells Angels down the street. There was always a surreptitious force lurking around the neighbourhood, but the RCMP's Operation Hammer was closing in on the Angels leaders. It was the kind of thing that someone like Wortman, always on the alert, might well see coming. On October 29, 2001, Wortman, then thirty-three, bought the two burned properties at a reduced price. . . .

In December 2003, there was another damaging fire at 191 Portland Street. This time the building was finally rendered unin-habitable. Wortman wanted the city to pay to tear it down. He put up a weak fight for awhile until the city ordered him to demolish the structure, which he did in April 2004.

Wortman had his land. He had a vision for a lucrative develop-ment that would include his dental clinic. But he had overlooked one important factor. In summing up Wortman's boondoggle, Tim Bousquet quoted Dartmouth historian David Jones: "Given the lengthy record of the discovery of human remains on the St. James Church hill (from 1844 and potentially earlier to 1954) and the 1894 discovery of a stone hammer at the site of the Church Manse, it is highly recommended that the Nova Scotia Museum, Special Places and the Mi'kmaq be contacted ahead of any potential further ground disturbances in the area of the hill," Jones wrote. "Wortman never applied for a development permit for the site."

All of this happened during the first three years of Wortman's relationship with Banfield. They struck me as an unlikely couple. What was the glue that kept them stuck together? Were they like-minded soulmates? Was she camouflage for a man who didn't want anyone speculating about his complicated sexuality? Or, as the RCMP and the news stories suggested, was she cowering in fear, ter-rified of stepping out of line? After all, Banfield had told various people over the years that Wortman was demanding, controlling and difficult to live with.

Banfield's sister Beverley Davidson and her husband, Dale, revealed a little more about what was going on in Wortman and Banfield's every-day lives in their April 19, 2020, interview with RCMP constables Holly Murphy and Denis Chartrand.

While the Davidsons admitted that they weren't the closest of Lisa's siblings—three brothers and four surviving sisters—they still were tapped into the family grapevine. They were impressed by all the money Wortman appeared to have and the fancy and frequent trips he and Lisa took. They knew that Wortman had recently bought "$800 of gasoline" and that other Banfield family members had bought ammunition for him. Beverley had Lisa's photos of the replica police car on her cellphone. Years earlier, during a visit to Portapique, Wortman had proudly shown them some of his illegal guns, including one with a banana clip. The Davidsons also knew the location of some of the secret compartments Wortman had built into his various properties.

Beverley didn't see Wortman's potential violence toward Banfield as much of an issue. She did recall an incident many years earlier when her daughter, Stephanie, Banfield's niece, had to go pick Banfield up at Sutherland Lake at 2 a.m. because of a fight. This caused Dale to blurt out to his wife and the Mounties: "I didn't know he was beating Lisa until you just said it." (His brother-in-law Brian Brewster said much the same thing in a separate interview with the RCMP.)

When pressed to describe Wortman's personality, the Davidsons said he was very intelligent but paranoid, a common view. Beverley said he showered Banfield with money and trips, and that Banfield was in a dependent relationship with him. In a *Seinfeld*ian moment during the interview, Beverley also said she believed Wortman was gay: "I mean, not anything against gay people, because I don't. But that was his circle." She wasn't the only one who thought that, but it was both more and less complicated than that, as we'll see.

The Davidsons said they saw few signs of discord between Wortman and Banfield. There was even a plan for the Banfield siblings to buy adjoining properties in Portapique and build a family compound where they could live and take care of each other in their later years. In March 2018, Maureen Banfield paid $6,000 for a 1.4-acre lot just south of the driveway to Wortman's warehouse on Orchard Beach Drive. It was the same amount Wortman had paid for the property two years earlier through his New Brunswick company, Northumberland Investments. Cheap as the land was, the Davidsons didn't like the idea and declined to get involved.

In the initial media depictions of Gabriel Wortman, he was described as a wealthy Dartmouth denturist who had a problem with alcohol and misogyny and who had lost his mind over his fears about the COVID-19 lockdown. He was a skinflint hoarder, which was undeniable, and a generally unstable personality, which proved true.

Lisa Banfield, meanwhile, was portrayed as a fragile, trapped and beleaguered woman who was controlled by her oppressive partner. The media, therefore, treated her with deference. However, some of the emails released by the commission test those assumptions.

On May 6, 2022, two months before Banfield was scheduled to appear before the inquiry, the commission released a rich package of documents that included Warnell's interview with the RCMP as well as emails between Wortman, Banfield and a Toronto lawyer by the name of Kevin Paul von Bargen.

◆

Von Bargen, whom Wortman had met in 2016, was a mystery in and of himself. Born and raised in the Niagara region, between Hamilton and Niagara Falls, he was an accredited lawyer in Canada and the United States. Although he had been a lawyer for more than a decade, there was almost no trace of him on the Internet. On LinkedIn, he is listed as a former general counsel for Brookfield Properties, a division of Canada's largest conglomerate. For years, Brookfield Global Relocation Services has held the contract to move Canadian government employees, including Mounties, wherever they might be headed. Was Wortman and von Bargen's meeting a coincidence, or part of something deeper and more complicated? After Wortman met him, von Bargen seems to have left Brookfield Properties to become a sole practitioner with no easily traced office.

Von Bargen's only statement to the RCMP was made on April 21, 2020, two days after the massacres. He was interviewed by Corporal Patricia Davis, along with Corporal Kathryn MacLeod, and seemed uncomfortable throughout, as can be seen in the following excerpt:

CPL. DAVIS: Right. Okay. Um, Kevin, you mentioned, I know you were back and forth with him a lot, um, through emails, um, would you be willing to provide the emails that you were back and forth with him about regarding police cars, regarding what we're talking about here today?

VON BARGEN: To the extent I can, I can, I can get them, yeah. Of course, um, again, I'm not sure to when, uh, I'm not sure how you know I, I would imagine over the last three years I have thousands of emails with him, I ju— . . . you know, if you want to, if you want all of them it's fine, if, if you want, if you want, uh.

Their correspondence, likely obtained from Wortman's computer, shows that both von Bargen and Banfield were kept in the loop when Wortman began collecting the decommissioned police cars. Although the public was sold the idea that Wortman was initially buying the cars to fix them up and resell them, the emails suggest there was something else going on. The following are some of the exchanges on the subject, which began on May 8, 2019.

In one themed collection from July 2019, Wortman, proud of his new replica Mountie cruiser, called himself "The Sherriff" [*sic*].

"Just call me Deputy Banfield," Lisa responded, as she posed in a police uniform.

"Detective," said Wortman, promoting her.

Von Bargen got into the conversation on July 26, 2019, in a message labelled "whoop woop [*sic*]," referring to the sound of a police siren.

"Looks like the RCMP finally caught up to you!!!" von Bargen said about Wortman's cruiser. "Did you bury the Mountie in the back 40?"

"I will now need a cellphone with your # on speed dial," replied Wortman, who purportedly never had a cellphone.

Banfield seemed to be into the game, whatever it might have been.

Whenever Wortman and von Bargen got together, it appeared, mischief was in the air.

In the following exchange from December 2019, von Bargen listed his address as 8700 Dufferin Street, the headquarters of land developer Greenpark Group, as well as an adjacent small strip mall. Greenpark is controlled by Italian-Canadian businessman Carlo Baldassarra and his family, none of whom appear to be involved in the larger story.

Like Tom Evans before him, von Bargen seemed to be a little slippery. A few months before the massacres, Wortman and von Bargen had jointly concocted a scheme capable of defrauding the Atlantic Immigration Pilot Program, a government initiative to help immigrants obtain permanent residency in Canada after working for a year at a sponsoring business. Wortman and von Bargen set themselves up as a dentist's office. They planned to charge immigrants an "administrative" fee, but they would never actually work at the office. Part of the plan was that Lisa Banfield would ostensibly give up half of her responsibilities at Wortman's denturist office to provide a job for an immigrant.

Here is an email exchange from December 4, 2019, between Wortman and von Bargen about the hiring of a dental assistant under the program. It begins with von Bargen copying Wortman on an exchange he was having with Maral Mirhosseini, an Iranian-Canadian lawyer in Toronto who specialized in immigration. To Mirhosseini, at 3:18 p.m., he wrote:

Mr. Wortman has confirmed the following to me:

He can advertise a position to best match her qualification, both as an assistant and office manager tailored to her background per her CV.

She will need to be in Canada for one year according to the Atlantic immigration program requirements. He will inquire if the applicant can leave to go home during Holidays/vacation without affecting her standing.

It is my understanding that once she is sponsored her husband can join her and ride on her coattails. It would be easier for him to seek employment once in Canada.

Please note that they will need sufficient funds to support their combined living expenses that will rotate back to her from her payroll, less deductions.

The administration fee of $40,000 is USD. Once we receive the $10,000 retainer and confirmation to move forward, Mr. Wortman will post the job offer on three different sites for the required period of time. (Mr. Wortman, can you please confirm how long the ads have to run for). Ultimately, she will be chosen as her qualifications will best tailer [*sic*] the advertised position. Once approved, the remaining $30,000 USD will be required to be paid.

Wortman replied directly to von Bargen at 3:50 p.m.

The job needs to be posted for a month. She will get the job offer, from there the Province of NS provides a certificate of endorsement verifying the position is legitimate. Then there is a needs assessment and a settlement plan.

   We are not the first to think of this scheme. . . . (i.e. "How an immigration scheme steers newcomers into Canadian trucking jobs—and puts lives at risk"—The Globe and Mail, October 5, 2019).

   Maybe we should reconsider if it is worth it?

   I think our plan is better tailored and not running a bunch of people.

Von Bargen answered Wortman at 5:22 p.m.

Fuck, I don't know about you, but I don't need the worry. The last thing I need is our names in the newspaper or claims of dishonesty with the Ontario Bar jeopardizing the last 15 years of my career. Sounds like there is or will be much extra scrutiny and they have basically already exposed every aspect of our scheme. What do you think?

Wortman answered von Bargen at 11:40 p.m.

Abort is my consensus. No good deed goes unpunished.

   I am in agreement, too much skin in the game and I don't trust the other lawyer.

   We will still sleep well at night.

The above exchange took place 136 days before Wortman's killing spree began, just prior to the COVID outbreak. The emails show that while Wortman thought like a criminal, he was anything but irrational. If he went along with von Bargen in the immigration scheme, it might have triggered prying eyes and a tax audit, especially if he reported salaries for the new employees that were higher than what he paid himself and Banfield. On the one hand, he was like a perpetual motion machine, bouncing from one activity to another, but on the other hand, he was cautious of being caught by authorities, always wary of his exposed backside.

Although the commission released these emails, they weren't a focus of the hearings. The commission didn't seem intrigued by what motivations this kind of behaviour suggested—or by Banfield's knowledge of and possible role in Wortman's criminal activities. Banfield's limited public statements leave these questions unanswered.

Interestingly, after the massacres, Banfield reached out to von Bargen for "some guidance" through her brother-in-law, Doug McGrath. Von Bargen said he put them in touch with Toronto lawyer James Lockyer, a renowned social justice advocate whose specialty was representing wrongly convicted persons. Lockyer's notable clients included US boxer Rubin "Hurricane" Carter, Guy Paul Morin, David Milgaard and, more recently, Nova Scotia's Glenn Assoun. Not only had Banfield not been wrongly convicted, but she hadn't even been charged with a crime at that point. (Though she would be in December 2020, when she and her brother James and brother-in-law Brian Brewster were each charged with illegally supplying ammunition to Wortman, some of which he used in the murders he committed that weekend. All the charges were later dropped.)

The Mass Casualty Commission didn't call von Bargen as a witness, likely for two reasons. When Banfield contacted him on her phone soon after the massacres, that established solicitor-client privilege. But there was also the possibility that von Bargen would lead the commission into forbidden territory: criminal activity.

In his only interview, von Bargen noted that, in the year before the massacres, Wortman was interested in buying, refurbishing and selling decommissioned police cars. But there was a problem with that narrative: although Wortman bought four decommissioned RCMP police cars, he never put one up for sale.

◆

When the federal and Nova Scotia governments set up their joint inquiry in 2020, its focus was not so much on the murders and the failures of the RCMP, but on domestic violence. Wortman certainly had concerning credentials when it came to women. As I first reported in *22 Murders*, women who had had relationships with him said Wortman advertised his vasectomy as a way to turn a maybe into a romp, and measured patients' mouths to see if his penis would fit inside. He was forward and unrestrained, and didn't care all that much about age, race or, it seemed, gender. At least eight complaints were filed against him with the Denturist Licensing Board of Nova Scotia between 1998 and 2020. In 2007, he signed a settlement agreement, but afterwards said he was innocent and griped about the mental health of the patients. This history looked like firm ground upon which the commission could anchor its domestic violence agenda.

Depending on the moment when one peeked into their relationship, it seemed like Wortman was always cheating on Banfield. In documents released by the commission, there seemed to be a more complicated relationship between Banfield and Wortman than was revealed during its hearings. Take this diarized entry that Banfield made on her phone on November 11, 2018, after a visit to Houlton, Maine, where they saw their friends Angelette (Angel) Patterson and Sean Conlogue. Banfield wrote:

> We are leaving Houlton, Maine, and I'm devastated by what I witnessed with Gabriel and Angel. She was putting salt on the steps outside and Gabriel went out to help her. . . . I had a feeling in my gut to check it out and heard her say 'I can't' . . . along with Gabriel grabbing her!!! She said she did nothing wrong. . . . But then later I heard the three of them out in the kitchen . . . she was by Gabriel . . . joking around and when he was leaving to supposedly go to bed they hugged and he grabbed her ass!! I'm sick to my stomach [at] the thought that he would hurt me yet again!!!!! I really felt our relationship had changed for the Better and that we were on the same page!!! Clearly I was wrong!

Throughout 2019, however, the publicly revealed emails between Wortman and Banfield depicted a loving, playful side, even though they effectively lived apart most of the time—Wortman mainly in Portapique, and Banfield in Dartmouth. Banfield was devoted to her sisters Maureen and Janice. They stuck together like their own gang, as one mutual friend put it, and were hooked on playing bingo on Friday nights.

The records seem incomplete, but the following are some revealing excerpts.

While her car was in the body shop after Wortman had the incident with the deer on Portapique Beach Road in 2019 (described in Chapter 6), Banfield was forced to drive one of his decommissioned police cars, which she said she hated. After Wortman had dealt with the insurance company to get her Mercedes back on the road, Banfield, who liked to refer to herself by her nickname, Lisasweeswee, expressed her deep love for him in an email.

"Why all the kind words? Nice finally that you respect me," Wortman replied on Wednesday, May 8, at 12:13 a.m. The message is littered with autocorrect errors. "Intern will respect you. I love you and will protect you. Ask yourself why I encourage you to get help you truly need from the chiro, and willing to pay for it rather than fine dine you. . . . I am not easy to deal with, but I am you Knight and tarnished armor fighting to get you through . . . this tough world that we are faced with every day. You have my back and that is the only reason I can forge through this tough would [world]. Bonne nuit Capitain. My lover my Friend."

"OMG . . . you drunk thing," Banfield replied three minutes later. "I love the man that you are and now that your in the cult . . . I love you TIL the end of time. Love your kind words. ♡"

At 3:52 a.m., Wortman emailed her again: "Do I make you laugh? How are you doing? I told Kevin that I hit a deer . . . no details. . . . I have some big plans! They all stem for the Source, Power of the subconscious mind. Did you win at Bingo? You need the uniform for the RCMP car. I told you you would be driving one some day. RED NECK BITCH."

There was clearly a plan for something, but we never learn what "cult" Wortman had joined. The RCMP?

"I hope you know how loved you are!!!! Because YOU ARE!!!" Banfield emailed Wortman on June 30, 2019, a Sunday morning on the Canada Day long weekend.

The next morning Wortman replied: "Love you."

"So, am I staying put here then?" Banfield asked. "I'm happy you're getting a lot done. . . . Love you."

On July 2, 2019, Banfield wrote at 9:05 a.m.: "Good morning sunshine. Do you want me to come up today? Hope you had a great sleep!!"

"No point coming up today I will be in Dartmouth tomorrow," Wortman replied nine minutes later. "Good morning. Love you."

He then told her that he had just lost out on buying another decommissioned police car that he was hoping to use for parts. "My bid was $2,127.00. Sold for $2131.33. there will [be] more in Dartmouth, not too upset."

"It's overcast but sunny a little nice and warm at least!" Banfield wrote at 12:59 p.m. that day.

That evening, Wortman emailed her at 9:29 to say: "Love you so much, you are my Primary!" The subject line of the email was missing and seemed edited.

Banfield replied: "Awe I Better be your Primary. ♡"

Two days later, Banfield appeared to be replying to an email from Wortman that was not included in the commission release. Its subject line read: "Nice seeing you today, you looked beautiful and sexy."

On July 8, at 3:47 a.m., Wortman told her: "Love you miss you."

Banfield replied: "Set up things for today. Love you."

The lovey-dovey chatter continued into Labour Day weekend. The couple had returned from another trip to Maine, and Wortman was staying in Portapique to work on completing the replica RCMP cruiser. Banfield was in Dartmouth.

"Do you want me to come up Monday or Tuesday??" she asked. "Are you working on the police cars today . . . or bike ride?"

"Studying air conditioner on u tube at the moment."

"So when do you want me to come up?"

"That is up to you," Wortman replied. "Got the cage in and the windows moved to the real cop car." He added later: "Yes, the stuff is out of the other cop car. Not much for food. Love you."

"Hi hon," Lisa emailed him back at 10:23 p.m., with a few typos: "I hope you hi miss you already. Love you ♡"

"I also washed the RCMP car very pleased," Wortman said the next morning, September 4, 2019. "It is back in the garage will wax soon, looks like new!"

As crazy and scary as he turned out to be, the emails seem to show that while Wortman had a voracious sexual appetite and played close to the line, he never quite went over it. He was never charged with a sex-related offence. As his first wife, Corinne Kincaid-Lowe, stated, he had a softer, gentler side, one of the reasons many women, including his patients, liked him and felt comfortable conversing (and beyond) with him.

After the massacres, Banfield was consistently called Wortman's common-law wife, which implied normalcy, as if they had a white-picket-fence life, living together without formal nuptials. The evidence suggests otherwise. Wortman showed signs of being a swinger, willing to swap partners for non-emotional sex. Banfield called Wortman "a nymphomaniac." There appeared to be a vibrant underground swinger community in Colchester County and across the province.

But Wortman and Banfield's use of the word "primary" comes from the language of polyamorous relationships. In that world of open relationships, there is theoretically no room for jealousy. Each person has their own side sexual partners—metamours—with emotional connections. The entire circle is known as a polycule.

Was that why Banfield stood by Wortman when patients lodged complaints against him?

One Halifax police interview released by the commission, which subsequently disappeared, indicated that Banfield had taken up with an old high school boyfriend around 2016. If Wortman was jealous and controlling of Banfield, why didn't he do something about that? He didn't because it was all part of their lifestyle.

While it sounds like Banfield was polyamorous, Wortman appears to have been that and a swinger, too, a hybrid I learned is called a swolly.

There is plenty of research suggesting that, rather than creating an idyllic world, polyamory increases the chances of violent behaviour because of repressed jealousy and other factors. But when it came to investigating the massacres, all the sex and talk of love and metamours complicated the narrative of coercive control and domestic violence. Who among the victims were part of the polycule? Who in the wider community would be dragged into the conversation if the commission chose to head down that road?

Wortman and Banfield had been "together" for nineteen years, but as the emails above indicate, Banfield was more like an occasional visitor to the Portapique cottage. She didn't share ownership of the property and, in fact, didn't like going there. She didn't feel safe there. According to Cyndi Starratt, a Portapique neighbour who was both a housekeeper and, along with her daughter, a sex interest of Wortman's, Banfield didn't keep any toiletries at Portapique. She and Wortman slept in separate bedrooms, and Banfield locked her bedroom door when she slept there. Starratt said Wortman spent holidays, even Christmas, alone while Banfield was with her family. Unsurprisingly, Starratt wasn't called as a witness by the commission; her story likely would have torpedoed its depiction of Banfield and Wortman's relationship. It would also have opened the door to revelations about Banfield's less-than-welcoming attitude toward Wortman's other girlfriends. She may have been Wortman's "primary," but her actions sometimes suggested that she wanted to be "the one." Starratt said Banfield was dismissive and rude to her.

In the notes on her phone, Banfield once remarked: "Some Michelle N . . . girl from Truro I found her number in Gabs truck897 . . ." That note alone speaks volumes about the true nature of her relationship with Wortman. The default story was that Wortman had never had a cell-phone, instead relying on Banfield to take messages for him. If he needed a phone, he would use Banfield's. But in that case, why would she leave notes on the phone that he could easily find? Was she just care-less? Or did Wortman not care one way or the other? The note also sug-gests that Wortman had his own secret phone.

◆

For Banfield, the real tension seemed to be with neighbour Lisa McCully. The RCMP knew that McCully and Wortman had had a relationship. Well before midnight on April 18, Sergeant Dave Lilly told his fellow

Mounties that McCully and Wortman had recently broken up again, and that Wortman had been bothering her. That news spread through the force. In his handwritten notes at 1:52 p.m. the next day, a little more than two hours after Wortman had been killed, RCMP inspector Rob Bell noted at the bottom of page seven of thirty-nine pages: "Goes to MacCauley [*sic*] res (former G/F) shoots her on step."

Leon Joudrey said that Wortman may have recently bought McCully a ring. Did Banfield know about that? Was the fact that Banfield had been living at the cottage for weeks during the COVID lockdown a point of contention between McCully and Wortman? Emails between the two women suggest there was some friction there. I wrote about it as part of a larger article about Banfield in *Frank* on March 31, 2022. Here is an excerpt:

> An eerie message from Portapique murder victim Lisa McCully to Lisa Banfield, the common-law wife of mass murderer Gabriel Wortman, suggests that there was a darker side to Banfield's personality than has previously been described.
>
> The brief message, released in a document dump by the Mass Casualty Commission, was dated June 30, 2018.
>
> In it, McCully was addressing Banfield's reaction to McCully's dog having wandered across Orchard Beach Drive and interrupting a party that was being held at Wortman's warehouse/man den at 136 Orchard Beach Drive.
>
> The message read:
>
> > I trust your weekend was successful and that you are satisfied with your party accomplishments. In regards to your communication with me, I can appreciate that your guests might not have liked dogs and I explained that I would make every effort to keep them in my yard. However, I think the manner in which you took it upon yourself to aggressively reprimand me for my dog's behaviour was unacceptable.
> >
> > I feel peace and happiness in my home and, to this point, have appreciated the camaraderie and support of my neighbours.

Gabriel has indicated that he enjoys the dog's company and has created habitual visits for a couple of years by feeding them treats, unrequested by me. This is an obviously unresolved issue between the 2 of you, and I would expect that he will stop visiting with them or will speak to me about changing the routine, if he wants it to stop.

Your sudden aggressive arrival in the dark on my deck at 11 p.m. was a poor choice, and will not happen, again. This is not how we interact with each other in Orchard Beach Estates. It is a community built on kindness and generosity, and I won't accept an assault a second time.

I was happy to accommodate your DJ music until midnight last night, knowing that you were celebrating a life, something that I know can be taken quickly.

I will consider our interactions as an error in judgment, however. I don't see that you have any reason to contact me again or ever come back on my property.

Thank you for respecting my standards.

-Lisa

That there was heat between the two women is a subject that has not been discussed in any depth by either the RCMP or most of the media.

Each has been portrayed as relatively harmless individuals who were one kind of victim or another. McCully ended up dead, while Banfield has been incessantly described as a helpless, battered woman suffering under the psychological and physical abuse of Wortman.

The truth is much more complicated. Wortman and Banfield certainly had a tempestuous relationship at times, which was well reported. There were largely third-hand allegations about him assaulting her years earlier, angrily putting her car up on blocks, paying her slave wages, controlling her finances and leaving her in fear for her life at all times. Feminist commentators continue to gnaw on that bone while choosing to ignore inconvenient facts. Although it appears that Wortman exercised some control over Banfield, she seemed content to play the role of his "primary"—a friend with benefits, as it were. And, as we'll see in Chapter 26, she spent her own and Wortman's money quite freely.

Many women contacted me to say they were offended by Banfield's story and believed it did a disservice to women who were truly abused. One was Carole MacDonald, whom I've never met, who wrote this:

> Most victims do not get to spend so much time away from the abuser. One thing Banfield said was that she didn't actually know many people in Portapique because she didn't go there all that often, preferring to spend her free time with family. Abusers usually work to separate victims from their families early in the relationship.
>
> She also had her own bedroom at the cottage. . . .
>
> Anyway, glad you are not letting this go.
>
> C

Even though the rest of the media had access to most of the information I have reported, not one other journalist wrote a skeptical or critical story about Banfield. And when the RCMP charged her, her brother James and her brother-in-law Brian Brewster in December 2020, the media attacked the force for "revictimizing" her.

Banfield's biggest champions among journalists were Tim Bousquet and his team at the *Halifax Examiner.* I had done many of my first stories about Portapique for the online paper, but found myself frozen out after I suggested writing about Banfield. At the time, I didn't realize two things about Bousquet. First, the highlight of his career had been a series of stories about the wrongful murder conviction of Glenn Assoun, who was eventually exonerated. Bousquet's work was nominated for a prestigious Michener Award (which he didn't win). One of Assoun's lawyers was James Lockyer from Toronto, who went on to become Banfield's lawyer in Halifax. The Lockyer connection made me question whether the *Examiner* had inside information that helped them so often front-run positive stories about Banfield. Later I learned that one of the biggest influences on Bousquet was a woman who occasionally wrote in the

Examiner but was never identified as his wife. She is Lisa Gannett, a professor of philosophy at Saint Mary's University in Halifax who specializes in the philosophy of biology, race, gender and science. One of her interests is "scientific racism."

Interestingly, when Banfield launched lawsuits aimed at claiming what she thought should be her share of Wortman's estate, she never purported to be a victim—"or at least not victim enough to count," according to the commission's final report. It went on to say that "self-blame by the long-time partners of abusers is not uncommon. While we acknowledge Ms. Banfield's self-assessment, we believe it is important to recognize that she is a survivor of the mass casualty, and she has also been failed by many people and institutions in its aftermath."

Likely true, but perhaps in ways not yet imagined. However, this perspective reigned supreme in the days leading up to Banfield's eventual appearance before the commission on July 15, 2022.

24

LISA BANFIELD WEEK AT THE SPINQUIRY

Lisa Banfield's appearance before the commission generated so much interest because, to date, she had, through her lawyers, declined to answer any journalists' questions or grant interviews. What I have written about her so far in this book has come from her statements, her appearance before the commission, and interviews done with those in her circle. Her only statement about the massacres was a comment relayed to the public by the RCMP in one of the two unredacted summaries of their early interviews with her, in which they said, "Lisa Banfield has had guilty feelings and wonders if Gabriel Wortman went to locations that Lisa might attend to get help and killed people as he went along. Lisa questions whether people would have died if she didn't run away."

Because the official RCMP narrative is largely a reconstruction of events based almost entirely on two early interviews with Banfield, let's take a moment to recap them here. As I wrote in *22 Murders*,

One was conducted sometime on April 19 by Constable Terry Brown, who, as you may recall, was also one of the two RCMP officers who mistakenly shot up the Onslow Belmont fire hall that same day. On April 28, Banfield was subjected to a caution interview by Staff Sergeant Greg Vardy, the Nova Scotia RCMP's polygraph expert. A caution interview is conducted when police have reasonable grounds to suspect that a crime may have been committed by the person being interviewed. The RCMP said afterwards that Banfield did not take a polygraph. Vardy conducted another caution interview with her on July 28, 2020. Banfield did try to hire a lawyer on the morning she was "rescued," but we do not know whether she was accompanied by a lawyer for any of the interviews. The RCMP has never released a transcript or recording of the interviews [until the MCC dribbled them out two years later].

At face value, the summaries of what Banfield told police portray an absolutely harrowing situation for the killer's common-law spouse. She said she and Wortman had a virtual FaceTime party that night with an unidentified couple from Houlton, Maine. [We now know this was Sean Conlogue and Angelette Patterson, whose ass Wortman touched, according to Banfield's 2018 note.] The occasion was a celebration of Banfield and Wortman's nineteenth anniversary together and was held at Lisa's Bar in the warehouse. Wortman and Banfield told the other couple that the next year they were going to have "a committed party" to celebrate their twentieth anniversary.

"Don't do it," [Patterson] said.

Banfield was upset by the comment and decided to go home, which was about 400 metres away through the woods. Wortman was angry that she had left. Halfway home, Banfield turned around and went back to the warehouse to apologize. Wortman was so enraged by then that she returned to the cottage, stripped off her clothing and tucked herself into bed.

Not long afterwards Wortman came into the bedroom, ripped off the blankets and started to beat her up. "It's done," he told her. "Get dressed."

At one point in the summaries, Banfield said Wortman tied her hands together with what might have been the cord from a bathrobe, but the statement was vague. There was no further mention of the cord or how she became unbound.

A representative sample of what Banfield said took place next is described in documents that the RCMP kept blacked out for many months. I've interwoven three sets of statements for clarity:

Gabriel Wortman poured gasoline all inside the cottage and told Lisa Banfield to grab the gun out of the cottage. They started to walk back to the warehouse so Gabriel could burn that.

Lisa Banfield said the floor was very wet from the gas being poured on it and Gabriel Wortman told her to be careful. As they exited the cottage, Gabriel told her to look back and she could see that he started it on fire but she could not recall seeing him with matches or see him light the fire.

Lisa Banfield said that she knew things were serious as Gabriel was proud of the cottage and the warehouse and now he was burning the cottage.

"I'm done, I'm done. It's too late, Lisa, I'm done," Wortman was quoted as saying.

She remembered seeing Gabriel put gasoline on a police car that was in the driveway but can't remember if it was on fire when they left.

Gabriel Wortman told Lisa Banfield to walk in front of him and she told him she promised to walk behind him but Gabriel wouldn't allow that and ripped her shoes off her feet . . . "now you can't run, you bitch."

Lisa Banfield got loose and started running but tripped and fell. . . . Gabriel found her easily and called her an idiot and told her that he had a flashlight. . . . Gabriel Wortman picked her up by the hair and started pulling her towards the warehouse. Gabriel Wortman tried to handcuff her but only got one handcuff on and then he started shooting at the ground around her.

At the warehouse Gabriel Wortman poured gasoline on the truck outside the warehouse. Lisa offered to move the Jeep and Gabriel said: "Do you think I'm stupid?"

Lisa Banfield watched Gabriel walk over to the bar area and she knew that he had guns there.

Lisa Banfield begged Gabriel Wortman not to kill her. He shot the firearm again and then put her in the back of the police car and then he went upstairs in the warehouse.

Lisa Banfield tried to kick the windows out and then was able to open the glass [the silent patrolman, as the barrier between front and back seats is known] and crawl through and escaped and ran into the woods.

Gabriel Wortman had put all the guns on the front seat of the car.

Lisa Banfield could see smoke and heard gunshots.

Gabriel Wortman had guns like the military people have. He had approximately 5 guns, two handguns with red lasers on them and a military firearm that took 32 rounds.

Lisa Banfield ran and remembered running past a blue shed and finding a truck in a grassy area and climbed inside but the inside light went on and she was concerned that Gabriel would find her, so she continued to run into the woods. She believed that she had a puffy jacket on and threw it in the woods hoping the police would find it.

Lisa Banfield heard shots and thought Gabriel might blow the truck up and she left that hiding spot and eventually came across a tree with an exposed root system and hid inside the cavity.

. . . Banfield's statements to the police were revealed slowly and teasingly every few weeks over nearly a year. For the first six or eight months, just about every newspaper and television station reported each new revelation uncritically. Eventually, Chad and I and other citizen investigators recognized that there was rarely much new in each supposedly new reveal. It was all the Monster and the Maiden tale and nothing about the performance of the RCMP—nor about the anomalies apparent in Banfield's statements.

The temperature that night hovered around freezing. It was bitterly cold, and the area was typically buffeted by strong and persistent winds associated with the rising and falling tides. In her stories to the RCMP, Banfield talked about running through the woods and seeing a truck in a grassy field near a blue shed. In the absolute darkness, how could she see colours and textures? More importantly, how could she safely run barefoot through those tangled, mossy woods in the middle of the night? I've been through them now a number of times—in shoes. The woods are difficult to navigate safely even in daylight. . . .

Banfield said she was there when Wortman poured gasoline around the cottage, covering the floors. If that were true, she likely would have reeked of gasoline fumes. She said she saw the fire start but didn't know how Wortman had ignited it. Fire experts uniformly agree that the method Banfield described would result in an explosive fire and likely injury to anyone who was not well clear of the site upon ignition.

Wortman allegedly told Banfield, "I'm done. It's too late, Lisa." There was no specific timeline or context for these statements. Had he already killed someone, or was he talking about other unknown forces bearing down on him?

If Wortman was intent on killing Banfield, why did he tell her to be careful not to slip?

Banfield said Wortman smashed her cellphone and ripped off her shoes, flinging them into the woods. Did the police ever recover these shoes? Were they tested for evidence?

The RCMP never mentioned finding Banfield's puffy jacket that she "believed" she had been wearing. That statement was made only a few hours after she had been found, and she wasn't sure if she had been wearing a jacket in the freezing cold? Did the police ever find it? If so, where? Was the jacket tested for forensic evidence? If not, why not?

Banfield said there were multiple gunshots fired at or near her on at least two occasions. Did the RCMP recover the shells or casings? Did it conduct forensic testing for gunshot residue on Banfield to try to confirm that story?

Banfield's reported comments about Wortman's guns suggest that she knew more about guns than a casual observer—"a military firearm that took 32 rounds." She knew where the guns were hidden, such as near the bar and in the bedside table. Wortman allegedly asked Banfield to get a gun for him as he was burning down the cottage, which she appears to have done. Were her fingerprints on one of the guns? If she had a gun in her hand and he was threatening to kill her, did she consider using the gun to defend herself, escape or even shoot him?

Banfield told the Mounties that she was hiding close enough to the warehouse that she could hear gunshots. She said she suspected that Wortman was going house to house searching for her. She said that during the night she could hear the police but stayed in hiding because she was afraid it was Wortman continuing to stalk her. After nineteen years with him, she didn't recognize his voice—even if it was over a loudhailer?

One curious thing Banfield said was that she feared Wortman would "blow the truck up" that she was hiding in. What did that mean? She said he had guns, but she told the Mounties that she didn't know anything about explosives, such as the two cases of grenades. Was "blow up" a Freudian slip?

And then there is her story about hiding in the roots of a tree. It's a scene that seems ripped from the pages of *The Fellowship of the Ring*—Frodo and the other hobbits, Sam, Merry and Pippin, hiding from the merciless Ringwraiths under the hollow of a gnarled tree root. Has she ever identified that hiding place to police?

There is also the bizarre and suspicious coincidence of the Mounties going home at 6:30 a.m. that Sunday morning and Banfield emerging from the woods at the same time. Banfield said she noticed the lights on at Joudrey's house and found her way there. She didn't see any police, she said. By her own account she had spent about eight and a half hours outside on a bitterly cold night. She had no jacket, shoes or gloves. She had seen a blue shed at one point and had walked and crawled through the woods and along dirt and stone roads for a considerable distance, perhaps one to two kilometres or more, in the moonless black of night, without the aid of a flashlight or even a cellphone. Going to Joudrey's house seems like an unusual choice. It was a long way from where she claims to have spent the night, but it was relatively close to Highway 2, from which access could be gained to Joudrey's property through Brown Loop. Did Banfield come from the woods or the highway?

◆

As the day approached for Banfield to appear on the stand, the commission was anything but subtle about its intentions. An entire week was set aside. Monday's topic was violence in Wortman's family life as a contributing factor to the massacres.

Tuesday was Brenda Forbes's day. Forbes was a retired army veteran who had lived for twelve years on Portapique Beach Road but had moved out in 2014, claiming that Wortman scared her into leaving the community. Her house was bought by John Zahl and Jo Thomas; Wortman murdered them, then set fire to their house. She was the keystone witness that Banfield had been a victim of domestic violence.

The retired soldier testified over a Zoom link from Alberta. Her lead interrogator was commission council Emily R. Hill, who was a senior staff lawyer at Aboriginal Legal Services in Ontario when she was selected to be part of the inquiry.

Forbes's story was that, in the summer of 2013, she had been told by Wortman's Uncle Glynn that Wortman had had a fight with Banfield, held her on the ground and choked her. She said the event had been witnessed by Richard Ellison, his sons, Clinton and Corrie, and others, including the elderly Elson Sutherland. Forbes said she had called the Mounties to report the incident, as well as the illegal guns Wortman had on his property, but the Mounties had done nothing.

I watched the gruelling three-hour interview with interest. The more the perpetually dour Hill tried to make her case, the more it seemed like Forbes had problems with her memory. When I reviewed the transcript later, it confirmed what I had remembered. The quality of Forbes's evidence can be summed up by the following exchange in which she explained that when she was first questioned by the RCMP, Constable Troy Maxwell said he needed proof of Banfield's assault. (You'll recall that Maxwell had responded to a complaint by Richard Ellison about Wortman speeding around the neighbourhood in 2013.)

"And who told you that you needed to have proof?" Hill asked.

"They did," Forbes replied. "I had to have proof that, you know, the stuff that happened, happened. Pictures, whatever, so . . . and if he had weapons, to have pictures of them. Really."

"And I think you'd said a little bit earlier that you may have received a picture of this assault, and so did you—do you recall if you have that picture, whether you gave that to the RCMP?" Hill continued.

"I didn't give it to the RCMP because it was after all that happened," Forbes said, garbling her words, not for the first time. "And I had it on my computer, but my computer—got spammed and everything, and I had to get it fixed and almost all my pictures and stuff that were on there are gone, so I don't have a copy of it. I wish I did."

"So you don't have a copy of that picture today, is that right?"

"No."

"Okay," Hill said. "And you haven't provided it to the RCMP or to the commission or anything?"

"No."

In further questioning by Hill and other lawyers, Forbes mentioned her background in the security business and how she had once done a criminal check on Wortman and found a notice about him threatening a police officer almost a decade earlier (which we'll get to later). She talked about being afraid of Wortman after she had told Banfield that he had other women around his cottage when she wasn't there. Forbes obviously didn't understand the nature of their polyamorous relationship, and Wortman didn't take kindly to her sticking her nose into his life.

At no point did any of the lawyers who questioned Forbes ask her about the rowdy and bawdy hot-tub parties at her house, which several people told me about, or what Wortman and others were doing at them. "Who wants a piece of these 44s?" neighbour Dana Geddes told me was something Forbes said that was etched into his memory after attending one of the parties.

The incidents of abuse may well have happened, but there was no recent or conclusive evidence of such behaviour. Objectively, Forbes contributed little of value to the overall story, but the media didn't see it that way. "Brenda Forbes Tried to Warn Neighbours and the RCMP about the 'Psychopath' in Portapique Years Before He Went on His Murderous Rampage. No One Listened," shouted the four-deck head-line over Joan Baxter's account in the *Halifax Examiner*. "Former Neighbour Stands by Story RCMP Did 'Nothing' about NS Killer's Spousal Abuse," the *National Post* blared in a story by Michael Tutton of the Canadian Press. "Mass Killer Had a History of Inflicting Physical, Sexual, Emotional Abuse on Others, Inquiry Told," Francis Campbell wrote in the Halifax *Chronicle Herald*.

After Forbes testified, Constable Maxwell was brought forward. With his notes in hand, the now retired Maxwell said he had met with Forbes at her then workplace in Debert. She had not complained about domes-tic violence but about Wortman speeding around the neighbourhood and endangering others.

"Brenda Forbes says that she told the RCMP officer who she met with . . . that the perpetrator physically assaulted his common-law spouse, Lisa Banfield, by choking her while she was down on the ground. Did Brenda Forbes tell you that?" Hill asked.

"No, ma'am," Maxwell said.

"She says that she told the RCMP officer who she met at Debert about the perpetrator having illegal firearms. Did she tell you that?"

"No, ma'am."

"Brenda Forbes says she told the RCMP officer who she met at Debert that this assault was witnessed by Glynn Wortman and Richard Ellison. Do you have a recollection of Brenda Forbes telling you that?"

"No, ma'am."

". . . I'm wondering what you say to the suggestion that Ms. Forbes makes that no one contacted her in response to what had happened with regard to her complaint."

"I would say that's completely false," Maxwell said. "I actually attended Debert. I went out there and spoke with the complainant myself, personally. I remember going out there because, being some-body from the area, I didn't know that the Debert airfield was still in use, so when I went out there it was . . . kind of cool for me to see that they were actually still using the airfield. I remember speaking to Ms. Forbes in a trailer type of thing that they had out there where her office was located. So I definitely know that I spoke and advised her of what my actions were in the complaint."

Those in our group who watched it live that day felt bad for Maxwell. Other Mounties who should have been subjected to hard questioning were given the Care Bear treatment, while the commission counsel grilled Maxwell, who is Black, as if he had done something wrong.

The fact of the matter was that in spite of Forbes's long-ago complaint, none of the witnesses she cited had supported her claim. Even Banfield said later that she didn't know about Forbes's efforts to help her. Nevertheless, that complaint, warts and all, continued to hold pride of place in the pantheon of the commission's preferred "findings."

That week, family members of the murder victims were in Halifax at the expense of the commission to be part of the spectacle. At one of the sessions, a police officer who had befriended Ryan Farrington, son of the late Dawn Gulenchyn, whispered something into his ear: "Off the record . . . We know that Wortman was working with the Mounties."

Was it a tease or the truth? Who knew?

◆

The third day of that week's hearings featured the RCMP video of Banfield, accompanied by Corporal Gerard Rose-Berthiaume, at the site of Wortman's properties in Portapique, describing her memory of what had taken place that cold, windy Saturday night. I had already watched the video and written about it in *Frank* three months earlier, commenting on how Banfield appeared unsure of many of the details and needed to be coaxed by her Mountie guide, who seemed at times to be suggesting to her what she should be remembering. For example, Banfield still could not find her way around Portapique or pinpoint where she had hidden in the woods. She mentioned a house bursting into flames near her. Which one? Where was she at that point? Was she even there that night?

The gaps in her story seemed obvious, but neither the police nor journalists were interested in exploring them. "Spouse of N.S. Mass Shooter Shows How Deadly Rampage Began in Video Re-enactment:

Lisa Banfield Told Police What She Could Remember about Portapique Events Months Later," the CBC's headline read.

The fourth day of Lisa Banfield week was devoted to two round tables with international experts and one local expert, Robert S. Wright, acting executive director of the African Nova Scotian Justice Institute. The topics were "Prediction and Prevention of Mass Casualty Events" and "Definitions and Psychology/Sociology of Perpetrators of Mass Casualty Events."

After that session, senior commission counsel Emily R. Hill was compelled to host a Zoom meeting with reporters to explain what the commission was thinking about Banfield's appearance the next day. "A public inquiry is not a trial," said Hill. "A public inquiry allows us to gather evidence and information in a variety of ways, not just through in-person testimony. This is so that witnesses and those most affected can share their best information, so they don't have to go through what they would in a trial, which can be unnecessarily stressful. Our approach is to get the best information from the witness. Cross-examination is not the only way to get the truth, nor is it always the best way."

The plan was for the family's lawyers to submit questions to the commission's counsel. The questions would be considered and, if deemed appropriate, the counsel would relay them to Banfield. Hill added that Banfield had co-operated extensively with the commission, and every-thing she had to say was contained in the foundational documents and the re-enactment video—"it's available on our website."

Lawyers for the families thought otherwise, of course. "From our perspective it was a pre-emptive decision that was made without consul-tation with the participants," lawyer Sandra McCulloch told Francis Campbell of the Halifax *Chronicle Herald*.

Her colleague Michael Scott, who had distinguished himself in the trying circumstances of the inquiry, said this to Campbell: "If there was ever one particular issue that would cause the clients [families of victims] to abandon the [inquiry] process altogether it would be a full pre-emptive and unexplained denial of any opportunity to ask that witness questions."

The stage was now set for the red carpet to be rolled out for Banfield, but not before the commission reminded everyone one more time about the ground rules. "Our goal, as with previous witnesses, is to build upon what we have learned from Ms. Banfield and others to date to add to our understanding, to seek answers and fill gaps," Commissioner Leanne Fitch said in opening. "We know that there are some people in the room who have not joined us in person before, and we thank you for being here today." The commission's intentions were noble and its methods exacting: "This morning, commission counsel will question Ms. Banfield. In serving the public interest, our commission counsel are instructed to engage in an objective and tenacious pursuit of the truth. As we have stated many times, an inquiry is inquisitorial and not adversarial," Fitch stated. Then she brought up the charges against Banfield. "We would like to note that our mandate, specifically Section G2 requires the commissioners to perform our duties in such a way as to ensure that the conduct of the joint public inquiry does not jeopardize any ongoing criminal investigation or proceeding or any other investigation. As Ms. Banfield's criminal court matters are yet to be concluded, we cannot pose questions about the purchase or transfer of ammunition that remains the subject of criminal charges," Fitch concluded.

As early as the afternoon of April 19, 2020, the RCMP had known about evidence suggesting that Lisa and her brother James and brother-in-law Brian Brewster had been providing ammunition to Wortman. Banfield's sister Beverley Davidson and her husband, Dale, told the Mounties about the ammunition in their interview. And they weren't the only ones who talked about it. It was no secret, but it took the RCMP eight months to lay charges. The Crown had an additional nineteen months to deal with the tardily laid penny ante charges, but they were allowed to linger, which protected Banfield from being asked any questions that might affect her case. So much for transparency. The charges were later dropped.

It was now July 15, 2022. For five months, the hearings had been all but devoid of drama. Hours would pass and daily attendees such as Scott McLeod and Darrell Currie would struggle to stay awake. Banfield was finally going to be seen in person. McLeod and Currie knew it was showtime when the Halifax Regional Police canine units came into the room at the Halifax Marriott Harbourfront Hotel and the dogs started sniffing around. Security that day was greater than it would be when the prime minister attended the final session.

25
HOW SHE CRIED

Lisa Banfield looked beyond stressed as she took a seat at the witness table, flanked by her sisters: blond Maureen on her left and raven-haired Janice to her right. Banfield was wearing a tailored black dress with a stylish scoop neck, and a light-pink blazer to go with her lipstick. Her forehead was furrowed, her fingernails chewed to the quick.

Nick Beaton had been itching to get at Banfield. He believed that, despite her protestations to the contrary, she was somehow complicit—that she had been Wortman's accomplice and had backed out of whatever he was planning to do.

Beaton, his mother, Bev, and a gang of their supporters showed up only occasionally at the commission sessions, but they always put on a show. On Banfield's day, Nick wore his signature summer wear: a black baseball cap with sunglasses riding above the bill, grey-and-white camo shorts and a T-shirt with the words "Everything's Still Fucked" across the chest. He brought with him a poster-sized photo of his late wife, Kristen, and their son, mounted on a board. First he leaned the photo against a wall where Banfield would be able to read the caption: "I miss my mommy ♡ We deserve answers and truth." Then Beaton moved it closer, placing it on a stand near where Banfield would be seated, so that she couldn't miss it.

"I think everyone in the room watched him and thought: 'I wouldn't want to be the person who is going to ask him to take that down,'" podcaster Jordan Bonaparte said. "To my surprise, no one did."

"It was the Beaton circus," said Scott McLeod. "I didn't want to get involved in that. I wanted to fight for the truth. I wanted to grab people and threaten them to make them give me the truth, but I couldn't do what the Beatons were doing. I thought it was wiser to control myself, be a good little boy and just keep pushing when and where I could."

The commission counsel designated to interview Banfield was Gillian Hnatiw, whose day job was as proprietor of a Toronto-based law firm that specialized in sexual, physical and psychological abuse. Hnatiw seemed relatively unprepared for the assignment, scrambling to find documents when she needed them, and handled Banfield as if she were a soufflé. Her questioning was also made awkward because of the commission's protocol that Wortman's name could never be mentioned, even by Banfield.

Hnatiw began by leading Banfield through her nineteen-year relationship with Wortman, skipping over much of what you have read here. There were no mentions of the previous fires at Wortman's properties in Dartmouth, his scams, her two colourful and deceptive small claims court experiences, as documented in *Frank* magazine and *22 Murders* (including the attempted fobbing off of a receipt for a ring purportedly signed and dated by lawyer Tom Evans 113 days after he had died), the guns, sniper rifle or grenades, their separate-but-together love lives, her precious Mercedes C 300, the apparent tax evasion, or all their love notes back and forth up to the end. Most of it (but not all) was condemned to the depths of the foundational papers, there to be found only by the curious with time on their hands. In that way, the commission could argue that it was being transparent while maintaining that none of this information was intended for public consumption because it might be triggering or be considered victim-shaming.

Banfield described how Wortman had brought her two dozen red roses on their first date, which she thought was charming, entirely unaware of the concept of "love bombing" by a controlling individual.

She was even more impressed that after their vehicle was rear-ended on Spring Garden Road that evening by a female driver, Wortman had taken it all in stride.

She confirmed what Rob Doucette and Cindy Starratt had said, that she and Wortman had separate bedrooms; she said it was due to Wortman's snoring, which didn't explain why she often kept it locked. Banfield also said she and Wortman had shared a great life together, even if it was not a full-time relationship. They saw each other a couple of times a week, though sometimes not for a week or even two at a time.

Hnatiw's primary interest was domestic violence. She homed in on the 2003 incident at Sutherland Lake previously described by Banfield's sister Beverley Davidson. "I understand that you declined to report the assault to the police that night," Hnatiw said.

"I didn't," Banfield said, her face contorting, something that would become a trademark that day. "Like, that's the first time anybody ever hit me, and I didn't want to get anybody in trouble. I just thought, I'll just walk away. Like, I'm just done . . . and I was scared. Like, I didn't know what he was going to do, so I just—sorry. I just wanted to get out of there."

"Okay, Lisa. Do you need a break?" Hnatiw asked.

"No, that's okay. I'm good."

"Sure?"

"Okay, yeah. If you don't mind, please."

"Yes, a break?"

"Mm-hm," Banfield said.

Banfield presented herself as an innocent: although she had counte-nanced wrongdoing by Wortman, she had never done anything wrong herself. She said she knew very little about the replica police car. When she and Wortman were in the United States and he would be smuggling things into Canada, she would warn him: "Well, don't get a firearms [sic] because . . . I don't want to be stopped."

"Do you understand that it was illegal for him to have those guns in his possession?" Hnatiw asked her.

"Yes."

"Did you ever think of reporting them?"

"No."

"Were you worried that he might use them to hurt others?"

"No."

"Were you worried that he might use them to hurt you?"

"Yes."

"Can you tell me a bit more about that?"

"Just give me a second," Banfield said, seemingly overcome by emotion.

"Yeah," Hnatiw said, waiting patiently for Banfield to get comfortable.

"There were a couple of times that he—if we had a fight, he'd put the gun to my head to scare me and he said that he could blow off my head. So I was scared. I'm not going to, sorry, I'm not going to say anything."

Rob the Carpenter had earlier recounted ear-witnessing that incident from another room in the house.

Banfield briefly described an angry Wortman firing off a gun inside their apartment in Dartmouth in June 2010, which was around the time when he had threatened to kill his parents. "'If anybody comes, I'm shooting,'" Banfield quoted him as saying. "And he was just pacing back and forth, and I don't know if he was trying to intimidate me or scare me. Sorry. I think it was just to intimidate me so I wouldn't say anything."

"What was just to intimidate you, Lisa?" Hnatiw asked.

"Shooting the gun in the house."

When they returned after lunch, Hnatiw mentioned an observation that had been made earlier in the week by former neighbour Brenda Forbes. "She said that you were like the perpetrator's Barbie doll, that he could do anything to you, move you around, whatever. You were his, nobody else. He had full control over you," Hnatiw said. "That was what she described observing about your relationship. Would you agree or disagree with that statement?"

"I would agree," Banfield said.

"And so that's a fair description from your perspective?"

"Mm-hm."

The Barbie doll comment got me thinking.

"She also described the perpetrator as being very possessive and that if you were having a good time, like if they were out and they were having a little garden party and stuff and that you were having a good time, that he would grab you and sort of put you back—pull you back to his place because he didn't like you having a fun time."

"Yes," Banfield said.

Had Forbes called her hot-tub events "garden parties"?

And so it went.

Seated at her table, Hnatiw meandered from one incident to another while Banfield was bookended by her sad-faced sisters, who, with their turned-down lips, served as both her guard and support dogs. At one point Maureen was chastised for nodding knowingly as her sister spoke. Another time, they all joined hands, only to have someone from the audience shout that it wasn't allowed. MacDonald reprimanded the audience member, and the Banfield sisters were asked to untangle their hands.

When Hnatiw lobbed tough questions about the potential contradictions in her statements, Banfield appeared prepared to hit them out of the park. Hnatiw asked her about the statements from various witnesses that Wortman had used his "police cars" to pull people over. Banfield said she knew nothing about that—only what Wortman had told her. He said that when he drove his decommissioned police cars, he would hang a "neon" safety vest over the back of the driver's seat so that passing drivers could see it, but Banfield said she was never there during those drives.

One delicate issue was the statements by Bruce Gilmour, the Halifax Mercedes-Benz service manager, about Wortman dropping Banfield off in the replica police car. Banfield had repeatedly said that she had never been inside Wortman's police car, only the other decommissioned ones, including one that had fluorescent stripes at the rear.

Banfield denied the incident. "Never happened," she said.

"Mr. Gilmour was firm in his recollection," Hnatiw said.

"I'm firm in mine," Banfield snapped, seeming to breaking character for a second or two.

Similar moments occurred when Lisa McCully's name came up. Both times, there were collective gasps from the audience, but Hnatiw wasn't there to press—that wasn't allowed.

Banfield told the parts of the story the commission had deemed safe for the public to hear. It was okay for her to recall that Wortman had an "ambulance" badge that he used to fob himself off as a former member of the RCMP in "J" Division in New Brunswick. He did that to get discounts and freebies at hotels and restaurants in the United States, Banfield said, but never in Canada. But she knew next to nothing about any other relationships he might have had with real Mounties or other police.

Instead of asking her a direct question and letting her answer, Hnatiw read from previous statements Banfield had made. "In the last year, he seemed more distracted and bored," she began. "The perpetrator was always doing something, but he stopped working on anything . . ." Hnatiw seemed to catch herself, realizing that she was talking to the perpetrator's girlfriend, then continued to parrot Banfield's words back to her: "The last year he was talking negatively and crazy about knowing when he was going to die and that he would go out with a bang. I would just block it out as crazy talk because when he started talking like that, he would just obsess and it scared me, so I tried to get him focused on something else. 'Don't talk foolish,' I'd say. 'That's crazy talk.' I'd try to get him to focus on the positive. I said, 'You have so much. We have a great life.' I loved him and people loved him and—but, but the last going off, he was just so different. He would tell me that he wasn't afraid of dying. He'd embalmed people and it didn't faze him, and this time he told me he knew when he was going to die . . ."

Banfield followed up in her own words, grimacing and seeming on the verge of tears: "He was just becoming really paranoid with the COVID. So he would listen to the news from morning to night. He would talk about the world's going to end. He would obsess about this kind of stuff, that he needed to protect what we had. And again, in my mind, he's talking crazy, so I was just passing it off because I didn't want to listen to what he was saying."

◆

It was well into the afternoon when Hnatiw got to Saturday night, April 18, 2020—the issue that everyone wanted to hear Banfield talk about. By then, she had taken off her jacket to reveal the sleeveless black dress.

In an earlier, rambling statement to Staff Sergeant Greg Vardy, Banfield had quoted Wortman as saying these words at the beginning of his rampage: "I'll be dead and, if you don't run away from me, you won't be." Whatever it meant, Hnatiw avoided stepping into those weeds. In fact, her line of questioning began *after* Wortman had dragged Banfield out of the cottage and set it on fire, because the commission had taken the position that the earlier events had been covered in the re-enactment video, shown two days before, and in other statements Banfield had made to the police and commission investigators. But in the view of many of the family members and the public, Banfield had never explained convincingly what had happened inside the cottage.

The structure of the questioning seemed designed to allow Banfield to tell her story unimpeded by facts that fuelled skepticism about her. For example, long after Banfield described how she had crawled and fallen everywhere, Hnatiw brought up the injuries and trauma that she had apparently suffered: two cracked vertebrae and a right rib fracture. A medical report said she spent five nights in the hospital. One of the first RCMP documents stated that her injuries were minor, but that was condemned to the "unreliable" basket. All of it begged for cross-examination.

Asked about long-term after-effects from her injuries, Banfield seemed to hesitate and gather her thoughts, and then said her back bothered her.

"Are you just talking physical?" Hnatiw asked. "You don't have to share if you don't want to."

Banfield stared.

"Do you want to talk about any other harms or the impact on you?" Hnatiw pressed.

Banfield let out a flicker of emotion, it seemed, but remained mum.

"You can decline," Hnatiw told her.

Banfield almost imperceptibly nodded in agreement.

Shortly afterwards, as Hnatiw scrambled to find a document, a member of the audience played the infectious theme from the television game show *Jeopardy!*. Even that didn't cause the three Stone-Faced Puppets, a.k.a. the commissioners, to break into a smile. "That was an appropriate tension breaker," Hnatiw said. "Thanks to whoever played that."

Hnatiw had misread the crowd. Minutes later, another vague response from Banfield caused Beaton to pick up his poster and leave the room, followed by members of other families and their lawyers.

"I just want answers and the truth, and we're not getting it," Beaton said outside the room.

Lawyer Michael Scott was unhappy that he was not able to cross-examine Banfield: "Right now, what we have is evidence from Ms. Banfield that is entirely untested. Some of it is contradictory, and it leaves us in a position where we don't know any more today than we did yesterday."

Hnatiw had Banfield touch briefly on this and that—a rather condensed and sanitized version of events—but never pressed the veracity of her statements.

I would have asked her: "You said you were in the cottage and that Wortman cautioned you not to slip on the gas. How did he start the fire? Why weren't either of you burned, and why did you not reek of gas when you showed up at Leon Joudrey's house?"

Banfield said she had escaped from the handcuffs that Wortman had placed on one of her wrists, leaving a scar, and had crawled through the silent patrolman in the police car, but in the re-enactment video she couldn't clearly describe how she had done that. More importantly, there was no record of a wrist injury in her medical record. A good follow-up question would have been: "Why would you struggle to escape from the handcuff when it was only on one wrist?" But Hnatiw let the moment pass.

Banfield also said that, during her escape from Wortman, she "started running through the woods, but then they were whacking me, like the branches, so then I dropped to my knees and I'm crawling, and then all of a sudden I heard gunshots, and there was a divot, and I went down into the divot. And I heard gunshots and it seemed like it was getting close, so then I just kept crawling."

The woods in that area are tangled, and the floor is moss-covered rocks and fallen limbs and trees. I couldn't walk through them on a warm, sunny day, fully dressed, without slipping, stumbling or getting entangled. Given that Banfield was in her bare feet in the pitch dark with no flashlight, it would have been reasonable to ask how she could possibly have run through those woods.

Banfield said she heard something like "'Hey, boys.' And *bang, bang* and then there was nothing. And then I just crawled back to the log and just hid there . . . And then I think I am hallucinating because I could see this shadow of somebody, like, with a short gun, like a rifle kind of gun, but I'm thinking, is my mind playing tricks on me?"

Sitting in the audience that day watching her, Scott McLeod thought that what she was describing sounded like it could possibly have been an accidental shooting of victim Corrie Ellison by the RCMP. No other known situation seemed to match that information.

"And then time went on," Banfield continued, "and then I can hear, like, it sounded like a blowhorn kind of thing, saying 'Colchester police' or something in the distance where those bullets were coming from . . . And then I heard this, like, a weird . . . kind of whistle that I've never heard before and I didn't know if he was there and trying to taunt me or—I was just scared."

Colchester police? There is no such entity, and the RCMP would never use those words to announce itself.

If there was one constant in Banfield's story, it was that she crawled from one place to another. She said she had hidden in a divot and the trunk of a tree. McLeod, like many, didn't believe that story. "The so-called trunk was one of those windblown trees that fell over, and its root system was like a flat wall of roots and dirt. There was nowhere for her to crawl in and stay out of the cold," he said in an interview afterwards.

Rob Doucette had spent much time at Wortman's cottage. In interviews, he had stated that Banfield was averse to the cold and used blankets inside the cottage, even on moderate days. Hnatiw never raised the twin issues of how Banfield had suddenly developed a tolerance to cold and had survived the night in freezing temperatures and, according to Leon Joudrey, wasn't dirty when she arrived at his door just as dawn broke that Sunday morning.

One of the most apt commentaries I've ever found about an analogous situation is in *All the President's Men*, by Carl Bernstein and Bob Woodward. The issue at hand was how people fail to use common sense when analyzing a problem. Woodward described getting a failing grade at Yale for a paper he had written about *The Road to Canossa*, which described Henry IV's visit to Pope Gregory in 1077 to seek his forgiveness. As the story went, Henry waited barefoot in the snow outside the Vatican for three days, and that's what Woodward wrote. The instructor failed him because he had not used common sense: "no human being could stand for days barefoot in the snow and not have his feet freeze off . . . the divine right of kings did not extend to overturning the laws of nature and common sense."

As I wrote earlier, that night in Portapique, Clinton Ellison was outside until only 3 a.m. and was treated for mild hypothermia—and he was dressed for the weather.

Hnatiw didn't question any of this, including Banfield's statement that she hadn't heard Mountie Trent Milton's drone hovering around the area in the still of the morning. Instead, Hnatiw seemed focused on constructing a sympathetic profile of Banfield. On the advice of Banfield's lawyer, James Lockyer, she quoted a report by Dr. Peter Jaffe, a Toronto clinical psychologist who is a go-to expert in domestic violence situations. "Dr. Jaffe talks about something called a fawn response to trauma, which he describes as sort of people-pleasing to the extent that a person disconnects from their own emotions, from their own somatic experiences and from their own needs," Hnatiw said. "And that fawning behaviour includes the belief that you can love someone out of abusing you. I just want to know if that observation resonates with you."

"If it what?" Banfield asked. "Sorry."

"If it resonates with you?"

"Mm-hm," Banfield said. "Mm-hm."

"Did you see yourself reflected in that observation?"

"Yes."

While that may be so, I'd talked to people who knew Banfield who thought she was anything but a fawner, and not as subservient as she may have seemed. But it's hard to know how relationships work when we only view them from the outside.

Going through her all her statements, there were a million questions I would have loved to ask Banfield, but the commission was more than satisfied with what it had accomplished. "This has been a very difficult day for many," chair Michael MacDonald said with a sympathetic face. "The pain and hurt here today has been palpable, and it emanates from everywhere, but it's been an especially difficult day for you, Ms. Banfield . . . Maureen and Janice, you are wonderful siblings . . ."

It was Banfield's first and last public appearance regarding the massacres. She left without expressing condolences to the families of the victims.

After the session, Dawn Gulenchyn's son, Ryan Farrington, said: "I don't think that we'll ever get the answer as to why all those people were killed that night."

Lawyer Robert Pineo couldn't contain his anger. In the hallway, he confronted Hnatiw: "You won't shut your mouth and listen to me, and you never have since the commission started. And you never have . . ." His colleague Michael Scott intervened and led him away, while Hnatiw stood there, speechless.

In the end, I couldn't get the Barbie thing out of my head. I had to wonder if the RCMP and the government had taken control of Banfield, just as Wortman had done in the past, and used her for their own purposes. As Dr. Jaffe said . . .

The official narrative was that Banfield was lucky to escape with her life. You would think she would never want to look back on her time with Wortman. But that wasn't the case. At the first opportunity, she had claimed Wortman's body and had it cremated. She then asked for his ashes, blocking his family from getting them.

It looked like Lisa really did love Gabriel. And, the evidence showed, Gabriel loved Lisa back. He didn't kill her.

Banfield's supporters couldn't understand why some people were upset that she had been protected by the government and the police. I could all but see James Lockyer's or the government's hand, or both, up the backs of Tim Bousquet and Stephen Kimber, each of whom lashed out immediately afterwards in the *Halifax Examiner*.

In his piece, Kimber, a university journalism professor, cited all the evidence that Banfield was a paragon of virtue and had done nothing but tell the truth. In his zealous defence of her, Kimber, too, failed to acknowledge any of the unflattering details about her, dismissing such reporting as—you've got it—conspiracy theory.

Bousquet outdid himself, however. Under the headline "The Witchification of Lisa Banfield," he wrote: "There is a campaign of lies, innuendo, misogyny, and hatred directed against Lisa Banfield. The goal, apparently, is to destroy her. After the murders, Banfield completely cooperated with investigators."

In the days and weeks afterwards, I heard countless people discuss her situation. Most had seen the TV news stories. "That poor woman" was a common refrain of those who sympathized with Banfield.

Then there were those who didn't buy in to her story. Their sentiment was perhaps best summed up by Pineo. When I asked him what he thought about her public interview, he uttered just five words: "She cried with her mouth."

Depending on the diet of information they had ingested and their personal and political biases, people saw Banfield in markedly different lights:

1) She was an unwitting victim who was trapped by a controlling, narcissistic predator. She had feared for her life for nineteen years and had no way out. She barely escaped with her life and has been traumatized forever by the experience.

2) Family members of those murdered, such as Nick Beaton, Ryan Farrington and Scott McLeod, among others, told me that they believed Banfield might have been a willing participant or accomplice in a scheme by Wortman, perhaps his faking his own death, but that somehow went wrong and exploded out of control. Although there is no evidence suggesting Banfield was an accomplice, the perceived dearth of information from her— not speaking publicly and hiding behind lawyers—suggests to them that she has something to hide.

3) She and Wortman had a special kind of relationship that suited them both, and they protected each other to the end.

4) She knows the real story about Wortman and wanted to tell it, but the RCMP and the federal government have kept her quiet with threats that she would be charged as an accomplice to the

murders and face life in prison should she breathe a word
about it.

Using Greek mythology as a metaphor for that final scenario, the
RCMP would be Cerberus, guarding the gates of hell and keeping
Banfield inside. The chimera, another three-headed beast that assisted
Cerberus, might well depict the Mass Casualty Commission.

◆

On July 26, 2022, nine days after she had spoken to the commission,
Lisa Banfield, her brother James and Brian Brewster had the charges
against them withdrawn after reputedly completing the restorative justice process. Since no one from the public was involved, there was no
clue as to what the process entailed. The Banfields and Brewster ended
up with no criminal record.

It was exactly what I had predicted would happen when the charges
were first laid, and it reinforced the view that the charges were a strategic tactic designed to keep Banfield from being questioned closely.

As for the commission, deep down on page 254 of Volume 7 of the
final report, they addressed the issue in what appeared to be a mere good-
housekeeping chapter, "Recommendations Related to Future Public
Inquiries." They wrote:

> We also encourage governments to provide clarity about the powers
> of the inquiry while ensuring it has as much flexibility as possible.
> Such clarity could assist others to address a challenge in which we
> were limited by a provision of the Orders in Council . . . directing
> us not to interfere with any ongoing investigations. This provision
> proved difficult because we did not know what investigations were
> under way and what charges were potentially forthcoming. This
> uncertainty held up some of our work and consequently fed a
> public narrative that our process could be manipulated by the
> laying of charges.

Isn't that precisely what happened?

One would think Lisa Banfield would have been pleased that the charges were dropped, but apparently not. On October 20, 2022, her newest lawyer, Brian Murphy, filed a lawsuit in Amherst, Nova Scotia, against both the federal and provincial governments. In his filing, Murphy contended that Banfield had been charged "in an effort to draw attention away from the errors committed by the Nova Scotia RCMP in their response to the events of April 18–19, 2020." Who was going to argue with that?

Both the timing and the out-of-the-blue choice of Murphy to represent her suggested that there was more going on here than might first meet the eye. Murphy was a former mayor of Moncton and a former Liberal member of Parliament for the riding of Moncton–Riverview–Dieppe. While in Ottawa, he had served as his party's justice critic and, as such, had close ties with the RCMP and the justice department. Furthermore, he had just been elected president of the New Brunswick Liberal Party. Time would tell if it was a bona fide case. To me, it looked like a smokescreen, but if so, for what purpose? Optics? To pretend that Banfield, the governments and the Mounties were on opposing teams?

The irony of it all was that Banfield had been fastidiously protected by the federal justice department, the RCMP and the commission to the point that her unwanted victimhood traumatized just about everyone else involved in the process.

As for the criminal charges, those laid against Banfield should be considered as similar to the penny-ante criminal charge laid against Leon Joudrey, but with a much different intent. Joudrey was the sole civilian witness who saw Banfield after the massacres, and he didn't believe what she said had happened. The charge against him was intended to discredit him, which it did. The charges against Banfield, which were allowed to meander slowly through the court system, were clearly designed to insulate her from probing questions by unfriendly lawyers at the inevitable public hearing, which they did.

26

THE IGNORED MONEY STORY
TELLS ITS OWN TALE

It almost always comes down to the money, doesn't it?

From the moment he made the news in 2020, Wortman was referred to as "a millionaire." The novelty factor was alluring. A millionaire-turned-mass-killer made for great headlines. It whetted the appetite of documentarists. You could all but picture Keith Morrison milking the irony with a sardonic twist here and there. But all was not as it seemed.

Wortman had plenty of money. Like most other participants in the buoyant Nova Scotian underground economy, he preferred bartering and cash. If a customer preferred to pay by cheque, he often asked them to make it out to him personally, not the company. He likely would have had two or three million dollars if he had cashed out his real estate and other holdings in time, but he did his utmost to hide his wealth. He told people he "didn't want to make too much money" because that would force him to pay more taxes. His ledger books from year to year were flat and steady. His official businesses made enough money to get by, maintaining an unnaturally low level of sales, profit and tax payments. Yet he and Banfield were swimming in money, as shown by a thorough examination of the financial records for their companies—Atlantic Denture Clinic, Northumberland Investments and Berkshire Broman Corp.

The name of Berkshire Broman Corp. alone made it sound reputable. It was anything but. One of the company's co-founders, along with the lawyer Tom Evans, was Kipling Scott MacKenzie, a known criminal who went by Kip and was a friend of Wortman's. Wortman had once paid MacKenzie to open a secret mailbox for him in Fredericton under MacKenzie's name. In November 2009, MacKenzie had signed over his shares in Berkshire Broman, then claimed that he was duped into doing so. This led to a fight between the men in which, MacKenzie said, he knocked Wortman out. On January 11, 2011, a bank account for Berkshire Broman was opened and the company was registered as both a used car dealer and electricians. You will recall that it was also the name of Wortman's account at GCSurplus.

What would happen to all that money now that Wortman was dead?

◆

At 7:58:38 p.m. on April 20, 2020, Maureen Banfield began a series of texts to Staff Sergeant Greg Vardy on behalf of her sister Lisa, who, a day after the massacres, was in the hospital. The texts seemed innocuous enough. Vardy had asked for certain information, such as photos of the cottage, and now Banfield was answering.

The commission documents indicate that Banfield had been interviewed twice on April 19, 2020, once immediately after being rescued and later at the hospital. Nine days later, on April 28, she was interviewed under caution by Staff Sergeant Vardy. And then there was the video re-enactment on October 23, 2020. There was something about Vardy that caught my attention. Not only was he one of the creators of the RCMP's pure version interview style, but sources inside the force told me that one of his duties was interviewing potential entrants into the witness protection program, the kind of thing the force would not confirm or deny—or would lie about.

In those first texts to Vardy, Maureen Banfield asked a string of questions, some of which seemed unusual in the context of the situation.

"How can Lisa get access to his remains?" Maureen asked. "What is the protocol?"

"When can Lisa go to the Dartmouth home/Denture Clinic location? She would like to get a few things even if somebody could escort her."

"When will Lisa be able to see and have access to the Portapique residences?"

"When Gabriel was apprehended, was he in civilian clothing or in the uniform?"

"Did he say anything? Last Words?"

The next morning, April 21, having not heard from Vardy, Maureen texted him again. "Any word on her questions?" she asked. "One more: Will she receive any autopsy reports or is that sealed?"

Three days after that, Maureen asked: "Lisa wants to know if she was a casualty in this if you're able to share that."

During the interview, Vardy played it close to the vest the entire time, the pure version style of interrogation, never revealing what he was thinking. At one point, he was trying to get Banfield to explain what happened before the killing started. His successive questions were as follows:

"Okay, that's really good. It's a lot of detail, right? Um, so I just want to take you back, Lisa, I want to take you back to, when you went back to the cottage, okay, and you were lying in bed . . ."

"Mm-hm," Banfield said.

"I want to take you to that point and tell me everything, just take your time here. Okay? I really want you to take your time, take me from when you got in bed . . ." Vardy continued.

"Mm-hm," Banfield repeated.

"Until you," he said, correcting his approach, "he was hauling you outside. Just that area. Take your time. Okay? Slow it down and tell me everything that happened. Take your time, don't leave anything out."

"I just remember being in my bed and [redacted] and, I heard him come in the door and I just laid there pretending like I was asleep . . ." Banfield began, as Vardy took it all in, occasionally interjecting an "Mm-hm" here and there.

While the focus has been on what the RCMP asked Banfield, her inquiries of the police have been largely overlooked. In those texts, she seemed keen to know if Wortman had had a Rosebud moment before he died. She also wanted access to his body and the autopsy report, which isn't so unusual for a loved one, but contrast that with her later colourful statements about Wortman's abuse and control. Note, too, that the autopsy report would give her the all-important death certificate, enabling her, as executor of the estate, to move forward.

She wanted to go to Portapique. How did she plan to do that, and when, considering that she was hospitalized because of her injuries? It was all over the news that the house and warehouse had burned to the ground. The only thing that had survived the fire was the $705,000 hidden in a munitions box in a wall outside.

Her question about whether she was *officially* being declared a victim sounded to me like her lawyer talking through her.

One of the first things Banfield did after her release from the hospital was to sell the remaining decommissioned police car that hadn't been destroyed. She transferred it to her name on May 8, 2020, claiming that it was owned by Wortman, who had given it to her as an inheritance. In fact, the car was owned by Berkshire Broman Corp. and she had no right to sell it. On June 30, 2020, the Department of Service Nova Scotia ordered reversal of the transaction.

I got the sense that Banfield was laser-focused on money, which was not out of character for her.

◆

A detailed examination of Wortman and Banfield's finances would reveal a lot about them, but the highest priority of the RCMP, the Attorney General of Canada and the Mass Casualty Commission was to protect Banfield—and perhaps the RCMP—from further harm. As such, they released the financial records in the same way they released foundational documents: in dribs and drabs and sometimes in clumps.

It seemed to me that the documents flowed when the commission appeared keen to make the point that Wortman was even worse than people thought. At other times, the releases trickled slowly. For example, the RCMP's 199-page forensic accounting report, by the Forensic

Accounting Management Group, a federal government agency, was completed on February 23, 2021, nearly five months before Banfield testified, and yet the commission released it on July 19, 2022—four days *after* Banfield's appearance—which meant she couldn't be questioned about it. An extremely critical analysis of the RCMP report was reduced to "supporting documentation" and wasn't dribbled out until August 19, 2022, and so was entirely ignored by the media, which had long since moved on to other matters.

Here, though, we'll cover both the report and the analysis. Let us begin with the RCMP forensic accounting report, which the commission numbered COMM0013939. (It must be noted that there were no documents listed for the previous number, COMM0013938, or the two succeeding ones, COMM0013940 and COMM0013941.) At first blush, the report appeared to be an examination of the financial records of Wortman, Banfield and all their companies from 2015 to 2020. During that five-year period, Wortman's denturist business generated average sales of a mere $166,910 per year. More than half of his profits came from $434,406 he received between 2015 and 2020 from the Nova Scotia Department of Community Services to treat marginalized and disadvantaged people who needed their smiles repaired. That's not enough money to get rich on while maintaining multiple properties, paying business expenses and salaries, and travelling first class.

To his neighbours in Portapique, Wortman looked like the wealthiest man in the neighbourhood, but that wasn't the case on paper. The audit revealed that he paid himself and Banfield poverty-level incomes. Between 2012 and 2019, Wortman's average salary was $39,316 a year, while Banfield brought home $15,288 a year, a total of $382,228, according to the seven years of tax returns the report included. But from December 2017 to May 2020—a little over two years—they and Wortman's companies spent $1,160,621, with almost $400,000 attributed to personal spending by Wortman and Banfield. They were spending far above their salaries, which raised the question: What were their other income sources and where were those records?

the detailed findings in Section 6 for additional information which is not included in this section.

3.1 SOURCE AND USE OF FUNDS

During the Period of December 1, 2017 to May 7, 2020, Gabriel Wortman, Lisa Banfield, Northumberland and Atlantic Denture had combined deposits of $865,591 and combined withdrawals of $1,160,622. Table 3.1[8] provides details as follows:

Table 3.1 – Source and Use of Funds

Classification	All Accounts	L. Banfield Accounts	Accounts less L. Banfield
Opening Statement Balance	$ 470,126	$ (17,588)	$ 487,514
Sources of Funds:			
Deposit - Known	557,944	77,354	480,000
Deposit - Cash	166,455	79,670	86,785
Deposit - Unknown	138,292	-	138,292
Deposit - Lisa Banfield	2,900	2,900	-
Total Sources of Funds	**865,591**	**160,424**	**705,167**
Uses of Funds			
Withdrawal - Cash	(614,306)	(1,776)	(612,339)
Withdrawal - Known	(681,419)	(360,099)	(321,320)
Withdrawal - Gabriel Wortman	(40,314)	-	(40,314)
Withdrawal - Paypal	(19,386)	(1,933)	(17,453)
Withdrawal - Lisa Banfield	(2,862)	-	(2,862)
Bank charges & interest	(1,609)	(2,583)	974
Investment Income/Loss	(918)	-	(918)
Missing Statement	(4)	-	(4)
Withdrawal - Atlantic Denture Clinic	(1)	-	(1)
Total Uses of Funds	**(1,160,622)**	**(166,385)**	**(994,237)**
Internal Transfers:	**(1)**	**20,288**	**(20,289)**
Closing Balance	**$ 175,094**	**$ (3,061)**	**$ 178,155**

See Schedule 1.0, differences are due to rounding.

All Accounts

The opening balance is predominately comprised of $400,000 in a GIC held by Atlantic Denture on information within the financial statements as well as the information provided by CIB... investment was made on April 26, 2017 with funds from Atlantic Denture's CIBC account 101...

Deposits

The "known" deposits of $557,944 are from 100 different payors, the top five are (see *Schedule 1.1* for a complete list):

The forensic accounting summary of spending submitted to the Mass Casualty Commission.

What I found suspicious about the RCMP report was that the federal government auditors tightened their focus on Wortman's and Banfield's personal earnings and expenditures to only the most recent twenty-nine months—from December 2017 to May 2020. Why didn't they go back seven years, like tax auditors do, to find more accurate patterns of deposits and expenditures? For example, I was familiar with the tax investigation many years earlier of a Tim Hortons franchisee who had claimed all his expenses but skimmed huge amounts of unreported cash. Based on the amount of coffee he had purchased, the Revenue Canada investigators extrapolated how many cups of coffee could be made and sold. The franchisee could not explain the huge discrepancy in his financial records.

Even the truncated version of the audited Wortman-Banfield financial records provided startling evidence of Banfield's spending habits.

Her first husband, Mike Wagner, told me she was obsessed with shopping, which had helped to drive them apart. Wortman, on the other hand, seemed willing to indulge that passion.

While Banfield's supporters decried her pay of a nearly static $300 per week at the denture clinic, with a small raise in 2020, they didn't know the whole story. Banfield had three personal bank accounts, into which she made $79,670 in cash deposits from unknown origins during the time period examined. She enjoyed a line of credit backed by Wortman that gave her access to money any time she needed it. She used it frequently. During that twenty-nine-month period, the rolling debt went as high as $33,700 on January 16, 2020, after she withdrew $4,000. The line of credit was paid down when required with fifteen cash infusions ranging from $1,000 to many around $5,000 to $12,000, with a one-time high deposit of $29,545.00. At the time of the massacres, Banfield owed $12,200 on the line of credit. She also had a small registered tax-free savings account (TFSA), which she dipped into now and then to access more cash. For example, she deposited $8,000 into her TFSA on February 6, 2018, and then withdrew $5,000 on March 6 and another $5,300 on August 9, 2018. When the TFSA account was closed on May 1, 2020, it held a balance of $2,969.99, the commission's public disclosures showed.

Banfield bought her 2015 Mercedes C 300 new after being in a relationship with Wortman for about fourteen years. He clearly had enough money to buy it for her outright—it cost about $48,000, taxes included. Instead, Banfield financed the car through Mercedes-Benz credit, which, based on her salary, she couldn't do without Wortman as a co-owner and co-signing for the loan. She made automatic withdrawal payments of $574.79 a month for the vehicle over a five-year period. Those payments alone represented almost half of her reported gross monthly pay, but Wortman helped her out. According to the notes stored in Banfield's phone, in 2018 Wortman had made her car payments "'til the end of June 2018." Later, she noted that she had reimbursed him for paying for her insurance.

Banfield couldn't assess patients but seemed to all but run the other aspects of the denturist operation. In early 2018 it appears she looked for other work, likely around the time Wortman "fired" her in a heated moment, which was revealed in a statement and messages released by the commission. "Nice guy wants someone to run his office—warehouse interior design," she noted in her phone. That rift seemed to pass, and she stayed with Wortman and continued to burn through money.

In that same twenty-nine-month period before the massacres, Banfield wore out her credit cards, one of which was in her name and the other shared with Wortman. These were not their high-flying days, filled with first-class travel and multiple visits to Caribbean resorts in a single season. Most, if not all, of the spending appeared to be by her, a total of $160,099.11, or about $5,521 per month. That included $22,804.36 at Atlantic Superstore, presumably for groceries. That's $786 a month for two people, when by all accounts Wortman lived on beer and takeout food while in Portapique. She dropped $14,246 at Costco and another $6,687 with Prüvit Ventures of Texas for keto supplements to control weight.

In *22 Murders*, I wrote about a washroom on the first floor of Wortman's warehouse that was lined with Rubbermaid containers filled with clothes, many with the store tags still on them. There was never an explanation for where those clothes came from until the financial records were released. Between December 2017 and May 2020, Banfield spent tens of thousands of dollars on clothes, including $20,001.85 at the Winners discount clothing store. Were the clothes for her or intended for someone else? Some families of the victims thought this seemed suspicious, but we don't have enough evidence to say whether such suspicion was warranted.

Banfield regularly visited hairdressers, aesthetic studios, tanning and nail salons, perfume retailers and jewellery stores. She was into self-help books and New Age thinking, cleanses and weight-loss clinics, as her records show. "I quit drinking Diet Coke since Jan 16, 2016," she reminded herself in the notes on her phone. That was around the time scientists reported finding that diet drinks caused belly fat. "I started eating healthy on January 8, 2020." She bought herself a treadmill. She was reading Joel Osteen, among others, for inspiration.

She seemed hard-wired to pursue whatever she wanted, writing, "My life moves forward through desire . . ." Hardly a day went by, it seemed, without her pushing a cart around a store or picking up something new. When she stayed home, she exercised her PayPal and eBay accounts.

Banfield often made twenty-five to thirty transactions a week. She occasionally made multiple purchases—five or six sometimes—on the same day at the same store. The $160,099.11 excluded any cash purchases she might have made. Multiple sources said that Banfield liked to shop at the Lululemon store on Spring Garden Road in Halifax, for example, but the RCMP records indicate that she used her credit card there only for a single purchase of $112.70.

There seems little doubt that Wortman indulged his "primary."

During that same period, Wortman spent at about the same pace as Banfield on his personal credit cards—$168,828.27, or $5,822 per month. Much of his outlay seemed to be for the business or for his home projects, such as the charges for building supplies from Kent and Home Depot. He clearly claimed many personal items as business expenses. His largest single expenditure was on June 12, 2019, when he paid an unexplained $51,219.30 into the trust account of law firm Landry McGillivray of Dartmouth. Was it for real estate, unknown civil litigation or a retainer for criminal defence services? We may never know because of solicitor-client privilege, which extends beyond death.

Wortman had constructed a comfortable world for himself and Banfield, flying under the radar of the tax authorities. They filed their taxes separately, not as a common-law couple. Later, as she fought for what she claimed was her half of Wortman's estate, Banfield said she didn't know why that was. Every year, they received tax refunds. On March 12, 2020, for example, Wortman got a $4,035.47 refund from the federal government.

The release of the RCMP's forensic accounting report on July 19, 2022, generated a few news stories. One long and seemingly exhaustive report was by the CBC's Catharine Tunney. It was headlined "N.S. Mass Shooter Had a History of Financial 'Misdealing,' According to New Documents." The story ran for fifty-eight paragraphs. The focus was almost entirely on Wortman. When Banfield was mentioned, she was described as Wortman's unwitting gofer. Not a single paragraph referenced her spending. The rest of the mainstream and alternative media took a similar approach, not reporting anything about Banfield that might be perceived as negative.

But there was one person who questioned the RCMP's report. Commission investigator Dwayne King had spent the last of his twenty-six years in the Toronto Police Service investigating money laundering and now worked for a leading forensic accounting firm. He reviewed the RCMP report, which you'll recall was issued on February 23, 2021, and wrote an explosive criticism. He filed it on June 1, 2021, but it wasn't released until August 19, 2022, a month and four days after Banfield sat down with the commission.

Again, the timing bears scrutiny. The commission had thirteen months and eighteen days to absorb the contents of King's report before the hearings began, yet it didn't release the analysis ahead of time. It didn't even release his report along with the RCMP forensic report on July 19, 2022, which would also have made sense. The way the MCC handled King's report calls into question its lament in its final report that the RCMP and the Attorney General of Canada were playing games with documents. It seems like the commission was, too. Despite its protests to the contrary, the MCC was its own obstacle to transparency and justice. Its stage management of the releases had the effect of making King's report disappear—until now.

◆

In his analysis, King cited the flagrant spending by Wortman and Banfield, whose personal disbursements far exceeded their individual incomes, and spelled out that he thought both parties were involved in tax evasion, noting: "tax evasion is a predicate offense of money laundering [and] all cash deposits are considered from unknown sources."

King was also curious about Berkshire Broman Corp. The RCMP mentioned the existence of the company's bank account on page 104 of its 142-page Information to Obtain a General Production Order and a Sealing Order, which was submitted by Sergeant Angela Hawryluk to Justice of the Peace Lisanne Jacklin on December 21, 2020, but none of the financial records were included in the report; it was as though the RCMP had made them disappear.

75.5.4. Gabriel WORTMAN placed both parcels into what appeared to be an old laptop bag and then placed the bag in the trunk of his car;

75.5.5. The transaction between Gabriel WORTMAN and Brinks is on video;

75.6. An account for Berkshire Broman Corporation was opened on January 11, 2011 and is registered as a used car dealer;

75.7. An account for Northumberland Investments Incorporated was opened in May 2017 and the description associated to the business is other health laboratories;

75.8. Gabriel WORTMAN has the following with CIBC:

75.8.1. Joint chequing account with Lisa BANFIELD;

75.8.2. TFSA, RRSP, GIC, mutual funds, Visa, and a line of credit;

75.8.3. Gabriel WORTMAN is authorized to use to the Visa belonging to Lisa BANFIELD; OR

75.9. Lisa BANFIELD has been a client with CIBC since 2005 and an employee of Atlantic Denture Clinic and has a Visa;

This excerpt from the Information to Obtain a General Production Order and a Sealing Order, dated December 21, 2020, shows that the RCMP had details of the bank account for Berkshire Broman Corp. After that date, the RCMP and the Mass Casualty Commission said it could find no such bank account.

King's skepticism about the RCMP was so obvious that it would be a disservice to both him and the reader for me to paraphrase what he said. Here, then, are excerpts from the six-page report "Investigations: Supplementary Report," dated June 1, 2021:

Writer's comments on RCMP Investigation:

The documents provided to the forensic accountant encompass two different timelines. The financial records [bank statements and supporting documents] span a period of 28 months [actually 29 months] and the personal tax returns and corporate filings span seven tax reporting periods. Financial investigations may be useful in determining the timeline of criminality and is useful in identifying any changes in financial behaviour. Both of these determinations can offer insights that can be used to drive the substantive investigation. It is my opinion the timeline chosen by the RCMP for the examination of financial records is not lengthy enough to allow for any significant investigative finding, especially when considered against the seven-year timespan of the tax records requested and received.

RCMP Follow up in relation to the Financial Investigation:

An exploration of the mindset of the RCMP at the time of the investigation is required to better understand the rational [*sic*] for the financial investigation and the investigative timelines chosen.

What were they hoping to accomplish?

Why was the banking timeline limited to twenty-eight months?

Was there any request for further supporting documents made by the forensic accountant during the review?

As an example, an $8,000 CAD draft was deposited into the personal TD account of the perpetrator on March 13, 2018. There is no information on the draft in relation to the payer. Did the forensic accountant request a production order be sought on Scotiabank to learn more details about this draft?

If not, did the RCMP review the documents prior to submitting those to the forensic accountant?

Were any accounts linked to Berkshire Broman Corporation located?

If not, what attempts were made to locate these accounts?

Why did the RCMP accept tax return documents from the accounting firm without a production order being sought?

Writer's comments

The financial investigation to date suggests that:

- The spending habits and lifestyle of the perpetrator exceeded his reported income;
- As an example; from December 2017 to May 2020, the perpetrator alone spent $19,386 CAD on PayPal and $23,585 CAD at GC Surplus. This amount totals 87 per cent of his disposable income for the same time period.
- That would suggest that the perpetrator had sources of income that were not reported to Revenue Canada;

- The spending habits of Lisa Banfield exceeded her reported income . . .
- This would suggest that . . . Lisa Banfield had sources of income that were not reported to Revenue Canada;
- There was evidence of tax evasion in the joint personal account of the perpetrator and Lisa Banfield. As an example;
- There were several internal banking transfers from the Atlantic Denture [account] into the joint CIBC personal account of the perpetrator and Lisa Banfield followed by an immediate cash withdrawal of a corresponding amount. This activity is consistent with known typologies of tax evasion and money laundering. These transfers were not part of Lisa Banfield's regular pay cheque.

PERSONAL TAX RETURNS

The personal tax returns filed of the perpetrator and Lisa Banfield categorized them as single. It is my understanding that the perpetrator and Lisa Banfield would have been involved in a relationship that met the definition of common-law. . . . Canadians are required by law to state their marital status on their tax return. This includes common-law relationships which are defined as two people living together in a conjugal relationship for twelve months.

King's report ended with suggested avenues of investigation that should be followed up by the forensic accountants. The first nine questions involved a more thorough examination of Banfield's role and activities.

King wasn't the only one who seemed skeptical of Banfield's story. Inside the RCMP, sources say, some members and officers suspected she might have been Wortman's accomplice, but that possibility was never thoroughly investigated, so we don't know whether there is any basis for those suspicions. Lawyers for the families certainly thought as much. They launched a civil suit against Banfield alleging, among other things, that she "was aware of and facilitated Wortman's preparations, including but not limited to, his accumulation of firearms, ammunition, other weapons, gasoline, police paraphernalia and the outfitting of a replica RCMP vehicle." The case is one of many by parties, including Banfield, that are still wending their respective ways through the courts. Banfield has denied these allegations.

The last question King asked was: "What understanding or information [do] they have related to Berkshire Broman Corp?" King smelled something very wrong with the company and wanted to know why so little effort was being expended to find out what had really been going on with it. It had a bank account, but where? In whose name or names? All good questions, but the commission took the position that Berkshire Broman "did not have any bank accounts."

Kip MacKenzie would not say what the purpose of the company was. Through an intermediary, he told me that "the company had a special purpose. I was there. I know what it was set up to do, but I'm not telling you." Whatever that purpose might have been, it certainly wasn't to conduct a legitimate business. Nothing about the company's existence or raison d'être made sense. It looked like a front company or a money-laundering vehicle.

The activities of Berkshire Broman are critical to understanding Wortman's world, and perhaps his motives. If Wortman had a secret relationship with the RCMP, they needed to pay him. Berkshire Broman was based and registered in New Brunswick. The Nova Scotia RCMP said it could find "no evidence" of such a relationship, but at the same time, it did not find or disclose the financial activities of Berkshire Broman. One would think the RCMP would want to know everything there was to know about Berkshire Broman. After all, the company was the registered owner of the replica police car and Wortman's fleet of decommissioned RCMP cars. Was Berkshire Broman where the Big Secret was stored?

We may never know. On December 20, 2021, the company was finally dissolved.

27

A MOUNTIE, WORTMAN AND THE EVEN MURKIER PAST

After Banfield's appearance in July, the rest of the summer passed for the Mass Casualty Commission with various hearings. The last live witness directly connected to the massacres—Halifax police chief Dan Kinsella—testified near the end of August after appearing to unheroically stall and duck the commission for months before being subpoenaed. Then there were three public sessions featuring advocacy, gender-based and police-related organizations.

It was easy for anyone not paying full attention to lose the plot. Public interest in the commission's work had never been that high. The commission had closed its office in Truro because even those who lived closest to Portapique couldn't be bothered to show.

But there was one more important witness to hear from.

It was Tuesday, September 6, 2022, the day after Labour Day, when most elementary and secondary-school students in Canada returned to class. The three commissioners assumed their normal positions at the draped head table, with Michael MacDonald in the centre, Leanne Fitch to his right and Kim Stanton on his left. Once again, the place was anything but teeming with interested parties. By now the commissioners had perfected their game faces: intense, earnest and glum.

That day, Commissioner Leanne Fitch opened the proceedings in the usual custom, by acknowledging that the setting in downtown Halifax was on the unceded ancestral territories of the Mi'kmaq. There was a solemn twenty-second moment of silence for the dead, their families and others affected by the Nova Scotia massacres, which had now been overtaken in the news by another massacre.

"Today our thoughts are also with the people of James Smith Cree Nation in Weldon, Saskatchewan. The events of this weekend only strengthen our resolve to come forward with recommendations that will help make communities across Canada safer."

Two days earlier, on September 4, 2022, another multiple-victim murder rampage had begun around the James Smith reserve, 200 kilometres northeast of Saskatoon. In many ways it echoed what had happened in Nova Scotia twenty-nine months earlier. Myles Sanderson stabbed and killed eleven people and wounded eighteen others, both on the reserve itself and in the village of Weldon, 25 kilometres away.

As in Nova Scotia, the RCMP response had been slow, tentative and underwhelming. Sanderson roamed around the province until he was identified driving a vehicle near Wakaw, about halfway from Weldon to Saskatoon. A Mountie used a pit manoeuvre to cause the vehicle Sanderson was driving to spin off the road. It looked like another RCMP disaster and seemed to show that, since Portapique, the force had done nothing to improve its response in similar situations.

Unlikely as it might seem, there was an upside for the Mounties in the Saskatchewan events. The massacre and the ongoing manhunt for Sanderson served as a well-timed distraction that drew eyes and ears away from Halifax.

The morning of September 6 was spent on a presentation by organizations on either side of the firearms debate, a key component of the MCC's mission to make the world a better place. The highlight was a presentation from Professor Joel Negin from the University of Sydney in Australia. He was the co-author of a report ordered and paid for by the commission: "Firearm Regulation in Australia: Insights from International Experience and Research." The choice of Negin was much criticized because it appeared that the commission was cherry-picking experts it needed, like gun-control advocate Negin, to prove the case Prime Minister Trudeau had set out to make, that most guns in Canada needed to be banned, even if there was no evidence that legally owned weapons were involved in the massacres.

At 1 p.m., it was time for the main attraction: RCMP constable Greg Wiley.

While the commission had done cartwheels to accommodate the needs of most previous witnesses, Wiley was afforded even more consideration. The Attorney General of Canada had applied for a Rule 43 accommodation for a number of people, including Wiley. This allowed them to do their public interviews in groups, by video, with support dogs or with whatever other accommodation they might need.

Wiley's accommodation had been granted four months earlier, on May 24, 2022. Did he have a health issue, or was there an operational concern? Perhaps the then fifty-nine-year-old constable was working undercover. Who knew? Maybe the attorney general was worried that Wiley might inadvertently reveal something he shouldn't, violating the Security of Information Act. The attorney general didn't have to give a reason, and didn't.

What was highly unusual was this direction tucked into the Rule 43 decision: "the audio and video of the testimony of Constable Wiley shall not be disseminated, released, published, or shared and shall not be audio or video recorded for the purpose of being disseminated, released, published or shared. Any breach of this order of the Commission could result in a charge pursuant to (section) 127 of the *Criminal Code*." The maximum sentence for a violation was three months in jail. Wiley appeared before the commission, lawyers and the media via a closed video link.

Why was Wiley being given even more special treatment than all the others who got special treatment? When his Rule 43 accommodations were rendered in May 2022, three other Mounties—Staff Sergeants

Allan Carroll, Brian Rehill and Bruce Briers—received similar dispensations, but all then spoke to the commission in the ensuing days. Carroll, Rehill and Briers had also served for an extended period in the Nova Scotia detachment, knew the history of the players in the community and had played integral roles in the initial botched RCMP response. Wiley hadn't even been in Nova Scotia at the time. He now was working in federal policing at Toronto Pearson International Airport.

On the surface, at least, Wiley appeared to be just another disposable front-line Mountie. But was he? Or was he some kind of supercop, working in the shadows? Why was the government so eager to protect him? What did he have to say, or not say? And after the ruling to protect him, why did the commission wait for another fifteen weeks—105 days—exhausting its witness list, before it got to Wiley?

Was Wiley a minor witness? Or was there more to his story than we were ever going to be told?

◆

When Constable Greg Wiley talked about his experiences with Gabriel Wortman to the MCC in September 2022, he was recalling events that had taken place as much as fifteen years earlier. He said he had searched for but couldn't find his notes. He recalled no conflicts with Wortman, whom he depicted as a law-abiding citizen and a veritable gentleman. Wiley said he had been stunned to learn that Wortman was the one who had perpetrated the Nova Scotia massacres.

Wiley first met Gabriel Wortman a dozen years or so before the massacres. He was six years older than Wortman, who was around thirty-nine at the time, and so might have appeared to be an experienced police officer, but he was, in fact, a wet-behind-the-ears rookie. Like so many modern-day Mounties, Greg Wiley had come to policing later in life. He had been a farmer near St. Catharines, Ontario, then had earned a master's degree in education and taught children how to read and write. But Wiley's uncle had been a Fredericton police officer, a connection that attracted Wiley to the RCMP, which was looking for older recruits to fill its ranks. In the mid-1990s, the force relaxed its rigid age and physical standards because younger Canadians, its usual feeder stock, had lost the taste for Mountie-style policing. In 2005, Wiley enlisted for six months of training at Depot in Regina. At age forty-three and single, he graduated from Depot on February 27, 2006. He was assigned to the Bible Hill detachment in Colchester County, where every day a half-dozen Mounties patrol 3,600 square kilometres of north central Nova Scotia.

In his first two years, Wiley said, he aspired to trade on his background in education and join the red-rubber squad as a school liaison officer, but that was unlikely. In the past, those soft jobs were used as a landing place for front-line officers to rest and heal from PTSD. Today, red-rubber-gun postings seem to have become a career path almost exclusively for female members.

By his third year in the RCMP, Wiley had become interested in another way to get off the street. In his 2009–2010 annual evaluation, he wrote that he was aiming for Federal Policing, National Security and Covert Operations—including special entries and electronic and physical surveillance.

Wiley's disdain for journalism was apparent. Near the end of his interview with the commission, he said the media should recognize that being allowed to cover something like the MCC was "a privilege" and that "they should be held to a standard where they're going to report with greater accuracy." He thought the media got off too lightly for the mistakes it sometimes made, even if those so-called mistakes might be attributed to efforts to report information that the police were hiding, such as the release of the revealing Portapique 911 tapes by *Frank* magazine and the *Nighttime* podcast in June 2021.

"If there's a penalty box for hockey, there should be a timeout corner for media that are putting . . . surviving family members and friends of the victims on an emotional roller coaster," Wiley said.

Prior to being called before the commission, Wiley had recounted his version of events on two other occasions. The first time was in an interview with Ontario-based RCMP corporal Alan Foster, conducted at the Toronto Airport detachment, at 255 Atwell Drive in Etobicoke, five weeks after the massacres.

"I got a fairly decent memory for numbers, and I might have a chance to show it off," Wiley said, somewhat cockily, as he recounted to Foster how he had first met Wortman in 2007 or 2008 after responding to his complaint that someone had stolen tools from his garage. "I'm gonna guess that his, uh, address was Portapique Beach Road, I remember. Um, I went to the location, where there was a large, um, a log home type thing. Uh, a replica log home or a log home, and it was like 288 or something like that. I don't know whether that's correct or not."

It wasn't. Wortman's cottage was at 200 Portapique Beach Road, as the media had been reporting extensively.

Over the next forty minutes, Wiley recounted his version of what he remembered while Foster listened, interjecting every few seconds with a "yeah," "uh-huh," "hmm," "sure," "I know" or "absolutely." Then Foster "drilled down" on a few things, to little avail.

The one thing that leapt out about Wiley's story was that he had nothing negative to say about Wortman. He described him as "cultured," "polite," "had very good manners" and "a good host." He described Wortman and a woman he assumed was his wife as "a good couple . . . They were nice people, pleasant people and . . . came across as pro-police, um . . . not blowing a horn your way, but you were welcome into their house, and you could talk with them. They would share what he was doing around the house."

As for the theft of tools, Wortman had a suspect in mind and eventually recovered the items on his own. The matter seemed to have been resolved to his satisfaction, and the relationship between the two men continued afterwards.

Wiley stayed in contact with Wortman over the next few years, until late 2011, when he was transferred to remote Advocate Harbour in northwest Nova Scotia, where the RCMP detachment is a mobile trailer. Wiley said he had visited Wortman "no fewer than ten but no more than twenty times," always in uniform and driving a marked cruiser. "I would guess fifteen times . . . Make it sixteen. Round it off, and if the average visit was between five minutes or ten minutes for a short one and an hour for a longer one . . . let's pick half an hour as a . . . median number for the visit . . . I met him for eight hours over a period of years." Wiley had to do it from memory, he said, because he couldn't find his note-books from that period.

In Wiley's view, Portapique was so small and out of the way that it was all but invisible, a place hidden in the trees between the road signs on Highway 2 proclaiming its existence from east and west. "You wonder how it had a name," he said. "It wasn't a hoppin' place. It was Sleepy Hollow."

Although Wiley never responded to another call in Portapique, he deemed Wortman to be a useful contact. "I knew the value of having a few people in the community that you could go to. This is the irony of it: I was going to a guy—him of all guys—and asking, um, 'Is there anything that we should know about anyone—anyone that should be on our radar?'"

Wiley told Foster that Wortman was not an official or coded source, just someone who liked to help the police here and there when he could. But if Portapique were indeed a Sleepy Hollow, as Wiley put it, why would he need to cultivate Wortman to help him in the community? He never specified what Wortman helped him with, just saying Wortman was a contact, not an informant. Wiley may have simply been socializ-ing with a chatty, well-off resident, but there is another possibility: that he couldn't talk about what Wortman was actually doing. Recall the criminal turmoil in the area—Fargo, Nova Scotia.

Wiley's second interview was on June 11, 2021, with commission lead investigator Stephen Henkel, a retired Toronto police detective. It went on for almost four hours, and the MCC considered the transcript a foundational document. That transcript appears to have been done by an artificial intelligence program and is flawed to the point that Wiley complained about it: "My gosh," he said, after reading it. "Like, I must have been speaking gobbledygook the whole time . . . I had trouble read-ing my transcript, and I thought, 'Who transcribed it?'"

One of the first things Henkel focused on was domestic violence. He asked Wiley about his training and experiences in his twelve years patrolling Nova Scotia. "How many domestics would you say you have attended?"

"Couldn't even begin to tell ya," Wiley said.

"Because of the number?"

"Yeah . . . It's a significant number."

Wiley went on to discuss what he remembered about Wortman and Banfield. "I met her a couple of times," he said, adding [according to the wonky transcription], "She didn't stay in the room and talk with us or anything like that. She just bring in a Pepsi or whatever. And I have a chat with him that I feel any weird vibe between those two? No. Did she ever come in with her clothing, anything like that she'd been beaten up . . . or something like that? No. She seemed fine. They both seemed very polite to me. He was . . . exceedingly polite as a person, very well mannered. And so was she . . . like similar sort of personalities . . . I never detected anything hinky."

Wiley's positive descriptions of Wortman were the antithesis of the image that the RCMP, the government, the commission and most of the media were trying to convey.

◆

In his interviews with Foster and Henkel, and before the commission, Wiley could not explain one of the most curious episodes of the pre-massacre story.

On June 2, 2010, Wortman was briefly investigated after his uncle, Glynn Wortman, told police that Gabriel was threatening to kill his parents, who lived in Moncton, New Brunswick. Neither Wortman's cottage in Portapique nor his residence in Dartmouth were in the Truro police jurisdiction, so the RCMP and Halifax Regional Police were alerted. The Halifax police investigated and issued an intelligence report to all police agencies warning them about Wortman's behaviour and his suspected access to guns. No charges were laid against Wortman. Constable Wiley said he didn't know anything about that alert.

Then, in 2011, an unnamed tipster told Truro police corporal Greg Densmore that Wortman had a stash of guns and was threatening to kill a police officer. Densmore issued what he later described as a rare "officer safety" bulletin to all police forces through the Criminal Intelligence

Services of Nova Scotia (CISNS). Now there were two warnings in the system about Wortman and his guns.

Immediately after the massacres, a police officer in Amherst, Nova Scotia, remembered the Truro bulletin buried deep in his email history. A week later, Truro police found their copy of the same bulletin. CBC reporters Karissa Donkin and Elizabeth McMillan filed an Access to Information request looking for Truro police radio communications during Wortman's spree—which was a good idea, since the RCMP was releasing virtually nothing about what had taken place. Truro police complied with the request, and Chief Dave MacNeil threw in the bulletin as a bonus prize for the reporters. On May 29, 2020, under the headline, "2011 Tip that Warned N.S. Gunman Wanted 'to Kill a Cop' Was Purged from RCMP Records," Donkin and McMillan reported:

"This is the largest mass [shooting] in Canada's history, and it's a piece of the story," MacNeil said in an interview.

"What piece that plays, I don't know. I'm not at liberty to specu-late on that, but it's information that should be shared with the public . . ."

In the officer safety bulletin from 2011, Densmore writes that he received information from an unnamed source on May 3 saying that Wortman had "stated he wants to kill a cop" and was upset with how police investigated a break-and-enter complaint he made.

"He believes police did not do their job in relation to this investi-gation," Densmore wrote.

The tipster told police that Wortman was "under a lot of stress lately" and was starting to have some mental health issues, describ-ing him as "becoming a little squirrelly."

Wiley was the one who had investigated the break and enter at Wortman's garage. When asked by his various interviewers about the incident, he said he had no recollection of Wortman's ever making threats against him. "He was never unfriendly to me," he said. He had no notes, and he didn't remember the bulletin from the CISNS. "I wish I could remember."

The bulletin issued by Truro police corporal Greg Densmore in 2011.

Someone who did have notes was Cordell Poirier. A thirty-five-year veteran of the Dartmouth and then the Halifax police, Poirier retired as a sergeant in 2016. He was interviewed by MCC investigators Will Crews and Paul Thompson on January 12, 2022. While it was nearly twelve years after the event and a lot of water had passed under the bridge since, Poirier's notes helped him focus on what had happened back on June 2, 2010: "I was a patrol supervisor at the time, working out of the Dartmouth office . . . This would have been my first night shift . . . And in relation to this matter, I would have received the phone call at about 2 in the morning, which would have been the second of June, and that call was from Constable Len Vickers, who was with the Codiac RCMP in [Moncton] New Brunswick. And he was calling, basically advising our department that he had received a complaint several hours earlier from a Paul Wortman, which I learned . . . was the father of Gabe Wortman [The initial call actually came from Wortman's uncle Glynn Wortman] . . . He was angry at some kind of land deal that was going on between his parents and himself and he was threatening to go to Moncton and kill his parents . . . Gabriel was a bad alcoholic and has [sic] possession of several long-barrel weapons."

Poirier recalled going to Wortman's place of business at 193 Portland Street with another police officer at 3:30 a.m., knocking on the door and having a brief conversation with Lisa Banfield, who described Wortman as being drunk and passed out. Poirier left his card for Wortman. The next day, Wortman called Poirier and said he was in Portapique, but Poirier thought he was lying and was actually still in Dartmouth. Poirier insisted on talking to him face to face, which caused Wortman to become confrontational. "The conversation ended with him saying, 'Look, if you're going to charge, charge me,' and he hung up. So I checked with Dennis Desveaux from Firearm Registry, police helpline, who confirmed that there were no registered weapons to Wortman, Gabe Wortman."

The matter slipped away until a year later, when Wortman purportedly threatened to kill a police officer. Poirier saw Densmore's CISNS bulletin about Wortman and: "Ding-dong. I said, 'I remember him.'" He followed up with Densmore on May 3, 2011, then called Constable Wiley at the RCMP detachment in Bible Hill, "who happened to be a friend of Wortman. I advised Constable Wiley that it was a possibility that Wortman had numerous unregistered weapons at the cottage and I felt someone from Bible Hill should talk to Wortman. I have here in my notes, I never heard back from him . . . Until I finally had contact with him on [June] the 17th here. I [found] it strange that well over a month after Wiley getting the information, he still hadn't had the time to talk to Wortman."

Poirier wouldn't give up. He called RCMP member John MacMinn and explained the situation. "He advised me that he would review the file that Constable Wiley did and determine what action, if any, was taken last year . . . As well, he would speak to Constable Wiley and he advised me he'll get back to me with an update either tonight or tomorrow night. I never got that update."

Poirier told the MCC investigators that he talked to Wiley twice.

"And indications were that he was going to speak to Mr. Wortman?" Crews asked.

"Because he was a good friend, as he described it, right so," Poirier replied.

"He described it as a good friend?"

"Yes."

"And there is no indication that there were any firearms, or he had no indication that there were any firearms?" Crews asked.

"No. Again, going from my notes, not memory . . . He was just relaying that he'd been in the house a number of times and he'd never seen any. So, and that's all he basically said in relation to that."

When Wiley was questioned about this during his appearance before the commission, he drew blanks. He had no notes. He couldn't remember much, not even relating to a statement made earlier by Lisa Banfield that he had gone to Wortman's cottage to check for guns, was shown a pair of deactivated guns—an antique musket and a pellet gun—and then left after spending only five minutes there.

"I don't recall anything to do with whether I was contacted by the Halifax Regional Police or that I would have investigated anything to do with weapons, or that I would have gotten back to him," Wiley told Grace MacCormick, one of the Patterson Law lawyers acting for the majority of the family members of the victims. "Sergeant Poirier's account makes me wonder about things right away when he says I indicated I was a friend of the perpetrator. I would have never described myself—and I'm not trying to distance myself—as a friend. I would have described it as I may be on a friendly basis with him. I have a good rapport with him, something like that. A friend is somebody you see in your off hours in your civilian clothes or do social things with. I never did anything like that ever on any occasion with the perpetrator. I was always in uniform, always in a vehicle, and always on the clock . . . So, at the end of the day, I don't have memory of a gun complaint."

◆

Wiley's incredibly blank memory suggests that there may well be an alternative interpretation of the murder threat story that no one has bothered to pursue. No police force is that nonchalant when it comes to threats against its members' lives. They would take it personally, and rightfully so. The media, however, interpreted the saga as an example of RCMP incompetence and duplicity—a sign that Wortman was getting special treatment from the force. They never considered that he might be an agent or informant.

The RCMP knew full well that its security was easily penetrated, especially by the Hells Angels and other criminal groups. To defend against such intrusions, one way to protect an agent or informant is by creating a viable legend for them. In 2011, the Truro Police Service and the RCMP worked together in the local office of the CISNS. Dave Melanson, one of the RCMP constables involved in the pursuit of Wortman, worked there from 2008 to 2013. There is no evidence, however, that Melanson was involved in the CISNS bulletin.

Having Truro police investigate the "complaint" was an elegant cover story. Recall that the information was anything but solid. It came from an "unnamed tipster." As serious as the matter might have seemed, it was outside Truro police jurisdiction. Nevertheless, as a matter of policy, they would have to create a file and disseminate the information to other police forces by putting out a CISNS bulletin, something a criminal mole or their friends in policing would see. Wortman's threat to kill a Mountie would give him street cred with criminals seeking to "vet" him. That would help to explain why the Mounties didn't do anything about Wortman's threat against Wiley: it wasn't real.

The forensic examination of Wortman's accounts found that on August 10 and August 23, 2010, Wortman made two large cash deposits, totalling $200,000, to a Toronto Dominion Bank account in the name of Northumberland Investments Ltd. He then took out the cash and deposited it into his and Banfield's personal accounts. Commission investigator Dwayne King could not determine where the money came from. It was around the time that Wortman allegedly stole lawyer Tom Evans's estate, but that source wouldn't explain Wortman's anxiety during that period.

Whatever was going on in Wortman's life in 2010 and 2011, it scared him enough that he started thinking about the future. He was stressed, and he visited his doctor twelve times between February 2009 and October 2012, complaining about, as the doctor described it, benign essential hypertension—high blood pressure. On March 29, 2011, he hastily scribbled out a four-page holographic will that was witnessed by Lisa Banfield's sister Maureen and her husband, David McGrath. Wortman designated his "dear friend" and, later in the will, his "friend-companion" Lisa Dianne Banfield as his executor and sole beneficiary. ("Dianne" was spelled incorrectly. The RCMP spells her middle name "Diana" most of the time, and occasionally "Diane.") He never referred to Banfield as his wife.

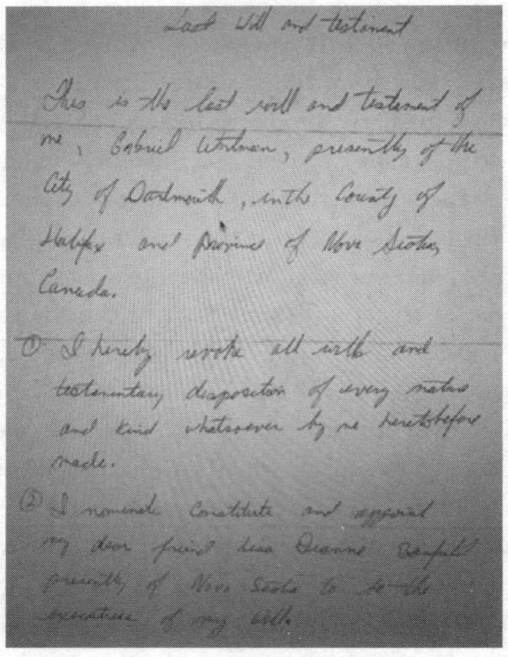

The first page of Wortman's hastily written four-page last will and testament from 2011. (MCC)

Wortman was clearly spooked. Was he a confidential informant back then?

Wiley, though, apparently didn't notice anything unusual about Wortman. Or perhaps he couldn't read Wortman's poker face.

Wiley did remember running into Wortman years later, once at a Canadian Tire store in Truro, and another time near Portapique in 2017. The second occasion was a curious encounter. Wiley had stopped to relieve himself in the woods just off Highway 2, several kilometres west of Portapique. He said Wortman emerged out of the woods on an ATV and the two men had a brief conversation, which Wiley recalled went like this:

"Hi," Wortman said. "I haven't seen you in awhile. You're back?"

"Yeah, I'm working in the area again," Wiley said.

"You should stop by sometime if you are down in the area," Wortman told him.

Wortman then left "because it was getting dark, and he wasn't going to see where he was going on his ATV."

Commissioner Leanne Fitch was perturbed by Wiley's testimony. "I'm just going to be very straightforward in saying," she stated, choosing her words carefully, "part of what I'm troubled by is that your recollection that you've shared with us has been fairly detailed in some encounters that you've had with the perpetrator, whether it was the ATV incident on the side of the road, the Canadian Tire incident, conversations you had with him, descriptions of inside—of going inside of the house. But, yet, this one particular officer safety–related bulletin and also the uttering of threats in 2010 and the firearms and the information that we've obtained that suggests that you were in fact involved in those, you have zero recollection, and I'm struggling with that. I don't know how there can be that gap."

Lawyer Michael Scott, acting for the majority of the victims' families, afterward described Wiley's testimony this way to reporters, including Haley Ryan of the CBC ("RCMP Officer Who Considered N.S. Gunman a Contact Has No Memory of Threats Complaint"): "There are times where what we want from a witness is new information. There are other times where the fact that they're not giving you clear answers, or they're taking a somewhat reactive posture to questioning, tells you what you need to know. And I think Const. Wiley falls into the latter category."

◆

So why was Greg Wiley called as a witness and given special treatment? Was it because he had only good things to say about Gabriel Wortman? Or did he get special treatment because he might have said the wrong thing if asked the right question?

The answers might lie in Wiley's annual evaluation records. Evaluations are done every year on the anniversary of the member's joining the RCMP. Occasionally, they might be delayed a short time through oversight, incompetence or other factors. The commission posted Wiley's evaluations on its website as foundational papers. It seemed entirely transparent.

Wiley joined the RCMP in 2006. His assessment for the period from February 2006 to February 2007 was numbered COMM0063642. In it, he was described as an average police officer, both sincere and dedicated. He had had positive and negative experiences in his first year. He was the subject of a public complaint for making an inappropriate comment "to a female client." There was another complaint against him for what was perceived as inaction on a file and, oh, he accidentally fired a shotgun round into the ceiling at the detachment. No one was injured. He took remedial training. That and all the other issues were resolved.

Missing in the foundational papers are Wiley's evaluations for the two years between 2007 and 2009. In fact, three documents seemed to have disappeared during that period, because the numbering of the foundational papers jumps from 63642 to 63646. This was the period when Wiley said he first met Wortman and continued to visit him. Where did those evaluation reports go? We know that, based upon the 2020 RCMP "moratorium on the destruction of evidence," there is a strong possibility that the force did destroy documents in the case. The very word "moratorium" implies that destruction was going on. Therefore, it's logical and reasonable to ask whether Wiley's missing assessments were included in that destruction. The commission didn't seem all that eager to find out.

In Wiley's evaluation for February 2009 to February 2010— COMM0063646—he was described as a pleasant and helpful Mountie. He was praised for his sensitive handling of some difficult situations, including helping a spouse after the sudden death of her husband. He had taken some courses and was now interested in jobs elsewhere in the system that would take him off the streets—such as the air protection detail.

Also missing from the foundational documents were evaluation records for Wiley for the period between February 2010 and July 17, 2011. This was the time frame during which Wortman made unusual cash deposits into his bank accounts, drew up his last will and testament, and threatened to kill a police officer—likely Wiley—which Wiley said he knew nothing about. Would his assessment have contained clues about what Wortman was really doing?

The last assessment the commission released was for the period between July 18, 2011, and March 31, 2012—COMM0063648. It described how Wiley had grown into the job, was personable and responsible, and had even participated the previous Halloween in a Spook-A-Rama dance in Parrsboro. Wiley listed two career goals in this evaluation. One was to write his first search warrant by June 30, 2012. The other was to develop effective sources and "to have coded at least one effective/valuable source before March 31, 2012."

None of Wiley's other evaluation reports were made public. We weren't told what he did to qualify for a federal policing posting at Pearson Airport. But the evaluation reports we were shown, combined with Wiley's porous testimony, strongly suggest that there was more going on than the RCMP and the commission cared to admit.

28

A "DOCTOR" AT THE AIRPORT:
A POSSIBLE ALTERNATIVE NARRATIVE

When Lisa Banfield's sister Beverley Davidson was interviewed five hours after the massacres ended, she speculated about what had driven Wortman to commit such a heinous series of acts. She offered, "Somebody must have been after him for something, and he retaliated, is what's going through my mind."

"Yeah," said Constable Murphy. "Who do you think might be after him?"

"I think he has to do with the Mafia . . . Something's not right," Davidson said.

Her impressions may not have been far off the mark.

In his intelligence report about Wortman in 2010, Halifax police sergeant Cordell Poirier entered something unusual that has never been explained. Under "Particulars" (the basic identifying information for a suspect), Wortman's ethnicity, height, weight and hair colour are recorded, along with his occupation and employer. Poirier filled out the form this way:

Occupation: DENTURIST
Employed by: DOCTOR 1 BELL BLVD

The address Wortman gave for his employer was Halifax Stanfield International Airport in Goff's, Nova Scotia, the next exit south on Highway 102 from where he was killed by police at the Irving Big Stop.

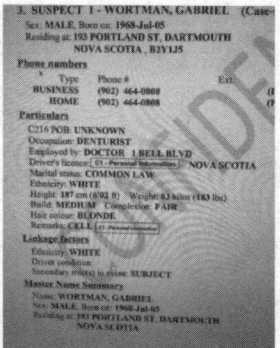

From a Halifax Regional Police document after Wortman was investigated for uttering threats in 2010. (Palango)

At the time, there were several businesses located at the airport that used the same address: the chapel, various stores and restaurants, including Tim Hortons and Burger King, the RCMP airport detachment and the Canada Border Services Agency (CBSA), to name some, and likely CSIS.

A photo of the RCMP detachment list in Nova Scotia from 2009, showing the address of the RCMP at Halifax Stanfield International Airport. The list was found by citizen investigator Ryan Potter using the Internet Archive Wayback Machine. (Palango)

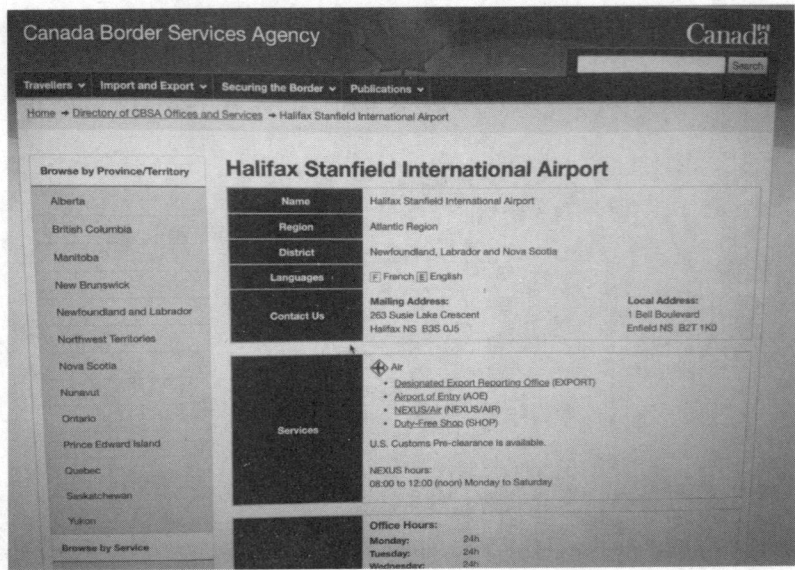

The CBSA address, as listed on the agency's website in 2023. (Palango)

Why did Wortman say his work address was 1 Bell Boulevard? Was this a clue that couldn't be buried, erased or redacted by the RCMP or the Attorney General of Canada lawyers because it originated with the Halifax Regional Police?

Was "Doctor" Wortman's code name, or that of his handler?

Recall that Constable Greg Wiley, in his yearly evaluation for 2009–2010 expressed an interest in air protection detail and federal policing. The RCMP had a federal policing unit inside the airport. Was there a connection?

"It's not an address you just pick out of a hat," said former Nova Scotia police officer Jimmy McNulty. "It served a purpose. It suggests to me that he might have been an informant, and that was a signal for help in that situation."

If so, which agency was he an informant for?

"I suspect he was with the Mounties," McNulty said, "but he could have been a formal or off-the-books informant for a variety of agencies, all at the same time. He could have been working for the Mounties or border security or Halifax police or even CSIS, and none of them would know about the other guys. That's how things get really fucked up. I suspect he was off the books. If he isn't coded, it's easier to hide him."

McNulty said several things make him suspicious about what Wortman was doing with the police: "He was under a lot of pressure in early 2010. It was reported that he was threatening to kill a cop—Wiley—but Wiley says he doesn't remember anything like that. How can you not remember something like that? Cops always remember who threatened to kill them or their brothers. They steer clear of the guy making the threats. Wiley goes back and they're buddies for awhile. It makes me suspect that if Wiley wasn't actually Wortman's handler, he was grooming him to be an informant. Then something happened. Did Wortman get pushed into a dangerous place? Is that why he lashed out at Wiley? There's no way it was over the break-in. Wortman got his stuff back. It was something else. And then it all went away. I think Wiley handed him over to someone else, and he got shipped out to the boonies—Advocate Harbour—to sit in the penalty box until things cooled off."

Calvin Lawrence concurs. Lawrence served for thirty-six years as a police officer, initially with the Halifax police and then with the RCMP, and is the author of the 2021 book *Black Cop* and a frequent commentator on policing. He told me: "I always had the feeling that in the Nova Scotia incident some members had the shooter as an off-the-books informant . . . so that they can enhance their careers. There used to be close supervision regarding informants, but that's gone down the drain like most of the RCMP. If Wortman was off the book, he may not have been given money . . . However, he may have been allowed to commit small infractions like assaults, drugs or gun violations."

Whatever the case might be, the two warnings about Wortman, issued in 2010 and 2011, were good for five years. Before they expired, on March 19, 2015, Wortman applied for a trusted-traveller NEXUS card for himself, Banfield and an unnamed third person, which would make it easier for them to cross the US–Canada border. Even though the weapons warnings were still in the system and he and Banfield had previously been flagged at the border, the CBSA issued a card to Wortman, but not to Banfield or the unnamed third person. No reasons

were given for the rejections. After the NEXUS card became an issue
the CBSA released an undated statement to the commission which was
numbered COMM0053648. It read, in part:

> Wortman applied for his Nexus card on March 19th, 2015. His initial
> risk assessment was passed on March 24th, 2015 and his U.S. risk
> assessment was passed on April 1, 2015. These risk assessment(s)
> included checks in Canadian and American criminal databases, spe-
> cifically CPIC [the Canadian Police Information Centre] and NCIC
> [the US National Crime Information Center]. All indices checks
> were passed.
>
> Wortman did have an assault charge from 2001 for which he
> received a criminal discharge. Wortman was on an order of no con-
> tact for one female in 2002 that expired the same year.

CBSA spokeswoman Karine Martel told the Canadian Press on April
7, 2023 that although the CBSA had "had access to the 'Firearms Interest
to Police' reports since 2007 . . . intelligence officers didn't check for it
because employees who screen for NEXUS cards still aren't allowed
access to the firearms warning because 'it would not be appropriate
under current legislations and rules.'"

I ran that story by several police officers who are familiar with the process. None of them bought it. Nova Scotia outlaw biker cop Danny Gunn
(a pseudonym) said this to me in an email: "That's bullshit! The fact he
crossed so many times is very strange to me. The USA border guys have
access to criminal records on people entering USA and also CPIC warnings et cetera. I would suspect the USA folks had info on him which leads
me to think the RCMP who run CPIC took the warnings off the system.
This actually makes sense. They could have done it intentionally for their
working agent to move a little freely around provinces as well as USA. The
fact he crossed so often, had criminal interactions with police, was flagged
on a national database as a firearms threat also against law enforcement!
And he skates through the border fifty times, seems very, very suspect."

Wortman wasn't registered crossing the border quite that many times,
but he was very active. Based on all the available evidence, it's impossible

to discern his true intentions. Was he a good guy pretending to be a bad one, or a psychopathic maniac who lost his mind? What if it's more complicated than that? What if he wanted to be the good guy and naively trusted the police, who took advantage of him? What if he was a dead man walking, desperate to save his own life, and felt that to do so he needed to take the lives of others? Maybe he was an injustice or grievance collector, as the RCMP initially suggested, exacting revenge against his tormentors. Or maybe his intended target was the RCMP. Did he dress as a Mountie and drive a replica cruiser to pay the force back for destroying his life?

The answers to those questions are likely lost forever because much of the evidence has been manipulated or hidden by the RCMP, the Attorney General of Canada and the Mass Casualty Commission. The authorities proclaim that they were entirely transparent in their subsequent investigation, but the fact that we're not allowed to see everything suggests that something more sinister is going on.

From a journalist's point of view, this is an incredibly challenging story to attempt to tell: there is a huge story here, but no one involved is willing to talk. Think of it as a puzzle whose parts are strewn about a walled room behind a series of three locked glass doors. We can see pieces of the puzzle through the glass, but we can't see them all. Some pieces are piled on top of others. Some are hidden in the corners of the room, out of view. To see all the pieces, we need a key that gets us through all the doors. That key is perspective. With the proper perspective, every piece of the puzzle should fit somewhere.

One theory is that Wortman was a criminal who was being targeted by the RCMP for crimes he had committed and was about to be arrested. That gets us through one door, but we still can't see the entire puzzle. If Wortman had indeed been a target of investigation, then logically the RCMP should have been happy to discuss his history. Instead, it made his criminal activities all but disappear. The police never explained, for example, where his smuggled sniper rifle(s) ended up, or the origin, history and final resting place of the grenades. Disclosure of these details would seem to be in the public interest.

The preferred perspective of the government and the commission was that the massacres were triggered by a combination of COVID lockdown paranoia and a fight over an offhand comment during a FaceTime chat. While this narrative cracks another door open, we still can't see through the layers of evidence or find out what puzzle pieces are hidden in the corners. And there are fundamental flaws with this perspective. One is that Wortman didn't follow the playbook for cataclysmic arguments: kill the spouse and *then* everyone else. Killers typically don't put their spouse on hold until the very end. Nor did there seem to be enough fuel in their lovers' spat to generate such a murderous inferno. Wortman had expressed jealousy toward Banfield, especially in the early years of their relationship, but they seemed to have come to an accommodation—each was the other's "primary," and they talked about "committing" to each other on their twentieth anniversary the following year.

Polyamory sounds like a cool, calculated and modern way to conduct a relationship, but what if Wortman's numerous lovers had become an aggravation to Banfield? Was she upset when Angel Patterson discouraged commitment in their FaceTime chat, because she had caught Wortman with his hand on Patterson's rear end seventeen months earlier?

As intriguing as these scenarios might be, they don't explain the actions and inactions of the government, the RCMP and the commission.

What if Wortman and others around him were police informants and something dramatic happened to knock him off-kilter? Wortman's medical records, as revealed by the commission, show that between June 2018 and January 29, 2020, he once again sought treatment for high blood pressure, seeing two doctors for a total of five visits. It's circumstantial, yes, but it seems to mirror his mental state in 2011, when he purportedly threatened to kill his parents and Constable Greg Wiley. In this scenario, we can surmise that Wortman may have been burned by a blown undercover operation or a series of operations that exposed him to very dangerous criminals.

If he were an informant, he would know he had a stay-out-of-jail card. The authorities portrayed Wortman as a one-dimensional psychopath, but he was anything but stupid, according to people who knew him. He had likely figured out that he could do whatever he wanted—even kill as many people as he needed to—and the government and the RCMP would be the ones with the problem. They could do little about it. The precedent was the Dany Kane case. Kane had murdered eleven people while working as an RCMP informant. When he was caught red-handed in the 1997 murder of Robert MacFarlane in Halifax, the Attorney General of Canada's office set him free.

Viewing the case from that perspective, every little nuance seems to fit neatly into place. Beginning in 2010, Wortman's most erratic behaviour paralleled contemporaneous high-stakes RCMP investigations in the Truro-Portapique area, such as those that led to arrests in the Mersereau murders. From 2015 on, there were operations aimed at the Hells Angels and at Nomad Robin Moulton's activities. In the lead-up to the massacres, Wortman liquidated his assets and withdrew his cash from the bank via Brink's. In the aftermath, the police, the Attorney General of Canada and the commission may have destroyed and suppressed evidence. In this version of the story, there are no loose ends that cannot be explained—the very definition of Ockham's razor.

So let's now draw logical inferences from the facts—and lack thereof—and do what the commission essentially did in its final report: *speculate* a little. If Wortman were an undercover informant whose cover was blown, he had likely been threatened with death, which the RCMP or whatever agency he was working for would have known. Perhaps they were planning to move him into witness protection, but it couldn't happen immediately because of the COVID lockdown. Borders were closed. There was nowhere to go, even for the police. Everything was in a holding pattern.

If Wortman couldn't bear the pressure and couldn't wait, he may have decided to make a run for it and fake his suicide. His original plan may have dovetailed with his previous experiences, as it were: he could burn down his two Portapique properties and make it look like he had been incinerated in the conflagration. To sell the story that he had committed suicide, Wortman may have left his old Remington Firearms Model 870 Wingmaster 12-gauge shotgun in the cottage as one of the few remnants that could be identified after the fire. In that vein, most of his available cash—$705,000 in eight banded and wrapped packages—was conveniently stored in a munitions box stuffed into a hidden compartment in a wall *outside*. More money was stashed at his denture clinic, waiting for a designated person—perhaps Banfield—to come back and retrieve it after his "death."

Wortman had the presence of mind to pack a change of clothing and a brick containing an estimated $20,000 in $100 bills in his fake Mountie cruiser when he set out on his killing spree. It seems doubtful that he was on a suicide mission. More likely, he was planning to survive—and never go back.

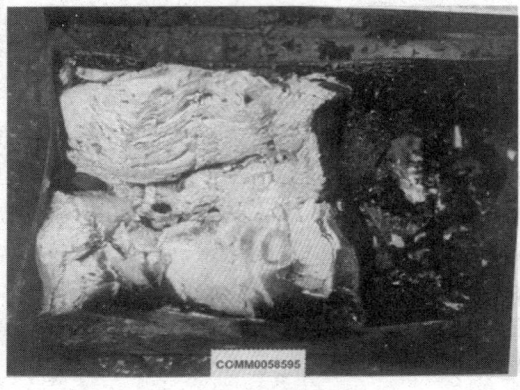

The burned cash found in a munitions box in Wortman's replica police car. (MCC)

But something must have happened at the last minute to alter this plan. If Wortman and Banfield's future was teetering on the brink, Patterson's comment about commitment could have triggered the rift. Viewed in a different light, perhaps an enraged Wortman was not trying to kill Banfield, but rather to make her go along with his plan.

An enduring enigma of Wortman's spree is that at least three of the women he murdered were former or current metamours in his polycule: Lisa McCully, Alanna Jenkins and Gina Goulet. Why them? A plausible scenario is that he wanted to prove his commitment to Banfield by eliminating her perceived competition. The problem with that theory is that their murders were secondary to his first burning down his cottage and warehouse.

Perhaps the fight between Banfield and Wortman was not about a commitment party a full year away, but about her not wanting to join

Wortman in whatever exile he was planning or was planned for him. Banfield wouldn't have wanted to leave behind her beloved sisters and the rest of her family. After the massacres, she told the RCMP that she had feared Wortman would head to Dartmouth to kill her sister Maureen. Why her? She seemed close to Wortman and Lisa. She had bought a property in Portapique to be near them. If Lisa backed out of Wortman's plan, was it because Maureen had convinced her to?

One would expect Wortman's 2011 holographic will to have been stowed in a secure place, such as a lawyer's office or a personal safe, but it was left essentially out in the open, in or on a desk at 193 Portland Street, where it could be easily found. Why?

Some witnesses remembered hearing shouting, commotion and the sound of motorcycles or ATVs on Portapique Beach Road at least an hour before the fires. But we don't know what was going on or what other vehicles were in the area at the time.

Banfield said she had gone to sleep at 7 p.m. Later, when Wortman dragged her out of bed, she quoted him as saying: "It's done . . . I'm done. I'm done. It's too late, Lisa, I'm done." *What* was done? We still don't know.

Wortman set fire to the cottage, then drove to his workshop with Banfield. While he rummaged around in the warehouse, Banfield said, she escaped out to Orchard Beach Drive and fled barefoot to the south, hiding in a pickup truck and then in the woods. If she indeed ran away, Wortman may have been forced to create a new narrative on the fly, to direct attention away from himself.

Wortman was friends with the Griffons, who had been connected to Mersereau and the Hells Angels for many years. Everyone in the community knew about Jamie Gratto Blair and the 1999 murder of Randy Mersereau. Is that why he went to the Blairs' house? But as we know, Jamie was able to call 911. Wortman was likely close enough to hear her telling the police who had shot her and Greg, and that he was driving a police car. He had to realize his identity was known. His problems escalated.

In line with its protocols for blown undercover operations, the RCMP did not call for assistance from other police forces but kept everything internal. In the same vein, Wortman did not kill anyone in areas outside RCMP jurisdiction—although he had opportunities to do so—inadvertently or otherwise ensuring that the RCMP had control of the entire investigation.

The two Blair children left their hiding spot in the closet. They had to move their mother's body to get out of the bedroom. They thought about taking her phone, but left it because it was covered in blood. On the porch, they searched for their father's phone but couldn't find it. Did Wortman take it?

After killing Greg and Jamie Blair, Wortman likely raced down Orchard Beach Drive to Cobequid Court, passing the residences of Richard Ellison and Doug and Judy Myers. He didn't stop to kill them. He wasn't killing everyone. On Cobequid Court, he pulled into the semicircular driveway of the Tuck family. Wortman no longer got along with Aaron Tuck, who had his own biker connections, albeit with the Outlaws, rivals of the Hells Angels. Wortman shot Aaron at the door and his wife, Jolene Oliver, in the hallway behind them. He then executed seventeen-year-old Emily Tuck in the living room at the back of the house, eliminating her as a witness. As I reported in *22 Murders*, sources say he was driving away from the Tucks' place when he noticed someone looking out the picture window of the Bonds' house to his left, at the end of the court. He drove there and shot Peter and Joy Bond.

Meanwhile, the Blairs' two young sons ran to Lisa McCully's house, seeking shelter. The McCullys and Blairs were distant cousins. She hid the Blair children and her own two in the basement, then went outside to investigate. Wortman was likely coming back up the road. If Banfield was where she said she was, Wortman would have passed her hiding place and then come upon McCully, who was found shot near the rail fence at the front of her property. It's surprising that McCully, an elementary school teacher and protective mother, didn't immediately call 911 before leaving the house. But the commission provided no record that she did.

When McCully didn't come back, the elder Blair and McCully children went looking outside and saw Wortman circling the neighbourhood. They hid in a chicken coop. At one point, they saw the interior light in McCully's car go on and the brake lights activate. Who was in the car?

Before leaving the area, Wortman likely noticed that the Gulenchyns had seen him, too. He killed them and set their house on fire. He would have known by then that the police were on their way. He parked his car in the Gulenchyns' driveway, likely pondering his next move. David Faulkner drove by, noticed the police car in the driveway to Wortman's warehouse and continued on to Leon Joudrey's house. The lights were off and he decided not to rouse Joudrey. Meanwhile, neighbour Andrew MacDonald (commission chair Michael MacDonald's nephew) and his wife, Kate, pulled up in front of the Gulenchyns' house. They were investigating the source of the fire that Kate had seen raging from her bedroom window. Wortman drove up beside them and fired a couple of shots at Andrew, inflicting a minor wound. By this time, Faulkner was behind them and heard the *bang, bang,* but he couldn't piece together what was happening.

MacDonald sped north on Orchard Beach Drive and then west to where it intersects with Portapique Beach Road. He was followed by Wortman and then Faulkner. Allison Francis, who lived across from the Gulenchyns with her husband, Bjorn Merzbach, tried reaching the Gulenchyns. There was no answer. She called 911: "I hear shots, or fireworks, or something. Three vehicles leaving Orchard Beach Drive. I hear the fire alarms. They're not answering. I texted . . . Just as I was calling you there, somebody's screaming, like, kids sounding, then three vehicles just left."

MacDonald went right toward the highway, where he could see the flashing lights from the first RCMP cars bouncing off the trees around the bend in the road. Wortman could see them, too. He slammed on his brakes at the intersection, something that Jerry and Florie Murphy heard from their house down the road. His sudden stop surprised Faulkner, who had to drive up on the grass of the house at the corner to avoid a collision. The replica police car was Wortman's get-out-of-Portapique ticket, but by then he may not have been sure that he could finesse his way out. If he had tried, he likely would easily have gotten the drop on the Mountie or Mounties up the road, but it seems he didn't want to engage them. He headed south on Portapique Beach Road. The time was about 10:28 p.m.

Wortman drove past his burning cottage and other occupied houses on Portapique Beach Road, including the Murphys'. At the bottom of the road, he went to the Zahl-Thomas house. Gunshots were heard around that time from that approximate area.

This description of the order in which Wortman murdered his victims largely conforms with the commission's version of the sequence. The MCC suspected that Zahl and Thomas were killed after the RCMP had arrived on the scene. To reiterate: like me, the commission could only *speculate* about most things, because there were no witnesses other than the few we have already met. So it had a lot of wiggle room.

Where the official story became murkiest was when the MCC tried to explain what happened between 10:26 and 10:45 p.m., the nineteen minutes between the first Mounties' arrival in Portapique and Wortman supposedly slipping out of the area unseen. The commission posited that he killed Zahl and Thomas around 10:30 and lit their house on fire; the problem with that theory is that the Murphys passed the house almost an hour later, and the fire was still contained inside. The commission concluded that Wortman got back into his fake police car and, as the RCMP described, drove down a narrow one-lane road through the woods that led back to his warehouse. I drove down that path. It was extremely narrow and rough. I was in an SUV and barely cleared some spots. Even though he knew the path, I wondered how Wortman could manoeuvre his way through in a Police Interceptor, which sits low to the ground, and not get his car dirty. Photos of his vehicle the next day showed that it was relatively shiny and clean, considering all the dirt roads and fields that the RCMP said he had driven through.

There was another significant unaddressed problem with the official story. Wortman knew the RCMP had been called by Jamie Blair and likely the MacDonalds as they raced away. Both calls came from Orchard Beach Drive. The police would normally head immediately to the source of 911 calls. So why would Wortman drive back across his fields to emerge exactly where Lisa McCully's body lay? Unless he had a radio, which the commission insisted he didn't, he couldn't have known there were no Mounties on Orchard Beach Drive. Assuming a normal emergency response, Wortman would expect the entire road to be crawling with Mounties, wouldn't he?

Given that, it seems plausible that Mounties, not Wortman, went down Orchard Beach Drive, encountered Corrie Ellison standing near the gate of Wortman's warehouse and, in a panic, shot him. The ballistic evidence was rather vague, leading to all kinds of speculation about what really happened. The RCMP and the commission kept everything close to the vest. Even the autopsy report, which detailed the wounds inflicted on Ellison appeared to have been accidentally unredacted and released before it was redacted again, but not before citizen investigator Ryan Potter had taken a copy. The official story was that Wortman had gotten out of his car to finish Ellison off. As one of my police sources put it: "Why would he have to finish him off?"

Wortman did not escape through the blueberry field road, as the RCMP posited, but drove right past the two distracted Mounties at the intersection of Portapique Beach Road and Highway 2. He then supposedly drove to the old Debert air strip and spent the night there. Why there? Was he expecting a rescue mission by air? Planes could still land there. The next morning, he knew the gig was up. The public knew his name. The RCMP, lackadaisically so, were looking for him. When he was finally killed, he was one highway exit north of Halifax International Airport. Was he headed there, back to 1 Bell Boulevard, or was he trying to get back into the city to burn down more buildings or kill Banfield's sister? Did Wortman do all these horrible things in a mad rage after an incidence of domestic violence or was he seeking revenge against the RCMP for ruining his life? We'll likely never know unless someone pops out of the Mountie woodwork and shows us everything.

The RCMP and the commission went out of their respective ways to *not* find any meaningful links between Wortman and criminals, even though his friend and so-called gardener, Peter Griffon, was a convicted drug trafficker with ties to Mexican cartels and the Hells Angels. In the intervening years since *22 Murders* was published, I continued to keep an eye on Griffon's activities. In early 2024, he was seen walking down a street with a ranking member of the Sea Titans MC, a Hells Angels puppet club in Nova Scotia. Shortly afterward, the Sea Titans were dissolved and its members were absorbed into the Red Devils, the primary support club of the Angels.

Shying away from what really happened before, during and after that terrible weekend in April 2020 seemed to be the goal of the RCMP and the media who covered the story. Scenarios and evidence that should have been questioned never were. As for the commission, it never investigated these discrepancies and closed its hearings on September 23, 2022. We waited until March 2023 for the final report, and then that was it.

◆

Throughout the process, the RCMP shielded *all* its officers and members from deep scrutiny, or for some, any scrutiny at all. Many were allowed to retire. Senior officers who were intimately involved in the case were transferred or given promotions before the commission hearings even began. After the massacres, the RCMP was rendered nearly catatonic in Nova Scotia. It didn't mount a single successful major case for years. What could those officers possibly have done right to warrant immediate, financially rewarding bumps? Was it because they closed ranks and kept their mouths shut?

As I wrote this, four years later, Brian Brennan was still in charge of contract policing. Darren Campbell was running operations in New Brunswick. The same gang was still in control of the overall story.

Brennan's subordinate for the previous past eight years or so, Dennis Daley, who was the last Mountie to be interviewed by the commission, on September 15, was promoted to assistant commissioner and took command of Nova Scotia. A few months later, he boasted that the Nova Scotia RCMP had gotten "its swagger back."

Nobody within the RCMP who was involved in the massacres paid a price for what happened that weekend and afterwards—except, perhaps, in terms of their mental health. "After Portapique, about seventy Mounties took the summer off work, and some even longer than that, claiming that they were suffering from post-traumatic stress disorder," my friend, a former RCMP deputy commissioner, told me. "I'm sorry, but I don't buy it. They fumbled the response. Those seventy Mounties didn't engage Wortman. They didn't see anything that police officers don't regularly see. All those seventy Mounties were not involved with the bodies. I believe the stress they were suffering from was due to the fact that they couldn't tell the truth about what really had happened. That's what was killing them."

Apologists for the RCMP were prepared to write off the debacle as an extraordinary isolated incident that could happen to any police force. Nothing to see here. Move on. In reality, it was an indictment of the RCMP policing model, from bottom to top—which, in spite of the dearth of evidence it had presented in public, the commission seemed to acknowledge in its final report.

Recommendations about how to fix the RCMP have been a regular feature of Canadian politics for half a century, and almost all of them have been ignored. The true test of the power of the latest recommendations, from the MCC, lay in how they were received by governments. Over the ensuing weeks, months and years, not a single pertinent question about the RCMP's epic failure was asked in either Parliament or the Nova Scotia House of Assembly by any politician. Everyone thought as one, as if Canada were being run by a cult. In fact, most politicians continued to support the RCMP as a contract police force across Canada: "We love our Mounties."

Five years ago, my antennae detected that something was amiss in the official narrative of the massacres. My suspicion was triggered by the actions of both government and the RCMP—it was obvious that their primary focus was on not causing further trauma to the families of the victims. Since when do the government and the police really care about the feelings of individuals? Their novel approach—viewing the RCMP's failures through a feminist lens—sealed the deal for me. The government had deftly employed the politics of the day to serve as a screen for its true activities. In my investigation and these pages, I've tried to bypass those sentiments, lean into my experience and knowledge, and deal with the facts at hand without allowing my emotions, fear or current political fads to dictate the course of my investigation. The families of the victims deserve the truth. So do the members of the public, who pay the bills. The story as told by the RCMP, the Mass Casualty

Commission and politicians is full of holes. It doesn't answer the question about a Big Secret, but all the finagling, subterfuge and loose ends shout that there is one.

Fabula ipsa loquitur.

EPILOGUE

As I write this, the fifth anniversary of the massacres is a few months away. Over those years, as I have chased, talked about and written about this story, many people have asked me if I am crazy to take on the RCMP. "Aren't you afraid?" is one question I've been asked many times. Others say, "You'd better get some dogs." I've also heard "Arm up" a few times.

I'm not easily scared. I've seen just about every dirty trick the RCMP can pull on a person. Character assassination is the force's favourite weapon. It prefers to smear and discredit a critic and kill their reputation, not their body.

But I've received threats, most of which I reported publicly, usually immediately. That alone generally served as warning enough for the perpetrator to back off. There was one incident, however, that I tried not to talk about or report because it went to the next level. It happened three weeks to the day after Lisa Banfield appeared before the commission.

In retrospect, in the days before Friday, August 5, 2022, the people around me were spookily prescient.

"Do you ever fear for your lives?" our friend Lyndsay Fraser asked over dinner with her husband, Scott, at the Seaside Shanty in Chester Basin, near where we lived, the night before.

"It gets scary sometimes," Sharon said, appearing to brush it off.

The next night, two more people echoed Lyndsay's concern.

John Fraser (no relation to Lyndsay and Scott) is a distinguished and worldly colleague from my days at the *Globe and Mail*. He was a renowned China correspondent and a long-time master at prestigious Massey College at the University of Toronto. "Palango, I actually worry about you these days. Do you watch your back or am I being paranoid?" he wrote in an email. "You are revealing stuff some people just don't want to hear or know, but surely it will explode sometime soon . . . Take care of yourself please. It's not easy being the sole investigative reporter left in Canada."

"Make that sole investigative glass artist, please!" I replied, pointing out that I had enjoyed another career over the past two decades before being dragged back into journalism.

A few minutes later, I received a message from lawyer Shirley Heafey, who had spent ten years as chair of the Public Complaints Commission. She was still active in policing and sat on the police services board in the Vancouver suburb of New Westminster. Heafey's stories about her experiences with the RCMP and the federal government, if ever published, could fill a shelf in a library.

Heafey had often expressed her frustrations to me about both the RCMP and the Mass Casualty Commission's apparent lack of curiosity and desperate avoidance of controversy. For more than a year, she had fretted about my personal safety. "It appears you are a thorn in the side of many people including journalists, the MCC, the RCMP, lawyers at the MCC, and likely lots of politicians. Have I missed anyone??? I don't know where to begin to try to clarify the mess that has been created by all the parties involved," she wrote.

"Shirley," I wrote back. "You have to admit that, until now, they have not had one of their cover-ups reported in real time as it unfolded with play-by-play commentary. That's got to be unnerving for them."

"The work you are doing at raising all the questions that are being ignored and relegated to the dust bin by the MCC is worthy of an Order of Canada!! I know that people who don't know, don't want to know and those who are too blind to bother paying attention to the story you are painting of the RCMP prefer to believe this story is too incredible to be true. The MCC members are so clearly in over their heads! It has become farcical. You and yours have my continued admiration for the courage you have shown and continue to show in this pathetic 'opera'!"

"Order of Canada? As has been said already by WC Fields, I believe: 'Any club that would have me as a member isn't worth belonging to!'" I flippantly replied.

The time of that message was 9:57 p.m., August 5, 2022, on an unusually hot summer night for the South Shore of Nova Scotia.

For Sharon and me, Friday night was reserved for *Real Time with Bill Maher*, which came on at 11 p.m. The guest that evening was actor David Duchovny, star of the weird and wonderful TV series *The X-Files*. It was after midnight when I plugged our cellphones into a charger in the kitchen. The ringers were usually muted. We also had land lines in the house. We headed upstairs to bed.

For you to fully appreciate what is to follow, I must make a confession about my bedtime attire that is not known outside the confines of my family. In addition to my other, previously documented health issues, including heart attacks and a bout with cancer, I'd had an operation in August 1986 that forced me to change my choice of sleepwear. I had undergone an emergency appendectomy at a hospital in rural Renfrew, Ontario, by a surgeon whose first name, appropriately enough, was Lance. In his rush to save my life, when I was still in the process of being anaesthetized, I could see Lance, gowned and masked, standing between my legs with a scalpel poised. "Can you let me go to sleep first, please?" I asked.

He did, but barely. He cut me from north to south in a long slash that ran just east of my belly button and down through my belt line. The resulting scar made it impossible for me to wear anything tight around my waist for a long time. I switched to nightshirts. Nineteen years later, courtesy of a pair of surgeons in Halifax, I doubled down on massive abdominal incisions in another death-defying medical procedure. For that performance, I earned an even longer scar that ran parallel to the first one and through the waistline.

My man-nighties, as I called them, became a running joke in the family. Years ago, my daughter, Lindsay, and her husband, Keith, then an avid moose hunter, bought me a ridiculous-looking lemongrass-coloured jersey nightshirt with a cartoonish wide-eyed giant brown moose on it and the caption "I Don't Moose Around." Sharon hated it, but it was comfortable and perfectly suited to hot nights like that one.

"It's a perfect night for the moose," I said, teasing her.

We had been lying in bed for a few minutes when Sharon heard something. She was always hearing things in the night, even more so in the past couple of years. My hearing was dulled by age and too many nights sitting near giant amplifiers in smoky bars, so I couldn't hear a thing.

Finally, she took executive action. It was exactly 12:30 a.m. She got out of bed and headed downstairs. She returned a few seconds later, pushing her cellphone toward me. She had a fearful look in her eyes. "It's Rob the Carpenter," she said. "He said: 'Hi, Sharon. I'm down the road and coming to your place.' And then he let out a dirty laugh."

"Shit," I said.

In a hurried moment weeks earlier, while my phone was charging, I had used Sharon's to send Rob Doucette a message. Now that he had her number, he was using it to get to me.

I didn't bother lifting my head off the pillow as I put Sharon's phone to my ear.

"Hey, Rob, what can I do for you?" I asked.

"Why aren't you answering my calls?" he asked.

"Well, it's late. I was half asleep and I didn't hear the phone ring."

"Why should you get to sleep when I can't?" he said, with a hint of menace in his voice.

Sharon was getting more and more agitated. "He's coming to the house," she said. "He's right outside."

"Where are you?" I asked in a matter-of-fact tone.

"I'm six miles from your house," he said, "and headed your way."

"If you're six miles away, you are in the middle of nowhere," I said. "So where are you, really?"

"Hubbards," he said.

Hubbards is a scenic village located on St. Margaret's Bay, an eighteen- to twenty-minute drive to the east along Highway 103, on the way to Halifax. I knew that Doucette didn't drive, and I wondered if he was bluffing.

"How did you get there?" I asked.

"None of your business," he said.

It was obvious that he had been drinking. I was trying to assess the situation, his actual location and the threat level. Sharon, meanwhile, just wanted to get out of the house.

"Let's go," she said. "NOW!"

"He's not here," I mouthed.

In the twenty-five years that I'd known Sharon, I'd never seen her in panic-stricken flight mode. She was determined to leave right away, but I was more concerned with neutralizing Doucette. I didn't want to run out of the house and right into him, or whomever might be with him.

His complaint was about the series of three stories about him that we had published a month earlier in *Frank*.

"You're a liar," he said repeatedly.

"What did I lie about?" I asked as calmly as possible.

"You made it look like I was helping Gabriel smuggle things across the border."

"I didn't say that," I said. "What I reported is what you said on camera: that you went to the border with him a couple of times but didn't cross it with him. He came back with guns and stuff and picked you up. That's what you said."

"You should have let me view the interview before you put it online."

"That wasn't going to happen," I said.

"You said I built the hidden compartment in Gabriel's truck," he said. "I didn't. It was already there."

"Rob," I said, "in the interviews, you said you built it. I later phoned you back for clarification and asked you who had welded it together, and you said that it wasn't welded but bolted together."

"I didn't do that," Rob said. "I didn't do anything wrong. I didn't do anything wrong."

Then the conversation took a dark turn. Sharon could only hear my side of it and was so stressed that she was clutching her chest as if on the verge of a heart attack. As bad as I felt for her, I couldn't hang up on him.

"My life is so fucked up now because of all this," he said. "I have to carry a gun on me. I almost shot someone yesterday over this bullshit. Can I bring the gun to you right now and you can keep it?"

"No, Rob, that ain't gonna happen. I'm not meeting you to get your gun." The comment made Sharon's green eyes almost explode out of her head.

"I know you told me you've had dealings with other hit men, but they ain't me," he said now. "When you disappear, I want you to know that it's going to be me. And they'll never find you."

It sounded like drunk talk, but even so, he appeared to be tapping into his inner thoughts. I could hear him pacing around a room. It sounded like he was wearing hard heels—maybe cowboy boots. The floor sounded like hardwood. There was an echo off the walls, like there was no furniture. I had been to the dingy motel room where he lived in Dartmouth. It was full of furniture and had curtains. It didn't sound like he was there. So where was he?

"I don't like to kill people, but I think I'm going to have to start killing some people," he said in a chillingly calm tone of voice. "I'm going to do it even better than Gabriel did."

"What do you mean?" I asked, trying to get him to elaborate.

"I told you," he said with emphasis. "I'm going to do it better than Gabriel."

Then he seemed to walk away from the phone and around the room. I tried to hear what he was muttering. He began cursing at Wortman. "Look what you've done to me, you white bastard," I could hear him say. "You've ruined my life, Gabriel. You've ruined my life . . ."

He seemed to be working himself up to something. I feared he might shoot himself, or someone else. In all, I spent twenty-six minutes listening to him before I disconnected the call.

Sharon was desperate to leave the house. "Let's go now," she demanded.

She wouldn't even let me put clothes on. I grabbed the shorts I'd worn that day. As she literally dragged me out of the bedroom, I reached for a short-sleeved shirt and slipped on a pair of sandals. I was still wearing the moose man-nightie, which I had forgotten about in the turmoil.

Most people in such a situation would lock their doors, call the police and wait for rescue. But in many rural areas in Canada, such as our community, we have no provincial or municipal police to rely on; instead, we get twenty hours of RCMP policing a day—and even then, not all the time. If you call the police for help, there's no guarantee they'll get to you in a jiffy. It's a bit of a crapshoot, and this was not the time to gamble.

Sharon wasn't waiting a second more. She wanted to hit the road immediately. She didn't know where she wanted to go, only that she wanted to go somewhere, anywhere, that wasn't our home. "Drive," she said. "Just DRIVE."

We lived two kilometres up a dead-end road. The Chester RCMP detachment was at the next exit to the east off Highway 103, about a seven-minute drive. I headed that way, causing Sharon even more agita.

"If you complain to the police, won't that just make him madder?" she asked.

"Maybe. I really don't want to have him charged. I feel bad having to do it, but after the things he said, I think we have no other choice," I said. "If he goes out and does something, then it's on us."

It was about 1:10 a.m. when we arrived at the detachment, an exposed-cinder-block building with an azure-blue roof and cladding. There were five cruisers parked in the lot, but no one was home. Not a Mountie in sight. Thank the Invisible Man in the Sky that we didn't call 911 and count on a prompt response.

The next option was Bridgewater, a twenty-five-minute drive to the west. The Mountie base in Lunenburg County was actually in Cooksville, just over the line from Bridgewater, a town of almost 9,000 that has its own twenty-five-officer municipal force.

It had been 839 days since Gabriel Wortman was shot dead by the Mounties. Almost from that moment, I had come out of retirement and begun chasing the story. Along the way, I had avoided direct contact with the Mounties. Now I was showing up at their doorstep, a dishevelled seventy-two-year-old man wearing a lemongrass moose mannightie, along with his obviously distressed sixty-six-year-old wife.

Constable Paul McCallion knew instantly who I was and acted entirely as one would expect of a professional police officer.

I soon found myself in an interview room, giving my statement, conscious of the camera high up in the corner where the wall met the ceiling, recording everything. I crossed my arms over my chest and then thought, "They must be reading my body language. That's what they do." I was just trying to hide the cartoon moose across my chest.

McCallion listened to our story, and then he and two other Mounties headed out to our house to check around the property.

Sharon and I were going to go to a hotel, but the three in Bridgewater were booked solid. Sharon insisted that I park our car under the big security light near the front door of the RCMP detachment, which I did. We locked our doors, reclined our seats and waited for the Mounties to report back. I dozed. Sharon didn't.

At 4:36 a.m., Constable McCallion called to say that our property was secure, and that the Halifax Regional Police had contacted Rob Doucette. McCallion said Doucette was in Dartmouth, at the motel where he lived. Doucette wouldn't open the door, so the police were going to draw up a search warrant and visit him later.

"He's not in Hubbards," McCallion said. "It's safe to go home."

We arrived home shortly after 5 a.m. and went back to bed.

But there was one more twist.

Another Mountie called later that morning to tell us everything was in hand. The police knew where Doucette was in Dartmouth and were on their way to arrest him.

Shortly before six that night, the Mountie called again and told us Doucette was now in custody and would be charged. The arresting officer was Constable Laura Adams.

As it turned out, like just about everything else in the wider story, nothing was as first reported. Doucette hadn't been in Dartmouth; the person who wouldn't answer the door was not him. He was, in fact, in Hubbards, not all that far from our house.

After a few hours at the police station, Doucette was bailed out, but he had to find his way back to Dartmouth, about 100 kilometres to the east.

Chad Jones texted Doucette at 9:15 that Saturday night. "What the fuck are you doing?? Christ man . . ." Jones wrote.

"Walking from Bridgewater right now . . . Christ man . . . long way to go . . . not sure if I should talk to you," Doucette wrote. "But guessing I got extremely drunk . . . I don't remember a thing the RCMP said I did. Guess I have to wait for the recordings."

The next day he continued the exchange with Jones.

"I should have never called the RCMP April 19 that year . . . I'm fucked . . . they gunning for me ever since . . . I know too much . . . thought Paul was on their side for a minute . . . until I received this today . . . A copy of Frank magazine was just sent to me. Received tonight at 6:55 p.m. . . . apparently the people making the threats on my life are misrepresenting what they've read . . . I realize now that Paul has not lied in these articles in Frank magazine … I seriously owe him a great apology . . . but I am under a court order to avoid him and the MCC . . . I guess the RCMP got the block they wanted . . . Wish I had these articles from the minute they were written . . . would have saved some of us shitty days."

Doucette even said at one point that he wanted to be on our team: "Let me know in a few months if you guys want an addition to your crew."

It was tempting to withdraw the charges at that point, but I couldn't do it. I felt that Doucette had to experience some consequences for his actions. By his own admission on camera, he had made a career out of scaring and threatening people. When we first met, he had given me a copy of his Gladue report, which is a type of pre-sentencing and bail hearing report that a Canadian criminal court can request when considering sentencing an offender of Aboriginal background. He openly talks about the report and its findings, which showed that he had had a rough-and-tumble upbringing. He'd been abused, undereducated and nurtured by criminals. That being the case, I suspected he would just get a slap on the wrist from the court, which didn't bother Sharon or me all that much.

I didn't want to write about the incident, but even if I had been inclined to, there was nowhere left for me to publish.

◆

On September 14, 2022, Andrew Douglas signalled to the world that the Atlantic version of *Frank* magazine was dead. In typical *Frank* style, the cartoon standard-bearer of the magazine was depicted as lying in a coffin with his eyes closed.

David and Diana Bentley had started the magazine in 1987. Douglas Parker Rudderham, who goes by his middle name, had owned it since 2010. (There continues to exist a separate, less newsy *Frank* magazine based in Ottawa that was, at the time, independently owned by Michael Bate.) In recent years, Rudderham had been mostly hands-off, leaving Douglas to his own devices and mostly alone, without much funding or staff.

In the time since the massacre, Douglas had transformed the satirical magazine into an investigative journalist's dream publication—an unformatted and freewheeling platform to develop and report on an evolving and complicated public interest story. Subscriptions were up and people were talking about the magazine in a new and respectful way, but Rudderham didn't seem to care. He didn't allow Douglas an extra dime to improve things, and he stripped the bank account of any excess cash when he could, Douglas told me near the end. Rudderham didn't say much about why he decided to stop publishing *Frank*, other than to suggest that it was either a business decision or succession planning.

I always suspected that it was the old invisible hand at work again. With what we were reporting, *Frank* was clearly getting deep under the establishment's skin, contrary to the usual way in which Canadians, particularly the media, deal with controversial stories, which is to ignore them and hope they go away.

The loss of the Atlantic *Frank* was a blow not only to the local community but to the country. Its underlying mission was to hold the powerful accountable. If I were younger, I could have envisioned growing it into something bigger.

The cover-up of the Nova Scotia massacres wasn't the only one the federal government was juggling at the time. The same issues that had bedevilled the RCMP were plaguing the federal corrections service and the military, multiple sources told me, begging me to write about it all. The federal government's handling of the long-running WE Charity and SNC-Lavalin scandals, and the failures of the RCMP to thoroughly investigate them, were also worthy topics deserving deeper exploration. Hell, the RCMP didn't interview Prime Minister Justin Trudeau about SNC-Lavalin, even though his office had been implicated in the case.

There was a slew of cases involving the Chinese, including the arrest of former Mountie Bill Majcher for allegedly spying for the Chinese government. He denies any wrongdoing. His case is still before the courts at the time of this writing. I had featured Majcher in *Dispersing the Fog* back in 2008, and having gotten to know him, I suspected there was more to the story than first met the eye. And one of the saddest commentaries on the state of the nation and the media was Trudeau's appointment of family friend David Johnston to be the special rapporteur in a scandal over interference by the Chinese in Canadian elections.

It was enough to keep a publisher's presses humming for a decade or two.

There were so many opportunities for journalists to hold the powerful accountable, but almost no one was applying for or capable of doing the job. When everyone is striving to be on the same page, it's a dangerous situation for a country: no one is there to see the emperor's clothing.

In Nova Scotia, meanwhile, the cover-up still needed covering up. It had moved into another stage. The governments had appointed Linda Lee Oland, a retired Nova Scotia appeals court judge, to a novel position: "founding chair" of the committee responsible for monitoring and reporting on implementation of the 130 recommendations made in the Mass Casualty Commission's final report. It would be a three-year process, proclaimed Brad Johns, the Nova Scotia justice minister and attorney general, and Marco Mendicino, the federal minister of public safety. Oland had married into a Maritime brewing family that has served as political kingmakers on the East Coast. In 2024, she was replaced on the committee by Myra Freeman, a former teacher, philanthropist and lieutenant governor of Nova Scotia: a pleasant society woman who would not rock any boats.

Based on history and the players involved, the implementation committee looked like just another stalling mechanism erected to protect the governments. It was designed to include the victims' family members, as if they would lend it credibility. Some declined to participate because they suspected the committee was a sham created to shut them up. Others, like Scott McLeod, volunteered because they wanted to get inside the tent and see what was going on. There wasn't much to see. The committee had no real budget, was disorganized, and had no power to implement a single thing.

On March 27, 2024, one year after the MCC's final report was published, the RCMP issued a "progress report" on the implementation of some of the recommendations. Interim Commissioner Mike Duheme and Assistant Commissioner Dennis Daley made it clear that the RCMP had interpreted the recommendations differently than the commission may have intended. The Mounties said, on behalf of the entire force, that they were sorry for what had happened in Nova Scotia, but they then equivocated on implementing drastic change. They suggested that the recommended changes applied to all Canadian police forces, not just the Mounties. In response to reporters' questions, they also made it clear that the force was getting no pressure from government at either the federal or provincial level. It seemed Canadian governments were interested only in maintaining the status quo. To that end, the RCMP leaders were in marketing mode. "As an organization, if we don't learn from this, this tragic incident happened for absolutely nothing . . . I don't want that to happen," Duheme told the CBC's Catharine Tunney. "For the most part, we are better off today than we were two years ago, or four years ago . . . We want to prove to people that we can change as an organization."

Ex-Mountie Calvin Lawrence didn't buy any of it. He said the force continues to be resistant to change. He criticized its "fear culture" and predicted that nothing significant would happen in the future. "An apology without change is just manipulation," he said.

Also in March 2024, the Canadian Press broke a story about a June 2023 report by the Security and Intelligence Threats to Elections Task Force. The group, created in 2019, had issued a warning about the lack of faith in government, the growth of conspiracy theories and the growing dangers for the Canadian way of life. The RCMP and CSIS were involved in developing the report. "While extremist narratives and conspiracy theories do not usually manifest themselves as an act of serious violence, 'they have the potential to negatively affect the fabric of Canadian society,'" reporter Jim Bronskill wrote, summarizing the report. He also wrote that he was unsuccessful in getting the RCMP to comment on it.

Given how the government and the RCMP handled the Nova Scotia massacres investigation, is it any wonder that more and more people distrust the government, the police and the media?

◆

A year after he was arrested, Rob Doucette had his day in court. It was another sunny late-summer day in Bridgewater. The courthouse on High Street was all but empty. Two Mounties were there: Constable McCallion, who had taken our statements, and Constable Adams, who had arrested Doucette. McCallion, a competitive hockey player in his younger days, was professional and friendly, while Adams looked like she wanted to be somewhere else.

The judge that Doucette drew was Catherine Benton, who in 2017 had become the first Mi'kmaq woman to be appointed to the Nova Scotia bench. Doucette showed up dressed in his favourite Mi'kmaq vest and acted as his own lawyer, which, as we all know, is never a good idea.

First, he tried to grill Sharon on the stand. He asked her the name of the bar where we had all first gathered, perhaps as a way to test her memory. He didn't appreciate that the question itself conceded that the meeting had happened.

"I don't know," Sharon said.

"You don't know the name?" Doucette said, in what he seemed to consider a gotcha moment.

"I don't go to a lot of bars," Sharon replied.

During my stint on the stand, he did much the same, incriminating himself with his own questions, which left Judge Benton no option but to convict him of threatening both Sharon and me and place him on probation, as I had expected would be the outcome.

As he questioned me, Doucette insisted that his call that night had lasted just fifteen minutes, not twenty-six. The proof was in my phone records. He tried to get me to admit that I had fabricated the statement I made to Constable McCallion that Doucette had claimed to be Canada's most prolific hit man back in the 1990s.

"Why would I say that to you?" he asked.

"I was kind of wondering that myself," I said, "but you did say it."

Finally, he turned to the demise of *Frank* magazine and claimed that he was the person solely responsible for having it shut down. "Did you know that?" he asked.

"No, I didn't," I said.

As he gathered his thoughts for the next question, I mused to myself that I now had a name for the invisible hand that runs Canada—Rob the Carpenter.

"The only reason you had me charged was because you were taking revenge on me for the closing of *Frank* magazine," Doucette said, finishing with a flourish. "Isn't that true?"

"No, Mr. Doucette, the reason I had you charged was because you threatened me, and especially Sharon, and I couldn't allow that to go unpunished."

Doucette paused, looked down and then looked back up toward Judge Benton. "I've had enough of this guy," he said. He swept his right arm across, like a baseball umpire making a dramatic out call. "Get him out of here!"

As pathetic as it might have been, the episode was the comedic highlight of the entire investigation.

In early 2025, a settlement was reached in the lawsuit between the families of the victims, Banfield and Wortman's estate, which was valued at $2.1 million. Banfield had reportedly sought half of the estate. Some sources report that she received $400,000, others around 11.5 percent, which would be about $241,500, with the remainder of Wortman's estate reportedly split between the fifteen families of the twenty-two victims. At the time of writing, the settlement had not been recorded in the court file, which could indicate this was a confidential out-of-court settlement.

Meanwhile, a class action suit brought by the families against the RCMP and the Nova Scotia government, alleging incompetence, appeared to be stalled, sources said. At the time of writing, it remains unclear whether the RCMP and the provincial government have responded to the allegations.

A NOTE ON SOURCES

By now, dear readers, you have come to realize that my approach to non-fiction storytelling does not follow the formats and conventions of the genre. There are no footnotes or endnotes. We live in a time when it is all too easy for people to be distracted. I believe that forcing people to take a break from the narrative is an invitation for them to put down the book and leave the story. I want them to stay riveted. To that end, I try to incorporate enough identifying details about published materials that anyone can easily find the underlying documents via the Internet or other means if they feel the need to do so.

Over the past five years, since I first became involved in this investigation, I have been treated as little more than an unhinged outsider by the corporatized mainstream and most of the alternative media. I'm not complaining; there are plenty of alternatives that worked well for me and others like me. The point is that the mainstream media has lost its way.

For example, although *22 Murders* was a number one bestseller in Canada, not a single mainstream or alternative media outlet interviewed me about it. I was not reporting the story they were telling; I wasn't parroting the official narrative provided by the RCMP and the federal and Nova Scotia governments. I was and continue to be critical of contemporary journalism in Canada and am attempting to hold the media accountable. In an ideal world, they should be big enough to face the music they don't like to hear.

To illustrate my points, I have used extensive chunks of reportage where necessary. I know from past experience that the media outlets I cite would not grant permission for me to do so. As I stated in *22 Murders*,

> Any news outlet ought to know that no institution has the right to go unmentioned in a significant public-interest story in which they are involved. One of the running threads of this book is the media's choices of subject matter and tone, as well as their deferential behaviour toward the RCMP. I have quoted from and highlighted various outlets' work to show what they were comfortable reporting, in contrast to my own work and analysis. In that way, I believe that readers might better understand the important differences.

After *22 Murders* was published, a number of leading journalists took issue with my approach. They were critical of me for not giving the RCMP, the Mass Casualty Commission or the governments involved the opportunity to comment on what I had reported. My position is that over the years this so-called balanced approach to journalism has led to distorted reporting. Much of *22 Murders* and this book challenges the official narrative. I am confident that my documentation of the lies, deceptions and misdirections has accurately refuted the original comments made by the various authorities. To give them another attempt to muddy the waters would be journalistic malpractice.

Another concoction perpetuated by the corporate media and many alternative outlets is that the only credible sources are those who allow their real names to be used. As I wrote in *22 Murders*,

> In my opinion as a long-time journalist, author and even former editor at a national newspaper, that approach is journalism as conceived and practiced by ivory-tower purists, accountants, lawyers and their insurers. In the real world, investigative journalism isn't and can't be conducted in such a neat and tidy fashion. It is the duty of any experienced reporter to be able to judge the credibility of the

source, the context of the situation and the quality of the informa-tion. Time will tell whether I have judged the viability of my sources well. Since I began writing this book, many things told to me off the record, such as the RCMP's destruction of evidence, have since been revealed to be factual. I am confident that other unnamed sources in this book will prove similarly prescient and invaluable.

In recent years, there has been a popular move in journalism towards stories being double- or even triple-sourced. The accepted wisdom is that if two or three people agree something happened, it is most likely to be true. Reality doesn't always play along. Sometimes there are not two or three people involved in or witness to a situation, and, all too often I suspect, even when there are mul-tiple sources, the second and third sources are merely agreeable people. Such requirements for overreporting would make it almost impossible to ferret out deep, well-protected stories.

Many of my sources for both *22 Murders* and this book were law-enforcement and government insiders who felt they had much to lose by speaking with me. Many feared being ostracized by friends and family. Many feared for their jobs; a few, for their lives. When neces-sary, I assigned pseudonyms to sources who needed to be protected, especially from the RCMP and its enablers in government, who have proven to be extremely vindictive and even vicious when dealing with so-called whistleblowers. The information and direction these sources provided was much too valuable to ignore just because I couldn't reveal to the public who they are.

As was the case in *22 Murders*, I once again relied upon citizen investigators—ordinary people who became invested in the story. I have named some of them, but others asked to remain in the back-ground. I know who each is in their everyday lives. Their collective desire can be summed up this way: all they want is justice for the dead, accountability and defence of the rule of law.

ACKNOWLEDGEMENTS

It's not often that an author gets two kicks at the same can, but after the publication of *22 Murders*, my editor, Craig Pyette, agreed that there clearly was a "Big Secret" and that more needed to be done in an attempt to find the truth. Pyette asked me to take on the task with the simple instruction that I show journalists how to investigate a complex story like this one. I've done my best to that end. I thank Pyette and publisher Sue Kuruvilla for affording me this unique opportunity, which was successfully presented to them by agent Rob Firing of Transatlantic Agency.

Pyette left Random House during the course of this project and was replaced by Sarah St. Pierre. I was initially concerned that the shift might prove detrimental, but I was pleasantly surprised by how St. Pierre brought herself up to speed and shaped this narrative in a most satisfying fashion. Thank you, Sarah.

Although I conceived, researched and wrote this book, I could not have completed it as quickly and with as much detail if not for the help I received from non-journalist citizen investigators who were committed to uncovering the truth.

After assisting me with *22 Murders*, Chad Jones continued to immerse himself in the record and develop his own sources as if he were a professional reporter. The irony was that Jones's day job was as distribution manager for the Halifax *Chronicle Herald*. Since we first met in

2020, I have called Jones "A.I." because of his extensive knowledge and understanding of the nuances of the case and his ability to pull it all up on a moment's notice. He was an invaluable resource who reviewed this manuscript word by word. The story is better because of him. I would also like to acknowledge his partner, Caroline Kuepers, for her important contributions. Thank you both.

Along the way, another A.I.-like researcher joined this effort to serve as a bookend to Jones. Ryan Potter devoted much of his spare time and energies to reassembling the evidence from the RCMP and the Mass Casualty Commission into comprehensive timelines. With them in hand, I was able to see through the fog into the heart of the story. Late into the evening, Potter and I often worked together, hammering away at the smallest details in every chapter until we both felt that we had it right.

I likely wouldn't be here writing this if not for Andrew Douglas and *Frank* magazine. Andrew recognized the importance of the story and put his money where his mouth was. After the magazine's untimely death, it was revived in February 2023 by Ottawa *Frank* magazine owner Michael Bate. He brought back the Atlantic version, allowing Douglas to do what he does best: hold the powerful accountable.

Since 2020, I have spent most Sunday nights doing the *Nighttime* podcast with Jordan Bonaparte. We were later joined by lawyer Adam Rodgers and renamed the podcast *The Sunday Night Show*. Together we have striven to highlight important stories and, when necessary, show our audience how they have been spun by governments, the police or the media—and to what likely end. Our audience has been small, but our victory is that we have always known we have the attention of the powers that be.

The legacy and alternative media have largely accepted the official narrative about the massacres, despite the obvious gaping holes in the story. An important contributor to getting the whole story out and helping to change public opinion has been Halifax talk-show host Todd Veinotte. He picked up where the late Rick Howe left off and is willing to be critical of the RCMP, which is a tough but necessary sell to many of those in his audience who don't want to hear that message. Thank you, Todd.

Jodie Mills has been a valuable addition to the team, with her background in criminal courts and legal documents. When I asked if I could cite her in the acknowledgements, she wrote: "After reading *22 Murders*, my journey in starting this was to prove you wrong by following the Mass Casualty Commission and doing lots of research with the documents, which I used in an attempt to debunk your findings. Instead, I found a whole lot of misinformation and distraction from what really took place and more of what you said was backed by evidence provided than what the MCC narrative was . . . These last four years have really opened my eyes to a lot of things."

I couldn't have told this story without the help of some current and many former police officers. Most insist on anonymity out of fear of retribution from their former colleagues, which in and of itself says much about the state of policing. "Bad cops should fear good cops—not the other way around," as former Alberta-based Mountie Josh O'Brien put it to me. Others were not so shy, speaking out in what they perceived to be the public interest. They include: Cathy Mansley, Edgar MacLeod, Calvin Lawrence, Dave Moore, Tom Juby, Monty Robinson, Josh O'Brien, Rob Creasser, Normand Devarennes and Tim Kavanagh. Thank you all for your courage.

Two people who provided me with deep insights into the RCMP, Shirley Heafey and Moira Webster, had worked closely with the force but were not members. I hope this book addressed some of your many concerns.

I was assisted extensively by a wide range of citizens. Some were family members, friends or acquaintances of the twenty-two murder victims, while others were interested strangers. They all contributed to the overall story in one way or another. Some asked not to be named, and I have respected their request for anonymity at every turn. Otherwise, my sincere gratitude to those who lent their names to the story: Scott and Charline McLeod, Darrell and Margaret Currie, Rhonda Adams, Greg Muise, Autumn Doucette, Gerald and Floria Murphy, Judy and Doug Myers, Dana Geddes, Pete MacIsaac, Michael Zareski, Michael Marshall, Sandy Meschefske, Brian Wason, Scott and Lyndsay Fraser, Evelyn Ramsey, Mike Wagner and Sherry Sutherland.

All things considered, a special mention of thanks to Robert "Rob the Carpenter" Doucette, who made the story even more interesting than it already was.

In 2020, I was involved in the first attempt to do a documentary about the massacres. After much effort, it was shelved because of the unwillingness of parties on all sides of the issue to co-operate with the production. It was also unclear what the underlying story might be. Nevertheless, I thank Chris Smith, Michael Kronish, Patrick McGuire, Allyson Luchak and their associates for the time and work they put in, which was very helpful to me. Perhaps this book will help to disperse some of the fog for documentary makers.

I would also like to thank my brother, Dave Palango, as well as Steve Jarrett, Katie Gorman and Melissa Bond for their help when I needed it. Thank you to Nathan Perrault for reminding me that I can always do better, and to Tama Tisam, Ava Tisam and Lee Tisam for always making me laugh.

Last but certainly not least, my deepest appreciation to my wonderful, courageous and ultra-patient wife, Sharon McNamara. She is the epitome of a great Canadian, a true patriot in a country of shrinking violets. She stood beside me throughout all this because she believed that someone needed to step up, address the facts and do the right thing, no matter the cost, because personal and institutional accountability is what the country needs. Someone has to do it. Thank you, Sharon, for being my totally supportive partner in this endeavour.

INDEX

PAUL PALANGO is a veteran investigative journalist. He started his career at the *Hamilton Spectator*, his hometown newspaper. In 1977, he moved to the *Toronto Sun*, where he covered the Toronto Blue Jays in their inaugural season. Later that year, he moved to the *Globe and Mail* as a reporter. Between 1983 and his resignation in 1990, he served as its sports editor, metro editor and, eventually, national editor. During his tenure at the *Globe*, Palango's reporters swept the Center for Investigative Reporting awards in five consecutive years. In 1989, he accepted the Michener Award for disinterested public service journalism on behalf of the *Globe*. He is the author of four previous books: *22 Murders: Investigating the Massacres, Cover-Up and Obstacles to Justice in Nova Scotia; Dispersing the Fog: Inside the Secret World of Ottawa and the RCMP; The Last Guardians: The Crisis in the RCMP . . . and in Canada;* and *Above the Law: The Crooks, the Politicians, the RCMP and Rod Stamler*. In 2025, Palango and lawyer Adam Rodgers began a new weekly podcast called *Dispersing the Fog*. Since 2000, Palango and his wife Sharon McNamara, have operated Kiln Art, a successful fused-glass studio. They reside in Chester Basin, Nova Scotia.